THE AGE

OF

PROTEST

DISSENT
AND REBELLION IN
THE TWENTIETH
CENTURY

Also by Norman F. Cantor

Church, Kingship and Lay Investiture in England
The English: A History of Politics and Society to 1760
How to Study History (with Richard I. Schneider)
Medieval History: The Life and Death of a Civilization
Western Civilization: Its Genesis and Destiny

Edited by Norman F. Cantor

Augustine and Thomas Aquinas (with P. Klein)
Dante and Machiavelli (with P. Klein)
The English Tradition (with Michael S. Werthman)
A History of Popular Culture (with Michael S. Werthman)
The Medieval World
Plato and Aristotle (with P. Klein)
The Structure of European History (with Michael S. Werthman)
William Stubbs on the English Constitution

THE AGE OF PROTEST

DISSENT
AND REBELLION IN
THE TWENTIETH
CENTURY

by Norman F. Cantor

HAWTHORN BOOKS, INC.

PUBLISHERS / NEW YORK

THE AGE OF PROTEST

The author wishes to express appreciation to the
following for permission to reprint copyrighted
material:

Lines from "L'Homme Moyen Sensuel" by Ezra
Pound, from *Personae*. Copyright © 1926 by Ezra
Pound. Reprinted by permission of New Directions
Publishing Corporation.

Lines from "I-Feel-Like-I'm-Fixin'-to-Die-Rag" by
Country Joe and the Fish. Reprinted by permission
of Tradition Music Company.

Lines from "September 1913" by William Butler
Yeats, from *Collected Poems*, reprinted with permis-
sion of Mr. M. B. Yeats; The Macmillan Company,
New York, N. Y.; and The Macmillan Company of
Canada. Copyright © 1916 by The Macmillan Com-
pany, renewed 1944 by Bertha Georgie Yeats.

Lines from "Inishfallen Fare Thee Well" by Sean
O'Casey, reprinted with permission of The Macmil-
lan Company, New York, N. Y., and Macmillan &
Co. Ltd., London. Copyright © 1949 by Sean
O'Casey.

Lines from "Kill, Kill, Kill for Peace" by The
Fugs. Reprinted courtesy of United International
Copyright Representatives Ltd., New York, N. Y.

Excerpt from *Waiting for Lefty* by Clifford
Odets, reprinted by permission of the Estate of
Clifford Odets.

TO HOWARD AND JUDY, YOUNG REBELS

PREFACE

Pᴿᴏᴛᴇꜱᴛ movements have become central concerns in our society, along with industrialization, urban problems, television, professional football, the pill, and pollution. The aim of this book is to provide the educated public with an historical perspective on this efflorescence of protest. The book shows that the techniques of protest and the style of life that protest movements both engender and depend upon have been ever-recurring aspects of the twentieth century. These techniques and this style have been used by both the Left and the Right, by suffragettes, Nazis, Communists, and students. The book reminds the reader that often the very group condemned in one generation for employing protest methods has in the next generation been part of the respectable establishment that is angered when the same methods are used by new dissident groups.

This book neither praises nor condemns protest but examines it as a social phenomenon and thus seeks to add to the reader's experience and sophistication when he encounters protest in his own life. The book should be particularly useful to bleeding-heart liberals, stony-hearted conservatives, the young and the old, the great middle class, and the literate poor. University presidents, chiefs of police, and politicians will find it immediately practical, and from reading it parents may come to understand their children better, though they will not necessarily be happier about the behavior and attitudes of the young.

This book draws upon historical and sociological scholarship, but it is not—and is certainly not meant to be—a definitive and authoritative treatise. Historians and social scientists are currently investigating the protest phenomenon in great detail, and this book could not be more than a preliminary survey of a very serious subject. I have concentrated on the most exciting and immediately relevant aspects of twentieth-century protest, and I have tried to give the reader some instructive amusement as he takes up his position on one side or the other of the barricades. I can deal only with the most consequential and—for an American—interesting protest movements in the twentieth century.

I wish to acknowledge the very valuable research assistance of Miss Carol Berkin, lecturer in history at Hunter College; Miss Zane Berzins and Miss Judy Walsh, holders of two highly regarded graduate fellowships at Brandeis and Columbia universities, respectively; Professor Marshall Shatz, my colleague at Brandeis University; and Mrs. Clarissa Atkinson. Mrs. Nancy Melia helped me prepare the book for publication, and Miss Marlene Aronin assisted in reading the proofs. I also am grateful to Mr. Tony Meisel for encouragement and advice.

N.F.C.
August, 1969

CONTENTS

PART THREE

PROTEST AGAINST CAPITALISM
AND IMPERIALISM

PART FOUR

THE ERA OF PERMANENT PROTEST

INTRODUCTION:
THE AGE OF PROTEST

THE twentieth century has been an age of protest. Successive waves of protest against oppression, exploitation, and social misery have dominated the history of the Western world since the early years of this century. Protest against tyranny in Russia culminated in the Revolution of 1917, and the Bolshevik triumph inspired movements for national emancipation and social improvement in the non-Western parts of the world, particularly after 1945.

In 1900 the greatest share of the world's wealth and power was in the hands of a small group of Western aristocrats, businessmen, and government officials. The ideas of liberty and equality that had been disseminated by the Enlightenment, the French Revolution, and the liberal movement of the nineteenth century had not by and large been put into practice even in the democratic countries of western Europe and America; outside Europe ruthless autocracy and imperialist tyranny ruled unchallenged by native peoples. In 1900 the world was therefore still under the sway of an "old regime," in which a narrow group controlled power and wealth, and the majority of people lived out their days with no control over their common destiny, enduring daily terror, hunger, and forced labor to satisfy the power elite.

With the spread of the ideas of liberty and equality by means of modern communication to increasingly literate millions around the globe, this old regime could not continue unchallenged in the twentieth century. Nineteenth-century liberalism had held out the promise of dignity and happiness for everyone in modern society. Twentieth-century protest movements demanded the fulfillment of this promise. Radical change along democratic lines could have been resisted only with continuous ruthless oppression. The old regime did resist democratic movements but only intermittently and never effectively for very long.

The relative weakness of the leaders of the old regime had many causes. In the first place, they often subscribed to liberal rhetoric themselves; when protest movements tried to turn this rhetoric into reality, the power elite was often too guilt-ridden to put up effective resistance for long. Second, the structure and self-confidence of the elite were vitiated by the chaos and demoralization brought on by two world wars. Third, the leadership of twentieth-century protest movements almost invariably consisted of particularly sensitive and energetic members of the middle class who had sufficient familiarity with the power elite not to fear them greatly, sufficient leisure to engage in dissident activities, and sufficient education and political experience to know where and how the power elite was most vulnerable.

Although the old regime was extremely oppressive and exploitative toward the working class and the poor and although protest rhetoric usually concentrated upon this social evil, the greatest weakness of the twentieth-century establishments was their inability to prevent the alienation of the middle class. Middle-class intellectuals since 1900 have usually been hostile to the prevailing power structure, and this hostility has provided a particularly fertile breeding ground for protest movements.

These protest movements have been of two principal kinds. First, there is a kind of general dissent among intellectuals and the well-educated, particularly in the rising generation, which capitalizes on the inevitable hostility of the young toward the old. This kind of protest movement has been expressed in literature, art, the popular press, mass entertainment, and novel life-styles. It has not included direct confrontation with power elites but has consistently undermined them by impairing their communication with the middle class and by making the literate working class receptive to radical ideas. This kind of intellectual dissent has also made power elites conscious of their backwardness in contemporary culture, made them realize how "square" they are, and thus demoralized their leadership and exacerbated their fatal sense of guilt.

The other kind of protest movement is more specific—organized confrontation with the power elite or some part of it. Through parades, strikes, sit-ins, vociferous denunciations, elaborate agitation, and often isolated (but celebrated) acts of violence these protest movements have challenged the power elite to repression, stirred the tender conscience of the middle class, and sometimes roused parts of the working and poverty classes to participation in protest. The techniques for twentieth-century confrontation have some precedents in labor-union agitation during the late nineteenth century. But carried out by middle-class people and intellectuals and generally directed against the institutions of the prevailing social order, rather than against specific working-class grievances, these techniques have become more effective and steadily more refined. The first such protest movements were those of the British feminists and the Irish nationalists. But there was never a more subtle theorist of confrontation than Adolf Hitler.

This paradox points to an important aspect of twentieth-century protest: Although more often than not it has been leftist in orientation, its techniques and style have also been used with great skill by fascist and other right-wing movements. The changes sought have been of many kinds, but the styles, the techniques, and the eagerness to change the regime of 1900 have given the different protest movements a common character.

How does protest differ from revolution? The word "revolution" is often used for any radical change in an aspect of government or society, but in its strict and more correct historical usage revolution is the great exception, whereas protest is the norm. Protest is an attack upon the prevailing system in an intellectual or organized way. Revolution is a sickness in society, a breakdown of the social order, the kind of general demoralization and civil war that the ancient Greek philosophers called *stasis*. Protest uses violence, but it is strictly controlled and specific in its purposes—the seizure of a building, a riot, a political assassination—designed to shock and bewilder the elite and to advertise a grievance. Revolution is unchecked violence in which social groups war against one another for dominance, although violence usually becomes an end in itself and the groups often lose sight of their original purposes.

Revolution occurs only when an old regime defends itself against protest by becoming more reactionary and oppressive but, once having radicalized the middle class and stirred the workers and the poor to involvement, is too inefficient or guilt-ridden to carry out the necessary slaughter and imprisonment of protesters. The political and legal system then splinters, and uncontrolled violence takes over. Finally,

some army or police leader takes advantage of middle-class fear of
extermination and working-class hunger and establishes a new tyranny.
Protest in the twentieth century has led to social change and, more
often than not, to social melioration; revolution has been the road to
chaos, civil war, and new tyranny.

The emergence of protest against specific injustices and inequalities
in the prevailing political and social system has been facilitated and
inspired by cultural upheavals, by shifts in values and ideas. The great
turning point in the history of modern thought occurred at the end
of the nineteenth century and undermined the intellectual foundations
of the old regime.

Nineteenth-century liberals had assumed that men can reason objec-
tively and make rational decisions about themselves and the world
around them. Even this philosophy could serve as an intellectual basis
for radical protest: The world of 1900 fell far short of the liberal
rationalist's ideal of a good and just society. But in the late nineteenth
century intellectual life was inundated by a new irrationalism and a
new perception of human consciousness. There arose a new view of
human nature, rooted in the thought of Karl Marx and Friedrich
Nietzsche and gaining impetus from Freudian psychology, empha-
sizing man's *feelings*—his fears, sentiment, will, and unconscious drives
—rather than his reason. Art and literature advertised feeling rather
than objective reasoning. Protest movements, particularly organized
confrontations, depend upon a view of human nature that gives value
to expression of rage, love, hope, and hatred. Protest is not polite
dissent or institutional political opposition—it is a passionate, aggressive
assault on the prevailing system. The style of protest always has
affinities with anarchistic joy in destruction of order, and the philosophy of anarchism propounded by Georges Sorel at the beginning of
the century appears, in controlled and muted form, in all protest movements.

The old regime of 1900 depended upon a view of morals and social
institutions as products of divine revelation, the wisdom of rational
and learned men, and the accumulation of the experience of centuries.
But science and skepticism vitiated the claims of revelation; the new
irrationalism enfeebled reason in the face of human desire and will.
Finally, the claims of tradition were eroded by a new, relativistic way
of viewing social institutions.

Karl Marx had made a great contribution to this social relativism by
insisting that the institutions and morals of a given society are the

products of environmental conditions and reflect the interests of the ruling class. Then around 1900 the new sciences of sociology and anthropology reinforced a strain that had been prevalent in Western thought since the eighteenth century: that institutions of Western government and society constituted only one system among many, none of which was innately superior or more ethical than any other.

The emergence of this social relativism reinforced the blow that the old regime had suffered from irrationalism: No aspect of the traditional order could any longer be defended on grounds of inviolable sanctity, morality, or tradition. The spread of this philosophy among educated people deprived the power elite of theoretical arguments against protest movements. The old regime could be defended only on grounds of group and class interest, and its leaders were themselves too enmeshed in liberal, moral, and Christian rhetoric to use this kind of Machiavellian defense with conviction or comfort. Furthermore, the new relativism attracted the most sensitive members of the power elite, making them reluctant to use maximum force against protest movements demanding radical change along egalitarian lines.

The old regime of 1900 depended on a classification of people as rulers and subjects, those with reason and knowledge and those without, as parents and children, as teachers and pupils, as rational males and irrational women, as self-reliant masters and dependent colonials, as responsible businessmen and improvident workers and poor. Protesters attacked the falseness of such dichotomies, insisting that all men are equal as lovers and haters. Primacy of will and feeling are inherent in protest, which refuses to recognize moral inviolability in the prevailing order. Protest is based on the prescriptive rightness of every individual's desire to be free. The new culture of the turn of the century attributed value to feeling and desire above reason, tradition, and power; it thus prepared the way for the protest movements of the first two decades of the century and all their successors, which in style and program have drawn upon the heritage of irrationalism and relativism that is central to modern thought.

PART ONE

THE EMERGENCE
OF PROTEST

INTRODUCTION

At the end of the nineteenth century militant labor unions in Britain, France, and the United States inaugurated new efforts to improve the wages and other material conditions of industrial workers. This movement continued until the outbreak of World War I, with very modest success. The failure of the labor movement to develop a coherent program of action against the old regime was dramatically demonstrated in 1914, when unions acquiesced in the recruitment of workers for the monstrous armies of the European powers. In fact most labor leaders, in Germany or in the Allied countries, became enthusiastic patriots and questioned the war only after its debilitating impact on their countries had become evident in 1916. The labor movement in the early twentieth century was deeply divided; the general strike of all workers, which radical syndicalists wanted, never occurred.

In the first two decades after 1900, successful dissent and rebellion against power and privilege came from groups largely outside the labor unions. These protest movements went far beyond efforts to improve the material conditions of the working class. They attacked the fundamental structure of the old regime, and they developed techniques that became essential to all twentieth-century protest. There were four important protest movements in the first two decades of the twentieth century. The suffragette crusade, particularly in Britain, not only attacked masculine privilege and inaugurated the emancipation of half of the adult population; it also called into question the system of values upon which the old regime rested. The Irish rebellion of 1916 established a pattern for all anticolonial movements in the twentieth century. The ill-fated mutiny in the French army was the only significant protest against World War I and against the militaristic power system of the European states. The overthrow of tsarist autocracy in Russia, in which middle-class intellectuals played the leading role, inaugurated a movement for social liberation that eventually affected all the non-Western parts of the world.

CHAPTER

I

The Feminist Crusade

IN 1906 the Liberal Party came to power in Great Britain, with a huge majority in the House of Commons. The Liberal government, which after 1908 was led by H. H. Asquith, a middle-class lawyer with beneficent inclinations toward workers, remained in office until 1916. The Liberals put through Parliament various measures inaugurating the welfare state in Britain, although the more radical unions were not satisfied with these paternalistic efforts. Asquith and his colleagues, including the aristocratic Winston Churchill and the Welsh demagogue David Lloyd George, were confident that they could domesticate and channel all revolt and assuage all discontent.[1]

It was not the ranks of labor but another army which brought perspiration to the brow of Prime Minister Asquith. The ladies were mobilizing, and he did not know what to do about them.

Asquith and his colleagues could face with some equanimity the revolt of the workers, who had shown signs of restlessness and discontent throughout the nineteenth century. But the revolt of women in petticoats was a thing entirely unprecedented. It was indecent. The shrill cry "Votes for women!" threatened not only the English Constitution but also the sexual identity of the latter-day Victorian male. But whereas the former, tempered in struggle over centuries, might survive, the latter might not. The struggle of the militant suffragettes for the franchise in the years 1905–1914 was half political, half sexual, warfare. It was not the sort of battle that government officials were mentally equipped to understand.

Before the agitation of the suffragettes was swept away by the Great War, it had turned into guerrilla warfare between the government and the ladies. The suffragettes brought both hilarity and brutality to English political life. It would be hard to say which was more repugnant to the constitution of a serious-minded English Liberal.

In the years after 1906 no government minister was secure from the harassment of these shameless militants. If he stood for a by-election, his speeches to the electorate were certain to be disrupted by at least one piercing female voice clamoring for an explanation of why women had no votes. Such interruptions could not be ignored. The lady would more than likely unfurl a huge banner to add a visual dimension to her demand. Police and ushers would have to be rushed in to remove the offender. Her removal was likely to take some time, for she had probably chained herself to her seat. When, still struggling and shouting, she was at last dragged from the hall, it was difficult to regain the attention of the audience. Should the speaker succeed, however, his next sentence was likely to be interrupted by another of "the shrieking sisterhood." The women worked these things as if they were relay races; as one was dragged off, another would raise her voice. Matters grew so desperate that, as one suffragette smugly noted, "womanless meetings" became the rule for Cabinet ministers. Even the categorical exclusion of women from meetings was of little avail, for at least one enterprising young woman was usually able to sneak into the hall hours before to bide her time behind a curtain or inside an organ. Finally, halls had to be searched before political rallies. Even then the roofs of adjoining buildings were likely to harbor one or two ardent suffragettes of gymnastic inclinations, complete with megaphones.

Nor did the suffragettes confine their activities to political rallies. A Cabinet minister seeking relaxation at the theater was likely to be spotted and hounded even in the middle of a performance. He could no longer even count on the solace of a quiet game of golf. "Votes for Women" or "No Votes! No Golf!" was likely to be emblazoned in acid on the green turf. In the bushes there might well be concealed a suffragette ready to flay the would-be sportsman with cane or umbrella.

Such heckling and harassment were constant. They were also, or so they seemed to the victims, irrational, for the women refused to distinguish between their friends and their foes. It was well known that Mr. Asquith's Cabinet was divided on the question of giving women the vote. Both Lloyd George and Churchill had long since proclaimed themselves the women's allies, ready to do all in their power to hasten the day of deliverance. But they were not spared. On the contrary, the women went after them with special relish, adding the charge of hypocrisy to the other items in their indictment. On one occasion Churchill was attacked at a railway station by a young suffragette wielding a dog-whip. On this occasion he managed deftly to wrestle it away from the lady. Lloyd George was less fortunate. Upon entering his car after a triumphant speaking engagement, he realized too late that it already had an occupant. A suffragette had locked herself in the back seat. While the chauffeur struggled to open the door the lady proceeded to vent her wrath on Lloyd George by giving him a good shaking.

At the height of their battle, in the years 1912–1914, the suffragettes' ingenuity in destructiveness was wondrous to behold. They smashed windows, not singly but systematically, by the streetful. The London *Daily Telegraph* reported such proceedings with thinly veiled amazement:

A band of women set out on such a window-breaking campaign in the principal streets of the West End, as London has never known. For a quarter of an hour or twenty minutes, nothing was heard in the Strand, Cockspur Street, Downing Street, Whitehall, Piccadilly, Bow Street or Oxford Street, but the falling, shattered glass. . . . Many of the finest shopfronts in the world had been temporarily destroyed. . . . The attack was begun practically simultaneously. It was one of the busiest periods of the day. Suddenly women, who a moment before had appeared to be on peaceful shopping expeditions, produced from bags or muffs, hammers, stones, and sticks and began an attack on the nearest windows. . . .

On stealthy midnight expeditions with brush and bucket the feminine protesters painted out house numbers. They slashed the upholstered seats in railway carriages and wherever else they could find them. They poured jam down mailboxes, uprooted municipal flower beds, invaded picture galleries and mutilated paintings, cut telegraph wires, turned in false fire alarms, and planted homemade bombs, one of which badly damaged a home that Lloyd George was building. Finally they began to set fires. Several railway stations, the refreshment pavilion at Kew Gardens, a football stadium in Cambridge, and even a few churches went up in flames.

Emmeline Pankhurst, the silver-haired matriarch of the suffragettes, sounded the clarion call. "I want to be tried for sedition!" she shouted gleefully. "Be militant each in your own way," she urged her devoted followers. "Those of you who can break windows, break them. Those of you who can still further attack the secret idol of property . . . do so. I incite this meeting to rebellion!" [2]

When arrested and tried, these women turned their confrontations with the law into forums, indicting their judges and the government as tyrants and morally responsible for all outrages committed. Nor were the women above assailing judges and prosecuting attorneys with tomatoes and other missiles, when they were not uttering stirring invocations of human rights for the benefit of the press.

When sentenced to jail terms, the women blackmailed the government into releasing them by refusing to eat. The first hunger strike began in 1909, apparently spontaneously. It soon burgeoned into the nightmare of prison officials all over England. Confronted with a suffragette prisoner who insisted on starving herself, the government could do one of two things: It could release her, or it could attempt to feed her by force. The first alternative had the disadvantage of turning the criminal loose to commit more outrages. The second proved even worse. Force feeding was an unpleasant process that involved pinioning struggling women while their mouths were pried open with objects of wood or metal, and tubes containing vile but nutritious fluids were forced down their throats. The women usually vomited up the unwelcome food as quickly as it was poured into them. This practice provoked letters from doctors claiming that such procedures were dangerous. The women described their agonies in gruesome detail for the press. The more chivalrous and humanitarian members of the House of Commons, even those who had no special fondness for the suffragettes, found this practice repulsive.

The Prime Minister and Home Secretary Reginald McKenna found themselves embarrassed in the House by awkward questions and sometimes more than that. "You will go down in history as the man who tortured innocent women," [3] bellowed one usually mild-mannered member of Parliament to Mr. Asquith after a particularly gruesome incident. This was not the reputation Mr. Asquith and his Liberal government wished to leave to posterity.

The militancy of the suffragettes did not reach this frenzied peak all at once. It developed over a decade under the inspiration and guidance of the Pankhurst family. Emmeline Pankhurst was the widow of a Manchester barrister of progressive views. Richard Pankhurst had offered a rather characteristic example of the English radical tradition. Active in such organizations as the Royal Statistical Society and the National Association for the Promotion of Social Science, he had stood unsuccessfully for Parliament both as a Liberal and as a Radical candidate. He had joined the Independent Labour Party shortly after its formation in 1893, had become a member of the Fabian Society, and had stood for election as a Labour candidate in 1895. Women's suffrage was only one of the "left-wing" causes that Pankhurst had supported in his lifetime. Emmeline Pankhurst followed her husband's political teachings. Their living room had been a popular gathering place for radicals of many persuasions.

After her husband's death, Mrs. Pankhurst had to struggle to support her four children. She tried running a small retail shop, but her interest in politics and civic questions was frustrated. In 1903 she gathered a small group of women in her living room—in those early days they were mainly the wives of Labour Party members—and founded the Women's Social and Political Union. Mrs. Pankhurst immediately struck a dramatic note. The goal of the organization was to be "immediate enfranchisement." She renounced "outworn missionary methods" in favor of political action and was soon referring to the older, established women's-suffrage organizations as "the old-fashioned gang." Nevertheless for the next two years the organization proselytized in the area of Manchester along fairly conventional lines. Militancy began in earnest two years later, when Mrs. Pankhurst's attractive oldest daughter suddenly discovered the women's cause. Christabel Pankhurst had previously shown no special talent or vocational aptitude. She had, however, too much intelligence and energy to wait demurely, as Edwardian young ladies were supposed to do, for some likely young man to marry her. She plunged into the agitation for women's suffrage with a vengeance.

In 1905 the Liberal Party was preparing for what, by all indications, was going to be a landslide victory at the polls. Reform was in the air. Christabel determined to wrest an immediate declaration of intentions from the Liberals on the question of women's suffrage. Her target was Edward Grey, a leading Liberal who was certain to be included in the new Cabinet. Grey was scheduled to speak at a rally at the Free Trade Hall in Manchester. Equipped with a large banner on which was printed the question "Will You Give Votes for Women?" Christabel and a friend set out for the hall determined to secure the immediate deliverance of women or to go to jail. Grey's pitch to the Liberal electorate was interrupted by the startling question "Will the Liberal government give votes to women?" Grey was understandably taken aback. The question was not on the agenda. It was known that leading Liberals differed on this question. Women's suffrage could not be made a party matter at the bidding of two rude and anonymous young ladies. But Christabel and her friend would brook no denial. They proceeded to make such a row that they were forcibly ejected, as Christabel herself put it, "resisting . . . strongly . . . and still calling out: Will the Liberal government give women the vote?" [4] Not satisfied with the electrifying effects of this, her political debut, she proceeded to spit on a policeman outside the hall, thus committing "technical assault" and ensuring her arrest. So commenced the new tactics of militancy.

A few months after this memorable incident Mrs. Pankhurst and Christabel dispatched to the south one of their most promising young recruits, a former factory girl from Oldham, with £2 in her pocket and instructions to "rouse London." Later, on the opening day of Parliament, the W.S.P.U. held its own "Women's Parliament" in Caxton Hall. News arrived that King Edward VII's speech had been read without mention of women's enfranchisement. Mrs. Pankhurst herself promptly led a deputation of women to the House of Commons to argue with as many M.P.s as possible. On that occasion, after hours of waiting, a few women were actually admitted to the lobby, where they dutifully collared embarrassed and evasive members.

The pilgrimages from Caxton Hall to Parliament became an annual event, but never again were they so peaceful and orderly. The women were unwelcome visitors at best. Their determination to accost government members physically was a breach of decorum and a confounded nuisance. Christabel Pankhurst described the sortie from Caxton Hall to the House in 1907:

The House of Commons was guarded by rows of police who resisted the women's advance. A long struggle followed, for the women would not abandon the attempt to reach their goal. Again and again, through the interminable afternoon and evening, this went on. Exhausted, coats rent, hats torn from their heads, the women would return to Caxton Hall for a rest and then set out again to renew the struggle. . . . Fifteen women actually got through the police guard, made a rush into the House and began to hold a meeting in the lobby, only to be violently ejected and arrested. Other women in their hundreds made the same attempt, till the Square had to be forcibly cleared and some sixty arrests had been made.[5]

In the meantime the harassment of all Liberal candidates standing for by-elections in the country continued. As long as the Liberals refused to make a party commitment to women's suffrage, the W.S.P.U. waged war against them. The suffragettes were not interested in the individual views of the candidates. As long as the government itself refused to back enfranchisement, they would wage war upon all its members. Their tireless whirlwind tours against government candidates probably contributed to the defeat of several Liberals, including Mr.

Churchill, who at that time was unlucky enough to have a constituency in Manchester, the home ground of the W.S.P.U.

The W.S.P.U. was not out to ingratiate itself with influential Liberals. Its tactic was the simple one of obstruction, as nearly total as possible. Its members sought to damage the government at the polls and in the public eye. Insofar as a philosophy underlay their campaign at all, it was that of Charles Stewart Parnell and the Irish Nationalist Party of the 1880s. Richard Pankhurst had himself been the victim of the Irish Nationalist vote, which had cost him an election in 1885. The defeated candidate had explained to his wife the strategy of Parnell and his party. Parnell had been the leader of a small group that had had to face the implacable hostility of a large majority. Conciliation and reason were no good to him. By constant obstruction he had hoped to demoralize his opponents; he had engaged in a war of attrition, a war of nerves.

Mrs. Pankhurst adapted Parnell's methods to her own purposes. She sought to shock and infuriate the Liberals into taking some notice of her demands. The Pankhursts belonged to that difficult group of implacable human beings whose minds take a very literal bent. Of the jockeyings of party politics the suffragettes purported to be ignorant and contemptuous. When a Cabinet minister piously expressed his vague conviction that the question of the women's vote could not be long postponed, they pounced on his words and demanded the immediate passage of a bill. Immediately. During that very session of Parliament. They waved aside the fears of Labour and the Liberals that women's enfranchisement would upset the delicate balance of parties in the country and cause an unnatural swelling of the Conservative electorate—women were supposed to have an inborn bias toward Conservatism (as it turned out, a highly plausible supposition). They sneered at the Conservatives' fears that any enlargement of the franchise would inevitably lead to universal adult suffrage. (They assumed a continuous reliance on property qualifications.) They scoffed at Mr. Asquith's pleas that he had more urgent priorities to attend to.

The years after 1909 were marked by a storm of agitation over the Lloyd George budget and the House of Lords' unwillingness to pass it. Mrs. Pankhurst and her disciples maintained that if Mr. Asquith had to save the country from the House of Lords or the House of Lords from its own more archaic members, he was free to do so—provided that he granted women the vote at once. Northern Ireland was planning sedition—most interesting. And how, pray, did Edward Carson, leader of the Ulster rebels, stand on the question of female suffrage in Northern Ireland? In her single-minded pursuit of women's suffrage

Mrs. Pankhurst gradually left behind her old Labour associates, even though the Labour Party was the only one officially committed to granting women the vote. Questions of class and economics could not be allowed to blur the issue of women's rights.

To Mrs. Pankhurst and Christabel, Labour's obsessive preoccupation with trade unions and the poor was selfish and narrow, if not a deliberate subterfuge to evade its responsibility toward women. Although individual Labour members had worked arduously and selflessly in the women's cause, they received small thanks from the W.S.P.U. Mrs. Pankhurst sought no allies other than her own devoted female followers. Sylvia Pankhurst, a younger daughter, remained faithful to her father's political credo and worked tirelessly to organize the impoverished women of London's East End; she was eventually expelled from the W.S.P.U. for undue preoccupation with economics and for her loyalty to old friends in the trade unions.

Although Mrs. Pankhurst harkened back to the precedent of Parnell to find some sort of ideological underpinning for her movement, Christabel needed no such prop. Her justification of W.S.P.U. policies was very simple and had been unwittingly provided for her by, of all people, Arthur Balfour, leader of the Conservative Party. In the early days of the W.S.P.U. Christabel had led a deputation to visit Balfour, a professed believer in women's suffrage. Why was it, she demanded, that the question of votes for women had not been raised by the Conservatives during his tenure as Prime Minister? Mr. Balfour's candid answer had been "your cause is not in the swim." [6] Christabel apparently never forgot his words. In the years that followed, the militancy of the W.S.P.U. was constantly being accelerated to keep the issue "in the swim."

In effect, the drive for women's enfranchisement became a protest movement with the advent of the Pankhursts. Throughout much of the nineteenth century the issue had been more an abstract question or the pet peeve of an occasional radical feminist. The question of votes for women had been raised regularly in the House by sympathetic private members; it had found eloquent champions, among whom the philosopher and economist John Stuart Mill—at the urging of his intellectual wife—was the earliest and the most famous. Mill had made it part of his election platform in 1865, and since that time there had been no shortage of articles and discussions of the "women's question." In 1867 the first permanent women's-suffrage society had come into existence. Soon the federated National Society for Women's Suffrage could claim branches in every major city in England. Englishwomen had obtained the municipal franchise in 1869. The Local

Government Act of 1894 had given them the right to vote for parish councillors and boards of guardians and even to hold offices at this level themselves. In 1870 a bill to grant women the franchise had for the first time passed a second reading in the House. The theory that women had the right to vote had thus been endorsed in official quarters. The House had expressed its approval. Unfortunately, however, such votes meant little as long as neither party was willing to back the bill and steer it through a third reading, which (if the House of Lords approved) would make it the law of the land. The House had done nothing more than endorse a view.

In fact, for thirty years before the coming of Emmeline Pankhurst the women's cause had been languishing. Arguments for and against and methods of mobilizing public opinion and influencing legislators were about equally stale. Although the dedicated efforts of a few tireless nineteenth-century women had ensured that a women's-suffrage bill was debated every year but one in the 1870s, such a bill came to a vote only once in the 1880s. There was in any event an inherent unreality in these proceedings. Throughout the 1870s, 1880s, and 1890s Parliamentary majorities for or against the enfranchisement of women waxed and waned for reasons that had little to do with the merits of the case. Members of Parliament were always fully aware that they were voting on a bill that would die at the second reading. The annual debate on women's suffrage provided comic relief from the serious business of governing the country. Often the women were not given even the meager satisfaction of being taken seriously. A favorite opposition tactic was ridicule pure and simple. The vision of England and its mighty Empire tied to the apron strings of simpering females was invoked *ad nauseam* as an "argument" against the women's claim.

Perhaps it is better that most of the arguments against the enfranchisement of women should have been stated jocularly, for today they inevitably appear to range from the silly through the fatuous to the insulting. There was, for example, the argument based on chivalry. Politics, it was maintained, was a squalid and unladylike business. Once women became registered voters, their homes would be invaded by canvassers and pollsters of every description, presumably intent on making unwelcome advances to the ladies.

A weightier argument had it that women, because they did not serve in the army and defend the realm, were not entitled to the vote. This argument based on physical prowess was nicely suited to the jingoistic atmosphere of the late nineteenth century. It elicited from one eminent M.P. the sarcastic suggestion that if physique were to be the criterion for the vote, he himself should be disfranchised, whereas a popular circus strong man of the day was clearly entitled to plural representation. Women were not slow to point out that regard for their physical delicacy had not kept them from being employed in nineteenth-century factories. To the argument that they did not serve in the armed forces they raised the more venerable and reasonable cry "No taxation without representation."

Another, more interesting—and more insidious—argument against granting women the vote was that women already had great influence on the political process because in the sanctity of their own homes they could make full use of their feminine wiles to influence the votes of their husbands and fathers. This bizarre argument actually had its origins in learned and long-cherished constitutional theory. Throughout the eighteenth century and well into the nineteenth, English political theorists had argued that not individuals but "interests" were represented in the English Parliament. This argument was a pillar of the opposition to enfranchisement of any new sector of society. It was argued, for example, that the agricultural laborer had no political interests distinct from those of his squire and that he was indirectly represented in his master's vote. By the same token women's rights and interests were supposedly included in those of their menfolk.

Against this theory—which has its modern counterpart in the idea of the corporate state—there stood the radical ideas of Thomas Paine and John Stuart Mill, ultimately derived from the French Revolution: The rights of women were championed as an extension of natural rights and the rights of man. English constitutionalists were always uncomfortable with political doctrines derived from the tradition of the rights of man, yet more and more it was on these very grounds that the women argued their case.

The arguments against giving women the vote essentially reflected prejudice and habit. They changed little during the course of the nineteenth century, and on the eve of the First World War they had become quite hackneyed. But they were hard to give up. More than the political hegemony of men was at stake. The entire Victorian conception of womanhood was threatened with disintegration. The suffragettes had shattered more than the expensive windows of Regent Street. They had smashed a Victorian icon: William Wordsworth's romantic Lucy, a demure and blushing maiden who busied herself with embroidery and garlands of flowers. The suffragette looked more like snorting Medusa. Those who could not face this new incarnation of woman retaliated by trying to desex her. One nineteenth-century leader of women's suffrage, a certain harridan named Lydia Becker, was said to be proof positive that human beings now came in three sexes—male, female, and Miss Becker.

It was freely stated in the antisuffragette press that the petitioners were old maids in need not of the vote but of men. The climax of this edifying line of argument was reached in 1911, when *The Times* saw fit to print a letter from a physician who argued a close connection between suffragette militancy and menopause. The learned gentleman suggested that no fewer than 50 percent of all women went somewhat mad in middle life and that, furthermore, the female mind was well known to be "not an instrument for the pursuit of truth but . . . an instrument for providing her with creature comforts in the form of agreeable mental images."

If the women were not mad to start with, this line of argument must have driven them very near the edge. In the days before anthropologists and psychologists had testified that the social roles of male and female are largely matters of custom and cultural environment, this quasi-scientific quackery was largely unanswerable. The virulent outrage of the W.S.P.U. must be seen as partly the response of women too long treated and depicted as special variants of the noble savage, endowed, to be sure, with a certain dumb wisdom but a wisdom never to be put to practical use in the world of affairs.

Nevertheless, though the gross exaggeration of the doctor's words needs no emphasis, they were not without their kernel of truth. The fanatical excesses of some militant suffragettes had psychological, if not physiological, roots. Some of these women were bent upon wreaking a terrible vengeance on the masculine world that had so long forced them into passivity and mindlessness. One of the clearest examples of aberration was the high priestess of the movement, Christabel Pankhurst herself. This remarkable young lady produced in 1913, at the height of suffragette militancy, a most peculiar book. *The Great Scourge* was nothing less than a documentation of the moral turpitude of men. The scourge of venereal disease, she reported, was directly responsible for a host of ailments suffered by women. It was a primary cause of infant mortality and childlessness. It was spread through the gross and uncontrolled appetites of males, and it afflicted a staggering percentage of them. Christabel's panacea for the world's ills was "Votes for Women and Purity for Men." It is difficult to escape the conclusion that for Christabel the enfranchisement of women was a means to castrate men.

Embarked as she was on a sacred mission, it is not surprising that she had little use for the punctilious tactics of the older suffrage societies. In fact such tactics had proved dolefully ineffectual. Throughout the nineteenth century dedicated ladies had worked with the diligence of termites—writing articles, giving public lectures, collecting signatures on petitions to Parliament. They had functioned much as does any other pressure group—with the great and fatal drawback that their pressure group could not translate its pleasures and displeasures into votes at the polls. They had reasoned patiently with people who insulted and mocked them tirelessly; they had adduced evidence to prove that the British Empire would be spared instant collapse if women were granted the vote. Mrs. Pankhurst and her daughters did not bother to restate the many arguments carefully developed by suffrage societies over a period of decades. They simply assumed that women ought to have the vote and proceeded from there.

Countless aspirations, some of the vaguest and most unconscious sort, were collected behind the banners of the Pankhursts and the W.S.P.U. The position of women in Georgian England was not enviable. Working-class women were menial drudges who labored for wages that averaged one-third of those earned by men. Although the argument that these women needed the vote to protect themselves economically was a favorite among suffragettes, few leaders of the struggle for women's emancipation came from the working class.

Most suffragettes were women of solid middle-class backgrounds, fighting as best they could to dispel the uselessness and meaninglessness of their lives. Nineteenth-century economic prosperity had greatly increased their numbers without any parallel expansion of the roles that they were assigned, or even permitted, to play.

The lowest stratum of the female middle class was composed of domestics. At the turn of the century virtually half the four million employed women were servants in other people's houses. Their status in the world was not of their own making; it was derived vicariously from that of the families they served. Their free time and even their dress were arranged for them according to their places in the servants' hierarchy. Underpaid, often treated with no more consideration than household objects, many of them nevertheless sought to partake of the gentility of their employers. They had the mentality of serfs and often nursed the secret resentments and grudges of serfs as well. One step up from the maid or the cook was the seamstress or governess—virtually the only "careers" open to respectable ladies.

The unmarried women probably suffered most. They were supposed to exist only as eccentric maiden aunts living out their lives as appendages to other people's families. According to social theory, women were supposed to be provided for by their fathers before marriage and by their husbands afterward—in a day when marriageable women outnumbered men by 9 percent, and the census tables recorded that between 12 and 15 percent of the adult female population of the country was unwed.

The lot of married women, especially if they were intelligent and educated, tended to be almost equally stultifying. The Prime Minister's wife, Margot Asquith, might find sufficient amusement in her activities as glamorous hostess and witty gossipmonger to the lords and ladies of England. Obviously, few women were in a position to emulate her. For the upper—middle-class lady the endless round of tea parties, sewing circles, and charitable activities must have created subliminal boredom of the most dangerous sort. Women's access to the masculine professional world was still very slight. Florence Nightingale had made nursing respectable, but in 1906 there were only about two hundred doctors and no lawyers among the women of England. The fashionable lady with a bit of capital might take refuge in opening some elegant little shop—Mrs. Pankhurst herself repeatedly harbored this fancy—but most of these feminine business ventures proved ephemeral and economically unsound. They were the desperate diversions of those who suspected their own purposelessness.

The battle to secure votes for women thus became important not only for its goal but also for the activity itself. The thrill of the struggle was its own reward. Women grew intoxicated with the pleasures of camaraderie experienced by any soldiers on the front lines. The Pankhursts often referred to their followers as an "army." Within its ranks all distinctions of age and class were abolished. The only hierarchy that they recognized was based on fidelity and sacrifice for the cause. Distinguished ladies of the realm discovered sudden affinities with factory girls from Manchester and milliners from the East End of London. The suffragette movement was a solvent for many constricting social barriers. Christabel Pankhurst wrote proudly that everyone belonged to the suffragette aristocracy.

As the militancy of the movement accelerated so did the desire to suffer and sacrifice for the cause. Women who had braved jail for their acts took to wearing badges. Although officially the W.S.P.U. continued to give lip service to the idea that there were many routes to the attainment of the franchise, the militants evinced only contempt for those who preferred the traditional one of negotiation and political compromise. There was coming to be a masochistic undercurrent in suffragette philosophy. Jailed suffragettes competed to see which one among them could fend off the feeding tubes the longest. To hunger strikes were added thirst strikes. Certainly the women abused themselves in order to secure rapid release from jail but also in order to share in the honor of having suffered for their cause.

With so much millennialism in the air it is surprising that the movement produced only one full-fledged martyr—and a dubious one at that. On Derby Day in 1913 young suffragette Emily Wilding Davison flung herself in front of the King's horse at Epsom Downs. Perhaps she had intended only to wave a suffragette flag—she had purchased a return ticket at the railway station—but her injuries proved fatal. She had been one of the most ardent of the Pankhursts' followers, an avid hunger striker, and the first militant to resort to arson. Miss Davison was instantly canonized by the movement. Thousands turned out for her funeral procession led by a standard-bearer with a banner on which was emblazoned: "Thoughts have gone forth whose power can sleep no more. Victory. Victory." [7] Christabel, though effusive in singing the dead girl's praises, took her death coolly in stride: "Probably in no other way and at no other time and place could she [Emily Davison] so effectually have brought the concentrated attention of millions to bear upon the cause," [8] she wrote.

To gain the concentrated attention of millions was the governing precept of the W.S.P.U. Christabel and her mother launched the politics of spectacular visibility. Unwittingly, perhaps unconsciously, they accepted the cynical adage that *all* publicity is good publicity. The press, long used to dismissing the suffragettes with occasional cartoons, awoke with a start. The escapades of the suffragettes quickly became front-page news. No one could resist the theatrics of it all. The W.S.P.U. developed its own pageantry and iconography. The suffragettes had their own colors—purple, green, and white. They designed suffragette parlor games, printed illustrated postcards, and produced lapel buttons, costume jewelry, banners, placards, and handbills to advertise their fight. When, in the later, most virulent stages of the campaign, arson was being practiced, a sheaf of suffragette leaflets was sure to be found near the scene of any such crime. A favorite pastime, one in which a suffragette was supposed to engage in as regularly as brushing her teeth, was the chalking of "Votes for Women" on sidewalks and park benches.

In their more peaceful moments the suffragettes delighted in staging huge public processions. In an age that has been exposed to innumerable peace marches and civil-rights demonstrations, it is hard to appreciate the impact that those early monster meetings had on the eye and ear. In 1908 the suffragettes organized a vast demonstration in Hyde Park designed to impress the government with the strength of numbers. Proceeding along seven different routes from all sides of London, the marchers converged on Hyde Park. Government officials were invited to attend by a lady with a megaphone who had hired a motorboat and was sailing up and down the Thames opposite the terrace of the House of Commons. "Come to the Park on Sunday," she urged, adding by way of reassurance: "There shall be no arrests. You shall have plenty of police protection." [9]

Sporting banners and sashes of green, white, and purple, the women flocked to the park to hear speakers on twenty different platforms call for an end to their bondage. It is a moot question how many of those present came as champions of women's rights and how many as Sunday strollers in search of entertainment. Anywhere between a quarter- and a half-million people attended. London had not seen a political demonstration of such dimensions since the days preceding passage of the Reform Bill of 1867. At the end of the day, just before the reading of the inevitable resolution demanding the immediate grant of the vote, a bugle was sounded to give the proper solemnity to the occasion. The attendance figures were more than impressive, even the most grudging observers had to admit, but what after all did they mean?

Inevitably it was argued by the sober and more dignified press that the suffragettes' tactics—the pageantry was excepted as simply the occasion for harmless merriment—hurt their own cause. Stone throwing, heckling, and arson would in no way help to convince the government that women were sufficiently rational creatures to be accorded the solemn rights of the ballot. The suffragettes were held to be irresponsible and frivolous, cheapening and sullying their own image—indeed the image of all womanhood. The inevitable cry arose from well-intentioned liberal moderates: Irrational extremism was weakening and confounding the cause. Friends were being rapidly alienated. Sympathetic allies were being acutely embarrassed. No politician could afford to stand by the side of a movement whose leaders were so clearly tinged with lunacy. In a word, the specter of a vast and angry backlash was raised.

There is some indication that dislike of the suffragettes' tactics actually did cost them a few votes during an important House division in 1912. Yet very few M.P.s could afford to cast votes based entirely on personal pique. The Pankhursts were not able to budge Asquith, but then before the war probably only an earthquake could have done that. With every step-up in militancy the ranks of the W.S.P.U. swelled, and its coffers bulged. In 1914 the suffragettes collected, despite government harassment, more than £37,000—more than in any previous year and much more than the sums obtained by the "constitutional" suffrage societies. Militancy won many converts. It unmasked but probably failed to create new enemies. In fact, it is likely that the efficacy of direct-action techniques was vastly underestimated in a society in which they were so new and so unorthodox. Guerrilla warfare does not accord well with the liberal persuasion. Even today chroniclers of the crusading feminists are reluctant to admit that tactics so deplorable, so destructive and neurotic, could also have been so effective. But they were highly effective: The question of women's suffrage was never treated as merely academic after the arrival of the Pankhurst family on the scene.

As with all twentieth-century protest movements undertaken by middle-class people, the suffragettes' campaign confounded the political ingenuity of representative and democratic government, which was caught between impossible alternatives. Being liberal and presumably humane and rational as well, its leaders could not engage in open repression of these noxious rebels. Repression would bring down the wrath of all liberal laymen, for laymen not personally connected with the Home Office were notoriously unappreciative of the difficulties of dealing with these hoodlums in petticoats.

Any sign of unusually firm handling threatened to swing public opinion into open sympathy with the martyred outlaw. Public opinion is in any case very unreliable when it comes to guerrillas. Anyone willing to take on all the government's pomp and majesty in ludicrously unequal combat is certain to win a certain amount of sneaking sympathy. Hurling stones through the windows of Downing Street had of course to be officially censored, but the newspapermen who wrote irate editorials against such vandalism probably chuckled after hours. The sheer bravado, the stealth, and the ingenuity of suffragette escapades often produced cheers from the public. A big shot slipping on a banana peel brings a sure-fire laugh in any movie. A Cabinet minister dodging a lady's boot or dog-whip was at least as funny. The laughter of the public incited the suffragettes to further efforts.

The women's antics were insidiously debilitating to the morale and the image of the government. Governments are most secure when surrounded by a considerable amount of *gravitas*. Mr. Asquith's government did not defend itself very well from the ladies. How could it? They were considerably more than a mere irritation yet very much less than a national menace. If leaders tried to ignore or minimize the feminine attack, they simply looked inept. If they used brute force, they were condemned as vicious and reactionary.

At the Home Office this dilemma produced legislation that attempted to be simultaneously coercive and humane. This brain child of the government's nervous frustration, promptly dubbed "The Cat and Mouse Act" by the suffragettes, was schizoid in its intent and only aggravated the government's problems. The Act empowered the government to discharge fasting suffragettes before the termination of their jail sentences if their health was endangered—but it also permitted the government the option of clapping them right back into jail as soon as their health had been restored. The law was designed to circumvent the nasty problem of force feeding. Just to keep his hands free, however, and presumably to hold this odious punishment as an ever-present threat, the Home Secretary insisted that the government retain the right to force-feed at its own discretion.

The effects of the law could not have been more unfortunate. Mrs. Pankhurst and her daughter Sylvia were imprisoned and released no fewer than ten times each within the space of a few months. Each arrest meant capturing the shouting, struggling women anew. The press was given not one but ten opportunities for front-page drama. At times the suffragette leaders were plucked from the sanctity of their living rooms or, worse, from sanatoriums where they had gone to recuperate.

Back in jail the women promptly recommenced abusing themselves. Sylvia Pankhurst took to pacing about her cell until she collapsed on the floor and passed out. When discharged, the women often had to be carried out on stretchers. Often they were similarly transported to meetings and rallies. If the law that permitted this sort of thing was designed to impress the public and the news media with the benevolence and humanity of the government, it could hardly have been less successful. The W.S.P.U. made glorious propaganda of its members' sufferings. Its newspaper was full of bloodcurdling descriptions of their treatment at the hands of the authorities. A suffragette poster of the day illustrated the Cat and Mouse Act: a young girl writhing in agony in the jaws of a cat.

The government made a last-ditch effort to cut off the financial sources of the W.S.P.U. by raiding its offices and attempting to seize its subscription lists. The authorities also tried to censor the militant newspaper, which nevertheless managed to appear regularly. In perplexity the House began to entertain suggestions that these female demons be deported to Australia, New Zealand, or some even remoter and preferably uninhabited corner of the Empire. Mr. McKenna was forced to point out the impracticality of these well-meaning suggestions to his colleagues. The women would never last long enough to reach these destinations; they would starve themselves to death on the boat, he whimpered. He was personally convinced that at least thirty or forty suffragettes were ready to perish for their convictions.

Foolhardy and reckless though the women may have been, they were also brave. When they appeared on public platforms, emaciated and carried on stretchers, they appeared to be the victims of the government's naked brutality. Mrs. Pankhurst thundered that the suffragette holy war could end in nothing less than freedom or death. In 1914 her sorry physical condition was already inviting remarks that the government's policy toward the women was one of murder by installment.

And then the Great War broke out, and the suffragettes' struggle came to an instant and voluntary halt. By September 1914 Mrs. Pankhurst was addressing recruiting meetings on behalf of the government. Lloyd George had become her idol. Publication of *The Suffragette* was temporarily suspended. When it reappeared it bore a new slogan: "It is a thousand times more the duty of the militant Suffragette to fight the Kaiser for the sake of Liberty than it was to fight anti-Suffrage Governments."

Impressed by the women's contribution to the war effort, Asquith announced himself converted to support of women's suffrage in 1917. An electoral bill granting the vote to all women over thirty became law in January 1918. It was an abrupt and anticlimactic ending to a heroic struggle. Yet Mrs. Pankhurst had declared even in her angriest hours that she and the women she led desired in the end not to destroy but to serve.

In 1930 a statue of Mrs. Pankhurst was unveiled in Victoria Tower Gardens by Prime Minister Stanley Baldwin. By then women enjoyed suffrage in Britain on the same terms as men did. In fact by then women had received the vote in most democratic countries. The unveiling of a statue of Mrs. Pankhurst by the British Prime Minister symbolized the success of the women's struggle for the vote; protest against their inferior political position was something in the distant, furious past. The image of the suffragettes had become greatly softened in the memories of posterity; their protest seemed to have been good fun, part of the high jinks and charming eccentricities of the glorious twilight years before the First World War. Especially because adding the female half of the population to the electorate had produced no significant change in the cast of political life—only a shift toward moderate conservatism, exemplified by Calvin Coolidge, Baldwin himself, and other drab, do-nothing politicians of the 1920s— the suffragettes could be remembered with amused fondness.

But both image and memory were false: The suffragette protest had been a harsh and bitter cry from the heart by members of the exploited and subjugated sex who found in the vote an issue worthy of energies too long sapped by the weary labor, terrible boredom, and sadistic copulative treatment that were their lot in a society completely dominated by the male sex.

The sadism of the bedroom was the dark thread that ran through all early twentieth-century female protest—the one injustice that they could not publicly denounce. The sadomasochistic proclivities of the suffragette leaders—how delightful to be forced to eat in prison, how sweet the joy of whipping Cabinet ministers!—were veiled protests against this sexual slavery. The emancipation of women from insults and terrors was made possible by the discrediting of traditional morality in the holocaust of the First World War and the new conditions of industrial society, although that emancipation is only now achieving its necessary fulfillment. The suffragette movement—concerned superficially with ballot boxes rather than with wombs—was the distant clarion call to this emancipation, using politics to disguise the underlying sexual battle.

The feminist political crusade was of crucial importance in another way: as a prototype for twentieth-century protest movements. All the methods of middle-class radical protest were employed by Mrs. Pankhurst and her corseted legions: obstruction, destruction of property, hunger strikes, occasional martyrdom. The suffragettes played upon the bad conscience of middle-class liberals and used methods that stung this sensitive conscience mercilessly. This pattern would recur continually in the Age of Protest.

CHAPTER

2

The Irish Model

THE Easter Rebellion is the stuff of which poetry is made. At about noon on Monday, April 24, 1916, 150 men carrying pikes, crowbars, shotguns, and German Mausers manufactured for the Prussian forces of 1870 marched through the center of Dublin, up Sackville Street, and into the General Post Office. Hastily ejecting indignant and disbelieving citizens who were waiting to buy stamps, they began knocking out the glass from the windows with the butts of their rifles and ramming heavy furniture against windows and doorways. The telegraph operator in the building felt a sharp object at his back. It was a pike, and it belonged to a man who told him that he was a "prisoner of war." [1]

Throughout the city another eight hundred or so civilian soldiers, many without uniforms and carrying a nightmarish assortment of antique implements that they were pleased to call "rifles," seized various key points: a brewery, a biscuit factory, a lunatic asylum. They set about building barricades of old furniture and personal possessions. In all solemnity the leader of this fearsome army declared war on the British Empire.

Earlier that day the birth of the Irish Republic had been momentarily held up by an unwelcome visitation of common sense. As the commander in chief of the Irish forces, Padraic Pearse, was preparing to march to the post office, he had been intercepted by a hysterical woman, his sister. For a brief instant the destiny of a nation faltered.

"Come home, Pat, and leave all this foolishness!"[2] she screamed. But the commandant faltered only a moment and then pushed on.

The post office was "seized," and Pearse emerged to read the Proclamation of the new Irish Republic. It proved impossible to impress the august solemnity of the words ("In the name of God and of the dead generations . . .") on the people, most of whom continued down Sackville Street heedless of this great moment in the history of their nation. The few people who gathered around were incredulous or merely curious. The response to this declaration of national independence could not have been colder.

Eamon de Valera, a thirty-four-year-old mathematics teacher who later became President of Ireland, led 120 men to Boland's Mills, a dreary complex of bakeries and granaries that commanded key entrance routes to the city. At their destination De Valera's soldiers encountered furious opposition: The bakers refused to abandon the thousand loaves of bread in their ovens. Only at gun point were they persuaded to evacuate the premises for the greater glory of Ireland. Even then four of them tried to persuade the insurgents to let them stay until the bread was done. Even in a republic people had to eat.

From eight different directions a hundred men advanced on St. Stephen's Green, the lovely Victorian park in the center of the city. Mothers with babies in perambulators, holiday strollers, and old men enjoying the spring sunshine on park benches were summarily ordered out. A few moments later trenches were being dug among the flower beds. Passing cars were waved down at gun point and their drivers ordered to deposit them at the barricades. The motorists were unimpressed by the soldiers' assurances that the Republic would reimburse them for all goods appropriated. Excited women and children pressed around the barricades for a better view of what was happening inside the park. They were oblivious to the urgent pleas of the soldiers that they go home, that showers of bullets were imminent, that everyone was in danger. This occasion promised to provide the best show that they had seen in a while, and they did not want to miss the fun.

Now and then someone furtively shouted, "Up the Republic!" but the predominant mood of the crowd that week was undoubtedly hostile. Playwright and novelist James Stephens kept a diary during Easter Week. He recorded the reactions to the rebels expressed by the average men and women standing on street corners and nervously relaying the latest rumors:

"I hope every man of them will be shot."

And:

"They ought all to be shot." [3]

That week Dublin housewives served tea to the British soldiers who were hastily dispatched to the city to put an end to this exercise in mock heroics.

The great mass of Irish men and women had neither expected nor wanted the Easter Rebellion. The Rising was not an outburst of popular discontent long smoldering beneath the placid surface of events; such explanations and justifications were made up long afterward by Irish historians uncomfortable about the implications of a flight to arms by so tiny and unrepresentative a minority.

In 1916 John Bull's oppression of Ireland was already more a historic grievance than a present fact. Irishmen could vote, join the British civil service, and enjoy the full protection of the British Constitution. Rhetoric alone could define England's administration in Ireland as tyranny. After decades of struggle Home Rule—the right of the Irish to their own parliament and to self-government in the form gained in the nineteenth century by Canada and Australia—was safely on the statute books at Westminster. Ireland had the English government's promise that it would be implemented as soon as World War I had ended. The great majority of the Irish people firmly supported John Redmond, leader of the Irish Parliamentary Party, which had secured this long-sought prize.

The war, furthermore, had brought considerable prosperity to Ireland. England's need of Irish foodstuffs and wool, as well as of Irish labor, meant steady incomes for many Irish families for the first time in years. At the outbreak of the Great War a member of the British Cabinet had reported to the House of Commons that the one bright spot in the miserable European scene was Ireland, whose loyalty to the British war effort was assured. Not two weeks before the Easter Rebellion British intelligence—with characteristic prescience—had reaffirmed that Ireland was loyal and content. In 1916 there were a quarter-million Irishmen fighting with the British army in the mud of France. There was probably not a family in all Dublin that did not have a son, brother, or father in the British service. To many of these people the Rising appeared not only mad but treasonous as well.

The Easter Rebellion was the work of a small group of middle-class intellectuals guided by a myth and a vision more poetic than historical. They were an unlikely band of men to seize arms. The military plans for the siege of Dublin had been drawn up by Joseph Plunkett, who was also one of the signers of the Proclamation. At the time of the Rising he was twenty-eight years old and already dying of tuberculosis. His knowledge of warfare came from an intensive study of Napoleonic campaigns and eighteenth-century Irish peasant uprisings. He wrote verse that sounded like Swinburne's and pored over Sanskrit and Egyptian grammars. Another of the leaders was a clerk in the city treasurer's office, where he earned £200 a year—a good middle-class salary—who also played the Irish pipes. A third was a lecturer at the National University in Dublin.

The leader of the Rising and the man chosen by his comrades in arms to be independent Ireland's first President was Padraic Pearse. To the men who fought with him he became the incarnation of the spirit of the Rising, and historians have on the whole tended to second this instinctive judgment. Pearse was also a poet, one who proudly proclaimed himself a fool:

> Since the wise men have not spoken, I speak
>   that am only a fool
> A Fool that hath loved his folly
> Yea, more than the wise men their books
>   or their counting houses, or their quiet homes. . . .
>
> I have squandered the splendid years
>   That the Lord God gave to my youth
> In attempting impossible things
>   deeming them alone worth the toil. . . .[4]

Pearse was a shy, austere man who dressed in black and ran a bilingual secondary school in one of Dublin's prettiest suburbs. To those who knew him—he was one of Dublin's lesser literary lights—he seemed an impractical daydreamer who would probably never amount to much. The great passion of his adolescence and young manhood had been the revival of Gaelic as a living language. His school had been established with that end in view. It was run along progressive lines, and many of Dublin's prominent citizens sent their sons to St. Edna's. Even so, Pearse was constantly in debt.

The men who planned and executed the Easter Rebellion were painfully aware that the country was not behind them. They knew too that their stand in arms would inevitably fail and that they would in all likelihood be shot. On the eve of the Rising, James Connolly, a tough-minded labor organizer, remarked casually to one of his men that they would all be slaughtered. Startled, his friend asked whether there was not some small hope of success. Connolly replied cheerfully that there was no chance of success and went back to his preparations for the next day's battle.

These men hoped that their insurrection would one day be counted as the first installment of an Irish revolution, but the Rising itself was conceived as a protest demonstration against British imperialism and

Irish degradation—a sacrificial act, sincere unto death but still only a gesture. Their deaths were intended to waken an apathetic people from its comfortable stupor. They believed that Ireland needed not Home Rule but redemption. The very date of the rebellion had been chosen with this idea in mind. To devout Roman Catholics Easter week is the time when death ends in regeneration. The Rising, no matter how dismal its immediate prospects might be, was not intended by its leaders as a nihilistic kamikaze action. It was undertaken in a spirit of hope and faith: faith that the Irish people would in the long run respond to the challenge of martyrdom.

This curious state of mind, in which an almost mystical faith in the awakened Irish spirit was combined with a loathing for existing political and social habits, had its origins in a cultural movement that had profoundly influenced Pearse and other men of his generation. He had for many years been a member of the Gaelic League, an organization founded in the 1890s to promote, preserve, and spread the Gaelic language in Ireland. Although nonpolitical, this organization had made its contribution to nationalism by unearthing, translating, and disseminating the Celtic folklore that came to form so important an element in the works of J. M. Synge, Lady Augusta Gregory, James Stephens, and the young William Butler Yeats. The League had made familiar the image of the Gael as he had supposedly existed in Ireland before the coming of the English conqueror and corrupter: a familiar compound of nineteenth-century romantic stereotypes, a kind of noble savage and village Milton in one.

In pre-Christian and pre-British days, so the legend went, Ireland had been populated by a race of heroic warrior bards who had lived in a democratic, classless society; pagan bravery and pantheistic piety had produced a race both rugged and refined, courageous, chaste, and chivalrous. The modern descendant of these ancient Fenians was the Irish peasant. His martial valor slumbered, but he was still wonderfully sensitive to the beauties of nature and utterly innocent of the false values of factory, Empire, and urban slum. He drew his enduring strength from the soil, to which he was mystically bound, and from his Roman Catholic faith. Anonymous, poor, and exploited, he was the carrier of all the finest values of Irish civilization. The romantic strain in the Gaelic Revival, its hostility to materialism and modernity, was combined with nationalist resentment of England, the hereditary foe. As a result, England came to be pictured as the boorish propagator of all the evils and false values of modern civilization.

Not everyone took the mythical Gael as seriously as did Pearse, who had over the doorway of his school a fresco of the ancient Irish warrior Cú Chulainn receiving arms. Synge brilliantly mocked the heroic peasant Gael in *The Playboy of the Western World*, which caused riots in the Abbey Theater when it was first produced in 1908. For the sophisticated and worldly the Gaelic hero was useful as a vehicle for magnificent poetry and stirring drama. Nevertheless the Celtic Revival and the movement to revive the Gaelic language impressed on the mind of an entire generation the possibility of another Ireland, remote from the sweaty, tawdry life of Edwardian Dublin, from the disputations of lawyers and the deals and intrigues that had characterized Irish politics since the death of its last great political leader, Charles Stewart Parnell, in 1891.

In the first decade of the twentieth century the search for Irish traditions was on. Pearse had founded his school to give Irish children a sense of their own history, to which the national, British-designed school system was oblivious. His arguments in favor of disseminating a history and creating a literature indigenously Irish are strikingly similar to those of militant civil-rights leaders who press for an introduction of Negro history and African studies into the American school system today. Pearse was struggling to give future generations of Irishmen a sense of their own dignity and worth. The Easter Rebellion was part of the same campaign to raise national morale.

To members of Pearse's generation the inert complacency of Ireland was proof of a spiritual squalor, a degradation that caused them acute personal shame. Such shame was a surprisingly prevalent theme in Irish writing of the decade, appearing even in the works of those who found the Celtic Revival itself silly and too parochial to sustain great art. James Joyce, who rejected the idea of Gaelic literature and national Roman Catholic art completely, wrote *The Dubliners* as a bitter ode to the city that he thought represented the center of the moral and spiritual paralysis that gripped his country. Yeats, who had mixed feelings about Celtic romanticism, produced one of his most famous poems on the same theme: the drabness and the moribund pettiness of Irish life in his own day.

> What need you, being come to sense,
> But fumble in a greasy till
> And add the halfpence to the pence
> And prayer to shivering prayer, until
> You have dried the marrow from the bone?
> For men were born to pray and save:
> Romantic Ireland's dead and gone,
> It's with O'Leary in the grave.[5]

With its bitter puns on the words "pray" and "save," Yeat's poem was not resigned but challenging. It was written only three years before the Easter Rebellion, which testified in blood to the vitality of romantic Ireland.

Pearse had repeatedly sounded the same despondent and angry note: His was an accursed generation, one that lacked all idealism and preferred seedy security to nobility of thought and deed. Shortly before the Rising he wrote this evaluation of the quality of Irish life:

There has been nothing more terrible in Irish history than the failure of the last generation. Other generations have failed in Ireland, but they have failed nobly; or, failing ignobly, some man among them has redeemed them from infamy by the splendour of his protest. But the failure of the last generation has been mean and shameful, and no man has arisen from it to say or do a splendid thing in virtue of which it shall be forgiven.[6]

Home Rule he regarded as the quintessence of ignoble failure. At least to some leaders of the Rising, Home Rule itself was less objectionable than the mean, haggling way in which it had been secured. It represented the complete denial of the heroic element in Irish history, and a rebirth of that heroic spirit was what they yearned for more than new constitutional arrangements. Their disquietude found no scapegoats among the leading politicians of the day. Nobody hated John Redmond; nobody accused him of betraying the hopes of his countrymen. His party had manifestly done its best to steer Ireland through the turgid waters of English politics toward Home Rule. Those nationalists who were interested in such things as elections had failed miserably in their one attempt to unseat a member of Redmond's party. Redmond could be accused of nothing worse than failure of imagination, but in the view of the romantics that failure had robbed the Irish of their pride, their manhood, their heroic tradition.

As for the English administration in Ireland, it was quite popular in 1916. Augustine Birrell, Chief Secretary for Ireland in Asquith's Cabinet, was known to be genuinely fond of Irish life. During his tenure in office he had piloted through the House of Commons more than fifty bills dealing with such vital matters as Irish education, agriculture, and housing. Birrell was a student of Irish culture and had helped to publish an anthology of Irish verse that contained several centuries of Irish rebel yell. He was rather pleased at being the last Chief Secretary: The Home-Rule Bill would abolish his office when it was implemented after the war.

Sir Matthew Nathan, the Undersecretary, who shouldered most of the day-to-day work, was, if anything, even more easygoing and amiable. He made himself completely accessible to Irish politicians of all stripes. He frequented the Abbey Theater and was on terms of friendly intimacy with some of Dublin's best-known literary figures. When the war broke out, Birrell and Nathan clamped down on the noisier nationalist newspapers, some of which were openly invoking the aid of Germany and the destruction of the British Empire, but they did so in a perfunctory manner. Neither man had a taste for such high-handed procedures. The militant nationalists who strutted about the country disrupting English recruiting efforts by sneering at Irishmen who were willing to fight with England for the liberty of small nations were very few in number, and recruits to the British army kept coming. Informers compiled rumors on the mischief being brewed in nationalist circles; the men in Dublin Castle (seat of the British authorities in Ireland) did not believe in getting overexcited. Nathan noted the names of some people who might eventually have to be arrested or deported, but that was as far as he thought it wise to go.

After the rebellion both Birrell and Nathan had to answer awkward questions before the royal commission set up to investigate. Everyone in the top level of British administration in Ireland resigned; after all, somebody had to take official responsibility for the insurrection. The laxity and genial laissez-faire attitudes of Birrell and Nathan came in for much severe criticism. Privately, however, many people admitted that it was difficult to see how they had erred. Irish observers tended to agree. The poet George Russell told Nathan that his policy of not forcing a confrontation with the extremists had been a judicious one. The rebel action was an efflorescence of irrationalism and could not have been anticipated. The fervor of their determination to strike a blow for freedom was not something that could have been suspected from the dry official reports of intelligence agents. And since when had civil servants and bureaucrats been expected to study second-rate Irish poets as part of their government duties?

The year in which poets had first become insurgent soldiers and cultural nationalism had buckled on a gun belt was 1913. In that year Ireland had begun publicly to arm, almost at the behest of the English. Constitutionalism was dealt a severe blow by—of all people—the British Tories. Badly in need of an issue with which to discredit the Liberal Party, the Conservatives took up the cause of Ulster, Protestantism, and the integrity of the British Empire. Traditional antagonism between Protestant Northern Ireland and Roman Catholic Southern Ireland was deliberately and violently exacerbated by Edward Carson, F. E. Smith, and other Tory rabble rousers who announced themselves ready to fight to the death to preserve the Protestant Northern Irish from Home Rule, which they liked to advertise as "Rome Rule." As soon as it became clear that Asquith's government was determined to push through a Home-Rule Bill, the Conservatives took it upon themselves to smash it. If need be, they were willing to go as far as condoning and even promoting armed rebellion. Carson and some of his friends drew up a document known as "Ulster's Solemn League and Covenant." It pledged eternal loyalty to the English Crown and a fight to the last man against the "conspiracy" of Home Rule. This impressive document was circulated at giant rallies in the North, where thousands of people signed it. The next step was the formation of a military vigilante organization, the Ulster Volunteers, designed to frighten the Liberals with the specter of civil war in Ireland. Large quantities of Tory money and guns smuggled in from England contributed to the buildup of this organization.

A few months later Southern nationalists of all stripes responded by forming the Irish Volunteers, pledged to the enactment of Home Rule and the integrity of the Irish nation. They claimed, with justice, that the secessionists in the North were a small dissident minority abetted by outside agitators. On paper, at least, the Southern Volunteers, unlike their Northern counterparts, existed only to preserve the British Constitution and to prevent the spread of sedition in the North. Psychologically, however, both military organizations served to undermine constitutionalism. Both bespoke an unwillingness to abide by the decisions of the conference table.

The glamor of guns suited those who dreamed of a rebirth of the Irish heroic spirit. Padraic Pearse joined the Irish Volunteers, but he would hear nothing against the Ulster militia: An Ulsterman with a gun was a much less ridiculous figure than a nationalist without one, he said. Redmond saw to it that many of his supporters were seated on the executive committee of the Volunteers to keep the organization defensive and moderate in its aims. Nevertheless, its mere existence represented an erosion of his authority. Inevitably it attracted such radical separatists as existed in Ireland at the time.

Irish radicalism was concentrated in the Irish Republican Brotherhood, a secret society that dated back to the middle of the nineteenth century. The I.R.B. had gone into eclipse after an abortive Fenian rising in 1867 and a brief dynamite campaign in the 1880s. At the turn of the century it consisted of little more than small scattered groups of bitter old men who met periodically to drink to the death of the British Empire. Only a few years later, however, the national revival had attracted to its ranks a few able and militant young men who had succeeded in injecting some life into the decrepit old-timers. The I.R.B., which had never been a legal organization and was officially

condemned by the Church, had few scruples about the use of terrorist tactics. It looked upon the creation of the Volunteers as a
heaven-sent opportunity to put guns into the hands of Irishmen and
quickly maneuvered its leaders into key positions on the Volunteers'
executive committee.

Secret societies had always proliferated in Ireland; throughout the
nineteenth century they had been the sole means by which the peasantry could organize itself against exploitative landlords. The I.R.B.
was numerically insignificant. As late as 1911 it numbered no more
than 1,500 members. Republican ideals had come to Ireland at the time
of the French Revolution and had been nurtured since that time by
no more than a handful of men in every generation. Because of its
roots in peasant riots and uprisings, the republican movement had acquired overtones of agrarian radicalism, but it stood remote from socialist doctrines developed in industrial states. The radicalism of the
I.R.B. drew its inspiration from Jean Jacques Rousseau and the Jaco-
bins rather than from Karl Marx; it had hardly been updated since the
eighteenth century. To members of the I.R.B., republicanism was a
mystique, to be watered by the blood of martyrs. Once the tyranny of
kings—at least of the British monarch—had disappeared from the earth,
the sovereign people would legislate with innate wisdom, the chasm
between rich and poor would disappear, and harmony and brotherhood would return to the land.

There was an Irish trade-union organization, as well as an embryonic
Socialist Party. The former suffered the handicap of being concentrated almost exclusively in Belfast and Dublin, whereas the latter
consisted mainly of James Connolly and his newspaper, *The Irish
Worker*. During the war socialism in Ireland joined hands with nationalism, for the capitalist exploiter and the enemy alien were one
and the same. Connolly reasoned that the first step toward economic
justice was withdrawal of the imperialistic power from Ireland, and
he drew closer to the militant nationalists. But the social gospel of
Irish republicanism never went beyond a vague and optimistic declaration about the Irish people's right to own their country and to
control their destinies. This gospel was eventually to produce a revolution with no social content at all. Such economic grievances and goals
as the left wing of the I.R.B. and the tiny Socialist Party did nurture
were subordinated to the political and national struggle.

To an embittered few, the Irish Free State, when at last it emerged
in 1922, appeared to offer little more than a change of personnel at
the top, leaving the class structure and social mores undisturbed. Sean
O'Casey irreverently parodied Yeats's great poem "Easter 1916," in

which the poet had heralded an Ireland transfigured by the birth of a terrible new beauty in the fires of Easter Week. The Irish Rebellion, O'Casey jeered, had in the end succeeded in making the world safe for top hats, starched collars, clerical tyranny, the banishers of James Joyce, and a new Irish bourgeoisie.

> A terrible beauty is borneo
> Republicans once so forlorneo
> Subjected to all kinds of scorneo
> Top-hatted, frock-coated with manifest skill,
> Are well away now on St. Patrick's steep hill
> Directing the labour of Jack and of Jill
> In the dawn of a wonderful morneo.[7]

In 1916, however, the I.R.B. was making plans for an insurrection. At the commencement of the First World War it had endorsed the theory of a stand in arms, typically enough because it accorded well with an old eighteenth-century rebel adage that "England's difficulty is Ireland's opportunity." But it was a long way from endorsing an abstract theory and planning an actual insurrection. The preparations for the Easter Rebellion were conducted by a handful of men on the military council rather than by a majority vote of the organization. They quite simply usurped power and made a private decision.

For months the vast majority of the I.R.B.'s membership, as well as of its executive committee, was deliberately kept in ignorance of the planned uprising. Eoin MacNeill, president of the Irish Volunteers and an eminent scholar and known moderate, was exploited as a respectable front to allay the suspicions of the British authorities. As for the rank and file of the Volunteers, how many of them would undertake actual combat? It was justly feared that many were only Sunday soldiers who enjoyed marching and drilling but would evaporate at the prospect of a real fight. The Volunteers' full strength numbered a scant eleven thousand, for the outbreak of war the original body had split, and many of the erstwhile Irish Volunteers were now crawling around in the mud of France.

Nevertheless, the men who planned the Rising were determined to make the most effective stand possible. A decision was quickly taken to secure German aid in the form of guns and, if possible, soldiers and military advisers. This decision was made not in sympathy with Germany but simply because it was traditional for Irish rebels to seek assistance from England's enemies (in the eighteenth century attempts had been made to secure a French landing in support of the Irish Rebellion of 1798). The German response in 1916 proved less than overwhelming, and in the end a promise of twenty thousand rifles was all that could be obtained. These rifles were to be smuggled ashore on the west coast of Ireland a few days before Easter. The rebels' plans were simple: They would distribute these guns among Volunteers up and down the country, strike simultaneously throughout Ireland, and hold out as long as possible.

But on the eve of the Rising these plans disintegrated. Thanks to poor communications between Ireland and Germany, the arms landing miscarried, and the ship carrying the German guns was captured by British authorities as it attempted to leave the Irish coast. As many of the Volunteers had nothing more than pikes and wooden sticks for weapons, this seizure was a real calamity. Worse followed. MacNeill suddenly learned of the plot. Outraged and horrified, he shouted that short of telephoning Dublin Castle, he would do everything in his power to prevent such madness from taking place. The president of the Volunteers had been nervous for a long time about what he considered the rampant neurotic romanticism around him. Months before he had sounded a warning against the dangerous daydreams of those who spoke of insurrection:

There is a feeling in some minds that action is necessary, that lives must be sacrificed, in order to produce an ultimate effect on the national mind. . . . To my mind, those who feel impelled towards military action . . . are really impelled by a sense of feebleness or despondency or fatalism or by an instinct of satisfying their own emotions. . . . We have to remember that what we call our country is not a poetical abstraction, as some of us, perhaps all of us, in the exercise of our highly developed capacity for figurative thought, are sometimes apt to imagine—with the help of our patriotic literature.[8]

Discovering that his worst fears had been only too well founded, MacNeill acted desperately on his conviction that the Rising would be a disaster. He sent messages to all provincial Volunteer commanders, as well as to the newspapers, canceling the "maneuvers" that Pearse had announced for Easter Sunday. In the early morning hours the men who for months had dreamed and planned this insurrection discovered that their plans were in ruins.

Nevertheless, despite the twin disasters of the failed arms landing and the countermanding orders issued by MacNeill, the conspirators decided that the Rising must go on. They postponed it for one day, long enough to give Pearse time to issue still another set of orders telling his men to disregard MacNeill. Contradictory messages arrived all over Ireland. Only in Dublin would it now be possible to mobilize effectively.

The hoped-for thousands were reduced to a few hundred Dubliners—those who had not taken the holiday weekend to go fishing. The original military plans had called for three thousand soldiers in Dublin alone; about eight hundred actually turned out. With this kind of manpower it was obvious that tactical decisions would have to be largely improvised on the spot, for the Volunteers had nowhere enough men to attempt to capture all the strategic positions that they had originally planned to take. Solitary snipers would have to do work originally slated for whole groups of riflemen.

The military forces of the Easter Rising included another tiny "army" besides the depleted Volunteers. The Citizens' Army, which represented Irish trade unionism and socialism, numbered at full strength about two hundred men and two dozen women. It was Connolly's own. It too had been born in 1913, following a bitter transport strike in Dublin. Along with Connolly it had been brought into the plans for the Rising some months previously.

In addition to the Volunteers and the Citizens' Army there were the Irish Boy Scouts. First organized in 1909 by a flamboyant Irishwoman named Countess Constance Gore-Booth Markievicz—who had abandoned the frivolities of salons, as well as a rather boring Polish painter to whom she was married, for the thrills of social revolution—the Irish Scouts called themselves the *Fianna Eireann;* they had been constituted as an eventual cadre of an Irish army. The Countess led the Boy Scouts to battle: She was dramatically arrayed in a dark-green woolen blouse, tweed knee breeches, a small automatic pistol strapped to her waist, and a black velours hat bedecked with feathers. Such were the soldiers who assembled on the morning of April 24 to vindicate the national honor of Ireland.

During the week that the rebels held out, Dublin was gripped in a kind of festive nightmare. The insurgents had seized several railway stations and had torn up rails to make access to the city difficult. Easter Monday was a holiday for most people, and many got their first inkling that something was up when they were unable to board trains home from outlying resort areas. Transportation within the city also came quickly to a halt as the rebels used cars and trams for barricades.

By Tuesday most stores and places of business were shut, awaiting the outcome of the revolution. Milk and newspaper deliveries ceased, and in some parts of the city food ran short. For the average man and woman there was nothing to do but exchange rumors. The rumors were fantastic: German submarines had landed; exiles in the United States had returned, bringing thousands to fight with them; the entire West had risen and captured everything English for a hundred miles around; the rebels had all been shot; the rebels had wiped out an entire troop of British cavalry.

The city's poor seized the opportunity to make their own characteristic protest: They embarked on an orgy of looting. Gold watches, beer, and candy—especially candy—circulated freely in the streets. Children ransacked toy stores and sweet shops. Children were in fact everywhere. Volunteer commanders holding buildings throughout the city had repeatedly to send home twelve- and fourteen-year-olds who wanted to join up. They did not always go home. Inside the post office, in the last desperate hours of the rebellion, a fifteen-year-old boy was elevated to high officer's rank.

The military kudos of the Rising, such as it was, belonged on the whole to the rebels. Hopelessly outnumbered, they fought with terrific bravery. Both sides made bad mistakes, and at times the warfare in Dublin had about it touches of comic opera. At the commencement of hostilities the rebels missed capturing the Central Telephone Exchange, which would have effectively cut off communications in the city. A small group of Volunteers had been about to take it when they were met by an old woman shouting, "Go back, boys, go back; the place is crammed with military." [9] They took her word for it. In fact, the exchange was totally unguarded and could have been taken without a shot.

Had the English troops decided on a full-scale direct offensive against the rebel strongholds, the rebellion could have been put down much sooner. But uncertain about the exact numbers of the rebels, the English preferred to send for reinforcements and slowly to draw a cordon around the city, isolating successive positions. This strategy led to some ludicrous mistakes. On Wednesday a British gunboat steamed up the Liffey and for hours on end shelled Liberty Hall, supposed headquarters of Connolly and the Citizens' Army. But Connolly was in the post office, and his troops were in St. Stephen's Park. Except for an old custodian, who managed to get away, the building was entirely deserted.

De Valera, holding out in Boland's Mills, had been under heavy attack all week. When it appeared that his position was hopeless, the young mathematics teacher ordered a green flag hoisted atop a nearby water tower. Instantly the British barrage was deflected to this arrogant banner. The tower finally collapsed, and the English soldiers almost drowned while De Valera and his men laughed uproariously.

Inside the post office, main headquarters of the rebel army, the chief danger for several days appeared to be stray bullets from over-eager Volunteers fondling their guns in expectation of the English charge that never came. A continual stream of messengers brought reports to Pearse and Connolly on the positions of other battalions. Food supplies, nurses, priests, and occasional wives and sweethearts slipped through the barricades. Now and then fifteen or twenty men were sent out to relieve snipers on the roofs of adjacent buildings. Hardly anyone slept at all. Volunteers inside the post office played cards with two or three English prisoners, including one unlucky English soldier who had come in for stamps a few minutes after noon on Monday. Even there, at the heart of the new Republic, there were some who could not believe in the reality of it all. On Wednesday a soldier respectfully went up to Connolly and requested permission to leave. He wanted to go back to his job, he said, now that the Easter holidays were over.

But by Friday the post office was in flames and had to be evacuated. The British had dealt with this key rebel post by setting fire to the adjacent streets and turning the center of Dublin into a blazing inferno. In some of the areas where the firing had been heaviest, bodies of dead men and cavalry horses lay in the gutter, unclaimed by either side. British soldiers played football on the tennis courts of Trinity College a few yards away from the worst of the carnage. Both Volunteers and soldiers had destroyed many private homes. Civilian casualties were high, and property damage was estimated at £2,500,000.

James Connolly, lying badly wounded in the post office, was perplexed. He had been certain that artillery would not be used by the British because capitalists would not wish to damage their own property. During the evacuation of the post office Pearse watched the military cut down a family fleeing in terror from its flaming home. Sickened and disheartened, he finally ordered surrender, "in order to prevent the slaughter of Dublin citizens. . . ."[10]

As the defeated rebels marched through the Dublin streets behind their captors, they were jeered and spat on by the people of the city. Pearse was haunted by a vivid dream that he had had since he was a small boy. In the dream a young boy on a platform was about to be executed before a multitude for some great and noble cause, but the crowd regarded him not as a martyr but as a fool. Dublin was placed under martial law, and four thousand people were tossed into jail. The press, Irish and English alike, called for stern handling of these criminals and lunatics. Redmond mourned the whole episode, which, he felt certain, had set back the cause of Irish independence by years.

Four days after Pearse signed an unconditional surrender, he was executed by a British firing squad. Fourteen other leaders of the Rising were shot soon afterward. De Valera was spared because, having lived a few years in New York, he happened to be an American citizen.

The jeers of the people did not last long. Within a few weeks the attitude of the country toward the Easter rebels had undergone a dramatic change. The excessive damage done by British forces and the swift execution of nearly all the Rising's leaders horrified and revolted the hitherto somnolent populace. Girls going to mass carried inside their prayer books printed cards with the names and pictures of the new martyrs. Stores suddenly found that they could not stock enough tattered copies of rebel song books and separatist pamphlets.

The general election of December 1918 marked the complete collapse of Redmond's Parliamentary Party. Sinn Fein, the "Ourselves Alone" separatist party, which had been languishing since its founding in 1905, overnight swept to power as the new political voice of the country. In January 1919 victorious Sinn Fein candidates assembled in Dublin and declared themselves to be the *Dáil Eireann*, the independent parliament of an independent nation. The I.R.B. was reorganized in prison camps by those leaders of 1916 who had not been executed. They also formed the Irish Republican Army, which led the country in what was soon to become a full-scale guerrilla war of national liberation, culminating in 1922 in the creation of an independent, though divided, Ireland.

It is a mistake to believe that independence would have been granted in any case and that the Easter Rebellion provided only an extra propulsion away from Home Rule and toward full independence. Those six fantastic days in April were crucial. They were the catalyst without which the popular support necessary to carry out an Irish revolution would have never been crystallized. Without Easter week it is more than likely that Irish politics would have continued to limp toward some emasculated version of Home Rule. The Easter Rising and the martyrdom of the insurgents radicalized the Irish people.

Not the least of the imponderables on which Pearse and Connolly had gambled was the stupidity of the British. In the months following the Easter Rising, English policy toward Ireland fluctuated between repression and guilty solicitude. The Easter-week prisoners were released within a year as a gesture of good will. Yet at any moment they were likely to be reincarcerated for singing a rebel song or making an antirecruiting speech. Immediately after the Rising, the Liberal Prime Minister Asquith declared what was already only too obvious: The English system of rule had broken down in Ireland. Yet after a brief period of military dictatorship and an abortive attempt to effect instant Home Rule, Asquith was forced to return to the old system for the duration of the war. The English were visibly fumbling the Irish football.

A month after the rebellion Asquith made a special trip to Ireland to study the situation at first hand. He toured the prison camps where the rebels were being detained and on impulse asked one young man whether the rebellion had not been a lamentable, foolish thing. The Irishman answered that, on the contrary, it had been a great success. The Prime Minister looked bewildered. But his very presence in the country was proof to the rebels of their success.

To good middle-class Liberals like Asquith and Redmond the Easter Rebellion seemed pointlessly tragic and Pearse and the other insurgents at best incredibly naïve romantics. By the time that Pearse had finally surrendered, the Volunteers were outnumbered twenty to one by the British forces, and of course Britain, engaged in the First World War, had committed only an infinitesimal fraction of its military power to putting down the Rising. Open confrontation when the balance of arms, soldiers, propaganda facilities, and even popular support was so unequal seemed the height of idiocy.

But the poets understood what the politicians did not. Pearse and his colleagues had sensed the boredom, alienation, and degradation inherent in modern industrial society and the failure of political liberalism to satisfy the deepest yearnings of ordinary people for membership in some great collective movement and participation in the corporate joy of national liberation. The common man really yearned to be a hero, like the Irishmen of old; he really hated the drab compromise that was the best that liberal politics could offer. Pearse penetrated to the inner truth of modern life; he was a prophet of the twentieth century. He was not naïve or stupid but astonishingly clairvoyant.

The Easter Rising was the model for all liberation movements against Western imperialism in the twentieth century and for all protest movements generally. Endless debate, piecemeal reform, tedious compromise—they did not bring social liberation and personal exultation, which can be achieved only through immediate confrontation, no matter how futile, and martyrdom, no matter how certain.

The common man in Ireland seemed totally emasculated by industrialism and bureaucracy; he still waited in the darkness of his prison for the call to freedom, for an appeal to his inherent urge to heroism, for a summons to participation in an immediate, ineffable act of collective emancipation.

By precipitating a confrontation in which, hopelessly outnumbered, they could only be crushed, the Irish rebels of 1916 forced England into the role of the large ugly beast. As the executions went on, protests poured in from around the world, particularly from the United States, where there was a large and vocal Irish immigrant population. The English government, anxious in wartime to be on the best possible terms with the United States, was profoundly embarrassed. President Woodrow Wilson kept talking about the rights of small nations to self-determination, and though he exempted Ireland on the grounds that it was one of "the metaphysical tragedies" of the age, many people, including Englishmen, failed to understand this metaphysical lapse.

England's spastic behavior toward Ireland in the months and years that followed the Rising was a measure of its own confusion. The country was divided on what was to be done about Ireland. The Tories in the War Office favored a straightforward draconic military solution harking back to Oliver Cromwell's savage repression of Irish independence in the seventeenth century. But the Liberal government was too sensitive to public opinion to pursue this policy. The doubts and agonies of the middle-class English Liberal conscience eventually forced the British out of the country. Ireland was the harbinger of the end of the British Empire. Imperialist faith in British manifest destiny was fatally impaired by this first modern colonial revolution.

Pearse and Connolly had set out to arouse public opinion in Ireland and around the globe. They hoped the Rising would capture the imagination of the world. By this standard the Easter Rebellion must be accounted a great—though posthumous—success. A handful of men succeeded in imposing their personal aesthetic and a messianic morality on historical events. They wrote the play themselves. It did not matter to them that they died in the first act, for after that the plot was set.

CHAPTER

3

Mutiny in the French Army

In August 1914, Europe went mad and inflicted upon itself crippling, nearly fatal wounds. The nations of Europe, for no good reason, indeed for no reason at all, chose to go to war against one another. The assassination of the Archduke Francis Ferdinand, heir to the throne of the Austro-Hungarian Empire—a silly, vain man hated even in Vienna—by Serbian nationalists became the pretext for unleashing all the violent instincts and arrogant attitudes upon which the Europeans had drawn so heavily in their savage treatment of Asians and Africans during the previous half-century. Now they turned their violence and arrogance upon one another in what seemed a suicidal mania.[1]

The stupid leaders of the European states issued calls to defend their respective national honors, and no less than 99 percent of the population of Europe, including liberals, socialists, and labor leaders—the last depositories of reason and beneficence—responded with furious enthusiasm. A few voices of sanity, like that of British philosopher Bertrand Russell, dissented from this lemming-like advance toward the precipice, but they were ignored or, if they persisted in affirming the dignity of humanity, imprisoned and forcibly silenced.

The only glimmer of sanity in the statesmen's eagerness for war lay in their belief that it would be a short one—all over by Christmas 1914 at the latest. Two or three big battles were to decide the hegemony in Europe. As so often before, statesmen and generals were fighting the new war with the techniques and strategies of the preceding one. They all thought that the Great War would be a repeat of the Franco-Prussian War of 1870, when a lightning Prussian attack had destroyed the French Army in a matter of weeks. Somehow, all the deep thinkers had forgotten about the American Civil War—modern warfare between industrial societies could be just as readily a savage and long war of attrition as a lightning campaign. By the fall of 1914 it was clear that the defense on both sides was superior to the offense. Instead of marching home in triumph, the German and Allied soldiers on the western front faced each other along a thousand-mile line of trenches, freezing in the stinking mud.

By the spring of 1917 the Great War had been grinding on for two and a half years; it had left three million Frenchmen dead, wounded, or imprisoned in German camps. In April 1917 the unimaginable happened: The cannon fodder revolted. To this day many of the facts about these mutinies in the French Army cannot be determined. Official military histories have understandably treated them as cursorily as possible. Generals writing their memoirs often had a vested interest in minimizing what was euphemistically called "disaffection." No one was exactly proud of the rebellion in the army, and it was obviously best to treat it as a temporary, though acute, lapse in troop morale.

Despite the secrecy that shrouds the mutinies of the French soldiers, it is clear that they were on a tremendous scale, infecting entire regiments and "contaminating" thousands of men. By June 1917 the entire rank and file of the French Army threatened to collapse, or even worse. No one knew how this plague would end—perhaps with the soldiers turning their guns on their own officers?

The French soldiers refused any longer to man the trenches, refused to return to the front lines when their rest periods were up. Shouting "Down with war!" and demanding death to those who could not or would not make peace, company after company of the French infantry erupted into furious choruses of the "Internationale" and spontaneous cheers for world revolution to end the madness and horror of a war that they no longer believed could be won. They had had enough of dying on the barbed wire of no man's land in futile assaults on impregnable enemy lines. They refused to advance again. If they agreed to move at all, it was only toward small railway stations where they might seize trains to take them to Paris, where, they shouted, they would march on the Chamber of Deputies and throw out all the scoundrels and liars who issued the orders that brought only defeat and slaughter.

By June such mutinies were erupting with terrifying regularity. The high command of the army was in open panic at the thought of not being able to find enough loyal companies to maintain even a strictly defensive holding action on the front lines. It was freely rumored that if the Germans picked this moment to launch an offensive, the French lines would dissolve into the spring mud, and the men would lay down their arms and take off for Paris. In the corridors of the Ministry of War the awful secret was whispered from ear to ear. Between Paris and the German lines—a distance of no more than sixty miles—there stood only two divisions that could be relied on absolutely and completely.

Outright mutiny was accompanied by wholesale desertion. Whereas in 1914 only a handful, not more than five or six hundred men, had fled, by 1917 desertions were occurring at an estimated rate of thirty thousand a year. The *poilus*, shabby-bearded trench solders, no longer responded to exhortations to martial valor. They were unmoved by appeals to their pride as fighting men and to their sacred responsibility to homeland and comrades. They were on strike, perhaps quitting for good. They wanted new jobs and new lives.

The mutineers did not write their biographies. When the war ended in joy and triumph for France, everyone wanted only to forget the grimly terrifying summer months of 1917. Those who wrote about the army revolts at all (generally those who had helped to suppress them) tended to place exaggerated emphasis on the petty irritations and familiar soldiers' gripes. It was alleged that amid the general weariness such gripes had caused uncontrollable exasperation. To French generals it was axiomatic that French soldiers had never questioned the rightness of their cause or the ability of France to triumph over its enemies in the end. The *poilus* had only clamored, rather loudly and inopportunely to be sure, for some attention to their own elemental and unglorious needs from leaders who were laboring to save France. A few material decencies were all that they sought. The French Army suffered from "disaffection," according to the official accounts of the mutiny, because the men needed more leave, better food, improved medical facilities, canteens, and a homey atmosphere in their rest camps.

When, at the height of the mutinies, General Henri Philippe Pétain assumed supreme power over the French armies, one of his first acts was to requisition a half-million cots for the rest camps to which the soldiers retired when they were relieved from actual front-line duty. Another of Pétain's reforms was to order the Y.M.C.A and the Red Cross to set up gaily decorated canteens in the little railway stations to which men on leave thronged for the long journey home. The implication was that, amid the noise of the big guns and the pressing need for more and better artillery, more railroads, and better roads, the ordinary soldier had not received enough solicitude and was simply feeling unappreciated.

It was also generally conceded that French soldiers had lost faith in those who commanded them. A new face at the top, a more convincing father figure, was urgently needed. This demand too was satisfied by the appointment of Pétain. Changes in personnel are, after all, rather easily effected.

The revolts in the army had begun in full force immediately after the failure of General Robert Georges Nivelle's offensive in late April 1917. This spectacular plan had called for a *Blitzkrieg* of the most violent and stupendous proportions over a front about seventy miles long in the area between the Somme and Oise rivers. General Nivelle, the prodigy of the Allied armies, insisted that the entire offensive should be conducted with the utmost violence, brutality, and speed. It was to bring to an end the hopeless stalemate that had existed on the western front for almost three years. No more nibbling at enemy territory, no more "victories" that gained nothing but a hundred yards of scorched rubble. One overwhelming lunge was to start the French rolling back the German armies within forty-eight hours. The war would then be as good as over. By Christmas the *poilus* would be home with their families.

In fact the daring reflected in the Nivelle offensive was little more than bravado. It was doomed from its inception, and Nivelle's success in foisting it on a government already experiencing premonitions of disaster was a measure of the desperation that afflicted both the civilian and military rulers of France.

The trouble was that no one else was offering a better alternative. Two and a half years after the "miracle of the Marne" that had saved Paris in 1914, the reputation of General Joseph Joffre, the miracle worker, had become tarnished. In Champagne and Artois, at Verdun and on the Somme, he had accomplished nothing to match the brilliance of his early victory. Dissatisfaction with the progress of the war was mounting everywhere, and Joffre could propose only more nibbling.

Joffre had been replaced by Nivelle. The new Chief of Staff was, despite his sixty years, one of the new men who had proved his mettle not in the classroom but in actual combat. His reputation was based on the spectacular recapture of Fort Douaumont at Verdun, which had been achieved by the concentration of tremendous firepower coupled with imaginative deployment of a few crack infantry divisions. The recapture of the ancient fort had been a great psychological victory for the French armies at Verdun, indeed for the nation. Militarily it was impressive, but it was too quickly elevated to the status of another miracle by a nation desperate for some sign of military genius. Nivelle's tactics soon acquired the rubric "the Verdun method"; they were considered a satisfactory improvement over the innate conservatism of the old men. On his promise to apply the Verdun method to the conduct of the war as a whole, Nivelle was made Supreme Commander of the French forces. Nivelle spoke English beautifully and so impressed David Lloyd George, who had just taken over in England, that he ordered Douglas Haig, commander of the English forces, to defer to the new military genius.

Nivelle projected a breakthrough to take advantage of a large bulge that had developed in the German lines during the battles of the Somme. The British were to attack in the north, the French in the south. Instead of seeking to advance arduously trench by trench, the French were to use artillery to bombard all the enemy lines at once, following which the infantry would smash through at a lightning pace, opening a huge gap in the German lines. The French soldiers, having penetrated the enemy lines, would be in open country, from which they could outflank or encircle the rest of the German armies. There was, Nivelle assured everybody, no chance of failure. To prepare the attack he was going to bring up more than a million men, 500,000 cavalry mounts, and unlimited supplies of artillery. French intelligence reported that the Germans had a scant nine divisions in the area; they were exposed and vulnerable. The French soldier, who would be carefully prepared, psychologically as well as militarily, could attack with every confidence of complete victory. He would fight like a man possessed.

This plan, which Nivelle sold to the Minister of War, the Prime Minister, and the President of France, was faulty even in its original conception. Even granting that the original breakthrough could have succeeded, the logistics of follow-up and supply had not been worked out, and everyone knew that an army that had advanced deep into enemy territory needed constant reinforcement in order to hold its vulnerable positions. Furthermore, the plan called for withdrawing French troops from other areas, thus exposing the latter to critical manpower shortages. From the beginning there were grumblings and doubts among the subalterns on the General Staff.

By the end of March the military situation had changed so dramatically as to render the original plan not only risky but also absurd. The Nivelle offensive had become an open secret among the French troops. As a result the Germans knew about it in almost as complete detail as did the French. The element of surprise vital to any *Blitzkrieg* operation was totally lost. The German high command prepared for the onslaught thoroughly and well. It withdrew its armies from their exposed position to specially constructed and all but impregnable fortifications. The retreat to what became known as the Hindenburg Line was accompanied by the burning of towns, poisoning of wells, and felling of every tree. The abandoned ground was turned into a desolate and ghastly wasteland.

Not only prudence but also sanity dictated a complete reappraisal of the offensive, which was set for the middle of April. But Nivelle, who refused to rethink any of his plans, was clearly engaging in a terrifying species of double-think. Disquiet in the upper echelons of the military was acute. It stirred everyone but the arrogant General and his minions. The truth was that Nivelle was too far committed to reverse his course. In the final days before the scheduled offensive a worried government summoned the General to an emergency conference. The statesmen had heard alarming reports, persistent murmurs that the offensive could not succeed. Timidly, almost apologetically, the President of the Republic asked his Chief of Staff to reconsider and modify his plans. Nivelle erupted in righteous fury. He would guarantee success. If he was not given implicit trust, he would tender his immediate resignation, he announced theatrically. France had been on the defensive too long. If the government succumbed at this late hour to a fit of nerves, he really could not be held responsible. Did it not have the guts to pursue true victory?

His challenge was blackmail, and Nivelle knew it. The morale of the nation would be shaken by another change of command so soon after the exit of Joffre, and the resulting demoralization, civilian and military alike, might prove irreversible. Burdened with the sickening suspicion that they had committed themselves to a doomed venture, the government officials decided that they had no choice but to continue. How could they announce at the eleventh hour that they had miscalculated? They would never be able to face the public again. Everything would be all right if only they maintained faith. The decision to carry out the offensive was a collective flight into irrationality, possible because no one had the courage to assume responsibility for calling a halt.

The attraction of the Nivelle offensive was its simplicity: It promised a quick end to the war. There was nothing that the French government would not try to end the existing stalemate and wearying attrition. Anything was better than the interminable agonies of the Somme. The influence of Nivelle himself, cockily insisting against all reason that victory could be had, was a measure of the demoralization that beset France.

The much-vaunted offensive of the spring of 1917 actually offered very little that was new. It was only an intensification, the maddest and most furious intensification, of the strategy that had already predominated for three fruitless years. Nivelle's slogan might well have been "We try harder." Dynamic rhetoric passed for military originality. The *poilu* in the trenches realized this aridity first and called his own halt. He balked at committing suicide at the behest of his leaders.

For three years before the advent of Nivelle the ordinary French infantryman had been paying the price for the faulty thinking of officers turned out by St. Cyr, France's famed military academy. The French Army had entered the war the hapless prisoner of its military theorists. In the twenty years that had preceded the outbreak of World War I they had developed a conception of modern warfare which distilled all military wisdom into a single word: "attack." Always attack, attack when the enemy is unprepared, attack when in a tight corner, attack when outflanked and outmaneuvered, attack when outnumbered. Always and forever attack.

This remarkable theory of combat had been inspired by a slender volume on military strategy written by an obscure colonel who had been killed in the Franco-Prussian War of 1870. By the time that the First World War broke out, it had risen to the level of dogma among the French General Staff. Infantry attacking at close quarters was invincible, so the theory ran. The daring and the *élan* of a bayonet charge would inevitably send the enemy into disarray and flight. The morale of the troops, their determination and faith in their own invincibility, were everything. Furthermore, the career of the great Napoleon had conclusively demonstrated that French military genius functioned best on the offensive. The shameful defeat in the Franco-Prussian War had largely resulted from abandonment of this wisdom. The enemy had always to be kept off guard. The side that kept the initiative had a tremendous psychological advantage. The state of mind of the charging French armies had always to be one of feverish exaltation; armed with a bayonet and enough patriotic fervor, the French soldier was believed to be invincible.

This theory was convenient and comfortable in a day when civilian government was notoriously stingy about providing the money necessary for development and mass production of new and expensive weapons. After the controversy over the Dreyfus Affair, which had split the country just before the turn of the century, the army had been much discredited. The succeeding governments, which tended in any case to be left-wing and pacific, gave short shrift to the demands of the generals. This attitude led to an unrealistic denigration of new armaments like machine guns and heavy artillery pieces. It was much more pleasant when theory could be made to fit the limits imposed by account books. According to the new school of strategists in the French Army, heavy weapons were to be used only in support and clean-up operations but were less important than the trusty—and cheap —bayonet. Similarly, the importance of field fortifications and earthworks was played down so much that the ancient network of French fortresses in the east was not modernized, and virtually nothing was done to secure a solid line of defensive fortifications along the northern border with Belgium.

The absurdity of these calculations was rapidly and brutally demonstrated within the first three weeks of the war, as French armies were hurled back and decimated by German troops unencumbered with Napoleonic wisdom. France almost lost the war in the first month. Winston Churchill pointed out with grim wit the incongruity of a situation in which, although the Germans were doing the invading, the French attacked. Spectacularly visible in dark-blue coats and red trousers, French soldiers advanced to the stirring music of the "Marseillaise" played by brass bands, while the Germans sat back and sprayed heavy artillery and machine-gun fire at these colorful targets. Young officers leading their troops in gallant charges seldom went more than fifty yards across the open terrain. Charge after charge was mowed down. Within six weeks of the outbreak of hostilities France had lost 600,000 men—nearly half the number that had been mobilized. Two-thirds of the junior officers in the French infantry had died. France, it was clear, could not afford such valor. The philosophy of perennial attack had to be modified.

By 1915 the modifications had been fully developed. An unbroken line of trenches from the North Sea to the Swiss border had been built. Along this line and often separated by no more than a few hundred yards of barbed wire, the two armies faced each other month after month, disputing every ridge and hillside in monotonous and meaningless attacks and counterattacks. Henri Barbusse, who immortalized in his novel *Le Feu* life in the trenches as millions of Frenchmen had experienced it, summarized the military situation with a wisdom that seemed to escape the generals: "Two armies fighting each other—that's like one great army committing suicide!" [2]

To the average soldier very little changed on the front lines during the course of the year except that the network of trenches became ever more intricate. No more than hastily improvised ditches at first, they soon grew into an elaborate maze. The front line, or "firing ditch," was typically a meandering tunnel about six feet deep and four feet wide. The soldiers in this trench were protected from enemy fire by parapets of sandbags or earthen ramparts about a foot high. These ramparts were studded with small holes through which their rifles could fire. Fifty yards or so behind the firing ditch was a "cover trench," where reinforcements stood ready to move up should the first line of defense falter. Farther back still was another support trench and so on for a couple of miles. Communications trenches laced through the earthen arteries, connecting the back with the front. Finally, there were the dugouts, large subterranean cellars where the men congregated when not actually on duty. Soldiers might spend days or weeks in these trenches before they were relieved and sent for brief respites to towns farther back in the war zone.

A constant accompaniment to life in the trenches was mud—mud that froze in the winter and oozed in filthy slime in the summer. The novelists, poets, and film-makers who have portrayed the quality of soldiers' lives during the Great War have unanimously been more impressed with the mud than with any other aspect of front-line life. In the mud huge, ugly rats bred, and when it shifted, the *poilu* could see the rotting bodies of comrades lost in previous attacks. Mud made weapons clog and stick, delayed the arrival of supplies and reliefs, and prevented rapid movement in either attack or retreat. When he was not under actual fire, the soldier's biggest enemy was mud—and the tedium of keeping the trenches in good repair.

In the trenches the idea of the offensive had not completely died, though it had come to seem a sordid and very unglamorous business indeed. Usually an attack wave would gain only the first line of the enemy position, that is, no more than a few hundred yards. And it almost always invited retaliation, so that the trench "captured" by a furious assault on one day might well be lost on the following morning. The return to the previous military positions would thus have been achieved at the price of a few dozen, a few hundred, even a few thousand soldiers on each side.

The secret of trench warfare was that it *was* possible to advance if one was willing to throw away enough lives in order to gain a few hundred feet of ground. On both sides aassaults quickly became standardized. They began with a concentrated attack of artillery fire designed to blast through the barbed wire that cordoned off the enemy lines. Enormous volleys of shells were poured on in attempts to prepare the ground for the infantry. When the big guns had done their work, the *poilus* took over. In groups of fifty or seventy-five men they sprinted from their ditches and dashed forward to gain as much ground as possible before being stopped by the enemy's machine-guns. When the first wave of attackers had been repelled or obliterated, a second followed and then a third. Finally, assuming that at least the first line of the enemy's trenches had been taken, a rear guard of moppers-up went in and with hand grenades and bayonet thrusts took care of any snipers who remained at their posts.

If a soldier was unfortunate enough to be in the first attack-wave his chances of survival were poor; the mad dashes were more often pitiful crawls through the ubiquitous mud. This pattern of fighting further-more made it virtually impossible to keep up a sustained attack for any period of time. The enemy could always regroup and reform farther afield. And as soon as the first thrust had been completed, the problem of ammunition and supplies usually became acute. Hand grenades ran short, and then men—attackers and defenders alike—lost contact with their officers and comrades. Too often at the end of such a rush all that either victor or vanquished could do was to cower, spent and wounded, behind some bullet-riddled parapet, waiting numbly for the inevitable counterattack, which would in all likelihood drive them back to their original lines. As neither side had the resources, either expendable manpower or artillery, to sustain such attacks, the war rapidly deteriorated into a stalemate. But it was a vicious and expensive stalemate; even on days when no offensive was launched by either side an average of 1,500 soldiers were killed by snipers and random shells.

Virtually the entire economic and military resources of two mighty nations were given over to trying to secure a few feet, at most a few miles, of shell-scarred terrain in northern France. The cost in francs and marks, in lives, and in human talent and energy was grotesquely disproportionate to the results obtained. The pressure on the military hierarchy to break the deadlock was overwhelming. It was felt by every officer who commanded a regiment, a division, or a platoon. But instead of a fundamental reappraisal of the logistics of the war, it tended to breed a perverse determination: A game with such rules would have to be won by those with the most single-minded will to victory. What this attitude too often meant in practice was the sudden prominence of those officers who most coldly disregarded the stagger-ing toll in human life that was believed to be the necessary price of victory.

The way had been prepared for the rise of such new men by the wholesale annihilation of officers in the autumn of 1914. It was inevi-table that rapid promotions should go to those who showed the most vigor in pursuing the war effort. How this vigor came to be measured is curious. Officers whose companies sustained only light casualties became suspect. On the other hand, the loss of many lives was taken as a sure sign that an attack had been pressed with commendable ardor. Officers ambitious for promotion vied with one another to achieve reputations for unflinching pursuit of victory—and death. Although the victory might prove elusive, the deaths were sure. The commander who could bully, cajole, flatter, or terrorize his men into the most reckless acts might come to the attention of the General Staff as a marvelous leader of men. Although there were undoubtedly still large numbers of officers who valued the lives of the men they led, there can also be no doubt that the new species of officer had every opportunity to rise to sudden fame.

Not infrequently it happened that officers pushed their companies beyond the point of physical and psychological endurance. One case, which became known as "the affair of the four corporals of Suippes," provided the subject matter of the well-known film *Paths of Glory*. This particular episode took place in the province of Champagne, where the 336th Infantry Regiment had for weeks been unable to penetrate the German lines. Attack after attack had been thrown back at an enormous cost in lives. When one particularly battered company that had sustained heavy casualties only two days previously was ordered by the general of the regiment to make another sally, the response was dispirited. Only a few officers charged, and most of the enlisted men remained in the trenches. The general, observing the whole operation through a telescope, became enraged and ordered the artillery to fire on his own men. When the scandalized colonel in charge of artillery balked, the offending company was sent on what was a clear suicide mission. In broad daylight it was ordered to slash the barbed wire barring the way to the German trenches. The hapless victims of this command managed to leave their trenches but were immediately pinned to the ground by enemy machine-gun fire. The general had seen all he needed to see. The men had failed to obey orders in the face of the enemy. Sixteen privates and four corporals were rounded up at random, court-martialed after a fashion, and ordered to be executed. The privates were spared in the end in deference to squeamish public opinion. But the corporals were shot as an example to the regiment. The blatant injustice of the affair caused anger that threatened to turn mutinous.

This instance, though it became especially notorious, was not unique. Court-martials and executions as object lessons were, if not precisely standard, at any rate not uncommon. Military justice is, of course, peremptory at the best of times.

It is likely that the French officer's demands on his men were more extravagant than those of his German counterpart only because the fighting was occurring on French soil. The Germans could claim a measure of victory if they simply held their positions. The French commanders thus acted under greater psychological duress, for they had somehow to drive the invaders out of France. It is not surprising that repeated frustrations made them turn to the court-martial as one more weapon of war: a prod to drive their own dumb cattle forward.

Morality aside, the difficulty was psychological. Although it is often possible to induce men to spectacular feats of heroism even in the sure knowledge that they will perish, it is not possible to do it day after day. A great burst of patriotic self-sacrifice can be obtained from almost any company for an hour or a day. An exceptional commander can perhaps sustain it for the duration of an entire campaign. But the French soldiers on the western front were being asked, ordered, coerced into keeping it up for months and years, and the prizes when they won were simply too meager to give them even the satisfaction of a job well done. Capture of a hillside or an old fort at Verdun, let alone a few feet of mud at the Somme, could not be passed off as reconquest of *la patrie*.

It was against this background that the Nivelle offensive was launched and the mutinies began. Although the mutinies were perhaps encouraged by pacifist propaganda, which was by 1917 coming off Parisian presses in torrents, their real cause was the endless months of pointless defeat and death from which there was no escape, and to which there seemed to be no end. The General Staff was to pay for persistently valuing life too cheaply.

At the end of its first day the Nivelle offensive had been clearly exposed for what it was, the self-delusion of desperate men. The French troops, who according to the plan were to have penetrated at least six miles behind the German lines, had picked up a few hundred feet here and there. The medical services, which had been alerted that they might have to treat 10,000–15,000 wounded, coped with 90,000 wounded and maimed men. The roads were jammed for miles with troops and artillery units awaiting the moment when they would sweep forward. But the moment never came, and the congestion and confusion behind the front lines became a nightmare. The few units that did manage to dent the German lines had no one to back them up. Such uneven advances as had been made were often untenable. Nivelle had promised that the Germans would be crippled and demoralized, but the French artillery had actually left most of the German machine-gun nests unscathed. Instead of streaking across the enemy trenches and easily routing the Boches, the French soldiers crawled once again through the mud to fall under monstrous artillery fire.

It had all happened many times before. The difference was that the average soldier had been led to believe that this time would be different. For months past he had seen enormous numbers of troops moving to make ready for the great day. Tons of heavy armament had been brought up for this attack. Everyone, even the densest private, had caught some of the excitement and expectation in the air. The post-office censors had confirmed their hopes: The letters that the men had been allowed to send to their families were full of a new optimism. Victory thenceforth was to be measured in miles and towns, rather than in inches and tree stumps. The war had reached a great turning point.

Nivelle had promised to bring his offensive to an immediate halt—within forty-eight hours—if unforeseen setbacks should occur. The promise was ludicrous. Even had the Chief of Staff wished to do so, there could be no stopping once the offensive had begun. To withdraw troops at this juncture would be to leave the French Army exposed to a rout. Nivelle refused to admit defeat. Day after day French soldiers were sent out to pound against the Chemin des Dames, the old carriage route of Louis XV, which constituted the westernmost sector of the Hindenburg Line. The casualties were always high, the gains small or nonexistent.

At the end of April the mutinies began. They erupted first in the Sixth Army, which had paid most dearly for Nivelle's fantasies. They centered around Soissons, the filthy little barracks town that housed the headquarters of several divisions and served as a military junction through which a constant flow of troops moved to and from the front. The soldiers simply refused to return to the firing trenches when they suspected that they would be ordered to make one more sally against the Chemin des Dames. Typically they would line up for the march back, late and grumpy, a little drunk and sullen, but no more than was to be expected. Suddenly an officer would notice something peculiar: They had left their rifles behind. Once the aghast N.C.O.'s had established that the men were not playing a practical joke, the soldiers responded with glassy-eyed stares. They were not going.

The ugly little towns a few miles behind the front lines which served as rest camps became the chief breeding grounds of mutiny. It was amazing how swiftly a perfectly reliable company could be "contaminated" by contact with the malcontents of some less-disciplined regiment. A truck with troops returning from the front lines would roll through a town, bound for heaven knew where. From the military van pacifist songs might be shouted and improvised red flags waved furiously. "Throw down your arms, brothers! Long live peace!" the troops would cry as the truck careened out of the town. It did not matter whether these troops were mutinous desperadoes being carried off to the stockades or loyal men engaging in intoxicated bravado. The effect was the same. Soldiers who had been awarded the Croix de guerre, men with exemplary military records, suddenly became stirring pacifist orators. Someone always had the death statistics of the latest charge. Awesome as these statistics were, they were invariably doubled and tripled by rumor and mistrust of the officials in charge of such matters. Every regiment harbored at least one unsuspected Communist, who urged his comrades to emulate the example of the Russian Revolution, during which the soldiers had turned their guns around. Russia would soon be out of the war, they shouted. France had no chance. Long live peace and international solidarity!

The mutinies, which were initially a response to the aborted hopes of the Nivelle offensive, spread like a brush fire or epidemic throughout the army. The mutineers discovered the strength of numbers. It was impossible to shoot entire regiments. No matter how severe the mutiny, the great majority of those taking part would go unpunished. Even an instigator might escape, for military justice was only a form of Russian roulette.

In railroad stations and at home on furloughs the soldiers discovered what their officers had desperately tried to keep secret. Not only their companies had refused to march. How could one feel shame over such outbreaks when they were epidemic? There were stories of how in another army in another part of France a regiment had seized an entire town, elected its own "revolutionary representatives," and sent out a delegation to negotiate with its erstwhile officers. Another battalion had marched itself off to the safety of an adjacent forest. Still another had captured a train and set out for Paris.

The impact of the Russian Revolution and the pacifist propaganda from the interior undoubtedly helped to instigate some of these revolts. The *Union Sacrée*, the great moratorium on factional partisan politics in France, had become a fiction by 1917. Socialists, trade unionists, and pacifists of every stripe, who had agreed, in the frenzy of August 1914, to put aside their grievances and support the government until France achieved victory, had one by one returned to their prewar ideological stances. Factions and dissensions had reappeared and intensified as the unsatisfactory progress of the war found a thousand different explanations and rationalizations.

Freedom of speech and press existed in France to a degree extraordinary in wartime. The Minister of the Interior was, to say the least, lackadaisical about rounding up pacifist agitators. Agitation against the war was carried on quite openly. Troops returning home on leave were greeted with leaflets explaining the hopelessness of their positions at the front. Union meetings often turned out to be giant peace rallies in disguise. The General Staff repeatedly urged the government to do something about the steady stream of left-wing pamphlets that came through the mails. These pamphlets inspired defeatism, said the officers, preying insidiously on the minds of the already demoralized men.

The argument no doubt contained some truth. Yet it had the faults of any effort to make scapegoats of convenient "outside agitators." It comforted the General Staff to believe that aliens and paid German agents were poisoning the minds of the *poilus,* for such an explanation relieved the generals of guilt and responsibility for their own failures, their own inability to bring victory or even to instill a sense of purpose in their men.

But the agitation for peace back home was not an alien growth fed by German marks. It reflected very real divisions within French society itself. By 1917 deputies in the Chamber were speaking out for peace, for an early and honorable negotiated settlement with Germany —and their speeches were being greeted with enthusiastic applause. Support for the war was eroding.

When the *poilu* sang the "Internationale" and hoisted the red flag it did not mean that he had become overnight a convert to Lenin. Red flags had been the emblems of protest in France since the French Revolution. The rhetoric of anarchism or communism rarely implied ideological commitment to an alternative system of government. It merely implied total and vociferous rejection of what was. It was a jeer and a spit in the face of traditional authority, which had led countless young men to death in the trenches.

Soldiers engaged in actual combat on the front lines are in any case a curiously apolitical breed, as anyone who has read Erich Maria Remarque's *All Quiet on the Western Front* will recognize. Stripped of their civilian roles and life styles, men quickly lost their prewar politics as well. Trench life bred, willy-nilly, a rough fraternity; everyone was, after all, equally vulnerable to a bullet. In the grime of the Western Front, political convictions became curiously remote and abstract; they were dispensed with along with other appurtenances of civilian life because they were so patently irrelevant to the daily life of the *poilus.* Ideology came to seem mere words, abstract disputations all equally false and hypocritical. George Orwell once wrote, "In trench warfare five things are important: firewood, food, tobacco, candles and the enemy." Except when the troops were actually under fire, even the enemy came in a bad last among these elemental pre-occupations.

The conditions of life in the trenches lent a permanent air of un-reality to the sort of intellectual verbiage with which civilian life is filled. The men responded viscerally to the material circumstances of their life and death. Their protest, even when it took the form of mutiny, was at least as much a physical as a mental revulsion. The soldiers regarded the propaganda-filled newspapers as items with which to line their boots against the mud. Their protest was almost purely negative: They denounced everything and were no longer willing to accept anything that was. They called for peace because it was the opposite of war. They waved red flags because through long tradition such flags had come to symbolize the opposite—whatever it might be— of any existing regime.

The limited, negative goals of the mutineers is attested to by the fact that when they seized power, they never did very much with it. Having fled to the forest, they were content to stay there until, surrounded by cavalry and military police or starved out, they simply laid down their arms and straggled back. The cries of "To Paris!" died away long before the soldiers reached their goal. They permitted themselves to be halted by a few cavalry troops hastily sent out to bar their way. Often a mutiny lasted only a day or two, during which time the men consumed much wine and savored—one imagines with mixed fear and joy—their new liberty. Then slowly they straggled back, first to the barracks and then even to the trenches.

Certainly naked force played a role in quelling the mutinies. An unlucky few always paid with their lives as grim examples to the rest. But the monopoly of force was on the soldiers' side had they themselves realized the possibilities in their numbers. Military discipline ultimately depends upon the willing compliance and submission of the majority, for the common soldiers always greatly outnumber their officers. In France, for a period of months, entire divisions were judged undependable and potentially mutinous. Yet most of the mutineers succumbed to the habits of obedience under which they had lived for months and years. Although some military police were roughly handled and obscenities were freely tossed at the upper echelons of the military, the soldiers did not shoot their officers and storm Paris. For the duration of a typical mutiny, officers were not so much defied as ignored. In this respect the typical mutiny resembled a work stop-page more than a revolution. Only the rhetoric was forcible and defi-ant. The men were too weary to wage war, even a war that would liberate them from the prison of the trenches.

The mutinies flickered throughout the summer months of 1917. By

September they were becoming rare. Their progress and ultimate collapse have often been described in metaphors of disease attacking the military body, running its course, and then fading. Credit for saving the French Army from dissolution has traditionaly been given to General Pétain, who inherited command from the fallen idol Nivelle while the revolts were at their height. Pétain combined carrots with sticks, or rather with firing squads, to restore order among the troops. Exactly how savage the repression was will probably never be known. But it is clear that only a small proportion of those executed were officially tried and sentenced before military tribunals. Death on the western front was such a commonplace that hundreds, even thousands, of men could simply be listed as dead or missing in combat, and no one in the interior would be any the wiser. Henri Barbusse, who himself spent months in the trenches on the western front, has left a celebrated story, "Vengeance from on High," about 250 mutineers who were rounded up, placed in trucks, driven around until they had lost their sense of direction, and finally dumped in no man's land, where they were told to sit quietly. According to Barbusse, the guards then departed, and artillery fire was opened on the men, who were all slaughtered. Military historians have, of course, denied all knowledge of such atrocities, but who is to say in such circumstances whether they or the imaginative writers are the better witnesses?

What is certain is that Pétain did a great deal to mitigate some of the more gross and unnecessary horrors of the soldiers' lives by drastically increasing furloughs, improving food, brightening up the rest camps, and eliminating some of the incidental squalor that was a daily accompaniment to the *poilu's* life. Probably most significantly, he called a halt to Nivelle's senseless campaigns and committed the French Army to only the most cautious and limited actions. Pétain stood at the opposite pole from Nivelle on military strategy. He did not like to squander human resources, and he did a great deal to improve relations within the army. Tirelessly he personally visited company after company, delivered pep talks, and sought to discover the grievances of the men and as far as possible to see that they were rectified. He also took swift steps to halt the flow of propaganda to the front, although this task was not fully accomplished until Georges Clemenceau took over as Prime Minister and began ruthlessly tossing dissenters into jail.

The combined efforts of Pétain and Clemenceau helped to stop the mutinies. By the end of 1917 order had been restored in the ranks of the French Army, but the old devotion to the cause of *la patrie* was gone. The *poilu* did not regain his enthusiasm for the national cause. Rather he finally came to see mutiny as only one more exercise in futility. Despair alone does not long sustain a protest movement. This despair remained pervasive in the ranks of the army, but the soldiers no longer believed that mutiny could prevail over the power of the generals and politicians. There was no escape from the brutality and horror of the war. The French Army returned to obedience but with a sullen rancor and bitter hatred for the leaders who had betrayed it.

Pétain and the generals sensed this attitude. They knew that they could no longer demand sacrifices from the army. They adopted a new strategy of defense; the attack program was abandoned. The generals waited until the Americans put their armies in the field, thus giving the Allies overwhelming superiority over the Germans. Not until the fall of 1918 did the French Army again advance, and even then it was with great caution, although the German military machine by then was crumbling.

The heritage of the mutiny was long and bitter in French history. What happened in 1917 was the beginning of that cancerous malaise that spread through French society in the 1920s and 1930s, that sullen resentment and hostility of the common man toward the politicians, that lack of faith in the destiny of France, that selfishness and privatism that vitiated the nerve of the French people and made them incapable of withstanding the German onslaught in 1940.

CHAPTER

4

The Russian Experience

IT is one of the tragedies of modern Russian history that no distinction between protest and revolution ever developed. Under the autocracy of the Romanovs political discontent found no legitimate means of expression. Rigid and narrow-minded, when not actually paranoid, the tsarist government relegated generation after generation of rebels and critics to the roles of heretics and subversives. The tsars viewed dissenters as cancerous tumors that had to be destroyed. Protest movements were thus spawned and nurtured only in a climate of persecution and lawlessness which made conspiracy the only viable means of organization. Dissent belonged to the underworld, and its adherents acquired habits of thought and action suited to criminals and prophets, outcasts and saviors. Those who opposed the government never learned to view themselves simply as politicians of a different persuasion.[1]

By the middle of the nineteenth century Russian protest had already acquired its characteristic apocalyptic style. With only rare exceptions those who wanted to refashion Russian society aimed not at a slow amelioration of the existing order but at its total destruction. The radical intelligentsia assumed that a life-and-death struggle was to be waged between the forces of absolutism and the forces of revolution. It was also understood that no compromise would be possible between the children of light and the children of darkness and that no quarter would be shown by either side. The code of Russian radicals called for a struggle against the government and the existing order of things until the last drop of blood was spilled and the last breath spent. Over and over again Russian radicals insisted on the absolute destruction of the old as a prerequisite to building any good society. "We do not build, we destroy; we do not proclaim a new revelation, we eliminate the old lie," wrote Alexander Herzen, the disenchanted Russian aristocrat who stood at the beginning of the modern revolutionary tradition.

The Russian tendency toward extremism was observed early by many Europeans, among them Karl Marx, who shrugged it off condescendingly as a kind of fatuous intellectual *gourmandise*. Marx believed it a sign of Russia's political backwardness that its intellectuals always took their lead from the most extreme Western ideas. In no country, he thought, was a communist revolution less likely than in this enclave of medieval superstition and despotism.

The popular image of Russian protest was Dostoevskian, which is to say half mad. The typical Russian revolutionary was pictured as a student who lived in a garret and fed himself on black bread and fevered visions of assassinated tsars. If he attended classes at all, it was only to disguise his true vocation and perhaps to organize illicit midnight seminars among his fellow students, whom he would initiate into the political underworld. More likely, he had already been expelled from the university, thanks to a subversive leaflet confiscated by one of his teachers. His life had become a fantastic round of forged passports, secret rendezvous with sinister bearded persons, laconic notes written in invisible ink and placed in suitcases with false bottoms, and bombs hurled at the carriages of government officials. One day soon he would disappear from sight, betrayed by a secret-police agent masquerading as another student. He would die alone in a dungeon or during his exile in Siberia, unknown and ungrieved except perhaps by some comrade living a similar clandestine life in another garret. His fellow revolutionaries, however, would have little time to mourn his death, for individuals were regarded as significant only insofar as they served the cause.

The chief weapon of protest in nineteenth-century Russia was terror, perpetrated by professional revolutionaries or by the "dark people," the nameless, illiterate workers and peasants whose despair swelled into periodic eruptions of rage and frustration. The most characteristic form of Russian protest remained the peasants' rebellion, which had changed little since the Middle Ages. After a poor harvest, when the price of bread soared or when a particularly vicious landlord committed one indignity too many, a band of peasants would rise up, burn the estate of the local magnate, and murder him for good

measure. They attacked the men and buildings that were the immediate objects and symbols of their oppression.

The professional revolutionaries were more discriminating in their
targets. They eliminated government ministers and on one occasion
even the Tsar himself. These assassinations were designed to avenge
the oppressed and to warn all future tyrants of the fate that awaited
them. Such sporadic recourse to violence was unhappily all that the
peasants and the revolutionaries had in common. The Russian intellectual loved "the people" in an abstract fashion, viewing them as keepers
of the Russian soul, as suffering innocents uncontaminated by Western
ideas and aristocratic shams. He wanted passionately to do something
for them. But between the militant intelligentsia and the "dark people"
there was little understanding or cooperation. The intellectual who
cast himself in the role of missionary and educator to the masses was
greeted with apathy or suspicion by those he sought to lead. When
student missionary work among the peasants was particularly in vogue,
in the 1870s, the students were often reported to the tsarist police as
suspicious troublemakers by the very people whom they had come
to save.

Isolated outrages and a millennial spirit characterized Russian protest. Ironically it was the very hopelessness of achieving any reform in
government in the foreseeable future that bred the conviction, increasingly prevalent in the nineteenth century, that Russia would somehow
short-circuit history and pass directly from the cruelest of despotisms
to a veritable earthly paradise. The Russian intelligentsia, with rare exceptions, displayed both great envy and great scorn for Western
government and society. Western Europe, most Russians on both the
left and the right agreed, was spiritually hollow and crudely material-
istic; its vaunted freedoms were fraudulent or at least superficial. The
idea that Russia's destiny was to bypass the pettifogging republicanism
of nations like France was shared by the Tsar and his most subversive
subjects.

Those who sought a new order in Russia at that time tended to
place their faith in individuals. Those who stood on the side of tradition yearned passionately for a wise and tender tsar who could restore
peace and harmony among his unhappy and rebellious children. Those
on the left longed for steely, ruthless, and omniscient revolutionaries
who would lead the people to the far side of a bloody River Jordan.
As no political mechanism existed for winning liberty and justice by
degrees, a cult of spontaneity and irresistible force developed. "The
Revolution," whatever its programmatic content (usually vague),
seemed, as befitted an apocalyptic vision, at once imminent and infi-

nitely remote. The Russian intelligentsia, longing for reform, became collectively manic-depressive in its outlook. Revolution was forecast as regularly as the Second Coming had been predicted in the Middle Ages, though as late as 1917 no less an authority than Nikolai Lenin pronounced it unattainable in his lifetime.

Because any opposition to the regime was so dangerous, Russia had few part-time revolutionaries. The early terrorists and the later Marxist organizers among the urban proletariat were alienated from the social order to a degree that would not have been possible in the West, where political radicalism did not as a rule cut men off completely from the society around them, denying them university educations, jobs, and opportunities to marry and raise families. Western revolutionaries were not pariahs; they could write, lecture, propagandize, and still live their private lives in much the same fashion as any other sturdy bourgeois citizen. If they happened to be colorful or dramatic personalities, they were often adopted by respectable society as amusing institutional gadflies. They might with luck become celebrities whose "advanced ideas" made them highly prized dinner guests and public speakers. The Russian anarchist Prince Pëtr Kropotkin became, during his west European sojourn, something of a darling among the *fin du siècle* aristocracy, which enjoyed titillating itself with various heretical ideas.

In contrast, the Russian socialist or populist was almost inevitably driven underground. His ties with his old school, job, and social circle had to be severed. Often he was cut off from his family as well unless it was willing to join him in the demiworld of conspiracy. A young man might suddenly find that circumstance and accident had driven him to a revolutionary career.

Vladimir Ilich Ulyanov, who later took the name Lenin, was the serious, scholarly younger son of a respectable provincial family of educators until the day that his older brother Alexander was executed for his part in a conspiracy to assassinate the Tsar. Vladimir, who was at that time finishing secondary school, had shown little interest in politics and knew nothing of the conspiratorial activities in which Alexander—a student hundreds of miles away in St. Petersburg—had been engaged. But once his brother had been apprehended, there was no hope that the younger boy could ever escape the suspicion and hostility of the authorities. Although, after repeated petitions, Vladimir was finally admitted to a law school, the authorities expelled him on the first possible pretext. Barred from the university and thus from any useful career, the young man played chess and read Karl Marx. There was little else for him to do. His mother wrote to the Minister of

Education, telling of the torture in seeing her son unable to make use of the best years of his life. Lenin's experience was repeated a hundred times over in Russia, where innocent youthful fraternization with any suspicious person or a mild college flirtation with socialist ideas could brand a young man for life, driving him farther and farther outside the pale of respectable society.

The tsarist police knew that Russia's universities and secondary schools were seedbeds of sedition. Their only solution for rebellious intellect was repression, although evidence that this solution was in fact no solution at all continued to mount. Still they persisted in dealing with the troubled universities by banning subversive books and assiduously weeding out professors and students who showed any signs of political deviation. The number of works banned in these institutions of higher learning shocks and amazes Westerners accustomed to read what they please. Such classic Western thinkers as John Stuart Mill, Charles Darwin, and Victor Hugo were considered too provocative—to say nothing of socialist writers of even the most utopian and benevolent sort. The students, of course, read anyway; often the forbidden works were painstakingly excerpted by hand and passed from student to student. School authorities were commanded to search students' briefcases and coat pockets tirelessly, but somehow the forbidden works continued to circulate. In the 1890s, when most of those who would make the Revolution of 1917 were growing up, repression in the universities was particularly severe. Liberal and progressive teachers were repeatedly fired, and student strikes against government intervention in their classrooms and dormitories reached alarming proportions. There were many instances of violence.

A few years before young Joseph Stalin entered a Georgian seminary, the students of that institution had assassinated the principal. Needless to say, this act led to mass expulsions, and the school remained closed for many months. By the time that Stalin arrived at the seminary, the expelled students had become heroes and moral authorities to the next generation of students. The school authorities were obsessively vigilant; the students sullen, bitter, and alienated. Their free time was carefully regimented, and they were watched like potential criminals, which indeed some of them were. It mattered little that many students were being educated on stipends from the government; almost without exception they loathed the school that hedged their lives with a thousand and one regulations and denied them the right to study what was vital and exciting in European intellectual life.

The ferment in the universities was such that political culprits sentenced to exile were often specifically ordered to stay out of university towns. It may well be that in the 1890s the students constituted the most dissatisfied class in Russia. Certainly universities and technical schools were to be the chief recruiting grounds for revolutionaries. As few sons of peasants or workers (Stalin was an exception) could aspire to higher education, most of the political termites came from the middle class and even the nobility. Like students everywhere they were sensitive about their own and their families' privileged status and attracted to doctrines that promised a new deal for the common people. Lenin made a virtue of necessity when he argued in favor of a small, highly centralized cadre of political sophisticates as the backbone of the revolutionary party; in his generation recruiting from the intelligentsia was easy, almost automatic, whereas proselytizing, educating, and training workers to the tasks of revolution was exceedingly slow and difficult.

Barred from achieving recognition or distinction in the society around them, often cut off from their indignant (or sympathetic but frightened) families, the youthful heretics formed a distinct subculture. A cult of personal sacrifice, heroism, and absolute commitment to "the Idea" or "the Cause" inspired them. They took pride in their ability to endure extreme material privation and constant comfortless loneliness. To be scorned by the respectable world was, they felt, an honor, a testament to their uncompromising dedication. Often they lived lives of almost monastic asceticism. This was as true of the turn-of-the-century Marxists as it was of the more emotional populists who had been the chief activists among the peasantry in the 1870s and 1880s. The Russian novelist Ivan Turgenev was fascinated with the mentality of these déclassé intellectuals, and in "The Threshold" he portrayed initiation into the revolutionary underground as the awful privilege of the strong:

"To you who desire to cross this threshold, do you know what awaits you?"

"I know," replied the girl.

"Cold, hunger, abhorrence, derision, contempt, abuse, prison, disease and death!"

"I know, I am ready, I shall endure all blows."

"Not from enemies alone, but also from relatives, from friends."

"Yes, even from them . . ."

"Are you ready to commit a crime?"

"I am ready for crime too."

"Do you know that you may be disillusioned in that which you believe, that you may discover that you were mistaken, that you ruined your young life in vain?"

"I know that too."

"Enter!"

The girl crossed the threshold and a heavy curtain fell behind her. Fool! said someone gnashing his teeth. Saint! someone uttered in reply.[2]

Although Lenin had little in common with either fools or saints and would have been impatient with the nihilistic posture of Turgenev's young revolutionary, his life was also marked by absolute dedication to his calling. A sometime ally once explained Lenin's ascendance over his fellow Bolsheviks by saying that Lenin more than any of them was occupied with revolution twenty-four hours a day; he had disciplined himself to think of nothing but revolution, and when he dreamed at night his dreams too were of revolutio.. Maxim Gorki recalled how Lenin, who loved classical music, refused to allow himself the pleasure of listening to it because it "makes you want to say stupid nice things and stroke the heads of people who could create such beauty. . . ."[3] Such conduct of course was inadmissible for a revolutionary whose energy must be spent in delivering blows, not caresses.

Dedicated revolutionaries like Lenin had at all costs to preserve and treasure their isolation, their sense of remoteness and alienation from the values and the experiences of other people. Leon Trotsky, reminiscing about Lenin in London, remarked that, as Lenin was conducting him on a guided tour of that city, he had referred to landmarks and art treasures as "theirs." "This is their Westminster Cathedral," he would say, meaning not the English but the ruling class against whom he had pitted himself.

Isolation and small numbers, though often sources of pride among the revolutionary flock, were also the most distressing factors in their lives. Often the revolutionaries' separation from their countrymen was not only spiritual but physical as well. Until the Revolution of February 1917 brought them streaming back, many of the leaders of the Russian revolutionary intelligentsia lived in permanent exile in Geneva, London, and Brussels. Georgi Plekhanov, who taught Marxism to an entire generation of Russian activists, fled his native country in 1880 and did not see it again until 1917. Boating in Geneva with his small band of disciples, he would admonish them: "Be careful; if we drown, Russian Socialism will perish."[4]

What the revolutionaries needed above all was to make contact with the Russian people. One reason why Marxism so quickly became the dominant credo of the political malcontents was its dependence on the working class as willing and eager makers of revolution. Although Russia remained an overwhelmingly peasant country well into the twentieth century, the intelligentsia had by the 1890s despaired of ever radicalizing the ex-serfs. The quiescence of the peasant masses was so demoralizing to the revolutionaries that it occasionally led them to applaud the anti-Jewish pogroms that regularly broke out in Russia. After all, although the bigotry that produced such pogroms was reprehensible, it *was* nevertheless able to produce outbreaks of popular violence and thus provided proof that the people *could* be roused from their stupor.

Lenin and the other ideologues of revolution were driven almost to despair by the Russian workers' disregard of Marx and Engels. In the opening years of the twentieth century the best way to rouse the peasantry to seizure of land and to assaults on local landlords and government officials was to tell them that such actions had the blessing of the Tsar! Although by the 1890s bitter industrial strikes had become commonplace in Russia, where factories and railroads were suddenly multiplying very rapidly, the workers showed a disquieting tendency to act independently of their revolutionary mentors. Their demands tended to center on redress of particular grievances in the factories: Like workers in the West they wanted more pay and shorter hours. Politely but firmly they told their intellectual friends that their help would only bring police interference. How was the Russian proletariat to escape the trade-union mentality that in the West was rapidly undermining the revolutionary teachings of Marxism?

The Marxists thought that they had devised a solution to this dilemma by shifting their tactics from supporting propaganda (the slow and painstaking education of workers in Marxist study circles) to partaking in agitation. Lenin and his friends reasoned that the workers' demands, even though they centered on the narrowest bread-and-butter issues, had to be supported by the revolutionaries lest the latter be left completely behind, with only one another to talk to. The hope was that the confrontations precipitated between the workers and the government when strikes were suppressed would open the proletariat's eyes to the true character of the state. Lenin thus gambled on the political hooliganism of the tsarist government, on its crudity and artless recourse to the tactics of frightened thugs. Bloody and violent confrontations between the people and the police would serve better than any copy of *Iskra* (Lenin's revolutionary newspaper, which first appeared in 1900) to educate the Russian worker.

At the beginning of 1905 an event proved the astuteness of Lenin's evaluation of the government as the hapless victim of its own repressive reflexes. "Bloody Sunday" horrified public opinion the world over, and, as Lenin said, "the revolutionary education of the pro-

letariat made more progress in one day than it could have made in
months and years of drab, humdrum, wretched existence." [5] The
demonstration that led to this highly instructive bloodbath revealed
many of the characteristic features of Russian protest, suspended as it
was between old and new traditions. Yet the ingredients of "Bloody
Sunday" seemed unpromising enough from the point of view of tough-
minded "scientific" socialists like Lenin.

On Sunday, January 22, 1905, 200,000 St. Petersburg workers turned
out with their wives and families for a giant procession to the Winter
Palace to lay their grievances before Tsar Nicholas II. It was, it is true,
the largest congregation of people in the streets that St. Petersburg
had ever seen, yet the tone of the march was anything but menacing.
The people were led not by a fire-eating Bolshevik but by a peasant
priest wearing a cassock and carrying a crucifix. Moving slowly
through the snow-bound center of the city, the huge crowd sang
hymns and carried religious icons. The workers of St. Petersburg were
carrying a petition to their Tsar. Like medieval peasants they were
ready to lay their miseries at the feet of the man whom they believed
to be the fount of justice and wisdom, who, when he had heard of
the sufferings of his patient people, would smite with a terrible hand
the bureaucrats, landlords, and capitalists who oppressed them. The
strains of "God Save the Tsar" repeatedly swelled through the crowd.
It was a pilgrimage of faith and hope, naïve and sincere. The plan of
the march called for the entire assemblage of people to fall to its
knees before the palace while their spokesman, Father George Gapon,
handed the Tsar the people's petition. This list of demands was suffused
not with class consciousness but with reproachful supplication. Militancy and pious humility had produced an incongruous blend of
modernity and medievalism.

"O Sire," the document began—a salutation hardly either defiant
or egalitarian—

we workingmen of St. Petersburg, our wives and children, and our parents,
helpless and aged men and women, have come to you, our ruler, in quest of
justice and protection. We are beggars, we are oppressed and overburdened
with work; we are insulted, we are not regarded as human beings but are
treated as slaves who must suffer their bitter lot in silence. . . . We have no
strength at all, O Sovereign. Our patience is at an end. We are approaching
that terrible moment when death is better than the continuance of intolerable sufferings. . . .[6]

In such language, biblical in inspiration, they requested an assortment of political and economic privileges such as a Western political

party of progressive leanings might seek through a constitutional convention. The requests ranged from a parliament elected by universal suffrage and secret ballot to a progressive income tax and cheap credit, universal and compulsory education, freedom of the press, and the like. The program requested in the document was in jarring contrast with its language and psychological well springs. Its tone suggested that the people of St. Petersburg sought nothing less than remission for all the sins of Adam and immediate passage to the far side of the Jordan River. The peasants' yearning for freedom and an end to human misery was about as sophisticated and "political" as that which had inspired the Negro spirituals of the nineteenth-century United States—with the difference that the slaves who sang "I'm gonna tell God how you treat me, one of these days Hallelujah!" addressed their sorrows to a more appropriate figure than the Tsar of Russia.

The petition ended with a declaration of popular intent should the Tsar fail to heed the words of his subjects. It promised not strikes and agitation, not barricades and revolution but one more Christ-like sacrifice:

. . . if You will not so command and heed our prayer, we will die here on the square, in front of Your palace. . . . Let our lives be a sacrifice for suffering Russia. We do not grudge it, but offer it willingly.

More dismaying still to any scientific socialist must have been the organizational origins of this weeping, worshipful throng, for the demonstration was the final product of what can only be termed "police socialism"—gone, to be sure, slightly beyond the intentions of its originators. Father Gapon, the man who led the St. Petersburg populace that Sunday, was a popular preacher who had been recruited by tsarist officials to form the "Assembly of Russian Factory Workers of St. Petersburg," an organization designed to drown political and economic disquiet in a bath of piety. The idea behind the Assembly had been to initiate self-help and educational activities among the workers so that they would be less likely to fall prey to socialist agitators. The police had helped Gapon to provide his workers with social clubs, tea rooms, concerts, and lectures—the better to keep them loyal and satisfied. Such state-sponsored "unions," which had as their sole purpose the neutralizing of workers' grievances and the channeling of their energies into safe endeavors, were, of course, the nightmare of every socialist revolutionary from Bismarckian Germany to Russia.

It was unfortunate for the Tsar's government that Father Gapon had let his role as savior of the lowly and downtrodden go to his head, so that by 1905 it was no longer clear to anyone, himself in particular, whether he was working to buttress or to subvert the old regime. Sincerely pious and devoted to the idea of the Tsar as the little father of his people, Gapon was evidently also moved by an ideal of compassionate, quasi-religious anarchy animated by genuine moral outrage at the plight of the St. Petersburg worker. The procession to the Winter Palace had been his own inspiration. Gapon had notified the authorities of the march and had emphasized its peaceable nature. The demonstration came at a time when strikes and work stoppages were breaking out all over Russia, and discontent in all classes of society was very acute because of Russia's bungling aggression in the war with Japan. The Sunday procession was a perfect opportunity to drain off some of the resentment and frustration peaceably. A few tokens of good will from the government might have converted the demonstration into a festival of thanksgiving and patriotic devotion.

Unfortunately Tsar Nicholas II had only contempt for the amenities of public relations. He was vacationing outside the city on the appointed day. The workers formed five columns in the great square before the Winter Palace to wait for him to welcome them, bless them, and soothe them. The Minister of the Interior had left special troops to deal with the procession, whose numbers alone made it seem menacing. Awed and alarmed by this great sea of humanity, the garrison responded in its usual fashion: It fired into the crowd. Instantly absolute pandemonium set in; the crowd was too packed to disperse or retreat. Soldiers' horses tore into the crowd along with bullets, and Father Gapon reported that he saw "men, women and children dropping to the earth like logs of wood, while moans, curses and shouts filled the air." [7] All told there were hundreds of dead and injured. "Bloody Sunday" destroyed for all time the workers' illusion and hope that reforms would come through an appeal to the conscience of the autocracy.

The butchery produced widespread protest and demands for constitutional reform from middle- and upper-class liberals. The capital's workers formed the St. Petersburg Soviet of Workers' Deputies in self-conscious opposition to every other element in the city; agrarian disturbances were sweeping the countryside; and the armed forces were faced with dangerous disaffection. Out of it all came the October Manifesto, whereby the Tsar guaranteed fundamental civil liberties and agreed to call a legislative assembly, the State Duma, representing all the populace.

Eventually loyal forces restored order. The Soviet functioned for a few months before it was decimated by the arrest of its three hundred leading members. The Duma malfunctioned for twelve years. Although the various Russian political parties fought one another to a standstill, the government enacted legislation over its head, introducing such reforms as it saw fit. Economic prosperity permitted the regime the illusion of immortality. Those who sought to use the Duma as an instrument for securing responsible government exhausted themselves in impotent debate. As soon as Russia entered World War I, however, unprecedented strains on its underdeveloped economy and administrative incompetence stripped away all illusions of the government's longevity.

Under the stress of the Great War Russia began to disintegrate. By 1916 trade, industry, and the army were all rapidly approaching paralysis, and opposition to the government again mounted. Military disasters had closed the vital ports of the Baltic and the Dardanelles, depriving the country of vital imports of such raw materials as coal, petroleum, iron, and cotton. The transportation system proved utterly inadequate to move troops, war matériel, and foodstuffs. The mobilization of peasants created universal manpower shortages. Farmers were unable to obtain the most elementary tools and fertilizers. The area of land under cultivation dropped, always a sign of serious economic dislocation. Bread lines appeared in every major city, but often the people waited in vain—flour mills were operating at only 40 percent of capacity. The price of milk, bread, and sugar skyrocketed.

In October 1916 the secret police reported to the Tsar that the people were on the verge of despair. In the face of this breakdown of national productivity, strikes, work stoppages, and disorders spread, despite severest repression by the authorities. Many industries were placed under martial law, and strikers faced arrest and deportation to the front. Nevertheless popular agitation continued to gain momentum. In 1915 a thousand strikes erupted in the factories of Russia. In 1916 there were 1,500, and in the first two months of 1917 the strikes threatened to exceed that figure. Especially in Petrograd (as St. Petersburg had been renamed in 1914 in the heat of anti-German sentiment) it was a rare week in which the workers of some factory were not in the streets.

In the face of these accelerating disasters, Duma leaders pleaded with the Tsar for a government that could command the confidence of the people; they themselves must be allowed, the delegates insisted, to take a more effective part in the nation's war effort. They were rebuffed at every turn. The Tsar could disguise but thinly, the Tsarina not at all, an utter contempt for these arrogant busybodies attempting to tamper with royal prerogatives. Nicholas responded to popular pressure for a more effective army by placing himself in supreme command of his troops! Ministers who inclined to sympathize with the Duma were replaced by more compliant nonentities. A French minister who visited Russia in the spring of 1916 sneered at the Russian self-confidence reflected in a government that had a premier who was a "disaster" and a minister of war who was a "catastrophe." [8]

The Tsar, assaulted on all sides with demands for reform, continued to regard himself as a man who endured these idiotic mutterings with the patience of Job. To every request for a constitution and rational government he reiterated with mindless vanity his sacred duty to pass his absolute power on to his son unimpaired. The minds of both Nicholas and his German-born wife, Alexandria, were not exactly astute; they were both, furthermore, prey to quasi-religious fantasies, superstitions, and prejudices which, they convinced themselves, were sanctioned by divine authority. Trotsky wrote of Nicholas that "between his consciousness and his epoch there stood some transparent but absolutely impenetrable medium." [9] Nicholas' insistence on the inviolability of his power was aggravated by his basic lack of interest in the problems of government. Only the saccharine joys of domesticity, along with romantic and hazy religious sentiments, stirred him. While all Russia seethed with frustration and rage, the Tsar made placid entries in his diary: "Walked along and killed two crows. Drank tea by daylight. . . . Bathed twice. It was very hot. . . . Went paddling in a canoe." A kind of vapid fatalism was the only response from the throne to military and economic catastrophes. The Tsarina, who wrote her husband letters calling herself his "silly little wifey," fussed like an offended peacock over the impertinence of those who dared to disrupt her domestic bliss. "I long to thrash nearly all the ministers," she wrote to her husband.

The wonder is not that the February Revolution came but that it did not come much sooner. The so-called Progressive Bloc of liberals and capitalists within the Duma exhorted the Tsar to reform. They feared, they said, a revolution of the "dark people." Privately even the highest members of the nobility liked to spend their evenings predicting the fall of tsarism. The hatred that the royal couple inspired became almost pathological. Popular rumors linked them with German agents in secret efforts to undermine the war effort. Assassination of the pair was seriously discussed among high civilian and government officials—indicating perhaps how deeply inbred in all classes of society was the terrorist mentality. Still the deputies of the Duma showed an incredible reluctance to do anything other than talk; they languished in pessimism.

In the middle of February came disorders in the streets, before which everyone trembled. They began, as usual, in the capital. On February 23 a few hundred men and women milled through the streets, singing the "Marseillaise" and shouting for an end to war and for bread. Minor skirmishes were fought between the crowds and the police and Cossacks, whose job it was to keep the city in order. By the following day at least half the city's working population was on strike. Workers mixed fearlessly with the Cossack cavalry troops and attempted to fraternize with them. On the following day soldiers joined the people in the streets, the work stoppage became general in the city, and disquieting rumors reached General S. S. Khabalov, who was in charge of the capital: Mutinies were breaking out among the garrison. Men and women were going up to the troops, touching their bayonets with their bodies, urging, pleading with the military to lay down their arms. Uncertain and embarrassed, a soldier would waver and slowly raise his bayonet above his head. In a moment he would be embraced, cheered, carried on the shoulders of the jubilant crowd. On the evening of February 26 a company of the Imperial Guard, the Tsar's own hand-picked bodyguard, mutinied. A day later Khabalov wired the government a curt statement that he was unable to re-establish order in the capital.

In the Duma the deputies were in a panic. Unaccustomed to ruling, indeed to assuming responsibility of any sort, they shrank from taking charge of the movement in the streets. M. V. Rodzianko, President of the Duma, wired the Tsar: "Anarchy in the capital . . . government paralyzed . . . shooting in the streets . . . supplies of food and fuel completely disrupted . . . universal dissatisfaction growing." The Tsar for once acted promptly and with resolution: He prorogued the Duma. Rodzianko pleaded pitifully against the inevitable. "I am no rebel," he said. "I do not want to revolt. . . . I am no revolutionary. . . . I will not rise up against the supreme power. I do not want to." Perplexed beyond measure, the poor man fired off another telegram to the Tsar. "Situation worsening," he reported. "Immediate steps are necessary for tomorrow it will be too late." The Tsar was losing patience with these tiresome reports of imminent disaster. The deputies had, it is true, been besieging him with false alarms ever since he had come to the throne. "That fat Rodzianko," he said, "has again sent me some nonsense to which I will not even reply." [10]

The Duma, in a fit of resolution, decided not to disband. It was aghast to find itself being waited on by 25,000 mutinous soldiers who spoke darkly of other sorts of governments if these men did not do something at once. Still the deputies' dearest wish was that the Revolution go away. They had secured Nicholas II's abdication on March 2 but still hoped to save the dynasty. They petitioned the Tsar's brother, Grand Duke Michael Alexandrovich, to impose military dictatorship on the city. Only when the Grand Duke refused, did they at last pronounce themselves the new "Provisional Government" of Russia. The very name indicated how little they wanted their new responsibilities, how devoutly they hoped to find a quick escape from their fate.

Within the Duma the idealism, the longing for liberty—for constitutional and civil rights—that usually animate revolutionary parliaments were almost entirely absent. The Kadets, the leading party of the Duma, and their allies within the Progressive Bloc had spoken eloquently about civil liberties, freedom of the press, and responsible ministers in prewar days. But when the mob hit the streets they were appalled. Under the pressure of events, at the moment of supreme crisis in February, the quest for liberty was all but forgotten. The leaders of the Duma were distracted from revolution by a concern to maintain order. Then men in parliament acted only when riots in the streets forced them to. They were not exhilarated by their new power. They shrank from their mission to make of Russia a democratic republic. They regarded this task in the critical hours not as their proud right and privilege but as an onerous duty imposed on them by a malign fate.

The "dark people" were nevertheless naïve enough to rejoice. Liberty could not feed them or give them land, but for a brief period it proved an acceptable dietary substitute. Although under the Provisional Government the bread lines in the cities grew longer and the ration per person was steadily reduced, newspapers were cheap and plentiful. Every political faction, every interest, every eccentric, seized the chance to argue, debate, and propagandize. John Reed, an American newspaper reporter in Russia at the time, noted how "every day tons, car-loads, train-loads of literature" saturated the land. Every street corner, train compartment, factory, schoolhouse, and barracks room became a public forum. Soldiers at the front, lacking boots and subsisting on biscuits, would rush up to visitors with the improbable entreaty, "Did you bring anything to *read?*" [11]

The new government took office amidst great good will. In Petrograd the workers all but danced in the streets at the news that the Tsar had abdicated. A portion of the garrison in the city was given leave to spread the glad tidings in the provinces. In the capital red flags waved, and revolutionary songs were intoned as if they were Christmas carols. The rest of the country took the news in stride— when they heard it. It took weeks for the new regime to make its authority known in some of the remoter areas: Transportation and communications were that fouled up.

The new government, which consisted overwhelmingly of Duma liberals, with Alexander Kerensky as its sole socialist member, promptly began to legislate. It worked with such alacrity that in two months its entire legislative program had been enacted—and exhausted. Political amnesty was generously extended to all, including both the far Right and the far Left. Capital punishment was abolished, as was exile to Siberia. All legal discrimination based on religion, race, and national origin was done away with. Freedom of the press, of speech, and of assembly was declared inviolate. The military code was revised, and soldiers were given the same personal liberties that civilians were to enjoy. An eight-hour working day was enacted into law. Indeed all the political amenities of Western liberalism were showered on the newly emancipated children of the Tsar. Lenin called Russia in the months following the February Revolution the world's freest country. But it was one thing to remove the anachronistic fetters of the old regime and another to govern a nation still stumbling along in a crushing war. Once the vestiges of Tsarist absolutism had been swept away, the new government faltered.

The problem, of course, was that the reforms were supremely irrelevant to the most urgent needs of the people. They did not provide land, seed, or tools for the peasants. They did not solve the problem of transporting bread to the towns and the front lines. Bottlenecks in distribution became more acute, and the cost of living kept rising. Critical industrial shortages of fuel, manpower, and raw materials did not diminish. Furthermore, the Revolution itself had been the signal throughout much of Russia for a popular free-for-all. Peasants viewed the installation of the new government as a blank check to even accounts with landlords. Under the new freedoms in the army, soldiers wandered off from their units in growing numbers. In the absence of positive leadership from the government, every group in Russia began to "do its own thing."

The Provisional Government could not make up its mind to halt the war. It did not even contemplate such a measure: How could it dare when the February Revolution had included elements of a patriotic campaign to rid the country of the Tsar, who was popularly suspected of intriguing with his fellow autocrats, Russia's enemies, the German Hohenzollerns? On the contrary, immediately after taking office the new government reassured its allies of its intention to pursue the war with new vigor. There was a short-lived popular belief in government circles that the Russian Army would suddenly find new vitality, even as the armies of France had done after the French Revolution, for it would now march as a democratic people's army and fight for national liberty. The politicians tried to forget that even a democratic army needs boots, as well as bravado, if it is to succeed.

The Provisional Government was incapable of solving the industrial crisis of the country. It could not build the necessary railroads, nor could it simply decree the existence of heavy industry. Clearly, if Russia continued in the war, its manpower and resources would have to be severely regimented; otherwise there would be no hope of avoiding military disaster. But whereas in France and England the progress of World War I was marked by the introduction of more and more coercive regimes and tighter government control and supervision of national economies in order to exact maximum output in labor and manufacture, Russia plunged willy-nilly, in the midst of war, into the most extreme kind of laissez-faire democracy. Suddenly, all over the country, in factories and barracks, everything had to be decided by vote before the wheels began to turn. Within the government the newly emancipated democrats were unsure of their own powers and understandably reluctant to commandeer, to dictate, to issue fiats, to push anyone around. This excessive reticence gave unlimited license to hostile elements of the Left and Right to attack the government and to show in the worst possible light its every vacillation, delay, broken promise, and contradiction. The government was thus in effect continuously on trial before the Russian people. The Tsar's ministers had abundantly proved that corruption and incompetence could not win the war, but neither could punctilious democracy. The Provisional Government was caught between its sincere desire to be as tolerant, uncoercive, and democratic as possible and the pragmatic necessity of imposing ruthless efficiency on the nation if the war was to be continued.

Russia suffered from an excess of democracy and from only partial representation of the people by Duma members. The factory workers of the capital and increasingly the Russian peasant army as well, looked to their own political organs—the soviets—for leadership. Reactivated in the first days of the February Revolution, these bodies, which were neither parliaments nor trade unions, functioned as a kind of alternative government throughout the melancholy months during which the Provisional Government sought to unite the country. But these attempts to unite Russia came too late. In Petrograd, the city that had been built as a monument to Romanov vanity, two nations lived side by side. Each tried, with considerable success, to ignore the other.

Moneyed, propertied Petrograd—represented in the Duma by liberal ministers (although much of it yearned for the return of the Tsar) —ignored the Revolution as much as possible. The events of February, to be sure, had "stuck little red flags in . . . the cast-iron monuments of the monarchy," [12] but otherwise life had not altered so very much. The daughters of the Russian nobility still came to Petrograd to perfect their French and to take piano lessons. Food shortages might be acute, but gambling and speculation had never been so exciting. In the back rooms of private clubs plenty of champagne could be had for a price. The theater was enjoying a brilliant season, and weekly art exhibitions drew hundreds of ladies of fashion. Although the Tsarina had been much despised for her dalliance with every sort of religious quackery, the Theosophists were enjoying a great vogue in cultured circles. The Tsar's generals sent their reports to Kerensky, but they were the same generals. Although the Petrograd workers were again taking to the streets after April, the commander of the Petrograd military district filed reassuring reports: He was fully prepared to deal with any outbreak of ruffians. The government lulled itself with dreamy reassurances that it had the support of all the respectable elements in the nation. Only an intransigent faction of socialists, the Bolsheviks, insisted on rude opposition. But everyone knew that the Bolsheviks were morally isolated from the Russian people.

Respectable Petrograd resolutely shunned contact with "Red" Petrograd. Across the Neva River the working-class Vyborg suburb was seldom braved by the police, who knew that they were not welcome there. In factory after factory men of fifty and boys of seventeen spent their lunch hours learning military drills and the care and use of rifles. They were members of the Red Guard—the military arm of the soviets—and they were readying for another battle. Every factory and virtually every regiment stationed in the capital regularly sent representatives to Smolny, the headquarters of the Petrograd Soviet. Under the old regime Smolny had been an elegant convent school for young noble ladies. Placards inside still designated "Ladies' Classroom Number 4," "Teachers' Room," and "Grade Superviser," but hastily improvised signs also announced headquarters of such mysterious groups as "Union of Socialist Soldiers," the "Factory-Shop Committee," and the "Central Army Committee." Inside Smolny working men in rough black blouses mixed with the future luminaries of the Bolshevik state. Smolny functioned twenty-four hours a day. Improvised cots, sofas, and mattresses lay in the halls. The once-elegant dining room downstairs offered soup and black bread. Red Guards checked the credentials of all who came and went. John Reed came to the doors one day to find a soldier at the entrance stubbornly barring the way of Trotsky, who was searching in vain through his pockets for his misplaced pass. "Names don't mean anything to me," said the guard, unimpressed by his petitioner's insistence that he was the president of the Petrograd Soviet.

From the first days of the Revolution the Petrograd Soviet had taken upon itself the countersigning of all important decrees issued by the government. This role gave it a de facto legitimacy in the eyes of the citizens, even in the early spring when the Provisional Government's prestige was still reasonably high. By fall, however, many regiments on the front lines, as well as in the capital, maintained more regular contact with the Soviet than with the government. Much of the army was taking its orders from the government, subject to the approval of the soviets.

The working-class population of Petrograd, that part of the city that looked to Smolny for direction, was self-consciously revolutionary. Gargantuan industrial enterprise had produced the Petrograd workers, a unique class within Russia. Only in this city had factory workers completely severed their ties with rural Russia, with the crude conservative mentality of the peasants. Outside this tight concentration of heavy industry Russia's workers were scattered; many continued to be off-season farmers. Petrograd had the kind of working-class ghettoes that made factory inspectors in nineteenth-century Manchester wince. Working-class suburbs segregated factory employees from the rest of the population but also gave them great cohesion. Largely ignored by the tsarist government and cut off from provincial roots, the people of this new industrial metropolis had long had to rely on one another for aid and defense. They had also been carefully and lovingly educated by the Marxist organizers, who had for long assumed an almost proprietary attitude toward the Petrograd proletariat. The workers of the capital were a cohesive group; the soviets were in a sense only the institutional embodiment of this cohesion. Strikes in the capital always threatened to spread and become more or less general, for workers in plant after plant would lay down tools in sympathetic solidarity.

In the early years of the new century, particularly during 1905, the St. Petersburg working class had become proudly conscious of itself as an avant-garde force in Russia. Like the Parisian artisans of the nineteenth century, it had learned to regard itself as the vanguard of progress. When the people bestirred themselves in sufficient numbers, they were accustomed to a response from the nation's rulers. In the newspapers of the Right, as well as of the Left, the worker could read about his own power; it was as clear to him as to anyone else that Russia feared a rising of the "dark people." The capital set the pace for the rest of the country. When it stirred, however slowly or unenthusiastically, the rest of the country followed.

Throughout the spring and summer of 1917 the temperature of the capital continued to rise. By the autumn of 1917 people were taking to the streets automatically; the city had become dangerously revolutionary. The workers had marched, assembled, and demonstrated so often in the previous months that such action had become almost a reflex response to any move made by the unhappy government. In April the people had taken to the streets to force the resignation of an unpopular Foreign Minister and the inclusion of six socialists in the government. In June the Bolsheviks urged the workers to demand the dismissal of the remaining ten "capitalist ministers." In July peace demonstrations brought hundreds of thousands out following a disastrous military offensive launched by the Provisional Government in hopes of regaining some of its rapidly ebbing prestige. Cries of "Down with the government!" rang through the streets. A few of the more radical regiments in the city clamored for immediate action, threatening to leave their "leaders" behind unless an immediate insurrection took place. Six thousand Bolshevik sailors rushed down from the naval base in Kronstadt to defend the new revolution, only to learn that there was no revolution to defend.

The July disturbances aborted thanks to lack of leadership and the government's timely publication of documents purporting to show that the Bolsheviks were all German agents. The revolutionary ardor of the people was momentarily checked—only to be revived two months later when the entire Left rallied to meet the threat of military dictatorship. One of Kerensky's generals made a premature bid to become the Russian Revolution's Napoleon. The people of Petrograd had sensitive nostrils: They detected the scent of decay hovering over the Provisional Government long before it penetrated to the more insulated ministers. In the rush to defend the city from a military coup d'état the workers had claimed arms from the government's arsenals, but they had not returned them. "For a month before the revolution in scores of shops and factories of Petrograd an intense military activity was in progress—chiefly rifle practice," [13] wrote Trotsky, who was in a position to know.

The diligent preparations had gone on for so many months that the actual takeover of power in October was something of an anticlimax. The revolutionaries, who for generations had been tempering themselves and carefully sculpting their ideological blueprints, were readying a last stupendous assault on the walls of Jericho. Then they found that the walls were made of sand. They huffed, and they puffed, and they blew the house down. In its last hours, the liberal, democratic, mildly socialist government of Kerensky could find no defenders. To be sure, one after another of the men designated to defend the city confidently asserted that the "rabble" in the streets was badly organized, uncertain of its own strength, vacillating, and sometimes actually cowardly. With "one or two reliable regiments" the insurrection could be instantly quelled. In a sense, these believers in law and order were right: The insurrection was largely improvised, and its leaders lacked technical know-how and made costly errors in judgment. Yet all these weaknesses only made the government's internal dissolution stand out more starkly. The "one or two" necessary loyal regiments never materialized. They turned "red" on the road or simply evaporated into the night.

On the morrow of the insurrection a Bolshevik soldier described to some of his friends the "capture" of a government building. "We walked in there," he said, "and filled all the doors with comrades. I went up to the counter-revolutionist Kornilovitz who sat in the president's chair. 'No more Council,' I says. 'Run along home now!' " [14] That was exactly the flavor of the insurrection. Across the city the government found itself dismissed, simply shooed out of office.

Until the very eve of the rising the Military Revolutionary Committee of the Petrograd Soviet had cloaked all its preparations in defensive language. Even among the Bolsheviks the majority felt queasy about initiating an armed uprising that might fail and precipitate a sharp right-wing reaction. Besides, the rising had not been voted on by the Congress of Soviets, which did not seem quite democratic.

The M.R.C. and Kerensky played cat and mouse, each waiting for an overt declaration of war by the other side. Finally, on the evening of October 24, Kerensky's nerve gave way. He ordered that *Pravda*, the Bolshevik paper, be shut down and that the telephone lines to Smolny be cut; he issued requests for reinforcements in the city; and he began legal action against the M.R.C. with the arrest of certain leaders. At 5:30 A.M. a government representative and some soldiers showed up at *Pravda*'s printing plant and declared the paper closed. Before departing, they smashed some machines and had the building sealed.

Once the forces of "reaction" and "counterrevolution" had taken the offensive, Smolny moved instantly into action. All regiments in the capital received orders to stand ready for further commands by the Soviet. Someone thought of fortifying headquarters. Machine guns were hastily brought and set up in the windows of the young ladies' finishing school. Barricades of firewood ringed the building. Food and munitions trucks were sent for.

The ancient symbol of tsarism, the Peter Paul Fortress, which had for centuries lodged political prisoners, had been secured by the Bolsheviks well in advance. During the night Petrograd, which was accustomed to long queues of workers awaiting the bounties of the government, lined up again, this time outside the storerooms of Peter Paul, to pass guns and ammunition from inside. The next day the occupation of buildings began. Under the leadership of soviet "commissars" created at Smolny as the need arose, small groups of workers and soldiers marched to the bridges, the railroad stations, the telephone exchange, the post office, the state bank, and the power plants. Everywhere the procedures were the same. The commissar exchanged a few words with the sentries on duty. The only resistance met was verbal. The revolutionaries talked their way inside, dismissed the guards, posted their own men, and sent back messengers to Smolny reporting the success of their missions.

At the first sign of serious trouble the Provisional Government had ordered the bridges of the city raised, a precaution taken only in times of grave peril. It was supposed to quarantine the insurrectionary disease and to hamper effective mobilization of workers who lived on the far side of the river. The bridges and railroads were reinforced by military-school cadets, called "junkers." There were about five thousand of them in the city, and they were supposed to be loyal and valiant young men. The myth of the ferocious, well-trained officer cadets had penetrated even to the Bolsheviks, who sent their own strongest and most revolutionary regiments to reclaim these vital posts. The contest for the bridges, however, consisted of heated volleys of investive between the cadets and the Red Guards. Each side berated the other for being enemies of the Revolution. In the end the junkers allowed themselves to be disarmed or simply walked off muttering. To restore movement on one especially vital bridge, Smolny instructed the gunboat *Aurora* to stand by as a threat. Dutifully the ship steamed up to the bridge, and sailors appeared on all the decks. By the time that it had dropped anchor all the junkers had vanished. Every now and then an ardent detachment of Red Guards took a group of cadets prisoner and marched them off to Smolny. It seemed the thing to do in a revolution. The terrified prisoners were lectured on their arrival at Smolny, by Trotsky or whoever else was available, on the villainy of resisting a people's revolution. They were then made to promise that they would no longer lift arms to help the government. After the lecture they were sent home. The cadets, who had been told that they could expect to be slaughtered, were amazed. A general in the War Ministry sent word to headquarters:

The troops of the Petrograd garrison . . . have gone over to the Bolsheviks. The sailors and the light-armed cruiser have come from Kronstadt. They have lowered the raised bridges. The whole town is covered with sentry guards from the garrison. . . . The Telephone Exchange is in the hands of the garrison. . . . The general impression is that the Provisional Government finds itself in the capital of a hostile state which has finished mobilization but not yet begun active operations.[15]

The diagnosis proved correct, but the Provisional Government was having a hard time seeing the situation in perspective. On October 25 no tumultuous throngs of demonstrators rioted in the streets. One had to look long and hard to find a barricade. Ministers moved freely from their homes to their offices. They held meetings and feverishly drafted appeals to the city to remain calm and to support the Provisional Government. The city was certainly remaining calm. People were going to work. Stores, schools, theaters, and restaurants were all open. There was no sound of rifle fire. How could it be a revolution?

By midday on October 26 the city was in the hands of the Bolsheviks. From the windows of cars packages of leaflets were tossed (there was no time to paste them up). The leaflets informed the Petrograd population that the Provisional Government no longer existed—which was not quite true. The Provisional Government was bewildered, frightened, and hiding in the Winter Palace while it waited for a miracle to rescue it. Kerensky was gone. He had departed, in a car commandeered from the American Embassy, to gather troops to march to the city. Friendly civilians and soldiers waved as he passed by, according to his own account. Cruel jokesters gave it out that he had fled dressed as a Sister of Mercy.

The resources at the command of the ministers in the palace were not impressive. They consisted in the first instance of cadets—like those who had only the day before melted away from the bridges and depots—a few armored cars, some special soldiers led by an officer with a cork leg, and a battalion of women (melodramatically designated the "Death Battalion"). Via a telegraph wire in the palace the government requested immediate relief for the capital. But the relief supposed to be even then speeding to the city was not overwhelming: It consisted of a bicycle battalion. The government supposedly also had the Cossack cavalry at its beck and call, but the Cossacks sent word that they considered the defense of the Winter

Palace too dangerous unless they could be guaranteed supporting infantry. In the meantime they were "saddling their horses."

In these circumstances it is not surprising that the insurgents over-estimated the difficulty of taking the palace. They were in any case having some difficulty believing the ease, the bloodlessness, of their victory. The Winter Palace, it was feared, would offer stiff resistance. The Bolsheviks decided that it must be cordoned off by overwhelming force. Special cannons were rigged up in the Peter Paul Fortress for bombardment. The *Aurora* was ordered to train its guns on the palace. The arrival of several thousand sailors was deemed essential before operations could begin. In the meantime soldiers began to station themselves in the palace square, and some cadets began to build wooden barricades.

Inside the Winter Palace the deposed government moved from its conference room, which unfortunately faced the river and the gunboat that was expected momentarily to begin shelling, to the former Tsar's private dining room. There it partook of a meal un-pleasantly reminiscent of the Last Supper. The Minister of Justice wrote little notes to himself: "To resist to the last man, to the last drop of blood? In the name of what?" The ministers waited for the bombardment to begin and repeatedly exhorted the cadets to do their duty. The response was more perfunctory than enthusiastic. An ul-timatum to surrender was received and rejected. The *Aurora* began firing blanks. Some firing in the streets could also be heard as mem-bers of the Red Guards and soldiers impatiently awaited permission to mount a full attack. Morale inside the palace was not high. Many of the cadets clearly wished themselves elsewhere. They had no pro-visions and were trying to keep their spirits up by sampling the former Tsar's wine cellar. Bolsheviks kept appearing in the building. They came in through back doors and windows, a few at a time. The cadets disarmed them but could not shut them up. The agitators began to explain the hopelessness of resistance to the military-school boys. Scuffles between attackers and defenders broke out in the corridors. The trickle of Bolsheviks grew to a flood. Cadets and Bolshevik work-ers and soldiers milled around in the impressive, plush-carpeted halls of the palace like tourists in search of a guide. The old servants, arrayed in flashy red, gold, and blue uniforms, were aghast at the muddy boots and the bad manners of these intruders. One of the min-isters committed an indiscreet thought to paper: He said that he felt as if he had been caught in a giant mousetrap. Nevertheless, during this vigil it was considered advisable to keep up the morale of the people, who presumably were bitterly bemoaning the fate of their trapped leaders. A dispatch was sent out describing the situation inside the Winter Palace: "The government is in full attendance. . . . The situation is considered favorable. . . . The Palace is under fire but only rifle fire and without results. It is clear that the enemy is weak." [16]

Inside the palace, in fact, it was no longer clear who was disarming whom. Bolsheviks outnumbered defenders. Troops in the Peter Paul Fortress fired some artillery, which did little more than rip plaster. The barricades in the square had broken, and Red Guards, soldiers, passers-by, and newspaper reporters swarmed into the former Tsar's palace. But the building was never officially "stormed." The cadets were disarmed; the ministers, determined to meet their fate with as much dignity as the circumstances permitted, assembled around a long table in postures suitable to a Cabinet meeting. The Bolshevik commandant of palace operations entered and announced that the ministers were all under arrest. A raucous exploration of the Winter Palace was underway. Desks, draws, china closets, and cabinets were pulled open. John Reed, the American reporter who had entered the building with the first "wave," came upon a room where two soldiers were ripping some Spanish leather upholstery from chairs. They explained that it was for boots.

Dissent and rebellion in modern Russia ran a different course than in the West, just as Russian government and economy departed significantly from the Western pattern. In the nineteenth century peaceful protest against tsarist tyranny had been impossible. Because of savage repression, middle-class protest had to take the form of revolutionary subversion and assassination. But as the tsarist government disintegrated after 1905 and after the Provisional Government of 1917 had completely lost control of governing the country, revolution became impossible in Russia because it was unnecessary. There was no force capable of withstanding the Petrograd Soviet's grasp for power. So in the end the famous Bolshevik Revolution was actually little more than a peaceful protest demonstration.

In the 1920s the Soviet government commissioned propaganda movies showing hordes of soldiers and peasants storming the Winter Palace. The truth is that the Bolsheviks and their supporters did not storm the palace; they drifted into it through several entrances. The Bolshevik Revolution was a sit-in.

PART TWO

PROTEST AGAINST "NORMALCY"

INTRODUCTION

In his proclamation of "a return to normalcy," one of the least distinguished of American Presidents, Warren G. Harding, spoke for the leaders of the old regime in the 1920s. Now that the holocaust of the First World War was over, these leaders intended to turn the clock back to August 1914. Public lassitude and confusion, coupled with a dizzying prosperity, seemed to justify their expectations. But, even in a decade dominated by political conservatism and selfish privatism, movements of protest against this specious "normalcy" heralded the coming disintegration of the old order.

The general strike of 1926 in Britain, although a miserable failure that demonstrated anew the gross ineptitude of labor-union leadership, reflected the anger and misery of the masses in the midst of the apparent triumphs of arrogant capitalism. More significantly in the long run, a new cultural phase was emerging among the young intellectuals of the Western world. This Jazz Age rebellion advertised the bankruptcy of the values of the old regime. The new values that were so apparent in the literature, art, music, and life style of the 1920s made a mockery of the intellectual and moral pretensions of the generation still in power and of expectations that the prevailing pastiche of liberal, capitalist, and imperialist ideals and institutions could recover their prewar eminence in Western society. The rot and sickness of the old order was most evident in Germany. Amid the chaos following the collapse of Kaiser Wilhelm II's government and the inept wallowing of the Weimar Republic, the German middle class came to express its anger at the old order and its simultaneous fear of change through allegiance to Nazi terror.

CHAPTER

5

The General Strike
in Britain

On Tuesday, May 4, 1926, England did not precisely grind to a halt; it just slowed down dramatically. Three million people, from Scotland to Dover, quit work. It was the most vast and concerted work stoppage that western Europe had ever seen. Motormen and conductors abandoned trains midway between stations, leaving passengers to fend for themselves. Tourists returning home from abroad on steamships found no porters on the docks: Pickets and policemen were the only people in sight. Trams, buses, trains, porters, and taxis had all but vanished from the streets. Newspapers were unobtainable; though most made some attempt to continue publication, only bizarrely diminutive editions appeared. On the other hand, the country received a surfeit of the government's emergency news organ—*The British Gazette*—which proclaimed loudly in every edition that a small band of miscreants was bent on plunging England into civil war. Of more than four thousand city buses normally operated by the London General Omnibus Co., not a single one moved. Of more than three hundred subway trains, fifteen moved uncertainly along their routes. A large proportion of all workers engaged in the building trades, in chemical works, in iron and steel, and in other heavy industries had gone "out." At Eccleston Square, London headquarters of the Trades Union Congress, telegrams and petitions poured in from all over the country—most from unions that had not been ordered out and were begging for instructions. For example, the Goldbeaters' Trade Society, 310 strong, wished to be informed of the role that it was to play in the great struggle.[1]

For the next nine days the streets of London and other large English cities had a bizarre appearance. Despite the shortage of public transport the streets were teeming, even though it sometimes happened that traffic slowed to the astonishing rate of one mile an hour. Pony carts, motorcars of every possible vintage, bicycles, and contraptions that seemed to have been lifted from Leonardo da Vinci's notebooks cluttered the streets. Everyone who had to go someplace hitchhiked freely. By the end of the week it was hard to find a bicycle for sale in London.

The B.B.C. broadcast appeals for volunteers of every description. Volunteers were urgently sought to drive buses, load freight, act as porters, serve as power-station attendants, set type, conduct traffic, and serve as constables. Improvised recruiting stations sprang up around the country. From the universities, from the stock exchange, and from the elegant town houses of Mayfair came relief of sorts. Up-and-coming young brokers in the City were informed that volunteer service to the nation during the crisis would look well in their dossiers when promotion time came. Undergraduates at the universities of Oxford and Cambridge forsook the charms of Plato and Milton for the more exciting tasks of driving engines. By the end of the week, although the strikers' ranks were solid, the London General Omnibus Co. was falteringly back in business. Under police escort a few fugitive, windowless buses, often sporting the college colors of their undergraduate drivers, chugged through the streets. True, they were occasionally stopped and overturned by angry strikers, and they were all rather breezy. On their sides the buses sported signs like "A stone in the hand is worth two in the bus" and "I have no pane, dear mother, now."

Hyde Park became a huge food depot, from which milk was distributed throughout the city. Periodically Londoners were treated to the sight of armored cars delivering food in convoy formation. Winston Churchill temporarily abandoned his duties at the Exchequer and proved his versatility yet again by turning newspaper editor. *The British Gazette*, which he edited and largely wrote, predicted dramatically that unless the strike was totally crushed, the appearance of "some Soviet of trade unions on which, whether under Parliamentary forms or without them, the really effective control of the economic and political life of the country" would devolve was a certainty. The *Daily Mail*, being produced in France for the duration of the strike, quoted William Wordsworth:

> We must be free or die, who speak the tongue
> That Shakespeare spake: the faith and morals hold
> Which Milton held.

The Conservative Prime Minister, Stanley Baldwin, maintained his usual equanimity yet declared that the country had not been so close to civil war for centuries. The Archbishop of Canterbury pleaded for moderation and negotiations but was denied a hearing on the B.B.C. and in the *Gazette*. A Roman Catholic cardinal who declared that the strike was "a sin against Almighty God" received prime coverage, however. The Russian trade unions sent their English brethren good wishes and a check for two million rubles, which was promptly returned. The government stopped all exports of coal from the country. To conserve power, stores and theaters were forbidden to turn on their neon lights. The leaves of all servicemen were canceled, and they were placed on alert for unspecified combat. The Home Secretary, though conceding that there seemed to have been little violence, pleaded for more volunteer constables to serve, he explained, as a "steady influence." In the meantime, in Plymouth strikers and policemen played a football match on the green. The kickoff was made by the chief constable's wife. The strikers won by a score of 2 to 1. It was virtually their only victory.

For nine days in May England endured this general strike. Living through a general strike, according to the folklore of the Left, was supposed to be like living through the Apocalypse. No political organism was supposed to be able to survive a general strike. The fact that as recently as 1913 Belgian workers had carried out a general strike in perfect order with excellent organization and considerable success had dimmed the myth not at all. The idea of the general strike trailing clouds of revolution and rivers of blood had been bequeathed to the twentieth century. Mr. Churchill and a considerable number of his fellows in the House of Commons professed to take the general strike seriously. On the other hand, the men who had given the signal for the workers to turn out insisted fervently that the strike was not an attempt to overturn the British Constitution. British coal-mine owners were threatening to cut wages and extend working hours in that industry. The prewar "Triple Alliance"—a federation of transport workers, railway men, and miners—obliged the Trades Union Congress to support the miners' decision to strike to halt the owners' plans. The work stoppage, the T.U.C.'s explained frantically, was an industrial dispute and nothing more. In fact, Mr. Ramsay MacDonald, who presided over the Labour Party in the House, and the Messrs. J. H. Thomas, Arthur Pugh, and Ernest Bevin, all of whom sat on the General Council of the Trades Union Congress, preferred not to use the unfortunate term "general strike." The strike was *national*, they insisted, not general, just national.

The words "general strike," as the General Council recognized only too well, did not evoke from most men a rational reaction. However much ink the theoreticians of the Second International had used in attempting to domesticate and define the general strike as merely a tactic, to be eschewed or adopted for purely pragmatic reasons, its vitality nevertheless came from a vision. The vision was simple and at least as old as *Piers Plowman*. It was the old medieval vision of princes, lords, and seigneurs toppling head over heels off thrones and pedestals, plunging into an abyss. The general strike seemed to a great many left-wing Europeans to be the quickest way to realize this millennial vision.

The scenario might read as follows: On a certain day, not necessarily designated in advance, the entire working population of the country would lay down their tools—all workers at the same instant—thus bringing chaos and ruination upon the country. In 1834 the Glasgow *Liberator* drew a graphic picture of the chaos: "Bills are dishonoured, the *Gazette* teems with bankruptcies, capital is destroyed, the revenue fails, the system of government falls into confusion, and every link in the chain which binds society together is broken in a moment by this inert conspiracy of the poor against the rich." [2] Capitalists, politicians, bankers, and lawyers—that entire segment of the nation that customarily wore frock coats and top hats—would be at once reduced to penitent suppliants, entreating the workers to restore to society their vital skills and muscle power. The magnanimous workers would do so but only on their own terms. Thenceforth the "productive classes" would control government, industry, and the destinies of the nation. The inevitability of this denouement was postulated on the belief that all workingmen acting in unison would exert a force that could be neither denied nor defeated. This conviction had been adumbrated as far back as the French Revolution by Honoré de Mirabeau, who had warned the privileged classes, "Do not irritate this people, which produces everything, and which to make itself formidable has only to become motionless." [3] It was believed that the people could effect a social revolution by simply becoming motionless. Faced by silent, inexorable, yet passive resistance from the workers, the paralyzed country would simply have to capitulate. In 1926 this belief did not seem entirely fanciful, for had it not been vindicated by the October Revolution in Russia? The English upper classes had not yet become inured to the Bolshevik menace; as late as 1924 fear of insidious

Bolshevik influences in Britain had helped Labour to lose an election.

Even in its bloodier versions—as advocated in the works of Georges Sorel, who wrote exultantly of "proletarian violence" as the rejuvenator of the class struggle—the dream of a general strike had overtones of gaiety. National holocaust or not, for the workers it was to be a joyous liberation. From the 1840s, when it was first preached by English journeyman shoemaker William Benbow, a Chartist, the general strike had seemed festive. In fact Benbow had not called this marvelous event a "strike" at all but a "grand national holiday":

A holiday signifies a *holy* day, and ours is to be of holy days the most holy. . . . In our holy day we shall legislate for all mankind; the constitution drawn up during our holiday shall place every human being on the same footing. Equal rights, equal liberties, equal enjoyments, equal toil, equal respect, equal share of production: this is the object of our holy day. . . .⁴

The English general strike of 1926, which fulfilled so few hopes—and so few nightmares—did at least provide the English people with an extended holiday. The undergraduates who flocked to the rescue of the British Constitution had, for the most part, only the cloudiest conception of the issues involved in the strike. Many of them found their volunteer activities not at all incompatible with sympathy for the miners. It was a lark, a chance to cast off one identity in favor of an earthier, perhaps more virile, role. Overnight it had become patriotic to cut classes. Most of these students did not work very hard during the strike. If they set out in the morning to drive a bus or train, they were as likely to have wandered off to a pub by midday. If they did not like the jobs to which they were assigned, they could always try others. There were no sanctions for failure or incompetence. If they were unskilled and bungled their tasks, who could blame them, raw and inexperienced as they were? Important people made speeches on the B.B.C. lauding these antics as selfless and courageous. Unexpected rewards were often lavished on the students. One novice bus driver in London, thrown into the gutter by the backfire of his own vehicle, found himself being dusted off by a peer and an admiral and then taken home to a sumptuous supper, which included wine bottled in Napoleonic days. Volunteer lorry drivers covering long distances found their journey pleasantly broken by respites in posh country houses set up as temporary canteens. Girl Scouts and debutantes alike served coffee, cooked dinner, even washed and darned the volunteers' socks.

Even for those who sat out the crisis—the nonstrikers and the non-volunteers—life became jauntier. No employer was likely to grumble if one turned up an hour late for work, transportation being what it

was. Workingmen of all classes—those who were still on their jobs—
accustomed to being treated as perfunctorily as the office furniture,
suddenly found themselves all but heroes just for being there. In the
evenings there was the excitement of gathering around the wireless to
hear the latest news or simply the small thrill of exchanging rumors.
Not since the Great War had ended had the average Englishman,
striker or volunteer, enjoyed so much solidarity and camaraderie with
his fellows.

Only those in positions of official responsibility—trade-union officials, members of Parliament, Cabinet ministers, and the like—failed to
enjoy the week. Least amused of all were the men who were supposed
to have decreed the strike: the General Council of the T.U.C. The
Council found itself in an unenviable squeeze between a high-handed,
righteous government on the Right and militant, desperate miners on
the Left. It was not a comfortable position. The General Council
wanted only one thing: to negotiate, to patch up a compromise, and
to end the whole thing as quickly as possible. Neither the government
nor the miners seemed interested in negotiation. The former had announced repeatedly that it would not negotiate under duress, that the
strike would have to be called off unconditionally before talks might
begin. The miners, as their leaders explained over and over again,
would not negotiate at all because they had nothing to negotiate. They
were already living on miserable wages, and the mine-owners, apparently with the government's blessing, were attempting to cut their
wages and increase their working hours. The workers would never
agree, and the General Council, despite its best efforts, had been unable
to avert the strike. The general strike made a fine threat, but many
union leaders had openly prayed that its power would never actually
be tested. The General Council was trapped when the government
had broken off negotiations. The order to "turn out" had been duly
sent forth. Many General Council members had feared that the strike
would be ineffective because of insufficient participation, but the turnout had in fact been overwhelming. The General Council then began
to fear a successful strike even more than it had feared a dud. Three
million Englishmen had left their jobs: How could a handful of leaders
in London hope to guide, check, and control them? Many more were
only awaiting the word to walk out. What was a good union bureaucrat to do?

The general strike offered an unpleasant irony. It had been called
by men who were themselves utterly dismayed at what they had
wrought. The general strike was—there was no getting away from it—
essentially a revolutionary weapon, but the English trade unions did

not want revolution. They wanted profoundly and rather desperately to evade the consequences of this fearful weapon of their own forging. They were frightened lest they prove unable to harness the discontent that they had unleashed. At the height of the strike, it was not the government but the General Council that, in something very near panic, begged the workers for continued maintenance of order and peace. The *British Worker*, the strike sheet of the T.U.C., daily carried heartrending pleas for the workers to eschew violence and to avoid any hint of politicizing their grievances. The tiny Communist Party strike sheet, the *Worker's Bulletin*, called the T.U.C.'s constant admonitions to the workers both obsequious and insulting to the men on the picket lines, and for once the Communist Party was right. In France, where workingmen imbibed news of the general strike with their daily liter of wine, people did not understand what was going on at all. Why had no policemen been killed? an audience of Parisian socialists queried one visiting British professor. And why were strike leaders telling men to stay quietly in their homes rather than to go out and harass the local authorities?

The doctrine of the general strike was profoundly uncongenial to English labor leaders, reared as they had been in the cautious atmosphere of Fabian reformism. In the 1920s Labour was committed chiefly to establishing its own respectability, good manners, and patriotism in the eyes of the country at large. Ramsay MacDonald had rushed to adorn himself in formal tuxedo when the first Labour government had taken office in 1924. Nothing in Labour's brief administration could have been construed as a serious attempt to alter the status quo among the classes in English society. Philip Snowdon, Chancellor of the Exchequer for the first Labour government (January–October 1924), had prepared budgets indistinguishable from those of his Liberal and Conservative predecessors. The general strike afforded die-hard Tories one more opportunity to hurl the charge of reckless radicalism at Labour leaders. Churchill and other hawks in Baldwin's Cabinet appeared ready to label the whole affair a "Bolshevik conspiracy." From the point of view of the General Council, the situation could not have been worse.

Through the Council the more affluent, conservative sectors of the trade-union movement were being implicated in the radicalism of the most aggrieved sectors. Prestige and solidarity demanded, of course, that the entire trade-union movement unite behind the sector of the working class that was receiving the rawest deal. In 1926 that sector was, without doubt, the miners.

Even before the war the mining industry had been plagued by

strikes and walkouts. Coal mining was rapidly becoming a depressed industry in Britain, as German inroads into the production and export of this most important industrial fuel put British mine-owners on the defensive. The miners had always been among the most militant groups in the working class, and their grievances, almost everyone conceded, were serious. The English mining industry was operated in a needlessly wasteful and inefficient manner. Every government commission that ever studied the problem had pointed out these flaws. The most famous commission, the one to which the miners' leaders always referred, was the Sankey Commission, convoked in 1919 by David Lloyd George. The commission had soundly reprimanded the mine-owners of England for operating irresponsibly an industry in which mistrust and recrimination between owners and men were constant. The commission recommended increasing the miners' pay and cutting their working day to six hours. It also called on the owners to reorganize the pits drastically and to see to it that "the colliery workers shall in the future have an effective voice in the direction of the mine."[5] Otherwise nationalization of the industry was the only solution, according to the commission's report.

Six years after the publication of this document not one of the miners' grievances had been assuaged. Even Conservatives admitted that the owners were among the most reactionary and uncooperative of all employers. One outspoken Conservative Lord had remarked scornfully that he had always thought the miners' leaders quite the stupidest men in the country—until he had had the displeasure of meeting the owners. In 1926, in the midst of rising prices and living costs, the owners were insisting that the problems of the industry could be solved only by cutting the workers' wages and increasing their hours. The coal industry had been controlled and heavily subsidized by the government during the war. Now that an economy drive was on and the government was about to withdraw this subsidy, the industry would suffer a difficult period of readjustment. The owners expected most of the readjusting to be done by the workers, who would simply have to tighten their belts. As for suggestions that the industry might be mismanaged, the mine-owners treated them as beneath contempt.

Actually the government was bent only on withdrawing the subsidy, which was costing it millions of pounds a year. No Conservative government in the 1920s was willing to assume responsibility for a faltering industry except under the most extreme emergency conditions. Baldwin's position and that of his colleagues was that the miners and owners had to iron out the matter between themselves in a spirit of compromise and conciliation. The government was perfectly willing to appoint commissions to study the problem and to make recommendations. But it would not coerce either miners or owners into accepting these recommendations.

The situation reached one of its many crises in the summer of 1925. Government subsidies were to expire at the end of July, and after that, mine owners announced, workers in the pits would have to agree to new contracts providing wage cuts of 10 to 25 percent or face a lockout. The government tried to keep negotiations moving, but the miners were at least as adamant as the owners. They believed, with justice, that an attempt was being made to force their living standards below subsistence levels. They were not, after all, waging an aggressive war for more luxuries. They were merely trying to hold their ground. They had, as their leaders kept insisting, nothing to concede.

The miners' leaders inhabited a different cosmos from the plush drawing rooms in which Stanley Baldwin and Ramsay MacDonald circulated. The secretary of the Miners' Federation was Arthur Cook, a onetime Welsh preacher who had lost none of his fire when he turned to labor agitation. The president of the union was Herbert Smith, a monosyllabic Yorkshireman. At the negotiating table he was as immovable as a mountain. When asked what the men were willing to give in return for accommodations by the owners, his answer never varied. "Now't," he said. "We have now't to give." The catch phrase of the miners became "Not a penny off the pay, not a second on the day." [6] Beyond that they had little to say.

Smith and Cook were almost as much of a nuisance to the General Council of the T.U.C. as they were to the government and the mine owners. They had both come up from the pits and had acquired no polish from their contacts with government dignitaries. Smith insisted on eating in coffee stalls instead of in restaurants. He had contempt for anyone who had never worked in the mines, and his advice to negotiators was often, "Git on t'field." Cook made a lot of unpleasant noise, proclaiming himself a follower of Nikolai Lenin and toasting the demise of the British Empire. Nevertheless, there was no denying the fact that the miners' demands were both just and urgent. For any union to agree to a depression of already low wages would be an intolerable precedent in the trade-union movement. The General Council met with the executive of the miners and pledged total support to resist "the degradation of the standard of life of their members." [7] If the mulish owners could not be bamboozled into modernizing their modes of production and pruning their profits, then the government would have to nationalize the mines.

A strike—a *general* strike—now appeared inevitable. Faced with this calamity, for which the government felt ill prepared in July 1925, Baldwin capitulated and agreed to extend the subsidy for another nine months, pending the findings of still another commission, this one under the chairmanship of the distinguished former Liberal Cabinet Minister Herbert Samuel. The unions called the day of Baldwin's capitulation "Red Friday"; it brought a victory for Labour, but there was little rejoicing. Nothing had been gained but time, and it was unlikely that the attitude of either miners or owners would change in nine months.

Indeed the grace period proved a boon only to the government. The Samuel report, when it was duly published, represented several steps backward from the Sankey report of 1919. Intended as a sop to both sides, it angered everyone. The commission did not recommend nationalization but made the inevitable suggestion that the industry reorganize itself posthaste. Small, inefficient collieries were to be eliminated, and profit sharing, family allowances, and better working conditions were urged for the miners. On the whole the commission believed that the working day should not be lengthened. But—and this was the fatal "but" for the miners—wages would have to be cut at least temporarily while the industry pulled itself up by its bootstraps. The miners would not budge. Not that they had expected much from the Samuel Commission's report. Months before its publication Cook had toured the country, predicting: "Next May we shall be faced with the greatest crisis and the greatest struggle we have ever known. . . . I don't care a hang for any government, or army or navy. They can come along with their bayonets. Bayonets don't cut coal." [8]

The difference between the General Council and the miners was the difference between a compassionate observer and the man who feels a bayonet in the small of his back. The General Council was willing to use the Samuel report as a basis for negotiations. Its members tried to reason with Cook, pointing out that the commission had recommended granting two-thirds of all his demands. "Three-quarters," Cook corrected them, "and we can't accept it." [9]

Throughout the protracted months of negotiations the General Council kept up a rather stupid optimism. Its members devoutly wished the strike to be averted and were blinded by their own hopes. How little they wanted a general strike can be gauged from the fact that absolutely no preparations had been made for propaganda, for communications among different industries and regions of the country, for distribution of essential foodstuffs to workers, or for any other exigencies of such a battle. In the agonized days just before May 3, the members of the General Council were still shying away from the words "general strike." The editor of the *Daily Herald*, the biggest news organ of the Left, reported that "the one speaker who advocated the use of the Big Stick—in other words the plain threat of the general strike—was heard with impatience, and only found one delegate to vote with him." In the last hours of negotiation Jimmy Thomas, of the railroad workers, a member of the Council, reported that he had never in his life "begged and pleaded for peace as I have pleaded and begged today." In an attempt to avoid the strike he "grovelled"—his own word —before the government. Later, during the strike, he was further to distinguish himself by answering charges that the unions were attacking the Constitution with the words, "I have never disguised that in any challenge to the Constitution God help us unless the government won." [10]

While the T.U.C., ostrich-like, had done nothing for nine months in the hope that the strike could be prevented, the government had prepared extensively and well to take over operation of vital services. It was determined to be ready for the worst. The events of the previous July, furthermore, had caused sufficient alarm among the upper classes so that they had begun spontaneously to organize for whatever challenge the unions might mount. By September 1925 there had blossomed a citizens' group called the Organization for the Maintenance of Supplies. Officially it was purely voluntary and received no government money, but it certainly had the blessings of every "right-thinking" Cabinet member. The function of O.M.S. was to train sufficient Englishmen in skills vital to transport and communications. Admirals, former Viceroys of India, and distinguished peers lent their names, talents, and funds to this organization, which set about compiling nationwide lists of volunteers willing to receive instruction in how to drive trucks, operate telegraph wires, and conduct trains and buses. Exactly how much training O.M.S. actually provided is dubious. Nevertheless, it did help to marshall public opinion and enrolled about 100,000 citizens. The names of these volunteers could be made available to the government instantly in an emergency. O.M.S. was not the only group ready to rally to the colors. A small group of English fascists announced that it was preparing more forcible means of dealing with the strikers. The fascists armed themselves, held weekly drills, and practiced for future hostilities by breaking up left-wing political rallies in Hyde Park on Sundays. To Labour the specter of the upper and middle classes organizing for class war was extremely disquieting. The aristocracy was supposed to be decadent and to await helplessly the coming showdown.

The government meanwhile drew up plans for swiftly provisioning

the country so that it would not be starved into docility by the transport workers. Agreements were quietly made with haulage contractors,
who consented to give the government's transport needs prece-
dence over all private contracts during a general strike. Just in case
this measure proved insufficient, the government was prepared to
requisition whatever it needed as the situation developed. The country
was divided into ten "divisions," each with its own commissioners of
finance, food, coal, and roads. The commissioners were given wide
discretionary powers to fix prices, arrest recalcitrant storekeepers,
and imprison local troublemakers as the need arose. Emphasis was
placed on putting the emergency plans into operation as soon as the
strike hit. There can be no doubt that these extensive preparations
gave the government a sense of confidence, perhaps even complacency,
in the last hours before negotiations broke down.

It was this knowledge of total preparedness which made Baldwin
seem so nonchalant about negotiations that at one critical stage in the
talks union leaders arrived with a written resolution in hand only to find
the Cabinet room dark and silent. The Prime Minister, they were
told, had gone home to bed. Baldwin apparently was not nearly as
squeamish about a general strike as were the men who called it into
being.

Once the strike began, the government assumed a position of absolute intransigence, insisting that it be called off unconditionally before
negotiations could proceed. Treating the whole affair as an attack
on the Constitution, the government managed to terrify the already
distressed General Council. On the third day John Simon, a former
Home Secretary, declared with righteous eloquence that the strike was
not only immoral but illegal besides. Every union official, indeed every
striker, Simon continued, could be sued for damages. Strike funds
could be attached, and even the personal property of union officials—
their homes, cars, and gold watches—could be taken from them. Simon's
opinion was reinforced three days later by an eminent English magistrate. Most subsequent legal opinion was quite the opposite, but it
came too late. For the men of the General Council the idea of being
party to an assault on the British Constitution was horrifying enough.
Now they were also being told that they were no better than criminals!
They reasoned that although the plight of the miners was indeed
pitiful, it would not be improved by the depletion of union treasuries
around the nation. Furthermore, it was being whispered that at any
moment the government would arrest key union figures. The English
union leaders thought back to another general strike—in Winnipeg,
Canada, in 1919—and remembered uneasily that Canadian authorities

had brought the strike to an ignominious end with just such tactics. Churchill and his friends in the Cabinet insisted on calling the strike "civil war," and, furthermore, no one knew how long the exemplary conduct of the workers themselves would continue. The General Council was inexpressibly grateful that violence had so far been minimal; there had been not a single death and only a few hundred arrests, but how long could this peaceful behavior go on? As the workers grew hungrier, they would also grow bitter and more belliger-ent. The government, it was well known, had readied tanks, battle-ships, and God alone knew what else.

The government, furthermore, was making it impossible for the unions to demonstrate their pacific and civic-minded intentions. Union leaders had, for example, offered to help in the distribution of food and certain other vital commodities. Mr. Churchill replied on behalf of the government that a Cabinet minister could not seriously be ex-pected to enter "into partnership with a rival Government." [11] Al-though the General Council kept protesting indignantly that that was not what it had meant at all, in some sections of the country strike committees *had* virtually begun to run the towns. Local strike com-mittees, for instance, issued at their discretion "permits" to move goods. This activity produced sudden humility in many English captains of industry:

Employers of labour were coming, cap in hand, begging for permission to do certain things, or to be more correct, to allow workers to return to per-form certain customary operations. "Please can I move a quantity of coal from such and such a place." . . . Most of them turned empty away after a most humiliating experience, for one and all were put through a stern ques-tioning, just to make them realize that we and not they were the salt of the earth.[12]

Obviously if such anomalous conditions continued for long, people could get all sorts of wild ideas. A great many British trade unionists of the 1920s had more stake in the status quo than they had consciously realized. In the 1930s George Orwell brilliantly characterized a cer-tain kind of socialist, a type that had flourished in Labour circles in the previous decade: "In his fight against immoveable tyranny . . . he is upheld by the consciousness that it *is* immoveable. When things happen unexpectedly and the world-order which he has known begins to crumble, he feels somewhat differently about it." [13]

The General Council confronted several alternatives, all about equally unsavory. It could continue the strike, in which case one of two things would happen: Either the strike would begin to crumble, or it would take a sharp turn to the left and grow into violence and even open revolution. The only other alternative seemed to be outright capitulation. The General Council tried, of course, to disguise its capitulation, but the government seemed unwilling to permit the unions even a semblance of face saving. Shortly after the strike had begun, a powerful trade unionist had called on the Cabinet to "find a formula." He was greeted at the door by Churchill, who demanded, "Have you come to say that the strike notices are withdrawn?"

"No, we" began the would-be negotiator.

"Then there is no reason to continue the discussion," snapped Churchill.[14]

Despite official denials, the General Council was negotiating frantically behind the scenes. It sought a straw to clutch, and toward the end of the first week of the strike such a straw appeared, in the person of Herbert Samuel. Samuel had cut short a pleasant Italian vacation to rush back to England and offer himself as a negotiator between the government and the unions. He and the General Council went into a secret huddle and produced a memorandum that was to provide the excuse for terminating the strike. It did not read very differently from the report of the Samuel Commission, which had already proved futile. It piously reiterated the necessity to reorganize the coal industry and opposed lengthening the miners' work day. On the question of wage cuts, however, it equivocated, stating that they could not be ruled out in advance, though they were ostensibly to be tied to a comprehensive restructuring of the entire industry.

Armed with the Samuel memorandum, the General Council presented itself at the government's offices to announce the cessation of the strike. The government was not about to make things either easy or pleasant for the union men. Members of the Council had to spell out the purpose of their visit to a secretary before they were given access to the Prime Minister. In its subsequent bulletins the General Council stated that it "assumed" that the miners could go back to work pending the outcome of full-scale negotiations. It assumed also that the government would continue to pay some interim subsidy.

The problem of this particular settlement, which even the General Council had difficulty in labeling a "victory," was that it had not been authorized by the miners; in fact, it had been negotiated behind their backs and against their express wishes. Furthermore, Samuel, as he made perfectly clear, was tendering proposals that had the official backing of absolutely nobody. Neither the government, the owners, nor the miners had given the slightest indication that they would cooperate in implementing his recommendations. The General Council's assumptions about the future course of negotiations, and especially its faith that the owners would withdraw lockout notices, proved utterly unfounded. Worse yet, the rank and file of the unions had not been consulted. Typically, one of the members of the General Council stammered his conviction that the government would respond "in a big way" to the labor leaders' gesture of magnanimity. Such is the power of self-deceit.

The following morning, newspaper headlines exulted at the humiliation inflicted on the unions. The *Daily Mail* called the settlement "Surrender of the Revolutionaries." Official statements issued by the Cabinet made it painfully clear that no "deal" had been made. Baldwin was vague about what he intended to do next and promised the unions exactly nothing.

The General Council faced the extreme embarrassment of explaining its action to the rank and file, most especially to the miners. Strikers around the country first learned that the walkout was all over from the radio or from bulletin boards outside newspaper offices. At least some of them assumed initially that a hard bargain had been driven and that some sort of victory had been won. When the exact "terms" for ending the work stoppage became known, victory parties gave way to bewilderment and rage. Early bulletins from the General Council had deliberately disguised the fact that the miners had never agreed to the Samuel memorandum or to the termination of the strike. Demands for an explanation of the surrender poured into the General Council's offices. Telegrams arrived saying that the local strike committee of such-and-such a town was sure that there must be some mistake. The Cardiff strike committee "deeply deplore[d] the action taken by the General Council" and called upon it "immediately [to] order a resumption of the general stoppage. . . ." [15]

In many towns the men simply refused to go back to work; some thought that the announcement of a settlement was a government trick. Those who did report to work on the following morning were confronted with rude surprises. Employers around the country had decided to go on the offensive by not hiring back known troublemakers, forcing pay reductions, and so on. In some places employers made rehiring conditional on the burning of union cards! Elsewhere men were threatened with loss of seniority, job security, and the like. Workers in all sorts of industries, men who had struck not for personal gain but in solidarity with the miners, found themselves abandoned by their leaders to make whatever settlements they could in local situations. What had begun as a labor onslaught threatened to become a rout. In such circumstances men everywhere refused to go back.

The strike had been called off, but two days after the official announcement it was estimated that 100,000 *more* workers were "out"
than had been "out" during the official nine days.

The tough line adopted by the employers was generally broken
down but with no assistance from the General Council, which issued
lame pronouncements about not succumbing to victimization; rather
the spontaneous solidarity and good sense exhibited by local strike
committees around the country were responsible. Finding themselves
in effect without leaders, they managed nevertheless to rally sufficiently
to avoid a total debacle. Even so, it was weeks before everyone was
back at work—everyone, that is, except the miners, who were still
locked out.

The fate of the miners was an embarrassing and pitiful epilogue
to a story that both the government and "responsible" sectors of the
trade-union community had treated as a triumph of national good
sense and political restraint. The miners stayed out for another six
months, and their leaders continued to fight on alone. In the end they
received far less than the Samuel memorandum had pledged or any
government commission had recommended. The eight-hour day was
reinstated in most places, no national contract was granted, and wages
were reduced. As for any fundamental reorganization of the industry,
the mine owners simply told the government to go to hell. Baldwin
informed the owners that they were "discourteous and stupid" [16]
and apparently thought that he had adequately discharged his responsibilities. His ideology and his temperament alike made him reluctant
to bring political pressures to bear in an industrial dispute. By thus
abdicating responsibility he effectively ensured the complete crushing
of the miners.

The country as a whole was both relieved and embarrassed. The
people had read enough muckraking descriptions of the dismal poverty
in mining communities to loosen their purse strings in expiation. The
general public subscribed generously to the miners' relief fund.
The government tried its best to forget the whole matter. Neville
Chamberlain, known in those days as something of a "Tory socialist,"
noted in his diary that the miners were hardly undernourished, let
alone on the brink of starvation. A million pounds was sent by the
Russian Council of Trade Unions for the relief of the miners and
their families as they fought their brave rear-guard action through
the summer and autumn. The acceptance of this money brought bitter
words from many Tory back-benchers, though King George V for
one condoned it. He did not apparently reflect on the implications
for British economic organization and statesmanship, when British

trade unions were forced to accept £1,000,000 from an alien government to save (as he himself admitted) the miners' children and wives from starvation.

The story of the miners' fate can be pieced together from statistics and reports by those who made periodic excursions to inspect depressed areas. School authorities in mining communities reported that vast numbers of children were suffering from malnutrition. In many mining towns shops were shut, windows were boarded up, and men sat silent in workmen's clubs, too poor to buy even a smoke or a drink. In some of the hardest-hit places, whole communities eroded as people moved to the cities or emigrated. The backwardness of the mine-owners continued to be a drag on the industry and in the long run on the whole nation. The already-overdue reconstruction of the collieries was put off for another twenty years while English coal mining proved less and less able to withstand competition from the more streamlined and rationally operated mines of the Ruhr.

The English general strike was a symptom not of revolutionary ferment, which is the product of dynamic, expanding cultures, but of profound economic and social malaise. It lacked the vitality for effective protest. Except among the miners it was an expression not of anger but of discontent, a gesture, and at least among the leaders, an unwilling one at that. The rank and file, it is true, responded with tremendous solidarity but without any real *élan*. They answered a call much as soldiers respond to a drill. But when the drill was over, they returned to their private grumblings. After the strike, British labor continued its already noticeable drift to the right. The strike was a kind of token farewell to the days when socialism had been less a matter of party platform and more a matter of passion. It was the last and seemingly the fiercest expression of the class animosities that lay just below the surface of English life in the postwar years. But the ferocity was an illusion, and the general strike, far from being a turning point, was more a kind of last hurrah. In the very short run union membership dropped, a number of unions disaffiliated from the General Council, and the Communist Party enjoyed a slight increase in membership. But the men who led the General Council, and their cautious campatriots in Parliament, not the Cooks and the Smiths, represented the wave of the future. The strike cleared the way for the undisputed reign of Ramsay MacDonald, whom Churchill described as a "boneless wonder," and others like him. For a moment the English Labour Party had conjured up the face of revolution and had found it ugly. When the strike was over, it sighed in relief and said, "Never again."

The British general strike of 1926 demonstrated the fatal flaw of the general strike as a form of protest—it was, in a sense, too effective. This fundamental and radical measure came close to the line between protest and revolution and thus frightened its own leaders into retreat. The leaders of British labor in 1926, with the exception of the leaders of the miners' union, were far from being revolutionaries; they were merely working-class Tories, humdrum radicals in blue-serge suits. The general strike was far too radical and explosive a vehicle of protest for them, for it carried them into direct confrontation with the whole social order, which they neither wanted nor knew how to handle. Although French labor leaders in 1968 were much farther to the left, they seemed no more comfortable about trying to control a general strike than had the pedestrian leaders of British labor in 1926.

CHAPTER
6

Jazz-Age Rebellion

In 1916 Candide's maxim about "the best of all possible worlds" was emblazoned on the American mind, for it was the day of the Progressive and of the Progressive mentality, when the human race was still thought to be perfectible and the history of the country's improvement could apparently be charted as a steadily rising graph line. The American Dream had been revivified, and the country had recommitted itself to ideals, a sense of purpose. Woodrow Wilson, the American Don Quixote, was setting the example and the pace. Even artists were optimistic. In Greenwich Village an energetic and committed group of writers and painters was working on an American *risorgimento* that would, Ezra Pound modestly predicted, make Italy's glory seem pale in comparison. In the days before the United States entered the war even the most critical American never doubted that a revival of the Good, or a new step toward the Better, was inevitable.[1]

When World War I began, Americans watched from across an Atlantic Ocean that they still considered vast enough to isolate and protect them. They were determined to remain neutral spectators: It was Europe's war, not theirs. The Rhine Valley was a vague area on a map to many Americans, and Dijon only a charming name. Sarajevo and Archduke Francis Ferdinand were no more real to Iowans than were Baghdad and its sultan.

But by 1917 American political leaders were urging the country to rise to its duty. And when the country finally did enter the war, its entrance was justified in terms that were the quintessence of Progressivism. With the Manichean simplicity of the committed idealist, Woodrow Wilson spun a tale of the forces of Evil (Germany, barbaric and antidemocratic) against the forces of Good (England and France, culturally advanced and humane). The work of many centuries seemed to hang in the balance and with it American integrity. Boys from Peoria and Birmingham, Boise and New York City's East Side, marched off to save what was fine in the world—not only to save it but also to participate in the ultimate triumph of Good, to win "the war to end all wars." They marched off in 1918 while women and girls threw roses, their heads filled with words like "courage" and "patriotism." Those who stayed behind tightened their belts and prepared to make sacrifices for the cause.

But the war turned out differently from what Mr. Wilson had planned. The average soldier discovered that he was no hero, that war was ugly and confused and irrational. The peace turned out equally badly, and evil persisted in the world just as before. War did not seem to have been erased by *the* war. And the American tradition—which men had fought to preserve—seemed not to have been involved after all.

By 1920 the country had quite frankly had enough. It was tired of duty and sacrifice and self-denial. It had served the cause of social progress. It had even given up alcohol! But the world was no better for it. Morality based on duty bored the younger generation. Young people traded in their parents' placards for hip flasks, the Socialist Party for the decade-long party called the Jazz Age.

Postwar technology seemed to conspire with the young. Urbanization had lessened provincialism and had fragmented family functions. In an automobile a boy and girl could escape their parents' watchful eyes, and the movies gave them lovely suggestions on what to do with their privacy. The rewards of heaven paled before those of material prosperity, and the weakening fear of hell left the minister with diminishing control over the American conscience. Manufacturers seemed able to supply new pleasures and novelties as fast as the fickle public could tire of the old ones.

The extreme mobility of the urban age helped to break down class distinctions and destroyed the authority of local leading families. Social authority passed out of the hands of Mom, Dad, the minister, and the local doctor and settled nervously in the lap of Hollywood. In fact, the old morality and the old traditions might have died natural deaths before the younger generation could enjoy the thrill of killing them.

The women led the 1920s revolution in morals, and in the vanguard of freedom was the flapper. Ideally she was, as F. Scott Fitzgerald, her virtual press agent, described her, expensive and just nineteen. She was modern with a vengeance. She smoked in public, she drank at speakeasies until she was "blotto," and she punctuated her sentences with "damn." She was unshockable; she was frank. Her skirts, like the stock market, went up, up, and up. Soon they hovered above her knees, revealing more leg than the American man had ever seen in public. Happily he rose to the occasion.

The flapper dropped her waist, rolled her flesh-colored stockings below her knobby knees, bound her breasts, and starved herself into the boyish figure of her new dreams. She abolished the hourglass figure, stripped off layers of chemises and petticoats, and casually checked her corset in the cloakroom at every college dance. Soon she discarded it altogether. Freedom: From neck to foot she was pounds lighter, and her movements were unrestricted. The next step was the barber shop, where long hair was disposed of without a tear. The "bob" was the look—no nets, no hairpins. The flapper topped the look with a knitted cloche, from which only an occasional stray hair escaped.

Cosmetics supplied the finishing touch. Rouge was no longer the monopoly of the chorus girl and the prostitute. The "best" girls—awaiting their prep-school beaux under the Biltmore clock, splashing in the Plaza fountain, or dancing cheek to cheek—sported bright-red circles on their cheeks and Cupid's-bow lips. Ministers wrung their hands in despair, beauticians in glee.

The keepers of the old morality could rage. The Y.W.C.A. could conduct national campaigns against immodest dress. Ohio legislators could introduce bills to ban the sale of any garment "which displays or accentuates the lines of the female figure" and to prohibit any female over fourteen from wearing "a skirt which does not reach that part of the foot known as the instep." But to no avail. Just as Prohibition made drinking seem more exciting, so perorations against the "jazz babies" only inspired them to further rebellion.

Furthermore, Science condoned it all! Science—the only thing left for the modern mind to revere—gave the young American woman Sigmund Freud, and Freud instructed her in mental health. Through a remarkably unanimous misreading of the good doctor's works, flappers joined the ranks of those who declared sexual freedom as essential to health as eating an apple every day. Repression was the new mortal sin. Freud had indeed explored and revealed that repression lay at the foundations of civilization, but he approved of civilization and thus considered repression essential. He merely explained the phenomenon but did not mount the crusade against it. No matter. The American flapper had her way: She emancipated herself, honest and unafraid. Sex was her obsession, and it was echoed and intensified through mass communications. *True Story* and a hundred other similar magazines told her tales of love and repression, and at the movies Clara Bow showed her how far a girl with "It" could go. From the silver screen the flapper received constant gentle reminders of the joys of uninhibited sex. There were tales of "neckers, petters, white kisses, red kisses, pleasure-mad daughters. . . ." [2] She went to the theater to see dramas of homosexuality or wished-for rape. She read novels of lesbian love and impotent men. She thought it a point of honor to read anything that the Church or Boston had banned, and *Lady Chatterley's Lover* rested proudly on every intelligent woman's bookshelf.

She could, according to Fitzgerald, "take a man—the man of the hour—at his face value, with no foolish promises that will need a disturbing and disagreeable breaking . . . she'll take everything you say the way you mean it, not getting 'sore' as her older sister did when that 'pious' older sister rested back seductively in the pretty green canoe with a pink parasol to keep off the healthy tan of the sun." [3] As Fitzgerald, pointed out, mothers had no idea how casually their daughters kissed.

But were mothers so upset, and if so, did they stay upset? What about the flapper's older sister? As Fitzgerald sadly admitted, the younger generation—whose innocence and exuberance made much forgivable—had made their rebellion too appealing. By 1923, he wrote, the older generation had moved in on it. The children's party had been taken over by the parents.

Fitzgerald credited young liquor as the elixir that could take the place of young blood. Again technology and revolution went hand in hand, for the older woman and the less wealthy woman had been slowly emancipated from the twenty-four-hour housekeeping day. Smaller homes, smaller families, and a world of gadgets gave her leisure. Canned foods and neighborhood bakeries diminished her mealtime chores. Commercial laundries, electric washing machines, and electric irons freed her from entire Mondays devoted to the family wash. With ready-made clothes, vacuum cleaners, and telephone shopping, the woman of the 1920s was ready to live her own life.

But as always her "own life" centered around the American male. The Jazz Age male wanted more than steady, responsible family life and more than a sturdy, proper, motherly wife. He wanted excitement and thrills, and so his woman turned flapper. She sought the aura of youthful freedom and to look like anything but someone's wife and mother.

It would be difficult to say how many maidenheads were lost before the wedding bells chimed or how many married men and women marched into infidelity as into a righteous cause. Did more teen-agers talk about petting and necking than actually joined in the games? One observer argued that the ratio of virtuous to frail women has probably been constant through all the ages. In small towns and rural areas it is likely that the stable, church-blessed double standard held its own. Yet change was coming; the old code was being repudiated, the old values dethroned. Unfortunately, the flappers and their mates were uncertain what the new code should be.

The couple spent their most risqué hours in the speakeasy or the "blind pig." Prohibition, the last gesture of Progressivism turned prudish, had been voted in almost absentmindedly by an urban population busy with a war. The "drys," who had turned the idea of temperance into a crusade for abstinence and finally into a witch hunt for drinkers, were surprised and delighted with their success. With that peculiar, naïve American reverence for the law, the usually rural and city-hating "drys" were certain that once a law was on the books it would be obeyed. Drinking would promptly cease, health would improve, moral fiber would tighten up. Fathers would return to their neglected families, and, most important, those liquor-loving foreigners in the eastern cities would learn who ran the country.

Unfortunately, it was a singularly bad moment in American history to hope for reverence toward the law, especially Spartan law. People were tired of "making the United States a land fit for heroes to live in." [4] They preferred a little fun.

It was clear—to those who wished to see things clearly—that Prohibition was a failure from the start. In the first few months of the "Dry Era," illegal stills proliferated. Everybody who was anybody in Texas seemed to have one. On one farm five miles north of Austin, a 130-gallon still was discovered operating full blast. The farm belonged to Senator Morris Sheppard, author of the Eighteenth Amendment.

Legislators and politicians of the 1920s did not seem to revere the majesty of law. A special train carrying the Massachusetts delegation to the Republican national convention in 1920 was stopped, raided by diligent Prohibition Agents, and relieved of the stock of liquor on board.

The discriminating drinker could, and frequently did, splurge at the local grocery store, buying essence of crème de menthe, Benedictine, or vermouth. All he had to do was take it home and add sugar and a little grain alcohol; the result was vastly superior to his neighbor's fermented grape juice.

All over America the evil saloon was replaced by the equally evil speakeasy. On New York City's Bowery or in Hell's Kitchen lawbreakers and law-flouters could hang out in dingy dives where "smoke," a mixture of alcohol and water, went for ten cents a slug. Uptown the "swells" sat on soft seats in soft light as waitresses served liquor for $1.50 a drink.

Who managed the speakeasies? The rebellion against Prohibition introduced a whole new subculture into American life: The criminal came into his own. The best drinking spots in New York were run by men like Arnold Rothstein, whose greatest feat was fixing the 1919 World Series, like Jack (Legs) Diamond, Buggsy Siegel, or Dutch Schultz. In Chicago, where Johnny Torrio and his Neapolitan lieutenant Alphonse Capone were consolidating their bootlegging empire, Prohibition provided upward mobility for Italians. By 1924 Capone had a staff of seven hundred. He tried to reduce his competition through individual murders and spectacular wholesale killings like the St. Valentine's Day massacre; his enemies returned the favor. In all, some five hundred gangland murders were committed in Chicago during the decade.

The "drys" were unwilling to concede that Prohibition was a failure. They refused either to allow the law to be altered or to increase the enforcement services to the staggering size necessary. And so, throughout the 1920s, the law that was no law remained on the books. Juries refused to convict bootleggers, young married couples set up their wedding-gift still in bathrooms, and congressmen sipped sherry at committee meetings.

The whole business added up to a rebellion of urbanites against the rule of rural America, of immigrants against third- and fourth-generation citizens, of sophisticated atheists or agnostics against the fundamentalists who sought to impose their standards upon the country. Reform was dead; it had been discredited in politics, and it would not be tolerated in matters of morality.

The flapper and her male companions flaunted their rejection of the country's morals and its laws. But most of these "jazz babies" really wanted no more than a holiday. There were other Americans who wanted a permanent release; the most thoroughgoing criticism of American society followed in the wake of the war, and it came from American artists and writers for whom the memory of the battlefield could not be drowned in the "orgy of pleasure" that F. Scott Fitzgerald recommended.

These men had gone to Europe even before most American soldiers, usually to serve in the French ambulance service. John Dos Passos, Ernest Hemingway, Malcolm Cowley, William Faulkner, and others had gone to fight—or to help others to fight—for a variety of reasons, often because of a romantic urge to be "in the thick of it," to be where adventure and excitement and danger were. Sometimes they had gone because of a pervasive Progressive sense of duty; they found it impossible to sit in Groton or Princeton classrooms while civilization faced its greatest challenge.

In Europe, however, these men found a new reality in war. Their shining clarity of purpose and neat justifications for the war crumbled on the European battlefield. It was difficult to remember—and harder to believe—why the war was being fought. Social platitudes did not survive the war. Wars did not, after all, consist mainly of bands playing and men performing noble deeds. War was not just adventure or excitement. It did not conform to the image of American propaganda, which pictured war as having a beginning, a middle, and an end, as well as a persistent leitmotiv. Instead it turned out to be a disconnected series of little personal wars between the bullet and me, the gun and me, impersonal, unreasonable danger and me.

These men soon came to believe that all experience must be viewed as personal and that there was no collective history from which men could learn. The isolated individual must, each moment, start anew, with no reliance on the descriptions or judgments of others. No man could tell another man what death or courage meant. All the codes and mores and scriptures designed to shelter men from reality by distorting it had been proved useless. Life demanded unceasing moral improvisation.

This revelation of reality cut these men off from their fellow countrymen and from all previous American generations. It was this knowledge that made them the Lost Generation.

They took refuge in art, which they believed was the only ultimate defense against the world of hypocritical men and impersonal chaos. Art became for the Lost Generation, as it had been for Gustave Flaubert, a way of life. All that remained to the sensitive man was pride in his self-knowledge and devotion to the integrity of his art; the only sensitive people in the modern world were artists.

"What," one character asks another in E. E. Cummings' introduction to *The Enormous Room*, "do you think happens to people who aren't artists? What do you think people who aren't artists become?"

"I feel they don't become: I feel nothing happens to them; I feel negation becomes of them."

These men turned a bitter and critical eye on their country, its culture, and its morality. They felt keenly the contradictions in American social values and the hypocrisy in the preachings of democracy. Their own commitment to individualism, to personal freedom, and to art seemed not only to be discouraged but also increasingly to be threatened by American society.

Their critique of that society rested first on an ahistorical and thus inaccurate perception of the Puritan heritage. Their search for the roots of American glorification of the practical, industrious, materially productive man and for the source of the American credo of self-abnegation, conformity, and repression led these writers of the 1920s to the Puritans' New England theocracies. The Lost Generation, believing in no gods and rejecting all neat teleologies, was unable to appreciate the Puritans' religious framework. They saw in the seventeenth century's "Holy Experiment" only hypocrisy and a self-righteousness cloaking a mania for oppressing nonconformists. American society, the offspring of the Puritans, seemed to interfere sadistically with the lives and personal freedoms of its citizens. The Puritan ideal of productivity came to fruition in the days of Calvin Coolidge, when the man who built a factory was considered to have built a temple and the man who had labored on a poem to have produced nothing of value.

The Puritan atmosphere had always stifled the artist, but postwar America seemed even more likely to strangle him. Men like Ezra Pound, Hemingway, and Dos Passos returned to a society in which the machine, mass production, and mass culture were moving people toward a regimented sameness. The day would come, wrote Pound,

> . . . when man
> Will long only to be a *social function*
> And even Zeus' wild lightning fear to strike
> Lest it should fail to treat all men alike.[5]

The second basis for these artists' condemnation of American society was an insight into the potentially oppressive nature of democracy itself. This insight was not new; as early as 1837 Alexis de Tocqueville had recognized and warned of the dangers of a system that preached the virtue of the Golden Mean and drew its strength from the mass of common men. It was but a short step from the glorification of the common man to the vilification of the extraordinary man. In the artists' view, all democracy's institutions were bent upon stifling the exceptional individual; the sensitive young mind, wrote Pound, was warped by

> These heavy weights, these dodgers and these preachers,
> Crusaders, lecturers and secret lechers,
> Who wrought about his "soul" their stale infection.[6]

In such a world, what were the sensitive man's options? He could keep up constant guerrilla warfare against his enemies, as H. L. Mencken did. Mencken, a Baltimore journalist who had fled to New York, began a persistent and vocal crusade against the stupidities of American middle-class society which remains unmatched in the nation's history. With George Jean Nathan, Mencken edited the *American Mercury*, a journal devoted to puncturing American complacency and "to exposing the non-sensicality of all such hallucinations [as Marxism, Prohibition, Populism, and the like] particularly when they show a certain apparent plausibility."[7] The *Mercury*'s audience was, in Mencken's words, the "forgotten Man"—the intelligent American. In his long-running battle with those who ran the country, Mencken examined and satirized the customs, ideas, and sacred cows of the hinterlands, the "Sahara of Bozart," Americana. He dismissed American patriotism "because it demands the acceptance of propositions that are obviously imbecile—*e.g.*, that an American Presbyterian is the equal of Anatole France, Brahms, or Ludendorff."[8] He freely declared his low opinion of the country's political leaders and announced that in the mind of Calvin Coolidge "the whole repertory of Rotary Club ideas is rehearsed and exhausted; the wisdom of an entire race is boiled down to a series of apothegms, all indubitable, all freely granted by every right-thinking man."[9] He created, through a single-minded distortion, a caricature of humanity which he labeled "the booboisie." He held democracy to be the great leveler to mediocrity and argued that laws, customs, and morals were designed solely to make mediocre men feel secure. Mencken thrived on his hatreds. "Why do you live here?" he was asked.

"Why do men go to zoos?"[10] he replied.

But other men found it more difficult to do daily battle with their oppressors. These men left their midwestern or southern homes, fled rural America, and sought refuge in isolated sanctuaries like Greenwich Village.

The Village, New York's ninth ward, begins at West Fourteenth Street and Fifth Avenue. It had once been an elegant community of town houses but by 1910 had become an inexpensive and picturesque haven for artists and Bohemians. These earlier artists, also conscious of the country's "aesthetic starvation," had come to the Village to work on a corrective for the nation's cultural diet. They were optimists. They lived in cheap walk-up flats; wandered the winding, irregular streets of the Village; and sat in cafés all night discussing art, its forms, and their plans to revive and perfect it. They were seeking in their everyday life the Bohemian ideal of a free and individual life, removed from all authority and all social restraints.

But in the 1920s artists came to Greenwich Village in despair rather than in hope. And close behind them came modern technology: The West Side subway brought the Village back into the city, ending its isolation, and the Bohemian utopia was invaded by the Jazz Age. Bohemia became institutionalized. The subway carried the curious middle-class tourist into the Village, and tea shops with fake atmosphere and "resident" poets replaced the old cafés. With Prohibition the Village became a paradise of speakeasies. The Bohemian either succumbed to patronage, or he fled. "We had," wrote poet Floyd Dell, "something which it seemed all bourgeois America—sick to death of its machine-made efficiency and sacred respectability—wistfully desired to share with us: we had freedom and happiness." [11] The freedom and happiness may have come from no more than a hand-to-mouth existence on a borrowed fifty cents a day. But there was romance to it, and none of the American middle-class routine. For lunch the Bohemian drank a bottle of cheap sherry; dinner was an extemporaneous communal affair. No one planned where or how, but somehow it appeared on someone's table, maybe in a stranger's house. The night was spent in one of two favorite Village bars and later at a party in some borrowed flat. Mattresses were laid side by side and end to end, and in the morning those who had stayed the night, tired or drunk, went home to write their poems or to pretend to write their poems.

More and more the Village was filled with those who only pretended to write poems, and soon even such pretense passed from the scene. The Village was filled not with artists or genuine Bohemians but with single young people from ordinary homes, holding ordinary jobs, who were anxious to "see life" before settling down.

Many of the artists and writers fled to Paris, to the Left Bank of the Seine along Montparnasse, Raspail, the "Boul Mich," and the Boulevard St. Germain. Paris was more congenial, more exciting, more romantic than the Village. It was also cheaper, and there was no Prohibition. The days and evenings could be spent in outdoor cafés, drinking openly without worry.

But the expatriate had not made Paris his second home because the wine and the whiskey were legal or because the river was lovely. For him France was the center of literature and arts, and French culture the antithesis of the Puritan tradition from which he was trying to escape. In Paris the artist and the sensitive intellectual did not have to struggle to remain himself; France accepted him almost casually.

The French attitude toward art, even more than French art itself, impressed and reassured these expatriates. Like Flaubert before them, French artists were certain that "art is vast enough to occupy the whole man," [12] and thus the Lost Generation's retreat into art was understood and condoned.

The American in Paris was self-consciously creative. He viewed himself as a contributor to that intellectual ferment that caused Gertrude Stein to declare, "Paris was where the twentieth century was." There the expatriate met and mingled with the Dadaists, the French surrealists. There he issued manifestoes on art. A typical proclamation appeared in *Transition*, one of the little journals, in 1929: "[The literary creator] has the right to use words of his own fashioning and to disregard existing grammatical and syntactical laws. . . . The writer expresses. He does not communicate . . . the plain reader be damned!"

In Paris the American writer also met other writers in the informal salons of Ford Madox Ford and Bill and Mary Widney. There were expatriates of an older generation in Paris, permanent residents who welcomed and encouraged the new arrivals. There was always a welcome or a *bon voyage* party behind the closed doors of Sylvia Beach's shop on rue de l'Odéon. And at the center of this world were figures like Gertrude Stein, "a solid block of a woman . . . her finely shaped masculine head with its short-cropped, grizzled hair, giving her the appearance of a Roman Senator." [13] It was Miss Stein who christened these wanderers the Lost Generation. Also in Paris was Eugene Jolas, whose salon became a gathering place for those who admired James Joyce.

The expatriates were generally in their twenties, young men and women with college educations, from eastern cities or from the Midwest. If they had jobs in Paris, they were usually journalists; they would go each day to the American newspaper offices in the Place de l'Opéra or write free-lance articles for glossy magazines. Sometimes they earned rent money by doing translations. The most ambitious edited their own magazines, publishing the works of Joyce, Stein, and the poet next door.

The most intense and productive of these expatriates proved to be the Midwesterners. They were the central figures in the intellectuals' revolt against the United States. So great was their hatred of the Midwest and so vividly did they describe its tortures and its dreariness that it became a metaphor for all that the artist despised—not just the rural world of Ohio or Minnesota but also the broader middle-class world of conventionality, false pieties, philistine tastes, and spiritual poverty.

Yet, ironically, it was of the Midwest that these authors always wrote, as if, "having physically removed themselves to Paris, [they] returned to the Midwest in imagination, there being no other place in their experience or in their minds." [14]

These authors, then, both loved and hated the Midwest. Although its crushing boredom had driven them away, from Paris or Spain or some small island in the Mediterranean they often looked back upon their childhoods with nostalgia. Even Ernest Hemingway, at that time engrossed in the violence of the Spanish bullring, sometimes harked back to days when "the hay smelled good and lying in a barn in the hay took away all the years in between." These Americans could not go home again, for the war had come between them and their country. But in their art they could preserve and reshape their memories. They still loved the United States, but preferably at a distance. For the expatriate there was no other way.

The Jazz Age ended abruptly in 1929. The prosperity that had made the decade-long holiday possible disappeared. The era of excess— when, in Fitzgerald's words, "the snow . . . wasn't real snow. If you didn't want it to be snow, you just paid some money" [15]—gave way to the Depression. The Jazz Age, Fitzgerald mused, had been "borrowed time anyhow," and "now once more the belt is tight."

In the 1930s the writings of the expatriates were filled with regret and remorse for past frivolities. Even Fitzgerald, looking back at how his friends had spent themselves—dying in drunken brawls, as suicides, or murdered by fellow inmates in asylums—pointed to a moral of "wasted youth" and aimless lives. A chorus of *mea culpa* rose from this sobered generation, criticized by leftists and liberals alike, who told them that their political indifference had somehow permitted, perhaps even caused, the tragedy of the 1930s. The artist had failed to serve as prophet, as high priest of morality. He had only fled. The criticism was, of course, unjust. The writings of John Dos Passos could not have kept the stock market steady, and the mouthings of stale morality could not have saved the nation.

The writers of the 1920s had rebelled—perhaps naïvely, perhaps too impatiently—against their own culture. Yet in the rebellion they had brought to fruition that very *risorgimento* of which Ezra Pound had once dreamed. Free to experiment and ready to criticize, they had finally excelled. Their poetry, their novels, and their dramas were uniquely American after all.

In the 1930s such issues were dead. Urbanization had taken cultural control out of the hands of the rural fundamentalists. Women had won their freedom. The machine age, though fostering uniformity, had not succeeded in killing off the creative artist. Most important, the 1930s were concerned not with morality but with economics. Politics was more pragmatic and less idealistic. Prohibition had been repealed. A new kind of revolution was beginning, and the flapper, the Bohemian, the member of the Lost Generation, were superfluous to it.

CHAPTER

7

Middle-Class Protest
and the Rise of Nazism

EARLY in 1934, just after Adolf Hitler's takeover of the German state and during the first few months of the millennium that was to have been the Third Reich, a sociologist from Columbia University set out to study the discontents and aspirations that had drawn the German man in the street to Hitler's movement. His method was ingenious: He sponsored a contest offering a first prize of 125 marks for the best essay on why the writer had been converted to National Socialism. Hundreds of entries came in. People were proud to tell their stories. Many had been faithful disciples through long years of struggle and darkness. Now that Hitler had come to power they felt triumphantly vindicated.[1]

The respondents to the professor's little essay contest came from all walks of life, all age groups. Nevertheless, there was a curious sameness, a drabness, in all the accounts. They were written by ordinary, undistinguished people, from solid *bürgerlich* homes. Typically the father had been a hard-working laborer or small-business man, often with socialist sympathies. The mother had been a devout *Hausfrau* who struggled to make ends meet but saw to it the children were always well dressed. The future disciple of Hitler had done fairly well in school but had been disturbed or uncomfortable about the ideas of some of his teachers. His generation had been much agitated by doctrines of socialism and class struggle. Sometimes the gospel of Karl Marx had aroused much excitement and enthusiasm by its promises to do away with the contempt and snobbery with which important people in the government or the military treated the hard-working ordinary citizen. But other aspects of the socialist creed were incomprehensible, even repulsive. The socialists jeered at patriotism and love of homeland, and the German bourgeois could not eradicate this love from his heart: He had learned it at his mother's knee and felt it to be true and right. He had finished school often pensive and troubled, trying as best he could to sort out the false from the true, not at all certain where his allegiances lay in questions of religion and politics. He had found a job as a clerk or had opened a business. Perhaps he had married. Then a cataclysm had occurred: the war. If he was not too old or too young, he had marched away to the trenches, proudly wearing his uniform. For four years he had suffered beside his fellows through the mud and the slaughter, uncomplaining, fighting for German victory and honor. He had felt very close to the men in his company. They became true comrades, all distinctions of rank and class forgotten. Their friendship had been sealed in blood. There was a certain exhilaration in that.

Suddenly he had been told that the war was over—and Germany defeated! He could not comprehend. How defeated? Why defeated? He had never considered the possibility of defeat. Surely there must have been some mistake. He had straggled wearily back home, a bewildered warrior, to be greeted in the streets of his town by jeering bands of ruffians who spat on his uniform and tried to tear the epaulets from his shoulders. In the name of Bolshevism and international revolution they told him that he was dishonorable. He had tried to go back to his old job but found that it had been filled in his absence. His family's savings were dwindling. Riots and strikes erupted everywhere. He did not recognize his country. Everything had changed. Kaiser Wilhelm II had fled; the soldier was told that he now lived in a republic. His army buddies, the only people he could talk to, said that this government had sold them out. The army had been winning, but these men had signed a peace and had let Germany be shamefully defeated. The government, in the person of the new Social Democratic President, Friedrich Ebert, offered him the patently ridiculous greeting, "As you return unconquered from the field of battle I salute you." [2] It was plain that such words could have been spoken only by a hypocrite or a liar. The world was in a shambles, and the ex-soldier grew very bitter. His bitterness led very soon to wholesale condemnation of "the system," by which he meant everything connected with the new regime.

The personal stories of these converts to National Socialism were so similar that archetypes are easy to construct. Indeed the records read somewhat like medieval chronicles; they are all eschatological to some degree, looking forward to that moment of regeneration when the author discovered and embraced Nazism and the Führer: It was the moment when "the scales fell from my eyes," the moment when it became clear, usually in one blinding flash, that National Socialism was the true path from which he had too long strayed. One man put most clearly the sense of something familiar about Hitler, the sense that embracing National Socialism was like coming home after years of wandering in the desert: "I was always a National Socialist," he wrote. "The name of the concept is immaterial. Today I know that I was a National Socialist before there was a name for that idea." [3]

Hitler and the Nazi movement capitalized, to be sure, on the economic miseries of the Weimar Republic, but, far more important, they exploited the frustrated yearning for respect and dignity of all those who believed that in politics and society they were held in contemptuous disregard. The German soldier who returned from the front after World War I had difficulty obtaining a job and keeping his head above water economically. What impressed him above all was the ingratitude of the government. This experience accounts for the whining note that recurs constantly in these accounts of postwar personal struggles.

People who were accustomed to regarding themselves as the salt of the earth found that the material and moral basis for their lives seemed to have vanished. Their indictment began to transcend purely political issues, and the suspicion grew that something was corrupt and rotten throughout German society, that a worm was not only eating away savings in the bank but also threatening to undermine family life, religious convictions, and moral standards. Many of the men who became activists in the Hitler movement were people who in normal times would have left politics and public life strictly alone, asking nothing more than to be allowed to rear their families and pursue their careers in tranquillity. They were people whose maxim would ordinarily have been "Don't rock the boat," but now the boat was rocking them; they felt seasick but determined to save themselves. In the 1920s and the early 1930s the German middle class was collectively haunted by a nightmare; it waxed and waned, growing particularly vivid during the inflation following French occupation of the Ruhr and again in 1930 when the Depression hit hard. But even during the late 1920s, the so-called good years of the Republic, it never completely receded. "Corruption and profiteering . . . prevailed; Jews and profiteers grew rich, and lived in ease and luxury as in the Promised Land. The newspapers denounced every effort at a national awakening. Germany seemed doomed." 4

The inability of the Weimar government to arouse confidence had many causes, which are lugubriously recited in all historical accounts of Nazism. There was the onerous burden of its "responsibility" for the Versailles Treaty, a myth that the republicans should have attacked at every opportunity—instead they allowed it to work its slow poison. There was also the inability to deal effectively with the Communist-led "revolutions" and strikes that plagued the government's early years. There were inflation and the painful question of reparations to the Allies. But above all there was a critical psychological factor: The Weimar government was completely unable to establish any mystique. Republicanism in Germany had no roots, no traditions, to which it could appeal. There were no republican barricades in German history to which the government could hark back: no republican songs, no slogans like "Liberty, Equality, Fraternity." Indeed all the German traditions ran counter to republicanism; the German Republic's constitution was drafted at Weimar, but its capital was Prussian Berlin. The proliferation of postwar political parties and the resulting practice of *Kuhhandel*—political horse trading—made the Weimar parliamentarians seem to be sordid political hustlers performing continual sleight-of-hand tricks to stay in office, apparently striving for no higher goal than that of simply hanging on.

The frustrated idealism of the generation that had swallowed the exalted shibboleths of wartime propaganda could not endure this spectacle. Ebert, Philipp Scheidemann, Gustav Stresemann, and later Heinrich Brüning and Franz von Papen, were only ordinary men, scuffling, improvising, wheeling and dealing, trying to do a job. The German bourgeois, who felt acutely his own insignificance, his own precarious hold on a livelihood, his own inadequacy at coping with defeat and the Depression, had no wish to see his own miserable struggles mirrored among the men who ruled Germany. The scorn that fell on Weimar officials was an elaborate form of displaced self-hatred. The German schools of the Kaiser's day had taught, and wartime propaganda had continually reiterated, the greatness of government. Now the government, like any petty shopkeeper, was having trouble fending off its creditors, paying its bills, and keeping its dirty laundry decently out of sight. The German middle class looked hopefully, as it had always done, to the government for guidance and edification and found only a reflection of its own confused and tawdry self. It felt abandoned, trapped in a kind of Hobbesian fight for survival, a war of each against the other, a situation painfully different from the image of a great and united German *Volk* which it had learned to live in school. A government founded on utility, on expedience, and on self-interest seemed to many Germans a travesty of morality and a betrayal of German history.

The foundations of the Weimar Republic, such as they were, were thus eroded by contempt. From its inception it was a lackluster political contrivance unable to inspire idealism or loyalty. It was proclaimed suddenly and reluctantly in November 1918 after the Kaiser had abdicated and while Bolshevik soviets were sprouting throughout the country and threatening to produce anarchy. Like the Kadets in Russia in March 1917, the Social Democrats were loath to assume responsibility. Ebert, who became the first President of the Republic, had tried frantically to prevent its birth and had searched earnestly for a monarch to fill the Kaiser's throne. He shuddered at the idea of republicanism in Germany. As for social revolution, "I hate it as I hate sin," [5] he confessed. The prestige of the Republic was low on all sides. It could not make a right move. If it acted with vigor and firmness to preserve law and order, which it very rarely did, it was accused of oppression. If it tried to ride out the storms created by left- and right-wing terrorists and political blackmailers, it was charged with impotence and vacillation. To a man, the Republic's ministers were regarded as "that pack of scoundrels." Parliament never lost its designation as the "twaddling shop." More than one observer of Weimar politics noted that any speaker on any platform could be sure of a response from a somnolent audience the moment that he attacked the government. That Germans nevertheless went to the polls and voted for one or another of the political parties meant less than one might suppose. People voted perfunctorily, apathetically, often resentfully. They voted more to keep one candidate out rather than to put another one in. Industrialists, landed magnates, and military men fearful of the Reds voted for the Conservatives to fend off the Social Democrats. Workers cast ballots for Social Democrats and Communists to keep the reactionaries at bay. But the feeling that all the candidates were really unsatisfactory permeated the electoral process. The choice, familiar in our own day, was only of "the lesser evil." When a government arouses no positive allegiance over a prolonged period, it is in very grave trouble. It stands only because of a kind of inertia. It exists on sufferance, is no more than an annoying habit, a liaison that has dragged past the point of ennui and must end.

For a politically jaded, cynical, and repeatedly disillusioned people, part of the attraction of National Socialism was that the Nazis promised to deliver very little in the form of goods and services. After the disillusionment with parties that had promised pie in the sky to suit every political taste from left to ultraright, people found relief in being addressed by men who promised them nothing but the opportunity to participate in a great common venture. Here was a party that spoke of struggle and hardship as glorious and thus lent new dignity to their own struggles to eke out their livings and to raise their families. In Germany in the 1920s almost everyone felt unjustly deprived. To people in this frame of mind a party that openly called for "sacrifice" automatically sounded more honest than did one dispensing promises as freely as worthless coupons. The German citizen called on to sacrifice felt proud, important, virtuous.

By unashamedly issuing this call for fortitude and dedicated self-sacrifice, the Nazis made themselves seem both more candid and more realistic than their competitors. Astute politicians in many different countries have made electoral capital out of this psychological truth. John F. Kennedy did so in the United States when he called upon the American public to "ask not what your country can do for you, but ask rather what you can do for your country." Such words, when uttered by a charismatic leader, have an almost magical effect upon people who suspect that they have been suffering and sacrificing anyway but involuntarily and to no purpose, in the name of no ideal, in isolation and obscurity.

While the average returned veteran was quietly nursing his grudges against the government of the "November criminals," a good many had more virulent feelings and were determined actively to defy and eventually to destroy the men who had brought the war to an end. These veterans were men who had first come alive in active combat. They had entered the war as nonentities and had found status and prestige in the army. They wanted above all to perpetuate the fierce fighting spirit, the rough camaraderie, of their wartime experience. They would not or could not "demobilize psychologically." The contempt of these men for the pacific government of the Social Democrats knew no bounds, and they took great delight in rendering the government even more contemptible in the eyes of other Germans.

These men, intoxicated with the lust for fighting, did not disband but re-formed in little private armies under the command of famous and popular ex-officers. Maercker's Volunteer Rifles, the Haase Free Corps, the Ehrhardt Brigade, and dozens of other private armies sprang up in postwar Germany. They were committed to nothing but the exhilaration of a good battle and tenacious loyalty to their own leaders. They prided themselves on marching at the leaders' bidding. They boasted that they would kill, pillage, and destroy on cue for anyone who paid them, for they believed that the world around them was so rotten that destruction itself was a glorious, liberating, and cleansing act.

The cadres of these private armies and virtually all the leadership came from among junior officers in the regular army. They knew that the sharp limits set at Versailles on the size of the Reichswehr—4,000 officers and 100,000 men were officially permitted the defeated nation— would prevent them from achieving distinguished military careers. The officer posts were sure to go to the old men, not to those who had proved their valor under fire—those who had thrilled most to the military life. Many of them had been part of the elite corps of the German Army, the Storm Battalions, special combat units that had acted as "shock troops" on the western front. Similar to the American Green Berets of today, they were soldiers of unprecedented toughness, ruthlessness, and cunning. They wore special uniforms and insignia, addressed their officers familiarly with *du*, and regarded themselves as a new—and invincible—breed of man.

It was singularly unfortunate for the new republican government that it was forced to begin its career under the auspices and even the protection of these "princes of the trenches." No sooner had the government taken office than it was faced with revolts throughout the country. Most were Bolshevik-inspired and -led. They erupted in virtually every city; Berlin especially was menaced. The new government was shaky, and the regular army was not yet back from the front in full strength besides being riddled with Bolshevik sympathizers. In an attempt to ward off domestic chaos and a full-scale Bolshevik revolution, the new government promised to pay and clothe the volunteer corps if they would rush to the rescue. The government hastily appointed Gustav Noske, soon to be christened the "bloodhound of the revolution," as Minister of National Defense. Noske set to work to rally the Free Corps to wipe out the Red menace. Placards sprang up all over the city urging enlistment once again.

COMRADES

The Spartacist danger has not yet been removed.
The Poles press ever farther onto German soil.
Can you look on these things with calm?
NO!

Think what your dead comrades would think!
Soldiers, Arise! Prevent Germany from becoming
The laughing stock of the earth. Enroll NOW in
the HUELSEN FREE CORPS.[6]

The Free Corps set to work with a vengeance. In January 1919 they restored "order" to Berlin. One could not expect such men to exercise delicacy in carrying out their mission. And, once they had been unleashed, the government could find no effective means to call them to account. In fact a reign of terror came to Berlin. The leaders of the Spartacists—the erstwhile colleagues of Ebert and Scheidemann in the days of the Second International—were kidnapped and brutally murdered. In the next few months, as revolts flared here and there, the Free Corps were sent to put out the fires. When the new National Constituent Assembly met in Weimar in February 1919, seven thousand freebooters encircled the city to prevent any disturbances. Other brigades were sent to Bremen, Brunswick, and Munich. In March, when Berlin again became restless, the Free Corps were recalled, and for a week the city was at their mercy. Any Berlin citizen could be summarily shot for carrying a weapon or merely for acting suspiciously. The Free Corps were there to do a job, and they did not scruple about the means. Full-scale massacres occurred in Berlin in March and in Munich in May. The commander of one unit dispatched to Bavaria advised his men, "Shoot them, and report that they attacked you or tried to escape." [7] When the atrocities became really excessive, the civilian government chided the captains and apologetically urged a little restraint. It could do little else, for its very survival at that point depended on these *condottieri* armies. By the summer of 1919 the Free Corps may have been the single most important power in Germany. They numbered anywhere between 200,000 and 400,000 men, and neither their respect nor their affection for the government of the Republic had increased as a result of the rescue operations that they had performed on its behalf. When they were not shooting Bolsheviks they were drinking toasts to the old fighting days, to their commanders, to the German *Volk*, to the Reich—and to the death of the regime of the "November traitors."

As it turned out, the day of reckoning was not long in coming. In March 1920 the first of several attempts to topple the Weimar government by means of a military putsch was made. The Kapp putsch—called after the Prussian bureaucrat who was placed at the head of the new "government"—was not a distinguished affair. It was ill timed and poorly coordinated—in fact, badly botched by the conspirators from the first. The would-be revolutionaries held power in Berlin for five days; the legally constituted government wasted no time in fleeing to the provinces. The military force behind the putsch was one of the most famous of the freebooter armies, the notorious Ehrhardt Brigade. Only a few months earlier it had been paid by the government to shoot Communists in Brunswick and Munich. Now it proposed to shoot members of the government. Five thousand men marched into Berlin, meeting no resistance at all, and declared the republican government defunct. That the Republic did not perish on the spot was the result of bad communications among the freebooter armies, which were subject to jealousies and rivalries and a consequent lack of coordination. The fact that some of the would-be assassins of the Republic were drunk the whole time did not help. Then too, from its hideout in Stuttgart, the republican government appealed for a general strike, and it was answered by virtually all the Berlin workers. This time the Republic had to turn for urgent assistance to the very Reds it had been wantonly shooting only a few months before! The putsch, though it failed ignominiously, did not enhance the prestige or the self-respect of the legal government. Nor were the Free Corps disconcerted. The government seemed to them a football that could easily be dislodged by a swift, well-timed kick. On this occasion the timing had been poor and the execution rather lackadaisical. One disgruntled freebooter lieutenant remarked, "Everything would have still been all right if we had just shot more people." [8]

The freebooters had good reason to feel unconcerned. When the government had brought its briefcases back to Berlin, one might have expected the courts to deal harshly with those who had blithely perpetrated high treason against the state. Initially 705 people were charged with treason, but somehow the charges melted away. More than four hundred people were granted amnesty, and others were allowed to disappear from sight. Indictments were dropped with astounding nonchalance. In the end exactly one person—the police president of Berlin—was actually sentenced. His punishment was five years' "honorary confinement." His pension, taken away apparently in a moment of excess cruelty, was ordered restored by the Prussian courts. Kapp himself was cleared of all charges. Ehrhardt and the other officers who had seized Berlin were allowed to go their merry way.

Eventually the Weimar government made feeble attempts to dissolve the Free Corps or to integrate them into the regular army. When not killing Bolsheviks they could be a serious embarrassment, as the Kapp episode had showed. The escapades of freebooter troops in the Baltic, where they were trying to seize the Baltic republics as compensation for Germany's losses in the west, were difficult to explain to the Allies. By 1920 orders for the dissolution of various Free Corps companies were being regularly promulgated. The captains and majors who commanded the brigades laughed—and cursed. If their men were integrated into the regular army, they often managed to have them retain their old identity and old name. The more dedicated Free Corps leaders simply went out and recruited anew. Rather transparent front organizations were set up, and behind them the freebooters marched and drilled as before. The existed in many guises: as fraternal veterans' organizations, trucking companies, road gangs, detective bureaus, and even "savings societies." Arms were shipped to new recruits under the bland label "machine tools." Not only did they manage to find sufficient arms for their own uses, but they were also able to raise money by selling the surplus to the government. The freebooters were in the habit of "liberating" arms from the Poles. First, guns were sold to Poles or Bolsheviks; then, when the cash had been pocketed, the arms were "liberated" in midnight forays. Afterward they could be sold again, stolen back, and so on. Properly managed, this was both a lucrative and entertaining sport. The same weapons could be sold half a dozen times yet end up back in the freebooters' possession.

The government's halfhearted attempts to eradicate the freebooter organizations did not appease them. On the contrary, the fact that the regime, so lately at their mercy, was now trying to dispense with them roused the brigands to new heights of rage. And underground their influence was, if anything, more sinister. At least some of them—the versatile Captain Ehrhardt was again involved—turned to political murder. An organization known as the Feme was established; its function was to dispense "folkish justice," by means of assassinating one after another of the "November criminals." These executions were meant not only to settle old scores but also to produce internal chaos, the fall of the Republic, and the rise of some freebooting chieftain.

Not all the victims of the Feme were statesmen. Many were deserters or informers from its own ranks, wiped out like faithless members of the Mafia. Others were simply hapless ordinary citizens guilty of some such atrocity against Germany as reporting the existence of an illegal arms cache to the authorities. A Munich servant girl unlucky enough to discover and report such an arsenal was found the next day hanging from a tree in a nearby park. A note was pinned to her chest: "You bitch, you betrayed your Fatherland, so you die by the Black Hand." [9] Conservative estimates of the number of Feme murders perpetrated are approximately three hundred in the early 1920s. The organization's most famous victim was Walter Rathenau, the man who had, as Director of Raw Materials, virtually organized the supply side of Germany's war effort. Rathenau was shot on a public street by two Feme agents who overtook him in a car. Years later his assassins, Erwin Kern and Hermann Fischer, became two of the brightest stars in the

Nazi galaxy of heroes and were personally honored by Hitler. The sinister irony of the affair is that Rathenau had enthusiastically supported the Free Corps idea at its inception, had raised more than five million marks for its support, and had contributed generously from personal funds. This record made no difference whatever; he was executed for the double crime of being Foreign Secretary in the Weimar government and of being a Jew.

The government dealt with the murderers with its usual incredible lack of energy and conviction. Murderers, if apprehended at all, were usually let off with fines or a few weeks' imprisonment. Thorough investigations were avoided whenever possible, for they were too likely to implicate distinguished people in high places. The revolution that had brought republicanism to Germany had not been very thorough. Most conspicuously the army, but also the judiciary, was full of unrepentant foes of the Republic. Everywhere in local governments, in courts, and in police offices there were men who sympathized with the freebooters and took an indulgent view of their excesses. The defense that the freebooter-turned–political assassin offered if he was actually hauled into court revealed the degree of his contempt for and alienation from the government—and equally revealed the lack of conviction and the temerity born of bad conscience with which the government defended itself. Inside the courtroom the accused would simply turn the tables on his judges and prosecutors. He would, in sincere and righteous wrath, declare that it was they and not he who were the true criminals. *They* were betraying the sacred cause of the *Volk; they* were destroying Germany by doling out mock justice to the only true patriots that the country possessed. They were not impressed by the courts, these defendants announced; in fact, they did not recognize the authority of the courts. They were acting in the name of a higher law and a higher justice. No threatened punishment could intimidate them. Let the courts menace; let them threaten the death sentence. These men were prepared to die. They would be vindicated by history and the undeceived German people. Furthermore, they were proud to die because their deaths would help to awaken the people, who would soon move to cast off the scum that now ruled them. The defendants always tried to brazen the charges out in this way, and usually the tactic worked. German courtrooms became forums for vilification of the state. It was no wonder that these trials were embarrassing to the Weimar government. Then too there was always the possibility that a friend of the judge had obtained a hasty passport for a fugitive terrorist because the man was an old army buddy. A few years later, when the Nazis were soaring to power, their sympathizers were so many and so highly placed that in many German states the outlaw and the magistrate began to look peculiarly the same. There was a complicity, a fraternal bond, between the underworld and the authorities. The hunter and the hunted shared the same moral code, the same set of political assumptions. Before they fled Germany, Bertolt Brecht and certain German film-makers made great and damning dramas depicting this corruption. But German audiences watching Brecht saw not a savage indictment but only a witty and realistic presentation of the world as it was.

In 1923 Hitler staged his famous but ill-fated "beer hall putsch" in Munich. The plot implicated numerous high officials of the state government and a number of military figures, including the great war hero, the old General Erich Ludendorff. Like the Kapp putsch it was a clear case of high treason, and the sentence dispensed was typical: Hitler received five years' "honorary confinement," with assurances that parole would cut the time to a few months. Ludendorff was acquitted entirely. Apparently the government could not admit that such distinguished and important men as the old General hated and despised it sufficiently to turn traitor. It seemed better to pretend that there had been no such intent.

Like various freebooter assassins before him, Hitler used the witness chair as a soapbox from which to indict the government. Like them, he had friends in high places. Numerous Bavarian officials had trafficked with him, supported him, encouraged him—and only at the last moment tried to check him. Many of those who had tried to forestall his coup did so only for tactical reasons; they considered the attempt premature or Hitler an opportunist. Some of the men who had dallied with Hitler's putsch were actually Bavarian secessionists working for a different sort of revolution. But none loved the Weimar Republic any more than he did. All could find in their secret hearts little to fault in his oration from the prisoner's dock: "I feel myself the best of Germans who wanted the best for the German people." [10]

The eventual outcome of the trial was a nine-month prison stay for Hitler, during which, living in all comfort, he set down his thinking in *Mein Kampf*. The publicity of the trial first made him a national figure, not just a Bavarian agitator. The press publicized his defense of himself and his motives and thus unwittingly helped to make him a hero to many who had previously never heard of him. There were many people in Germany who would automatically acquiesce in the proposition that anyone who was against the government had to have some good in him.

It was good propaganda and excellent psychology for every political thug and malcontent to portray himself as a member of a tiny band of outcasts and misunderstood patriots enduring persecution at the hands of the police and vilification from the mouths of Jews and Bolsheviks. It was part of the freebooters' public image and no doubt part of their self-images to seem to struggle in lonely isolation against a society totally hostile to them, a society that scorned them and rejected their martyrdom. In fact the self-proclaimed outcasts had collaborators and sympathizers on all sides.

One of the tragedies of Weimar was that the daredevil freebooter, the terrorist, became a culture hero to an entire generation of German youngsters in the postwar years. He was a glamorous figure—part Tarzan, part Robin Hood, part James Bond—and thousands of adolescents sought to imitate his style. Many boys who had been too young to fight in the war itself ran off to join the postwar brigand armies as soon as they were old enough to do so. Captain Ehrhardt, of the Kapp putsch and the Feme, became a particular hero. He was, they believed, "the very epitome of military loyalty and honor . . . the man who could form and direct all our youthful enthusiasm and young passions. . . ." [11] Students, finding university education increasingly irrelevant and boring, were particularly attracted to the colorful activism of men like Ehrhardt. Ernst Röhm paid grateful tribute to the large share that students had played in his building up of the *Sturm Abteilungen* (S.A.), or Storm Troopers, the Nazi paramilitary organization, which used violence to cow the party's political rivals.

In our own day, when there is little love lost between students and professional soldiers, the attraction of young intellectuals to the flamboyant militarism of the armed gang seems bizarre. But the children of Weimar sadly lacked glamorous models on the republican side. German universities after 1918 were seething with discontent. Intellect was in disrepute among the young. They yearned for action, and the war that they had missed was being served up to them by former soldiers as romantic and heroic. Many students came to regard what went on in the classroom as synthetic dross. They yearned for action and for involvement in the society around them. The young Joseph Goebbels, who had drifted in and out of half a dozen leading German universities before receiving his Ph.D. degree, recorded in his autobiographical novel, *Michael*, the sentiments of many students of his generation: "Intellectualism is becoming a big bore to me. I feel nauseous at every printed word. I don't find anything in it that could redeem me. . . ." [12]

Oddly, the revolt of German youth at that time had little social content. Although what we would now call the generation gap was much vaunted and loudly proclaimed, it was essentially a rhetorical sham. The life style, the mores, and the aspirations of the younger generation differed little from those of their elders. The stress on youth became an ideology in itself, something of a fetish in fact, which Hitler was to incorporate as part of the fascist image. German students, after the war as before it, sang paeans of praise to the *Volk*, the great German people pure and simple in heart. Before the war the quest for the unspoiled *Volk* had produced much harmless quasi-cultural activity of the sort that goes on anywhere when a people is in hot pursuit of its "roots." Many folk songs had been resurrected for performance around campfires. Students had organized long hikes to explore the verdant beauties of pastoral Germany. Sports and gymnasiums were in fashion, and ancient pagan holidays like the feast of the summer solstice had been self-consciously celebrated. These quasi-mystical celebrations of the *Volk* all looked toward the great "spiritual revolution" that the students and young people were supposed to be preparing. The myth of a great German, or Aryan, race was already blossoming, but neither before the war nor after did the young dissidents have any concrete social or political program. More significantly still, German students did not, in scorn of their society, drop out. Rather they competed for positions in the universities and for the best and most prestigious jobs that they could find after graduation. They complained a great deal but protested very little. They were, on the whole, simply middle-class youths, and many were bitter that the job market was so tight, that so many of the best positions in government service and business still went to what remained of the old Prussian Junker class and, increasingly under the Weimar Republic, to Jews, outsiders. "A few more semesters and we shall be unemployed" was a standing joke among the undergraduates, one which became less than funny when the Depression hit with full force. On the whole the students shunned politics and economics. As it is hard to be a rebel and still profess affection for the government, they generally mocked the Kaiser and his love for medals, monuments, and big ships. After the war they simply swallowed the going valuation of Weimar as a political conjuring trick foisted upon the people by the men who had lost the war, and antigovernment posturing became noisier and probably more sincere. Students who did not actively hate the Republic remained indifferent to it. They were too busy cultivating their "spiritual revolution."

One theme did grow louder and more shrill among postwar youth groups. Anti-Semitism had always been part of the *völkische* myth, but during the 1920s and the early 1930s it moved from a peripheral to a

central concern. It was the perfect foil for the bankruptcy of political
and economic thought which characterized the youth groups. Before
the war they had conducted soul-searching debates on whether or not
Jews were themselves a *Volk* and whether or not they could ever be
sufficiently assimilated to become part of the German *Volk*. The ver-
dicts had been various, though in the main negative. Around the turn
of the century a fierce debate had taken place on whether or not Jews
could participate in the time-honored university practice of dueling,
the question revolving around whether or not Jews had any honor to
defend. Jews were excluded from most fraternities, and in some universities the creation of Jewish fraternities was looked upon as a
provocative act. Periodically petitions would circulate in the classrooms, asking that Jews be excluded from government jobs and the
professions.

But it was during the Weimar period that "the Jewish question"
came to assume a kind of absolute prominence. The regeneration of
the *Volk* had once been the main motivation of the "youth movement"; a number of its leaders had looked upon the wrangle over Jews
as merely an annoying distraction from the main task. They had
wanted the self-consciousness of the German *Volk* to develop not
merely negatively—that is, in opposition to Jews—but positively,
through a rediscovery of roots, customs, and traditions. During the
Weimar period the old groups that had insisted on the importance of
the folk dances, idyllic rambles in the countryside, and celebrations of
festivals came to be regarded as naïve and silly. They lost members to
the more strident activist organizations. Anti-Semitism was no longer
a subject for debate; it had become axiomatic, part of the dogma. The
anti-Semitic obsession was exacerbated by general disrespect for the
government, which was supposed to be riddled with Jews. Anti-
Semitic riots became frequent in German universities in the 1920s.
Fraternity bylaws were tightened to ensure that no Jewish influence
could seep in. In 1919 the exclusion of people of Jewish descent was
broadened to apply to any person who had married a Jew. When in
1922 the University of Berlin proposed to hold memorial services for
the murdered Walter Rathenau, a riot erupted among the student body
and forced the university to cancel the tribute. The government's
occasional gestures to stem the tide of violence and enforce the constitution, which after all guaranteed equality, were ludicrously inadequate and ineffective. In 1925 the Prussian Minister of Education,
seized by a fit of resolve or perhaps revulsion, threatened to cut off
all state funds and subsidies to the students' organizations unless they
changed their discriminatory policies. The wrangle dragged on for

two years, at the end of which the student organizations polled their membership, which voted overwhelmingly to accept the loss of funds and official recognition rather than to bow to government pressure and modify their "Aryan clauses." The students could truly claim that they had put principle ahead of economic interest.

The spread of anti-Semitism, coupled with the discrediting of the cultural aims of the youth movements, the new insistence on activism, and the new restlessness and militancy, made it inevitable that German students should mount the Hitler bandwagon ahead of their parents. On this point there seems to have been a real generation gap. More members of the older generation had reservations about the new savior of Germany. Parents were often grieved and bewildered when their children rushed off to join the Hitler Youth Movement, but could they in good conscience stop them? The Movement seemed to be the wave of the future. German propaganda plays of the Nazi period are full of passages in which the young son, having seen the light, attempts to convert his entire family to National Socialism, always meeting particularly stubborn resistance from his old Social Democratic father.

Most of the German student fraternities and youth groups claimed to go only part of the way with Hitler. Their differences with this politician were real and earnest, they said. Sometimes they acknowledged that he was a demagogue who pandered to all comers at election time. Many students were hostile to all political parties, the Nazis included, as divisive of the *Volk*. Snobs were repelled by the uncouth manners of this former army corporal. Yet, despite the students' claim that their plan for Germany was significantly different from Hitler's, more and more of the membership preferred to gloss over differences and follow the Hitler caravan. The membership of other right-wing, *völkische* young peoples' organizations was eroded; their pamphlets and journals became more and more indistinguishable from those of the National Socialists. By 1928 the official organ of the German fraternities was proclaiming triumphantly, "Race not economics is our fate." By 1931, two years before Hitler came to national power, the conversion of the student organizations was already complete. At one student congress Gerhard Kruger, Hitler's nominee, was elected president. From that time on all communications dispatched by the fraternities ended with the salutation "Heil Hitler." After 1933, of course, the recalcitrant elements, such as they were, were brought into line. Capturing the universities had been a pushover. Rootless, politically naïve and inexperienced, receiving no leadership from leftist or republican faculty members, and bourgeois to the core—though ranting against bourgeois society—the amateurish fraternal organizations could not compete with the dynamism of the Hitler machine. Such ideas as they had which might have been inimical to Nazism were drowned, garbled, or suppressed. Right-wing conservatism, tinged as it had always been with anti-Semitism and militarism, became harder and harder to distinguish from Hitler's rantings. Once again, capitulation to Hitler seemed to many the last logical step on the long journey home; with Hitler they would ride the crest of history. As part of the National Socialist movement they were not merely students, by definition impotent dreamers, but were once again united with the *Volk*, which they so revered and from which they nevertheless felt remote. Hitler was the path back to a people transfigured in the fires of that "spiritual revolution" for which the students so ardently yearned.

Though jobless veterans, freebooters, and alienated students were all grist for the Nazi mill, it should be remembered that National Socialism did not become a truly mass movement until 1930, when the Depression swept Germany, wiping out jobs, savings, and self-respect. Some six million people who had slowly rebuilt shattered lives once before suddenly found themselves again overwhelmed by vast anonymous economic forces that they did not understand and could not control. Only in 1930 did the Nazis become a major party in the Reichstag, securing more than a hundred seats. The years 1924–1929, the "good" years of the Republic, had been disappointing years for Hitler. Still, even in that period of relative peace and prosperity, the party had continued to grow in size. In 1925 it had had a paltry 25,000 members—many of them with only dubious loyalty to Hitler. By 1927 the membership was up to 72,000; a year later it had passed the 100,000 mark. From then on the Depression and the parliamentary stalemate among the parties of the Left and the Center were to help Hitler's propaganda machine more than had all the S.A. rampages and all the torchlight parades of the Youth Movement. In the end Hitler was invited to assume power by the political hacks of the right and center parties, who had succeeded in carrying intrigue and political *Kuhhandel* to the point at which they had maneuvered themselves against the wall.

The growth of National Socialism during the years when it was short of funds, divided by factionalism, and outlawed from public platforms in many parts of Germany was remarkable. During those years, the apparently stable time of the Republic, such growth came principally through the takeover of parties and organizations already basically sympathetic to Hitler's ideology. The gymnastic clubs, the *völkische* fraternal organizations, and the veterans' groups all responded to the appearance of a truly dynamic, nationalist, and antirepublican party. The style of the old Right—frock-coated, supercilious, and severely contemptuous of plebeian enthusiasm—was obsolete. Hitler, though he shared many political ideals with conservatives, cast off their style and introduced a new, earthy, gutter rhetoric. He was utterly cold to all suggestions of restoring the Imperial order and the Kaiser. This attitude pleased the little shopkeeper, who had been only a nonentity in that order. Hitler promised not the restoration of privilege but a new order in which careers and rank would be achieved through talent. People left the Conservative Party and the established veterans' organizations because they were repelled by snobbery and ossified class consciousness. They joined the new movement, which promised that merit and loyalty to the great *Volk* ideal would be the only bases of distinctions. Hitler insisted that class conflict was unreal, a hoax perpetrated by Bolsheviks and Jews. The party, which combined in its very name the hallowed ring of "nationalism" with the equally venerable "socialism," seemed suited to cut across and if possible to obliterate all previous political and ideological distinctions.

There were other reasons why National Socialism continued to flourish during the years when it should have gone under. At least two of the parties that regularly sent representatives to the Reichstag—the conservative Nationalists and the Communists—never ceased to remind the people that they remained fundamentally unreconciled to the "twaddling shop" and openly longed for its demise. There were, then, even during the "good" years of Weimar, plenty of voices to keep fresh the impression that the republican regime had been perpetrated on the German people. The cautious republicans never fought back. Among their many miserable failures must be numbered an almost criminal failure in public relations. No republican ethos was ever developed. Weimar never tried to acquire its own symbols.

The Nazis, by contrast, were infinitely rich and imaginative in symbolism, mythology, and pageantry. They had insignia, songs, slogans, salutes, and uniforms, the function of which was not so much to convince as to bewitch. The most famous symbol, the swastika, came from the Free Corps, its red color from socialism, communism, and the blood of soldiers. The salute came from Italian Fascism and, according to legend at least, from ancient Rome. The fervent "Heil" came from beer halls and ancient public gatherings. When Hitler spoke on public stages—at the annual Nuremberg rallies, for example—the production trappings assaulted the senses as if they were part of a Cecil B. De Mille extravaganza. Thousands of torches held aloft by devout youngsters from the Hitler Youth groups lined the routes of march. Wagnerian music preceded the speeches. Despite the "paganism" of Nazi philosophy, traditional religion was pressed into service, and Nazi speakers in small towns regularly found priests and Lutheran ministers sharing their platforms. The whole panoply of bourgeois fetishes was brought onto the political platform. The family, the sanctity of the home, and motherhood were invoked. (Hitler once promised an audience that under National Socialism *every* German girl would find a husband.) Politicians of other parties talked politics, but the Nazis talked about the whole man—his family, his fireside, his pocketbook, his vague aspirations to status and glory, his inchoate religious sentiments, his sense of decency. Above all, Nazi speakers skillfully played on the deepest fears of the middle class: their fears of drowning in a Red bloodbath, of being unmanned, castrated by French imperialists, of losing their golden-haired daughters to inferior races (Julius Streicher, a fanatical early Hitler supporter, made his career as a journalist by "exposing" Jewish sexual crimes). The Nazis tapped them all. While other parties spoke of interest and expediency the Nazis spoke of blood and race and thus summoned up what Joseph Conrad once called "fierce mouthings from pre-historic ages." The mysterious and formidable powers of ancient rituals and others, of "blood" and "soil," evoked them all. This kind of appeal served the purpose of making National Socialism seem very much more than a mere political party. Hitler never liked the word "party." He led, he said, a "movement" that was in fact nothing less than the efflorescence of the ancient Aryan soul. He was no scurvy politician. He did not *represent* any group or individual; rather he *embodied* the essence of German man. That was the whole secret of the *Führerprinzip*. It enabled Hitler to boast, years after he had come to power, that he was like a tree rooted in the people, deriving his existence and his sustenance from them. According to this formulation, Hitler was nothing less than Frederick Barbarossa, the German King Arthur, the once and future king who wakes now and then in the course of history and rouses his slumbering people, summoning them to their destiny and glory. During the Weimar years the Nazis appropriated all the best myths.

Hitler devoted many pages of *Mein Kampf* to elaborating his views on human, particularly mass, psychology. Above all, he said, the man who sought to win over the masses could use only the crudest, most elemental emotions. He had to shun reason and anything that smacked of subtle analysis, for "the rabble" would respond only to passion, vehemence, and fanaticism. Violence, both verbal and physical, was to be the fount of wisdom, welding men together in public meetings as it had in the trenches. This use of violence would produce loyalty, faith, and unity. It was magnificent propaganda. Because National

Women's march for freedom. A suffragette parade in London. Mrs. Pankhurst is on the left. (*Brown Brothers*)

Masculine reaction. London police, with characteristic brutality, removing suffragette militants to jail. (*Brown Brothers*)

The Irish rebellion. Dublin during the Easter Rising of 1916. Note the crowd at the bottom of the photograph. (*United Press International*)

In memory of the Irish martyrs. March of the radical Sinn Fein Party in Dublin, 1917. (*Brown Brothers*)

The Bolshevik triumph, 1917. Red Guards protecting a Bolshevik orator who is haranguing a throng in front of the Winter Palace, Petrograd. (*Brown Brothers*)

The British general strike, 1926. Police in London preserving law and order during the general strike. (*Brown Brothers*)

The German protest against liberalism. Posters depicting Nazi ideology and glorifying Hitler. (*Brown Brothers*)

The American Left in the 1930s. May Day parade in New York City 1936. (*Brown Brothers*)

Working-class protest during the Depression. Union members smashing windows at the Flint, Michigan, plant of the General Motors Company, 1937. (*Wide World Photos*)

he protest against colonialism. andhi leading the Indian march the sea. (*Wide World Photos*)

Imperialist repression. A native mounted policeman, a servant of the British Raj, dispersing Gandhi's followers. (*Wide World Photos*)

Black liberation. Black sit-in at a lunch counter in the Woolworth store in Greensboro, North Carolina, 1960. (*United Press International*)

The new culture. "Death of the Hippie" parade down Haight St., San Francisco, 1967. (*United Press International*)

The student rebellion. Occupation of Hamilton Hall, Columbia University, 1968. (*Wide World Photos*)

The revolt against Stalinism. Defiant Czechs carry their nation's flag past a burning Soviet tank in Prague, 1968. (*United Press International*)

The French revolution of 1968. Students in Paris mounting the barricades outside the Sorbonne. (*United Press International*)

Socialism was viewed by its proponents as an apocalyptic movement, the bloodshed it wrought could be regarded as not only necessary but also as proof of the authenticity of its millennarianism.

This belief in the efficacy of violence was tested every time the S.A. Brown Shirts took to the streets. The German population seems generally to have responded to it just as Hitler foretold. It attracted at least as many people as it repelled. The S.A. ostensibly existed in order to "defend" National Socialists from the attacks of Communists and other evildoers whenever they spoke on public platforms. When Germany began to slip into the Depression, S.A. membership zoomed, and by the early 1930s it numbered more than 300,000. Whatever its members' pious rationales about "defense" and "protection," it was obvious, even in the very early days, from their very strutting about hallways and streets, steely-eyed, uniformed, ready to do battle with all comers, that they were themselves a provocation, not only to the ordinary citizen but also, and equally, to the authorities. Just as he believed in political violence, Hitler believed in provocation as a tactic. Unless the government responded with equal brutality—thus exposing liberal hypocrisy—it would be exposed as effete, decadent, cowardly. Violent confrontation was thus to be sought at every opportunity; it could in the long run only help, not damage, the cause. Defense was to be turned into offense at every opportunity. In retaliation for a Communist heckler at a Nazi meeting the Brown Shirts would invade the meeting of a Communist or Social Democratic group and forcibly break it up. At times the feuds between the S.A. and the Reds took on all the characteristics of medieval blood feuds, with each side exacting vengence for some "unprovoked attack" by a foray into enemy territory. In such cases indiscriminate reprisals were likely to be exacted against utterly innocent bystanders. The memoirs of S.A. men include innumerable anecdotes of the joys of breaking up political meetings and harassing left-wing or Jewish speakers. The apocalyptic approach did its work. Not only were political and racial offenders punished (a warning of things to come), but invariably the violence produced catharsis as well. Apparently it overwhelmed many people with its righteous splendor, for the wonder of these brawls was that they always brought converts to the Nazi side.

In the early 1930s, as the Nazi vote mounted, violence in the streets increased as well. Hitler remained quite unconcerned about the possibilities of a "backlash" in favor of law and order. In the spring of 1932 the government briefly turned "tough" and banned the S.A., but it was too weak and divided to persist in this decision, and the ban was soon lifted. Soon afterward the harassed police president of Berlin reported that between June 1 and July 20 no fewer than 461 political riots had occurred in Prussia alone, with more than eighty deaths and hundreds of serious injuries. A similar condition of lawlessness prevailed in other cities. One of the lessons of political violence, however, seems to be that it discredits not those who perpetrate it but those who tolerate it or are simply powerless to check it. The responsibility for the carnage was thus always laid at the doorstep of the government, which appeared to invite and to sanction such goings-on. The single biggest riot of the period, which left nineteen people dead in a suburb of Hamburg, resulted not in a crackdown on the S.A. but in the removal of the Social Democratic government of that state by the then Chancellor of the Republic, Franz von Papen, on the grounds that it was incapable of maintaining law and order.

Analysts of National Socialism are fond of calling it a nihilistic movement intoxicated with destruction for its own sake. The idealism that the Nazis galvanized is called idolatry, but such "explanations" are merely playing with words. Yet thousands of Germans echoed Goebbels, who wrote in his diary, "Adolph Hitler, I love you because you are both great and simple." The same men who killed and looted in the streets of Red suburbs stood to attention before Ehrhardt, Röhm, and Hitler's other lieutenants, animated by loyalty, respect, and devotion. Though they behaved as thugs and terrorists in the streets, they maintained strict order in their ranks, often, in their own words, sharing with their comrades "our last piece of bread, our sole remaining cigarette." Often they sacrificed their families and their jobs to follow their leaders, asserting over and over again that National Socialism was "a faith, a religion." Once converted to the movement, men and women devoted every spare hour to proselytizing among their fellow citizens. When the party was in financial straits, they often dipped into their own pockets to carry on the work of organizing rallies and distributing leaflets. The early freebooters may have been nihilists, but Hitler's disciples were believers. They saw themselves as heroes and idealists and were convinced that "some day we shall go down in history as the first champions and prophets of a new, better age."

It is still difficult to comprehend how a creed so filled with hate, so violent, and so vengeful could have represented to millions the way to "a new, better age." Many discontents and longings gathered under the Nazi banner in the dreary years when Weimar, unresisting and almost uncomplaining, was expiring from premature senility. The Nazis appropriated for their own the protest against Versailles and the humiliation of military defeat; the protests against inflation and unemployment, against Bolshevism, and against insecurity and drabness;

the protest of the imagination starved for myth and music. All these protests were harnessed to bring Weimar to its grave and Hitler to power. Hitler promised to render a world that seemed oppressive and incomprehensible once more susceptible to human control and effort. In postwar Germany millions of people felt that their lives were ruled by vast collective forces that they could not understand. The rise and fall of stock markets and the mysterious transactions and decrees of international congresses governed their fates. Hitler said that it need not be so. Under National Socialism Germany would again enjoy wealth and power. The irreconcilable antagonisms between bankers and ditch diggers would be reconciled. When economists or generals produced blueprints of insurmountable obstacles, Hitler said to hell with them all. Versailles had produced maps of Germany's borders, but they had only to be torn up. Hitler recognized no borders. All obstacles could be effaced through struggle, through a determined effort of the will. This philosophy conformed exactly to his own experience. From the penniless derelict at the Vienna Home for Men he had risen to be Chancellor of Germany. Struggle, effort, and will power were at the center of Hitler's political creed. He impressed the exaltation of struggle on his followers and disciples. His was a philosophy of self-reliance applied collectively to the German people, or the Aryan race. It declared directly and brutally that there were no barriers, no anonymous and transcendent powers to limit and curb human potential. To still any final doubts, Hitler confided to his followers that they were part of a superrace, that their triumph was preordained. German man was Prometheus unbound, and conquest was the test of virtue. Such was his creed: self-reliance, self-help, the will to succeed—the bourgeois route to success grotesquely inflated.

PART THREE

PROTEST AGAINST CAPITALISM AND IMPERIALISM

INTRODUCTION

The ideals and institutions of liberal capitalism, already discredited by the inexcusable horrors of the First World War, were driven further along the road to impotency by the Great Depression, which began in 1929. Left-wing protest against liberal capitalism in the 1930s, inspired and to a degree directed by the international Communist organization, became a movement of prime importance in the United States and Britain. It gained the allegiance of intellectuals, students, artists, and workers; and shades of red and pink protest became a way of life, a style of experience and thought.

While this rhythm of dissent and rebellion against capitalist institutions and conservative leadership was working its way into Western society, another protest movement of enormous influence was emerging in India. Mohandas K. Gandhi led the first successful attack by a non-Western colonial people on imperial power and European subjugation. The granting of independence to India in 1947 inaugurated the demolition of European domination over Asian and African societies. Thus between 1929 and 1947 unregulated capitalism and arrogant imperialism, which in 1900 had reigned virtually unchallenged, were thoroughly discredited and drastically altered.

CHAPTER
8

Communist Protest as
a Political Movement

THE dream of a cooperative utopia has always existed in the shadows of the American devotion to individualism and capitalist competition. From Brook Farm to the Oneida Community, from Nashoba to New Harmony, Americans born before *Das Kapital* was written and who had never heard of Karl Marx were experimenting in socialism. Sharing ownership of land or factory and dividing profits as they divided chores, these utopians took advantage of the American tolerance for experiment and variation. Most Owenites or Fourierites had no dream of converting the larger society to their communal life styles. They thrived, if at all, in isolation; they were content to struggle or to enjoy success as small sects.[1]

In the post-Civil War years, in that gilded age of unhampered capitalism, of tycoons, of mergers, of unorganized, exploited labor—during the time that Vernon Parrington has called "the Great Barbecue"—a more ambitious vision of socialism took shape. Critics observed the economic and social consequences of capitalism and concluded that only a revolutionary transformation could correct these ills. Edward Bellamy described a utopian world in *Looking Backwards*. His book was greeted enthusiastically by a large and anxious number of Americans, ardent men and women who formed socialistic societies pledged to plan and work for the new order. But Bellamy was first of all a utopian and only secondly a socialist; his vision was clear, but his economic program to realize it was not. Other men proffered carefully thought out economic schemes to equalize the distribution of wealth, pain, and pleasure in society. The most famous was Henry George, a respected economist and reformer, who proposed "a single tax" on land. By that time, too, Marxian economists were familiarizing American socialists with their prophet's analysis.

Reformers and utopians had long found allies in the working classes, among those who sought to escape their lot as laborers. The leading labor organization of the early 1880s, the Knights of Labor, called for worker ownership of the factory or farm, as well as for immediate reform of labor conditions. Ironically, as the socialist movement grew, a trend in labor was also growing, one that would operate against the socialists throughout the twentieth century. Members of the American Federation of Labor, founded in 1886 on the ruins of the Knights of Labor, accepted the permanent status of laborer and sought through unionization and bargaining to improve wages and win shorter hours. The immediate bread-and-butter goals of the utopians were the only goals of the A.F.L., which was determined to come to terms with industrial realities. This shift in emphasis created an incompatibility between the socialist and his rightful ally, the proletarian. It was to leave him in the same position as a doctor who has developed a cure for a disease on which his patients thrive.

The socialists did not give up, however. Because they sought to transform society as a whole, they entered the battlefield of politics. Henry George ran for mayor of New York City in 1886 and again in 1897. In the Midwest a new political party, the Social Democracy of America, was organized by a hard-headed and devoted Marxist, Victor Berger, and a romantic crusader, Eugene V. Debs. In the East the most original and brilliant Marxist that the United States would produce, Daniel DeLeon, organized the Socialist Labor Party. In 1901 a dissident faction of this party, led by Morris Hillquit and dubbed the "Kangaroos," joined forces with the Debs group. Out of this merger came the Socialist Party.

The early years of the twentieth century were the golden age of socialism in America. Between 1901 and 1912 the Socialist Party attracted almost 150,000 members, and in his 1912 Presidential bid Debs polled 6 percent of the vote. More than a thousand Socialists were elected to public office, and cities like Butte and Milwaukee had Socialist administrations. The party supported 5 English-language daily papers, 8 foreign-language dailies, 262 English-language weeklies, and

36 foreign-language weeklies. There were Socialist lyceums and Socialist Sunday schools.

Circumstances seemed to smile on the young party. It had strength in the Midwest, where former Populists (members of the agrarian protest movement of the 1890s), well-versed in the evils of the economic system, rallied to the new protest. The growth of socialism in Europe made the American party seem more attractive. Especially the movement's success in Germany, which was then the most imitated and admired culture in American intellectual and academic circles, drew Americans to the party. The European success also enhanced Socialist claims that society's natural and peaceful evolution toward a more rational state ensured the triumph of socialism. The party's scientific and evolutionary veneer appealed to people reared on Charles Darwin and Herbert Spencer.

But the greatest appeal lay in the Socialist alternative to the injustices of industrial capitalism. The first decade of the twentieth century was a time of questioning and criticism for many Americans. The intelligentsia viewed the industrial capitalist as a villain responsible for the erosion of social and ethical values. Muckraking journalists and novelists explored and exposed the injustices of a big-business society. Social workers and ministers found themselves face to face with the casualties of these injustices in slums, in tenements, in saloons. Socialism offered more than just an explanation for these ills; it also offered an alternative system, a cure and a preventative. Many men and women conscious of social ills in the United States thus moved naturally into Socialist ranks. Although the core of the party consisted of dedicated Marxists, the rank and file during the first twelve years were prompted less by belief in dialectical materialism than by "an impulse to moral generosity, a readiness to stake their hopes on some goal beyond personal success." [2]

The loose organization of the party enhanced its appeal. Unlike the disciplined and doctrinaire parties that were to arise after the Russian Revolution, the early American Socialist Party encompassed with tolerance a variety of shades on the left side of the political spectrum. At one end were the municipal reformers, the "gas and water socialists," so called because, when elected to office in the Midwest, they revolutionized their cities by installing street lights and sewers. There were also tame Social Democrats and the most radical syndicalists—organizers and supporters of the anarchosyndicalist union, the Industrial Workers of the World (I.W.W.).

But this harmony could not last. As the party grew and began in earnest to enter politics and to hold public offices, schisms arose over doctrine and direction. The party's right wing, more successful in electoral contests, yearned for respectability for the party and frowned on the revolutionary talk of the syndicalists. These "conservatives" wanted a popular party that would draw not only from the working classes but from the middle class as well. This group sought to work within the A.F.L. framework, where Socialist gains were being threatened by I.W.W. (Wobbly) terrorism. The left wing of the party approved the I.W.W.'s militant tactics and preferred dual unionism (setting up competing unions) to cooperation with the A.F.L.

Schism had long been the nemesis of radicalism, and argument and schism now began. The Socialist Party soon became a Roman forum of debates, intrigues, and accusations. At the Socialist Party convention in 1912 the right-wing sprang a coup and had a new clause forbidding sabotage inserted into the party constitution.

This move proved to be small gain for the party. Although it righted the Socialists with the vast majority of law-abiding laborers, it set a conservative tone for the party and marked it as simply another reform party in an era of reformism. It thus had no great luck competing for members with the Bull Moosers, the Progressives, or Woodrow Wilson's Democrats.

The expulsion of the left wing weakened the party. Further losses were suffered each time that a Socialist won office, for once he became involved in the practical problems of holding office, many a Socialist found the limitations of his party a hindrance and its remaining utopian demands unrealistic.

Other factors also operated against the party. Competing agrarian-reform programs of the second decade drew off support among farmers, and rising farm prices, especially in wheat, caused agrarian radicalism to wane. But the Presidency of Woodrow Wilson and the wave of reform legislation during his administration hurt the party most. Wilson stole the Socialist thunder, just as he stole much of the party's intellectual following.

The outbreak of World War I sealed the Socialist Party's fate. Its leaders were doctrinaire Marxists who could not support a war fought in nationalistic rather than in class terms. The intellectuals deserted the party and its pacifist stance, and by the time that the decade had ended, the composition of the party had changed considerably. Native American support had waned, and the party had become entrenched among the foreign-language minorities in the East.

It suffered harassment during the war and postwar years. The government raided its offices, jailed its leaders, and deported its spokesmen. The movement, which had begun with optimism and confidence in ultimate success, had peaked in eleven years and had faded quickly, destroyed by internal disputes, defections, uncompromising Marxism, and the war.

The war, however, gave birth to a new and more militant movement, far more potent and aggressive than any that the gentle Debs could have led. The February Revolution of 1917 in Russia and the later rise to power of the Bolsheviks moved the left wing of socialism into the Communist camp.

For a few brief moments the whole Western world seemed on the verge of revolution. The Russian uprising spread westward, rolling across Germany, where the Kaiser was dethroned, and reaching even to the democracies of the Allied world. In the United States the idealists and the opportunists, those who lusted for progress and those who lusted for power, the romantic and the doctrinaire, shared in an enthusiastic misreading of the American situation. They saw ripening revolution in every factory strike, proletarian class consciousness in every dissident worker. But the United States had endured neither Kaiser nor Tsar, and an American peasantry had never existed. The working class was busy seeking status as an estate, as part of a respectable partnership of big business and labor. The country was entering the prosperous 1920s. Artists and intellectuals might revolt against old art forms, and fashions might undergo revolutionary change, but the revolutionary situation of which Bolsheviks dreamed did not exist.

In September 1919 two rival Communist parties held conventions in Chicago. The first, the Communist Party, was composed largely of foreign-language groups. It elected Louis Fraina chairman. Fraina believed that the time was ripe for mass action. His arguments, set forth in 1918 in *Revolutionary Socialism*, were largely responsible for the Left's indifference to parliamentary reforms and electoral activity. Unfortunately Fraina enjoyed the chairmanship of a united party for only the briefest of terms, for at the same convention his Communist Party quickly split into three factions, which settled into debate on the niceties of doctrine.

The second faction constituted itself as the Communist Labor Party under the leadership of John Reed and Benjamin Gitlow. The two rivals then took to battle in earnest, forsaking attacks on the bourgeoisie to exhaust their energies attacking each other. The forensic dueling was temporarily halted in May 1920, when the Comintern ordered the two parties to merge. The result was the United Communist Party.

As if on cue, a dissident group bolted the unity convention and set up its own party. In 1921 the Comintern effected a partial working unity between the United Communist Party and the new Communist Party, yet the year ended with a rush of new schisms, and at least twelve separate Communist organizations appeared where once there had been two. Some operated underground, for the postwar witch hunt was still going strong in 1921; some operated openly. Although mergers and further splits occurred, the major division lay between two factions and two leaders. The first was led by William Z. Foster and his two lieutenants, Earl Browder and J. P. Cannon. Under Cannon several of the open Communist groups merged to form the Workers Party. The second faction was headed by Charles Ruthenberg and his assistant, Jay Lovestone. The quarrel was basically tactical. Lenin was proclaiming a one-step retreat; as it became clear that world revolution was not imminent, what had not been done in the initial stroke would have to be accomplished by slow and steady work. Lenin programmed a "united front," which would provide means to infiltrate such existing labor groups as the Farmer-Labor Party. Foster preferred to work within the existing A.F.L. and other established structures. In the 1924 elections he strongly advocated the "united front" tactic and went so far as to call for the endorsement of Progressive Senator Robert M. La Follette. Foster had the double advantage of being in tune with Moscow's new policy and with the realities of American politics.

Lenin's new policy should have guaranteed Foster's triumph and Ruthenberg's disgrace, but the day was passing when logic would be a decisive factor within the national Communist parties. By 1925 the "Stalinization" of the Russian party had been completed, and directives from Moscow—based on Russian needs rather than on local circumstances—were issued *ex cathedra*. Intraparty arguments were settled not by debate or leadership but by decisions from Moscow. Foster was ordered to give his enemy Ruthenberg a leading role in the party, and he concurred. Factional fights might continue throughout the history of the party, but they would have little if any effect upon party decisions.

This united front signaled cooperative ventures with labor and socialists, but the gains were minimal. The events of 1929, however, ushered in an opportunity for spectacular gains, and dreams of revolutionary glory were revived. In 1929 the American stock market crashed. The breakdown could be measured not only in financial terms —bankruptcies, mortgage foreclosures, and bread lines—but in emotional and ideological terms as well. There was a disintegration of belief, of trust in all the "givens" of American life. The effectiveness of capitalism and the beauty of the marriage between government and business could no longer be taken for granted. The venerable clichés of America-the-land-of-plenty and of Horatio Alger were recognized as only clichés that could no longer serve as foundations for a national myth. The center did not hold, and new poverty and chaos came to America.

The intellectuals of the 1920s—sensitive men like John Dos Passos and Edmund Wilson—had felt their helplessness before a strong and smug industrial capitalism. They took the apparent bankruptcy of the system as vindication. They were both frightened and exhilarated. There seemed to be a chance to rebuild and to reshape America. There was excitement, a sense that history could be remade. And the task could best be performed by men with a hard-headed, realistic program for the new utopia. The intellectuals sought such a program and found it in communism. While Democrats and Republicans floundered and Franklin Delano Roosevelt gave the country 3.2 beer, communism offered analysis and a plan of action. The cornerstone of communism was scientific economic planning, and in Russia there was no unemployment.

The uncertainty of the early 1930s drove men to take shelter in the apparent certainties of Marxism. "They wanted to feel that, at the very moment the world was being shattered, they had found the key to its meaning." [3] Those who joined the Communist Party were not alone in this desire. Others flocked to the standard of revolving-pension or share-the-wealth schemes.

The Stalinized Communist Party appealed to some strange corner of the intellectual's brain—a roped-off region in which he sought relief from the critical thinking and questioning which are the intellectual's *raison d'être*, in which he sought the comfort of declared truth and the security of submission. Under Marx's wing and Stalin's watchful eye, the intellectual could, in the name of the coming millennium, lay down his burden of doubt.

To the party flocked American writers, professors, and artists. Not all, not a majority, not even many of the best. But they came. Some joined the party, and others became the fellow travelers of that decade. With them came social workers, Christian moralists, lawyers, and doctors.

The highly romantic image of the party that these new converts held scarcely fit the reality. Some recruits were conscious of the party's shortcomings but came anyway. For them the crisis demanded revolutionary change, and the Communist Party was the only party advocating revolution. To be a socialist would not have been enough; joining the Socialists would have been, as Dos Passos declared, like drinking "near beer." Others were strangely blind to or naïve about the party's faults. Still others, as Granville Hicks would later confess, quelled their doubts, for "it was enough for us to believe that Marxism was in general right and that the Communist Party was in general Marxist." [4]

The party that they joined or supported was no longer the party of the mild "united front." The "third period" was underway, and the Communist Party had become an ultrarevolutionary party. Ironically its revolutionary direction was not one well suited to the American intellectual's radical dreams. The party line focused on cannibalism of the Left; the main enemy was not capitalism or fascism but socialism. Capitalism, the Communists assured their adherents, was dying, and the fascism then on the rise in Germany and Spain was nothing more than the last stage of its decay. The victory of the Left was thus assured, but it was important that the Communists emerge as the strongest party of the Left. The Socialists, as rivals for working-class loyalties, had therefore to be crushed. Such reasoning led to strange political bedfellows: In Germany the Communist Party joined with the Nazis to destroy the "social fascists."

In America the attack on the Left extended not only to socialists but to all existing organized labor groups. The Communists launched an aggressive program of "dual unionism," concentrated in the clothing, textile, coal, and maritime industries. By this campaign they hoped to draw workers out of the A.F.L.'s established unions and to compete for potential members. Rather than operating from within the A.F.L., the Communist Party was openly seeking to weaken and destroy the moderate labor movement—but it met with little success. Despite the Depression and fear of unemployment, the American worker remained a Samuel Gompers man. Even those members of the working class who were actually recruited to the Communist Party could not be held—less because of ideological differences than because ideology was involved at all. These men were uncomfortable with philosophy and mystified by it; they were bored by constant meetings and debate. A worker reared on bread-and-butter unionism could not easily be satisfied with dialectical materialism. After five years the Communist Party could claim only the New York fur industry. The price for this meager victory was a legacy of anti-Communist feeling throughout the labor movement.

But although the party had not yet won the working classes, its adherents among the literati were hard at work creating the image for the "new working-class man." These intellectuals worshiped at the feet of an idealized proletarian, a worker nobler, somehow more "real," than they, a man of instinctive and simple goodness who, if freed from his shackles, could and would fulfill himself. "Proletcult"—proletarian culture and the cult of the proletarian as well—was the creation of men who felt guilty about their upper- or middle-class origins. These men of letters encouraged and overpraised the trickle of art and literature produced during the period by bona fide workers. And men who in the 1920s had gloried in their roles as artistic rebels and nonconformists now preached art as a class weapon, an ideological tool. Their efforts, foolish though sincere, came to naught, however, and faded with the third period.

The ultrarevolutionary American Communist Party had little good to say about the new President. In fact, it viewed Franklin Delano Roosevelt as the country's leading social fascist. His New Deal, pieced together in the first half of the decade, was denounced as a clever capitalist ruse to lure workers from their true allegiance to the party of the proletariat and back into the exploitative system.

Yet despite the economic difficulties of the Depression years, Americans simply did not turn to revolution or to the Communist Party for relief. By 1934 the party had enlisted only 47,000 new members, and only 12,000 of the recruits had remained. The Communists ended the third phase with only 24,000 members, far fewer than the Socialists had boasted even in their radical syndicalist days.

By 1934 the Russians were reconsidering their foreign policy. Adolf Hitler's rise to power seriously threatened Russian national survival. Fascism no longer seemed the dying phase of capitalism; instead it had the look of a healthy beast of prey. The fascist takeover in Austria, which had destroyed the strongest Socialist Party in Europe, signaled an end to the third period. Stalin began to concentrate on military and political alliances with the bourgeois democracies. He justified this unorthodox class collaboration to fellow Marxists by declaring that the rise of Nazism had created a political crisis dmanding special measures. Stalin had ushered in the era of the "Popular Front."

In Europe and the United States, Communist parties took their cue. Emphasis on class struggle lessened, and by 1935 the rhetoric of class struggle and revolution had been stilled. Stalin was seeking to allay Western fears of Russia, and the Communist parties began to present themselves as national parties, patriotic supporters of democracy. The American Communist Party, like all other American groups, argued for defense of the country against fascism.

Doctrinaire American Marxists may have been troubled by the change in party line, for Marxism decreed that the class struggle should *never* be subordinated to nationalism anywhere. But the American Communist Party was above all a disciplined and dedicated cadre, loyal to Moscow's directives and devoted to the survival of the utopian experiment in Russia. Some members were party hacks, loyal only to those in power and unconcerned with ideological paradoxes or contradictions. Others, having once committed themselves to the faith—as a devout Roman Catholic commits himself to the Church—believed that submission was the test of their commitment. Others were troubled but found the Popular Front more amenable to their own tastes and so troubled themselves little with the less attractive implications of this drastic change in policy.

The Popular Front began modestly enough in the United States with a wooing of fellow leftist groups. There were overtures to the Socialist Party, reminiscent of the earlier United Front. But, as the Communist Party moved right, the Socialists were veering toward a doctrinaire left. In 1936 the Communists, after bigger game than sectarian leftist parties, unofficially supported Roosevelt for re-election. The Socialists, however—more determined than ever to be right doctrinally and wrong politically—ran their own candidate, Norman Thomas, who concentrated his attack on the widely popular Roosevelt and the New Deal.

F.D.R.'s great victory in 1936 ended any Communist Party doubts about the virtues of Popular Front politics. The Communists extolled the New Deal and its creator. Roosevelt's picture frequently graced the front page of the *Daily Worker*. The revolutionary struggle was forgotten as patriotic Communists worked instead through "progressive movements inside and around the Democratic Party. . . ." [5]

The party was careful to mend other old quarrels as well. Attacks on the Church stopped, and Church leaders shared the *Daily Worker*'s editorial praises with the President. The opiate of the people was no longer treated as unworthy of kind words. The party wooed Jews by soft-pedaling its traditional anti-Zionism and sprinkling the pages of its newspapers with favorable mentions of Jewish Palestine. It had great success, especially among the new Jewish immigrants.

The Communist Party wore a new face. In keeping with the new emphasis on national pride and patriotism, it Americanized itself. Rather than organizing as "fractions" within unions, it adopted the political structure indigenous to the United States: organization by neighborhoods or wards. Neighborhood clubs did not meet too often, and arguments on dialectics were replaced by arguments on when and where to hold club picnics. Like its Republican or Democratic counterpart, the local club had become a social center.

With that passion for extremes so characteristic of the party, its leaders molded an image of themselves as "just folks." The Young

Communist League at the University of Wisconsin described its members as "no different from other people except that we believe in dialectical materialism as a solution to all problems." [6] New members of the party were no longer expected to pass trial by fire before acceptance. The party had moved far from the cadre concept; it encouraged and accommodated itself to the demands of a mass movement.

This Americanization knew no bounds. Happily the family tree of party leader Earl Browder—whose extreme docility in obeying Comintern orders resulted in his being chosen, over Foster, to lead the party during both its ultra-left period in the early 1930s and its Popular Front period of the mid-1930s—could be traced back to pre-Revolutionary Virginia. The revolutionary blood throbbing in his veins was declared to be the same as that of Virginia's other famous son, George Washington. The Communist Party put the venerable Daughters of the American Revolution to shame on April 18, 1937, when it celebrated the anniversary of Paul Revere's midnight ride. Its unfurled banner read: "The D.A.R. Forgets but the Y.C.L. Remembers."

The party showed its new face to labor by dissolving its "dual unions." Its members rejoined the A.F.L. with a vengeance, pledging loyalty with the vigor of the prodigal son. In 1936, when John L. Lewis began his drive to organize mass-production industries and to draw unions into the new Congress of Industrial Organizations (C.I.O.), the Communists hesitated. Their unions refused to follow the C.I.O. out of the A.F.L., for they were inclined to conservatism while the grave of their dual-union radicalism was still fresh. By the spring of 1937, however, the party had realized that its greatest opportunities lay in the C.I.O. Lewis needed experienced organizers, and the party could supply them. He felt confident that he could "use" them to good profit; they felt the same about him. As a dowry the Communists brought the Pacific Maritime Federation and the Transport Workers Union into the C.I.O. Lewis took over the apparatus that the party had used in past attempts to invade unions, but his efforts were more successful. His victories were Communist victories as well, however, for the party gained new jobs for its own men. Party members managed to ensconce themselves in the national office of the C.I.O., and within two years Communists controlled several C.I.O. unions.

Many non-Communist members did not resist the Communist influx. First of all, in those days of the Popular Front, it was difficult to tell the party men from the nonparty men. It was not until the Hitler-Stalin Pact, which suddenly changed the Communist attitude, that many unions recognized the extent of party influence and infiltration in their councils. Some unions, like the United Steelworkers, were more alert and squelched Communist efforts before the party could become entrenched. At the height of the Popular Front and immediately before its sudden death, however, the Communist Party effectively controlled twelve unions.

Events abroad helped to swell the party's ranks during the early years of the Popular Front. When the Spanish Civil War erupted in July 1936 there were many men and women, especially among the young, who believed that the last great battle between fascism and freedom was being fought on the dusty yellow plains of Spain. Yet none of the democracies came to the Loyalists' aid. A great malaise seemed to infect the Western democracies; they seemed unable or unwilling to defend their principles. Only Russia offered money and arms to the Loyalists, and it was the Communist parties in Europe that organized the volunteer brigades to fight in Catalonia or along the frontier. These brigades were composed largely of Communist youths, many of whom died in battle.

The Communist Party seemed invested with an energy and idealism that were lacking among other Western parties and governments. Russia seemed the only nation worthy of praise. Later many would be disenchanted as news of Communist pressures on the Spanish government reached them and the realization came that Mother Russia could be parasite and destroyer as well as savior. John Dos Passos would tell these new American Communists that they had been cheated and that their devotion and admiration exceeded the worth of the idol. Many would leave the party in disgust. But initially the Spanish Civil War— and pervasive despair over democracy—caused party membership to multiply and attracted the sympathies of many nonmembers.

Finally, the Communist Party's success could not be measured in membership figures alone. Many American liberals, worried less now about poverty than about the threat of fascism and Nazi domination in Europe, found themselves supporting the Communists' antifascism. These men and women were not Communists or sympathizers with the party's economic doctrines. Many believed that a Popular Front program meant cooperation between Communist and Democrat or between Communist and Liberal or Independent. They saw it as a united effort, not as a process of absorption or political exploitation. It was this group that guaranteed the success of the party's most spectacular political innovation, the front organization.

Each front organization was devoted to a cause guaranteed to attract respectable citizens. It was not difficult for the Communists to retain control of the organization and to direct its actions, despite the number of non-Communist members, for whereas most members joined as individuals, the Communists were trained as a unit, voted together, attended every meeting, served on committees, and were always ready with proposals and debate. These front organizations served the Communist Party well, not only as pressure groups for any given policy helpful to Russia, but also as entrées into respectable Federal- and local-government circles.

One such front organization, the League Against War and Fascism, was organized in 1933. Its membership on paper was extraordinarily large, for it accepted indirect and group affiliations. Hundreds of rank-and-file members of other organizations might thus be included without their knowledge, through the decision of their presidents or executive committees to affiliate.

The semantic history of the League reflects the changes in policy and purpose in the ensuing six years. The original League Against War and Fascism, a third-period creation, was both antifascist and anti-capitalist. By 1937 the Popular Front phase was in full swing, and the organization had become the American League for Peace and Democracy. Thus it now advocated peace, but it advised a policy of collective security in case war might be necessary to defend the United States and democracy. The League's shift in emphasis fitted many Americans' own shift in attitude. It attracted the support of men in government like Harold Ickes. At its fifth congress in January 1939 the national president of Hadassah, the Grand Exalted Ruler of the Improved Benevolent and Protective Order of the Elks, two congressmen, and delegates from the Y.W.C.A. were present. This meeting was the League's greatest and most illustrious and was also its last, for the Hitler-Stalin Pact demanded the League's hasty and indecorous demise.

The Communist Party took great interest in minority groups. During the Popular Front period it extended a hand to the American blacks, and many black leaders, though wary of Communist motives, took the calculated risk that cooperation might be profitable. In 1936 Ralph Bunche and A. Philip Randolph helped to organize the National Negro Congress. Although a majority of the original membership was not Communist, the Communist Party's organizational talents and experience soon gave it effective control. This Congress, like the League, suddenly collapsed after the Hitler-Stalin Pact. Many members had taken the stated goals of the Congress seriously and had believed that they were working toward equality for their race. The expendability of their organization and the abrupt about-face of supposedly devoted organizational leaders left these blacks angry, disillusioned, and bitter.

In 1935 the party enjoyed its first significant success on college campuses. Through a merger of Socialist Party and Communist Party youth groups the American Student Union was created. Socialist youth had been wary of the merger, as well it might have been. Although part of a united effort at the Union's inception, Socialist members very quickly found themselves outmaneuvered, outvoted, and finally dethroned.

But control of leftist student groups was less valuable to the party than was control of respectable liberal organizations like the American Youth Congress. The Congress—"started by vague young liberals and . . . soon captured by specific young Communists" [7]—received blessings and support from Mrs. Eleanor Roosevelt herself. Its members were invited to advise New Dealers on youth problems and policies. Again, although Mrs. Roosevelt suspected that Communist influence was present, many Youth Congress leaders seemed—and were —patriotic Americans genuinely concerned with problems of youth unemployment and schooling.

In all these instances, the Communist Party's success resulted not only from a Svengali-like influence over naïve Americans. The causes and concerns of the organizations founded were above reproach and attracted many devoted men and women. That Communist Party members were too sharp in debate, too talented when talent was needed in the organizational areas, and more willing to work for the organization than others were, meant their inevitable success in controlling the group. Paradoxically many of these American Communists —more utopians than Stalinists—believed in the goals of the organizations that they controlled, and it was not unusual for a man to renounce party membership when it threatened to harm his front organization's work.

The Communist Party made inroads to real power in only two major New Deal agencies: the Agricultural Division, led by Jerome Frank, and the National Labor Relations Board. In both cases the party's gains were measurable in terms of personnel rather than of ideology. The only opportunity open to these secret Communist Party members was to support strongly the most militant of what were essentially liberal options. They could take their extremist stands only within a liberal framework. Jerome Frank's Communist aides thus could and did ardently support what F.D.R.'s administration would have called a leftist position: a demand for increased government control of farm prices and a program of aid to Southern sharecroppers. This position was hardly Marxian, and Frank himself was anti-Communist. On the National Labor Relations Board the situation was similar. Communist members took a strong pro-C.I.O. stance, the most radical position available to them.

The liberalization of Russian control during the Popular Front period ironically coincided with the ideological witch-hunts in the Soviet Union. In 1936 the Russians began to exhibit their bountiful catch, and the heresy trials began. These Moscow trials shook the intellectuals in the American Communist Party. Leaders of the Revolution, with honored names, heroes of the not-yet-cold past, were accused of betraying that Revolution. They were accused, and they confessed.

The trials spurred anti-Communist intellectuals in the United States to assert themselves. John Dewey chaired a commission of inquiry, which traveled to Mexico to hear testimony from the exiled Leon Trotsky. The second volume of the two-volume report of this investigation was entitled *Not Guilty*. Then Communists and fellow travelers, led by Malcolm Cowley, sprang to Stalin's defense. A round-robin letter of protest was signed by 150 men and women in the arts. The doubts of some sympathizers and party members were forgotten in the heated activity of defense.

By 1939 the pro- and anti-Communist intellectuals were engaged in open battle. Sidney Hook and John Dewey formed the Committee for Cultural Freedom, which issued a statement carrying 140 signatures and decrying the blindness of those who denounced the suppression of intellectual freedom under fascism but accepted or failed to recognize equal repression in the U.S.S.R. The Communist Party promptly gathered four hundred signatures for its rebuttal, which accused the Committee for Cultural Freedom of spreading a "fantastic falsehood" and of undermining the united front against fascism. This letter, with its star-studded list of signers, was issued on August 14, 1939. Not two weeks later the Hitler-Stalin Pact was announced.

"The masquerade is over," [8] wrote Heywood Broun. The Hitler-Stalin Pact put an end to the innocence, real or pretended, of Communist intellectuals. Most deserted the party in disgust, yet the core members dutifully made the necessary change in party line. It was the greatest test of their capacity to accept anything on faith, and the Browders and Fosters passed that test.

It was not without regret that the American Communist Party packed away the costumes, banners, and organizations of the Popular Front era. They had been years of plenty for the party. Its tactics had worked well and had rewarded it with power and prestige. Slowly, however, the editorial gears of the *Daily Worker* shifted: The war in Europe was described as "imperialistic," not antifascist, and England was accused of having "unleashed" the holocaust.

The party's new task was to keep the United States out of the war.

It was to function as chief propagandist for isolationism and as a proponent of pacifism. This approach resulted in a new kind of Popular Front—a "Keep America Out of War" front. The old techniques were salvaged, and new front organizations were set up.

The League for Peace and Democracy was resurrected as the American Peace Mobilization. Its slogan was "The Yanks are not coming," and it set up a "perpetual peace vigil" around the White House.

The new Communist front organizations set to work to turn well-meaning members of the old organizations on their well-meaning heads. Support for collective security and F.D.R. had to be programmed out and a passion for isolationism and hatred for F.D.R. programmed in. A new ditty was taught to former Roosevelt lovers:

> Oh, Franklin Roosevelt told the people how he felt,
> We almost believed him when he said:
>> Oh I hate war
>> And so does Eleanor
> But we won't be safe 'til everybody's dead.[9]

The Hollywood Peace Forum was organized on the West Coast; at the other end of the country the Brooklyn Community Peace Council was called to order. This policy about-face was accomplished with many sympathizers still intact, for the myth of Soviet progress was still strong, and the joys of fraternal efforts for a cause were still sweet.

No sooner had the party settled into the new role than everything changed again. On June 22, 1941, Hitler's armies invaded the U.S.S.R. In Washington the "perpetual peace vigil" vanished. The American Peace Mobilization became the American People's Mobilization. Aid to Britain became the rallying cry. Communist strike agitators became union peacemakers and accused John L. Lewis of being a fascist, a pro-Nazi organizer of strikes.

It was a happy time for party members. Although they worried for the safety of their Russian comrades, they must have delighted in the new turn of events. They could again be Russian patriots and American patriots at the same time! They could throw themselves into a patriotic mass movement, a mainstream effort, and still serve Stalin loyally.

The war years saw a rise in Communist Party membership. By 1944 it had almost doubled and stood at eighty thousand, but membership was no longer a true gauge of the appeal of Marxism. Most new recruits joined the party as a gesture of friendship toward Russia and the gallant Red Army. By 1944 the party was no longer demanding that a potential member be a Marxist at all. In fact in that year the Com munist Party dissolved itself and was reborn as the Communist Political Association. The Communist Political Association campaigned actively for F.D.R.'s re-election. Once again, the more "American" the party became, the more it prospered.

The American people were obsessed with all things Russian during the war years, from folk songs on the balalaika to Dimitri Shostakovich. And, through some fantastic capacity to twist reality, the enthusiastic American public even "Americanized" the Soviet Union. Articles were written describing modern Russia as a "modified capitalist set-up." The Communist system did, indeed, seem to be evolving into a fraternal, if not identical, twin of Anglo-American democracy. In 1942 a D.A.R. member blithely announced the demise of Soviet Marxism: "Today in Russia Communism is practically nonexistent." [10]

If in the 1920s and 1930s Americans had worshiped Russia for its differences, in the 1940s they adored it for its similarities to the United States. The non-Marxists in this country had co-opted their utopian brothers' Russia.

At the end of the war the party line changed again. In the Cold War the United States became the capitalist-imperialist enemy once more. There was, however, a fatal lag between the new policy decision and the American Communist Party leaders' shift in gears. Even as the United States and the U.S.S.R. were drawing spheres of influence on their respective maps, Browder was still preaching peaceful coexistence. Browder, too much associated with the wartime slogans of national unity, too slow on the ideological uptake, was dismissed. His death sentence came to him secondhand, for it was first issued in a letter, composed by the French Communist leader Jacques Duclos, which appeared in April 1945 in the French magazine *Cahiers du Communisme;* in May it appeared in the *Daily Worker,* so that Browder could read the news in his native tongue. Browder's old rival William Z. Foster, long browbeaten, humiliated, and ignored by the party, was chosen to lead it again.

American Communist members were bewildered by this sudden change in leadership, which implied, frighteningly, that in loyally following a heretic they too had been guilty of heresy. *Mea culpa* was uttered for sins not understood by the penitents. One by one and then in droves they came forward publicly to repent and to denounce their "Browderism." On February 5, 1946, Earl Browder was expelled from his party as a "social imperialist."

What was to replace "Browderism"? The party's job was to arouse opposition to American expansion and American policy toward Russia. But the American Cold War mentality drove Communists out of positions of influence in government and labor. By fair or, frequently, foul means the C.I.O. began a wholesale ousting of Communist Party members from its ranks. The C.I.O. Executive Board passed a motion calling for all its members unwilling to enforce the U.S. Constitution to resign. The purged board then ruled that no union consistently working on behalf of a "totalitarian movement" could continue membership in the C.I.O.

In 1948 the party made a last-ditch effort to re-enter American political life. A new "people's party" was conceived, and Henry Wallace was touted as a potential Presidential candidate. Wallace was an ideal front man for the Communists; he had "a readiness to believe the best about the worst aspects of the totalitarian world—indeed there was something about Wallace that simply yearned to be deluded." [11] The Communist Party actually cared little about Wallace's thoughts on Russian society. It was concerned only with his ideas on foreign policy vis-à-vis that society, and Wallace was a "dove" in the Cold War.

New front organizations arose. (The tactic was stale by that time, but the Communists had lost their creativity.) The Progressive Citizens of America, a new "liberal" group, urged Americans to elect Henry Wallace, the hero of the common man.

The small number of Communists still in the C.I.O. opposed the third-party drive, for they knew that it would split the labor organization. When plans proceeded nonetheless and the founding convention of the Progressive Party nominated Wallace for President, many Communist union leaders left the party rather than jeopardize their union work and their positions.

Wallace polled one million votes, not a bad start for a new party, but the Communists were not interested in the slow process of building a long-term political party. Their goals and purposes were more immediate. The movement crumbled, in any case, for Wallace deserted it to support American involvement in the Korean War.

The Communist Party was dead as a force in American politics. All that was left was its public execution, and the executioner arrived in the person of Joseph McCarthy.

Karl Marx spent much of his life in London. And it was a society like that of Britain that he envisioned as the setting for the proletarian revolution. But the British continually disappointed Marx and his disciples. Although a socialist organization did spring up as early as the 1880s, the members of the Social Democratic Federation were content with a vague understanding of the gentleman's theories and were, in fact, archconservatives when it came to words like *riot* or *revolution*.

At the turn of the century a whiff of the radical spirit did reach Britain from the highly industrialized United States. Daniel DeLeon's "one big union" concept inspired Marxists in the industrial Clydeside area to action. A militant group formed a British Socialist Labour Party in imitation of DeLeon's own Socialist Labor Party. In the depressed and depressing industrial sections of Wales and Scotland, this militant group had some success. Most important, its efforts brought into being a nucleus of working-class Marxists who could provide leadership at opportune times for arousing and organizing the proletariat.

During World War I, the Labour Party—which espoused gradual socialism through legal trade-union activity and often showed a greater affinity for Gompers than for Marx—agreed to cooperate with the war effort. The trade-union leaders accepted restrictions on their activities for the sake of the nation's safety. Not so the socialist militants, who organized groups like the Clydeside Workers Committee, threatened strikes to protest wartime working conditions, and continued the task of strengthening unions despite the war then raging. Quite understandably, their class consciousness made the war between worker and capitalist seem more important than the war between Kaiser and King. The British government, however, valued this ideological consistency but little. In 1917 the militant Clydeside leaders were exiled from England.

That same year the Russian Revolution was applauded by Labour Party leaders and radical socialists alike. This united rejoicing was sweet but brief and ended with the Bolshevik coup. Again the Labour Party and the rest of the British Left eyed each other from opposite sides of the political fence.

The radicals began to debate their position vis-à-vis the Revolution and the new Communism. As in America, the Left in Britain was a motley collection of tiny parties, each with its own point of view. The major difficulty was to unite these groups, for otherwise there could be no effective political action or influence at all. But unification would not be easy. The British Socialist Party, an expanded version of the Socialist Democratic Federation, was pro-Russian but definitely not of a revolutionary turn when it came to Britain. It preferred parliamentary action. Its intentions to work from within the system were clear, for it had reaffiliated with the Labour Party in 1916.

Such other parties as that led by suffragette Sylvia Pankhurst preferred the formation of revolutionary cadres unsullied by association with conservative trade unionists like those in the Labour Party. Miss Pankhurst took matters into her own hands, and on July 16, 1919, wrote to Comrade Nikolai Lenin himself. Lenin, impatient to see the

British Left united, responded on August 28 that he preferred Communist participation in anything—elections, existing trade unions, the Labour Party—that might gain power for the Left but that he placed immediate unity above all other considerations. In other words, he would approve any workable compromise.

The British parties once again began their meetings, debates, and arguments. A unity convention was called, but the Pankhurst faction refused to attend. With its main antagonist absent, the British Socialist Party was able to persuade the convention to attempt affiliation with Labour. It assured its fellow leftists that collaboration with the gradualists would be only superficial. The idea was to affiliate "first of all to help the Labour Party get into office, and then, when they have got into office, our first act is to kick them out." [12]

Out of this meeting came the Communist Party of Great Britain (C.P.G.B.). Its only militant rival was the Pankhurst party. Miss Pankhurst, however, came around when the Labour Party rebuffed the C.P.G.B.'s petition to affiliate; the tactic she disapproved was harmless if the Labour Party refused to permit it. By 1921 a shaky but formal unification had taken place. The new party's structure reflected the still-strong individualism of each faction. The executive committee was elected partly on a geographical basis and partly by the participating groups.

The second unity convention was held, appropriately, at the Victory Hotel in Leeds on January 29, 1921 (prudently the party had booked rooms in the name of the National Fruiterers' Association). Old enemies toasted one another as new friends: "The Communist Parties are dead: long live the Communist Party." [13]

On the whole, the new Communist Party of Great Britain's membership was not English. Many members were Continentals. The great majority were of the "Celtic fringe": Clydeside Irish, Scottish, and Welsh. A third group consisted of young people and intellectuals Britons who admired Russia's overnight industrialization and her utopian promises.

The Bolshevization of the party during the 1920s was not easily effected. Democratic centralism—which encouraged discussion of issues *until* the party hierarchy endorsed a position, and then demanded unquestioning obedience to that decision—with its inhibition of free discussion, did not sit well with the strong nonconformist tradition of the British Left. Yet the Comintern's Second Congress had set down twenty-one principles outlining a strict, almost military organization each national Communist Party would have to conform to them in order to affiliate with the Third International. The small British party realized that it would have little influence on Comintern decisions, but it was eager for membership and so set about to complying with the directives.

In 1922 a *troika* was selected by Russian leaders to reshape the British party. The restructuring amounted to the establishment of a governing Central Committee. The main activity of the party would be trade-union recruitment and infiltration. As in the United States, party units, or "fractions," would be organized by factory or industry rather than by neighborhood or ward. Once this reorganization and redirection was complete, the party's Bolshevization could be declared complete.

The postwar period in Britain, as in the United States, was a difficult time of restriction and harassment for the party. The Communists thus rejoiced in the Labour Party's victory in 1924. They were hopeful that the government of Ramsay MacDonald would lift police restrictions on party activities. Although MacDonald himself proved to have little sympathy for C.P.G.B. members, there was sympathy to be tapped among liberal Labourites concerned with civil liberties. Unfortunately the Labour Party was in no position to risk aid to the radicals. MacDonald did not have a parliamentary majority, and his government's survival depended solely upon the good will of the Liberal Party.

The Conservatives were eager to detect any "soft on communism" moves among Labourites. They would hope to use such moves to frighten the Liberals, paint the Labour group as near-revolutionaries, and thus drive a wedge between the two allies. The Conservatives did not have long to wait. In 1924 J. R. Campbell, editor of the *Workers' Weekly*, published an antiwar appeal, "Don't Shoot." When MacDonald permitted charges of incitement to mutiny against Campbell to be dropped, the Conservatives immediately rose in Parliament to protest.

Parliament was dissolved and a general election called for October. While the candidates campaigned a scandal hit the newspapers. A letter from Comintern General Secretary Grigori Zinoviev to the C.P.G.B. was "intercepted" and made public. The Zinoviev letter (actually a forgery) instructed British Communists to do everything they could to paralyze British military operations in case of war. Guilt by association defeated the Labour Party, and Conservative Stanley Baldwin took the reins of government.

The Labour Party could not help but look upon its fellow Marxist party as a political albatross. This attitude was to hinder and eventually to defeat the Communist Party in British politics. The immediate effect was a tightening of restrictions on Communist membership in the Labour Party. Whereas once Communists had been permitted to join the Labour Party as individuals, now they were barred completely.

The Communist Party then shifted its attention to the Trades Union Congress. The moment was opportune. A coal strike was on, and it threatened to burgeon into a general strike if settlement was not forthcoming. The Conservative government would not compromise with the coal miners; instead it busied itself with preparations for a national emergency. One of the by-products of these tense months of 1925 and early 1926 was a new "Red scare." Twelve Communist leaders were prosecuted for sedition under the Mutiny Act of 1797. Communist Party headquarters was repeatedly raided, for the Baldwin government recognized that the Communists were taking an active part in fomenting the strike.

On May 4, 1926, a great general strike did begin. Nine days later the T.U.C. General Council made its peace with the government, and only the miners remained out. Throughout the next six months the Communists bitterly attacked T.U.C. leaders for their betrayal of the miners. The party thus gained popular support among these coal workers for its loyal and militant stand, but this support faded as the strike drew to a close. The Communist Party's advocacy of militant action had, in the end, proved a bankrupt tactic.

Party membership declined in 1927 and 1928, a serious problem for a group that had boasted only five thousand members in 1924. Moscow took the matter into its own hands and swept away the entire British party leadership. By this time Moscow had, of course, taken everything into its own hands, and the choice of new leaders reflected the Stalinization of the party. With the help of the British Young Communist League, Moscow reorganized the party and set up the presses of the *Daily Worker* as its chief propaganda organ.

Third-period politics were now underway. The sharp lines of battle drawn by the class-warfare rhetoric forced the extreme left wing of the Labour Party into the Communist Party. Within the labor movement dual unionism was revived, and two breakaway unions, the United Mineworkers of Scotland and the United Clothing Workers of the East End, declared their independence from the T.U.C. But party gains were actually small, and the only real success came among the unemployed. The National Unemployed Workers Committee Movement was Communist-controlled, and Communist leaders did demonstrate and agitate for the rights of the unemployed. But, despite hunger and depression, the jobless could not be transformed into the revolutionary masses for which Stalin yearned.

As early as 1931 Moscow realized that the class-against-class tactic had not and could not consolidate Communist control of the working classes. The ultrarevolutionary rhetoric and dual unionism had only alienated the Communists from their natural allies in factories and government. The only important membership gains had been made in the defection of Labour Party socialists to the Communist Party after MacDonald had compromised his party in a coalition government.

Party membership stood at six thousand when, in 1932, a mild united-front policy was revived. It was not intended to include cooperation with the "social fascist" trade-union leaders, but instead it was to be a "grass roots" movement, a "united front from below." But these efforts to win local organizations and to build support for unseating the union bureaucracy reaped few rewards.

It was Adolf Hitler's rise to power and the inauguration of the Popular Front which brought new life to the floundering C.P.G.B. The menace of a goose-stepping fascism made the Communist Party popular in Britain. As in the United States, the crisis drew intellectuals and students to the party. A whole school of socially conscious poets turned to political verse. W. H. Auden, Cecil Day Lewis, and Stephen Spender began to compose couplets around *Das Kapital*. Scientists, under the spell of technocracy, were also drawn to the party of the Five Year Plan. The rapid and rational development of natural resources in Russia contrasted sharply in their eyes with the chaos and economic waste of Great Britain.

These gains among humanitarians and scientists were not balanced by gains among the working class. The General Council of the T.U.C., still smarting from the attacks of dual unionism and Communist infiltration, issued a "Black Circular" in October 1934. This circular forbade trade councils to accept Communists as delegates and urged all unions to exclude party members from office. The strong T.U.C. organization and the existence of a Labour Party that espoused the workers' cause through peaceful parliamentary processes continued to defeat Communist efforts. Even the sympathy won by the party during the Spanish Civil War could not shake the worker from his established allegiances.

The Communists made continual overtures to the Labour Party. They withdrew their own candidates from opposition to Labourites and actively campaigned for the latter. But MacDonald's party continued to hold the Communists at arm's length. An application to affiliate was rejected once again.

The Popular Front period proved far less successful for the British Communist Party than for its American counterpart. Nevertheless membership had trebled, reaching eighteen thousand in 1939, the peak year.

The Hitler-Stalin Pact did more damage to the C.P.G.B. than to Browder's party, for England was soon at war, and Communist Party propaganda damning Churchill and Chamberlain as social fascists was not well received by a nation at war. When the *Daily Worker* applauded the Russian invasion of Finland as "liberation," the British public responded angrily. Mobs broke up Communist Party rallies, and Communist speakers were booed everywhere. Only pacifist students rallied to the party's antiwar banner.

On January 12, 1941, a front organization, the People's Convention met; its two thousand delegates claimed to represent more than one million workers. This convention issued a manifesto calling for friendship with the U.S.S.R. and a "people's government" in Britain. Less than a week later the British government retaliated by banning the *Daily Worker*. The Communist Party judiciously began making plans to go underground.

Once again Hitler saved the party from oblivion. Germany invaded Russia, and within a month the nations of Churchill and Stalin were allies in the war against the Führer. The C.P.G.B. applauded Churchill's coalition government, took its new patriotism seriously, and pledged an end to all strikes during the war effort. The party organization and nomenclature were quickly anglicized.

The enthusiasm for the Red Army and all things Russian which had given Browder's party wings swept across Britain as well. Communist Party membership soared. At the end of 1941 the rolls showed 22,70 names; by September 1942, 65,000. The *Daily Worker* was again hawked on London streets. C.P.G.B. members gained the respect of fellow factory workers for their war efforts, and the T.U.C. was forced to withdraw the "Black Circular" in 1943. This opened the way for the party's fantastic success within the unions. Before the war ended, the Communists controlled nearly the entire labor movement.

The Communist Party again eagerly petitioned the Labour Party for affiliation. If ever this final touch of respectability were to be had it was then. The fight within the Labour Party was fierce, for the dissolution of the Comintern and the apparent decentralization of Communist control had weakened conservative Labourite arguments against the foreign-dominated Communist Party. Nevertheless and despite popular support of the Communist Party, the Labour Party rejected the C.P.G.B. petition. The Communists remained outside the pale of national politics.

The Communist Party's decline began in 1943. Its new members, motivated by affection for the Red Army and not for Red economics, began to drift away. The second front was opened, and the public grew more intent upon the progress of the British and American armies than on that of Stalin's troops. The new labor recruits grew bored, as the American laborers had, with party meetings and political responsibility. And the party had gone too far in its support of Churchill's government. Its patriotic stance had left it little room for radical criticism on major domestic issues, and thus its appeal as a creative opposition for intellectuals and workers had died.

In 1945 the nation faced its first postwar general election. The C.P.G.B. staked its political future on this campaign, hoping to gain seats in Parliament and a role in a coalition government as reward for its wartime loyalty. But the Labour Party was shrewd; it realized the likelihood of victory even without coalition. Military success in Europe and current popular enthusiasm for a planned economy spelled political rewards for the Labour Party, and its leaders agreed to no united effort. The Communist Party suffered the consequences: Only two Communists won seats in Parliament.

The Labour victory left the C.P.G.B. still politically impotent, and the Cold War mentality caused trade unions to ferret out and expel Communist members. Communist control in unions faded. The rash of postwar social-service programs like the National Health Service convinced many British ex-radicals or potential radicals that revolution was no longer necessary. The Labour Party youth organizations, devoted to socialization through parliamentary reform, sapped the Communist Party of new blood. Finally, the new Communist line, which required the party to attack the American Marshall Plan as imperialist and the Labour government as reactionary, antagonized the generally optimistic and patriotic Britons.

As in the United States, the party of revolution succeeded best when it preached revolution least. It yearned for the loyalty of the working classes but had its greatest success among poets and middle-class humanitarians. The intellectuals always needed the party more; the working classes enjoyed the alternatives of the Labour Party and the T.U.C. Because the Communist Party of Great Britain was never master of its own fate and owed first allegiance to another nation, it was never free to adjust its tactics to the realities of Britain. But perhaps even if it had been left free, the desire to see the Russian Revolution re-enacted in Britain would have led its members to that same misreading of the national mood and circumstances which proved fatal time and again.

CHAPTER
9

Students, Artists, and Workers: Left-Wing Protest as a Way of Life

DURING the 1930s protest became a national pastime, rivaling baseba and cricket for the devotion and participation of the American an British peoples. The poor were protesting—marching on Washingtc to demand bread, jobs, and bonuses or on London to plead for th salvation of entire cities; parading down Pennsylvania Avenue wit banners and placards or chaining themselves to palace gates. And eve the workers—sitting down in factories and stores, fighting hired Pinke ton police, and picketing on the docks, all for twenty-five cents mor a week and the right to organize.[1]

But middle-class protest reached new heights. Spurred on by write and other intellectuals, exiles turned from the frivolity of the 192c and its personal preoccupations to soberer social obligations. Th middle classes were aroused—and from their number came picketer paraders, organizers, lecturers, young revolutionaries, and audienc to fill New York City's Union Square and London's Albert Hall wit thunderous applause for Communist speakers. The rise of fascism an the threat of war had activated the middle class, the Depression ha awakened fears and guilts, and social consciousness seemed to be o the move. Many people turned to the left, discovered Marxism in pure or diluted form, and joined the Communists in choruses of the "Internationale." With commendable energy and imagination—though little success—they sought to prove their solidarity with the proletariat, to make up for past dastardly deeds, to ensure the triumph of the inevitable workers' revolution, and thus to become part of "the mainstream of history."

Protest spread like an epidemic over the two countries, and neutrality seemed to vanish. Men spoke up for or against communism, fascism, capitalism, unions, peace, war, and dishwashers in university dining halls. With marching feet and chanting voices they lobbied for and against anything. The Communists set the pace with their May Day parades, overshadowing the humbler efforts of the socialists before them. Thousands gathered in New York's Union Square to cheer revolutionary orators while policemen leaned nervously on machine guns atop surrounding buildings. After the speeches came a parade, in which red banners were waved, placards announcing the coming of the workers' state were held high, and Communist youths led proletarian adaptations of bourgeois football cheers: "Are we in it, well I guess! Communists, Communists, yes, yes, yes!"

On any ordinary day passers-by at Union—or "Red"—Square could hear Marxism, single-tax theory, and overthrow of the government propounded by soapbox philosophers, each clutching the required American flag in his hand. The *Daily Worker* was sold, and radical theater, art, and dance groups clustered in office buildings near the square, turning it into a Communist commons. Nearby, serious young revolutionaries turned out polemical pamphlets by night, rushed them to printers in the morning, and paid for them with promises of a new classless society and I.O.U.'s.

Mass rallies filled London's Albert Hall, where the Left Book Club held mass educational forums for its readers. Left-wing orator J. B. Matthews followed the usual sports events in Madison Square Garden, describing fascism as "essentially . . . capitalism turned nudist" [2] to thunderous applause. In more genteel and cultured tones, a Boston Brahmin returning home from a white-tie dinner stopped to preach socialism to the available members of the proletariat in the city park.

The wealthy and the cultured paid to attend dinners, cocktail parties, garden parties, concerts, theater benefits, and lectures which donated all profits to causes. Collection plates and pails turned up at every gathering of the socially conscious rich, and money was given to finance peace programs, to raise arms for Spain, and to make possible more dinners, garden parties, concerts, and lectures.

In England in 1934 Canon Richard ("Dick") Sheppard invited men who cared for peace to send him postcards saying, "I renounce war, and will never support or sanction another." Within a year his Oxford Peace Pledge Union had eighty thousand members, and soon there were Peace Weeks and Peace Marches through such unlikely towns as Bury, England.

Protest seemed a palliative for the doubts and fears in the minds of men of the 1930s. And the illusion that one was Doing Something Significant was a universal salve. With furious energy, with naïveté, and with foolish gestures middle-class men and women took up protest as a way of life.

No group more vigorously adopted the spirit of the times than did the radical college students. This college generation was far different from that of F. Scott Fitzgerald's Dick Diver. The Depression-era diploma had diminished in value, and the graduates of the 1930s were aptly dubbed the "locked-out generation." One-fourth of all the unemployed were between fifteen and twenty-four years old, and jobless days often followed the glory of degrees *magna cum laude* from Columbia University, Brooklyn College, or Yale University. More than one forlorn pundit sang,

> ... in praise of college
> Of M.A.'s and Ph.D.'s,
> But in pursuit of knowledge
> We are starving by degrees.[3]

The harsh realities of life seemed to have crept inside the ivied walls. The Princeton frolics of the 1920s seemed more and more inappropriate in an era of bread lines, the Works Progress Administration (W.P.A.), and the Third International. The politically concerned students were a sober lot: In the early hours of the morning they argued the advantages of socialism and communism, contemplated the virtues of the working classes, and vowed to cast off decadent bourgeois habits for the Spartan life of the revolutionary. Small bands of young Socialists and Communists—and even F.D.R. Democrats—journeyed among the people, traveling to the Harlan Company coal region in Kentucky, to Appalachian schoolhouses, or to Harlem. In comparison with real-life struggles against fascism, poverty, and capitalism, the sonnets of Shelley and the soliloquies of Shakespeare seemed irrelevant.

Bourgeois campus traditions were the first focus of student protest. The attack was launched in 1932, not by a revolutionary, but by the crusading editor of the Columbia University *Spectator*, Reed Harris. Harris was, if anything, a progressive, a serious young man troubled by the stupidities of college life. In the pages of the *Spectator*, he lampooned that sacred collegiate cow, the fraternity system; shocked conservatives by urging the election of Socialist Norman Thomas; and finally brought the university administration to the boiling point by satirically denouncing "King Football." When Harris turned his eye on evils like labor conditions in the dining halls, the administration laid its heavy hand upon his collar. On April 1, 1932, Harris was expelled.

Communist and Socialist students, who heartily supported Harris' attack on college follies, sprang to his defense. A mass protest, which drew large numbers of nonpoliticals and nonradicals, was organized; a strike was called; and students demanded that Harris be reinstated. At campus rallies radicals delivered impassioned speeches in defense of freedom of press and speech. The defenders of the administration, "the Spartans," were masters of laconic understatement—"It's a lot of bull." They registered their opinion by heckling the radicals, hurling eggs into the crowd, and occasionally beating up picketing students. In the end, the protesters were victorious, and Harris was reinstated.

The student Communists, proponents of the working classes and opponents of bourgeois games like football, celebrated the blow struck for freedom. Unfortunately the only true sons of the proletariat among the students were football players attending Columbia on athletic scholarships—and they were not impressed with the glorious victory.

The only other members of the working class on campus were university employees. Although students picketed and petitioned for the sake of these underprivileged and ununionized workers, they had no luck in bridging the communications gap between the workers and the "enlightened" bourgeoisie. Each year Communist Party students went among university employees to recruit. In the first five years of the Red decade only two workers were persuaded to join the Columbia branch of the party, and, as James Wechsler sadly recalls, the students always felt uncomfortable around these members of the proletariat.

The "Reed Harris strike" ushered in a decade of spring protests. As Nicholas Murray Butler, Columbia's patriarchal president, lamented the bad manners of the youths who continually cluttered his campus with picket signs and rallies, Communist and Socialist students continued to mobilize general student discontent and social guilt in bigger and better demonstrations. In 1933 students struck over the dismissal of the one known Communist instructor at the university, Donald Henderson. The administration had lamely accused Henderson of being a boring classroom lecturer, but protesting students showed a willingness to name large numbers of tenured bores on Columbia's payroll. On this particular administrative decision, the university stood firm; no number of mass meetings, petitions, and stupendous torchlit parades could save Henderson.

The students had their revenge the following spring when they rocked Butler's bastion with not one but two strikes. The first centered on a campus issue of freedom of the press. The second was a strike against war, for by 1933 the Oxford Peace Pledge had reached American students. On campuses like the University of Wisconsin, City College of New York, Brooklyn College, the University of California at Berkeley, and Columbia University, antiwar strikes became regular features of the academic year. In 1937 students staged a peace-pledge gathering of five thousand, all swearing the oath against war in unison, despite a faulty public-address system and a barrage of eggs hurled by men of the R.O.T.C.

For the committed radical student there was little time for classes and studies. There were demonstrations to organize, meetings to attend, opposition meetings to spy on, leaflets to write, slogans to invent, and recruiting to be done. Days were filled with debate or picketing. There were rallies or lectures to picket, even movie premieres. When *Red Salute*, billed as a "slashing satiric attack on undergraduate radicalism," came to the Rivoli Theater in New York, conscientious students responded with a picket line. When there was no strike, no "fascist" speaker to protest, no movie theater to cordon off, no convention or conclave to plan, the daily life of student leaders of such organizations as the American Student Union resembled the more familiar bourgeois routine called office life.

As the Communist Party's Popular Front phase moved into high gear in the 1930s, attacks on the collegiate life style began to fade. One did not have to be a fanatic about a little honest collegiate fun. At the 1938 A.S.U. convention, after clearing away the serious business of censuring Columbia's *Spectator* for carrying Horn & Hardart ads during an automat strike, delegates found time to relax at a good old-fashioned college dance, swing band and all. For entertainment a skit was presented—"The Marxist Brothers Still at College"—and *The New Masses* writer Joseph Starobin reported that students came away singing the catchy lyrics of

> Alma Mater's going modern,
> Old Man Reaction's feeling blue,
> It's the academic epidemic:
> Gonna join the A.S.U.

Before the conclave ended, students danced the traditional snake dance around a bonfire on Vassar College's Poughkeepsie campus.

Protest was increasingly becoming a form of social gathering; young radical boys fell in love with young radical girls on picket lines, passed notes at "bureau meetings" of the Young Communist League, and expected a swing band at every convention. In 1939, just as the A.S.U. was to make its final bow on the academic scene, the conventioneers held a rally replete with confetti, ushers in caps and gowns, and cheerleaders shouting "Go Democracy, Beat Reaction!"

More seriously than the young people on college campuses, authors, dancers, playwrights, poets, and intellectuals dedicated themselves at the altar of the social revolution. Gone were the selfish days of the 1920s when art had seemed to exist for its own sake and the artist had felt no obligation to anyone but himself. The artist—with his penchant for extremes—now longed passionately to serve society, to awaken the masses, and to dramatize Marx in story and song.

A revolution began to unfold in the world of *belles lettres*. Art was declared a weapon to be turned against bourgeois traditions, just as the peasant might brandish his pitchfork against Cossacks, or the worker his tools against Henry Ford.

Not only did artists pledge never again to write decadent bourgeois pieces; all such works were to be denounced in full. Granville Hicks, of *The New Masses*, made a public apology for having loved the work of Marcel Proust before his conversion to communism. Writer Mike Gold, the most outspoken supporter of proletarian art, donned metaphoric sackcloth and ashes for continuing to admire Gilbert and Sullivan. "To me," the novelist Jack Conroy said in 1935, "a strike bulletin or an impassioned leaflet are of more moment than 300 prettily and falsely written pages about the private woes of a gigolo or the biological woes of a society dame about as useful to society as the buck brush which infests Missouri cow pastures and takes all the sustenance out of the soil." [4] So deeply ran this sense of commitment that a symphony-orchestra musician might refuse on principle to play if the conductor programmed a composition by a known aristocrat or reactionary.

In England a new school of poets challenged the restrained and aristocratic style of such Bloomsbury predecessors as Virginia Woolf. These new poets—W. H. Auden, Stephen Spender, Cecil Day Lewis, Louis MacNeice—gathered around them young men and women who hoped to speak with a political consciousness.

With enthusiasm the artists of the 1930s began to rattle their weapons. Radical magazines carried tales entitled "Monday Morning in the Machine Shop" and "Overtime on Aero Engines." In England left-wing theater groups were organized. The Group Theater was formed in 1932, and its playwrights tried to produce socially conscious drama. Auden and Christopher Isherwood contributed *Dance of Death*, in which fascism and the cult of athletics—both apparently major threats to England at the time—were condemned. In the Auden-Isherwood drama all attempts to solve social problems fail until at the end Karl Marx appears as a *deus ex machina*, escorted by two young Communists. As Marx smiles benevolently upon the audience, a chorus sings the praises of the prophet who revealed the meaning of life:

> Oh, Mr. Marx, you've gathered
> All the material facts.
> You know the economic
> Reasons for our acts.

The Group Theater had difficulty sustaining devotion to the propagandistic rather than aesthetic aspects of drama. Throughout his career "Uncle Wiz," as Auden was called, was more than willing to serve as the poetic voice of "the people," but he never developed an affection for the people for whom he spoke. When in 1936 he journeyed to Spain to serve as an ambulance driver, he came in close contact with the workers and peasants whom he had glorified. After only two months he returned to his England—never to speak publicly of his Spanish experience.

Although the Group Theater lapsed into aestheticism, its rival, the Unity Theater, stuck to a regimen of plays dramatizing the struggles of the labor movement. When the Group Theater made arrangements to stage a production at the Unity playhouse, the politically pure Unity group boycotted the performances.

In the United States left-wing theater groups also flourished. Angry young playwrights often began careers at the Workers Laboratory Theater, located reassuringly near Union Square. Among them was Clifford Odets, who at twenty-eight and while living (it was claimed) on ten cents a day, had written his first play, *Awake and Sing*. His second effort, *Waiting for Lefty*—about a taxi strike—was hailed as the finest proletarian drama of the era. Lefty, spokesman for the striking drivers, never returns to his waiting comrades. He has been murdered by the hired goons of the employer. The drivers resolve to continue their struggle. As the play ends, one of the workers steps forward to shout across the footlights to the audience: "Hello, America, hello. We're stormbirds of the working class. . . . And when we die, they'll know what we did to make a new world. . . ." And the audience, many members of which had no doubt taken taxis to the theater, shouted their solidarity with the workers: "Strike! Strike! Strike!"

Odets himself had never seen an actual strike. His next play, *Till the Day I Die*, which laid bare life in Nazi Germany, was inspired by a letter published in *The New Masses*. Like many of his colleagues, Odets willingly devoted his life during the thirties to writing about revolution and sacrifice, although his experiences with those on whom he based his characters were few and limited.

If Auden remained an aristocrat by temperament and Odets had no personal experience of proletarian life, there were talented young working-class revolutionaries determined to create a new literature. For a brief moment "bottom dog" literature came into its shaky own, nourished by the Communist-run John Reed Clubs and encouraged by the kindly Marxist editors of magazines like *The New Masses*.

The new writers gathered in cafeterias on Fourteenth Street, in club lofts above the Chicago Loop, or in *The New Republic*'s Washington, D.C., waiting rooms. Each longed to write the proletarian novel, poem, or play on the experiences of the disinherited.

All these young writers were drawn to the Communist Party, which provided a political justification for their literary efforts. The party gave these writers a sense of community, through the John Reed Clubs, and a chance to publish, for each club put out its own magazine. Proletarian efforts filled the pages of *Blast*, *Dynamo*, and *Anvil*.

In return, writers marched in May Day parades, aspiring poets wrote beautiful slogans for picketers' placards, and both joined the American Writers' Congress. Yet more was demanded of these men, and in the end the Communists squeezed writers into a mold that made creativity impossible. The demands of proletcult, of art as a social weapon, proved to be a conspiracy against the talented. Rather than drawing upon their own experiences, they found themselves writing the same tale of class struggle, with the same moral, again and again.

At its best the proletarian novel was a disaster. In 1935 *The New Masses* awarded its first—and last—prize for a "novel on a proletarian theme" to Clara Weatherwax's *Marching, Marching*, the tale of a young mill worker, Pete, in whose veins course the proletarian blood of his mother and the capitalist blood of his unlawful father, the mill owner. To which class will Pete swear loyalty? The working-class heritage proves triumphant; Pete joins the Communist Party and shows his devotion by assaulting his father. Throughout the book Miss Weatherwax depicts the trials of the harassed but undaunted workers. A Mexican Communist worker is kidnapped and beaten; vigilantes raid the homes of the innocent; and the book ends with unarmed strikers marching on the militia to suffer certain massacre.

Rarely did the class struggle, so vividly portrayed in *Marching*,

Marching and *Waiting for Lefty*, touch the daily lives of its propagandists. Once, however, in June 1934, Publishers' Row enjoyed its own strike. The Macaulay Company, a small publishing firm, was struck by its editorial and clerical staff. Writers hurried to the scene to lend support to strike leaders Isidor Schneider and Susan Brown. The picket line soon boasted such literary luminaries as Malcolm Cowley, Matthew Josephson, and Mike Gold. Josephson later described the scene as "a sunlit day of late spring; and for us, who habitually worked alone, it was a joyful occasion to come together outdoors and give expression to our public spirit and our fellow feeling for the Macaulay clerks." [5]

The strike had an air of merriment, of a social gathering to be joined for thirty minutes or an hour, as one's schedule permitted. When the police finally moved in and arrested eighteen authors, Cowley kept the group in high spirits by singing sea chanteys in the cell. After two hours the judge dismissed them all.

Although the intellectuals' experience in the class struggle proved slight, the challenge of educating others to the task remained. In 1936 Victor Gollancz took up that challenge in earnest. Gollancz, an Oxford-trained Jew-turned-Christian Socialist, circumvented the English booksellers' ban on Marxist literature by establishing the Left Book Club. The club required no dues. For 2/6 a month members were sent the monthly selection in a soft orange binding. With the books they also received *Left News*, a combination magazine and catalog. Gollancz conceived of the club as a means to educate and then to organize ordinary men and women in a united front against fascism. He found in this second half of the decade an eager market among the alienated and crusading English middle class. Within six months twenty thousand people had joined the club, and only twelve months later the monthly choice was sent to fifty thousand Britons.

Left Book Club readers not only read the works selected by Gollancz, Harold Laski, and John Strachey; they also formed local clubs to discuss the merits of these books. The local groups numbered more than one thousand at their peak and served their members not only as open forums but as social gatherings as well. The *Left News* called upon each to pass out leaflets and to proselytize in other ways, encouraged summer conclaves, and urged regular membership drives.

Gollancz's readers took debate and discussion seriously and were more than willing to travel to London for the mass club meetings held in the Albert Hall to protest the Japanese invasion of China or to raise funds for the Republicans in Spain. Yet these social critics took pains always to mix pleasure with business. A glance at any summer edition of the *Left News* reveals reports of "open-air events" like the meeting of the Sevenoaks Group in the woods at Roughetts Platt. "This is an enchanting spot," says the report. "The rhododendrons were in full bloom and the weather was perfect. Miss MacNaghten spoke on Amber Blanco White's book and her address was greatly appreciated." There seemed no reason, in that decade of protest, not to enjoy good, right-thinking company and the open air in the grand British tradition.

While students protested *for* the working class and intellectuals urged the working class to protest for itself, British and American workers were simply doing their best to survive. With shockingly little knowledge of Karl Marx and of their heroism as documented by Miss Weatherwax, desperate workers attempted their own modest upheaval in the 1930s.

Alas for the intellectual revolutionaries—and perhaps for the workers as well—the miners in Harlan County, Kentucky, and the welders in the General Motors plants in Detroit had no visions of overthrowing the capitalist system, destroying the bourgeoisie, or establishing a workers' state. Their goals were modest, their problems mundane: They sought jobs, food, higher wages, and shorter hours.

For these modest goals they willingly protested and often devoted their lives to the task. That the risk for these men was greater in real terms than any that Victor Gollancz would ever know did not make miners, riveters, or the unemployed the stormbirds of that revolution to which middle-class Marxists subscribed.

The most common kind of protest in the 1930s was the strike. But in Jarrow, in the north of England, there was no employer to strike against, no factory or job to walk out on. In 1934 Jarrow was a dying industrial town; 80 percent of its work force was unemployed. Neither the British Trades Union Council nor the British government offered help for Jarrow's revival. Petitions were met by silence from the Board of Trade; Jarrow, said the Board's president, must save itself.

To save itself, Jarrow decided to bring its case before the nation, to protest its neglect in some spectacular manner. The town began a crusade. Two hundred of its citizens made ready to march on London; £800 were raised for the journey, and £1 per man was carefully set aside for the long train ride home. With the rest of the money the townspeople bought leather and nails (to repair boots along the road) and waterproof groundsheets (to double for sleeping and as rain-capes). The British Boy Scouts donated field-kitchen equipment. And, with the last of the funds raised, Jarrowites purchased a secondhand bus to carry their supplies.

On October 4, 1934, the Jarrow-to-London march began. The town bid the men farewell with cheering and a brass band. At the same moment, ten similar marches were beginning in ten other English towns; all converged on London to protest the Means Test (the financial investigation to which applicants for unemployment relief were subjected). London was about to be besieged by bedraggled and lean armies of workers.

Along their route the Jarrowites were greeted warmly. Towns gave them food, lodging, and money. M.P.s of every political party outdid one another to organize the welcomes. The British government, however, was less than cordial. The Cabinet issued a statement while the men were still on the road: The marches were condemned as disruptive, and it was announced that no delegation would be given audience.

Despite this statement, the Jarrow crusade continued. One month after the men had begun their march, they reached London's Hyde Park. Thousands turned out to greet them, banners were raised, and songs were sung.

The government did, after all, see the Jarrow delegation and read the town's petition. The men returned home; the crusade had ended. No help came to Jarrow.

For some workers, especially in the United States, help came in the second half of the decade. In 1935 John L. Lewis and his C.I.O. began to offer greatly increased opportunities for self-help to industrial workers. And in 1936 strikes broke out in industries all over the country: Especially in the towns that Henry Ford had built, in the automobile factories of Detroit and Flint, a workers' rebellion was on.

Throughout its history the automobile industry had tried its best to discourage unions. A man overzealous in union activity usually found himself unemployed. Leaders of the abortive strikes in 1932 were blacklisted at Briggs and General Motors. Men did organize secretly, but even so the risk was great: General Motors was inclined to put labor spies in all its plants and in fact spent twice as much for private detectives as it paid its president. In three years, $419,850 went to the Pinkerton Agency, the private police force to which Henry Ford was partial.

But in 1936 the National Recovery Administration (the N.R.A., or, as the workers called it, the National Run Around) gave its blessing to unionization. At the same time the United Auto Workers broke with the A.F.L. and joined the more active and radical C.I.O.

In December 1936 the U.A.W. began an organizing campaign in earnest. Union leaders went to General Motors Executive Vice-President William Knudsen to ask for a conference on collective bargaining. Knudsen said no. At a Fisher Body plant in Cleveland, Ohio, Knudsen's loyal workers heard the news and sat down. The battle was on.

Fisher Body Plant No. 2 in Flint was the next to go. The sitdown began with a carnival air. It was New Year's Eve, and the men decided to celebrate with liquor and two obliging prostitutes. The next day, when the celebration ended, the neutral and casual protestors drifted out, and a hard core of about one hundred men settled in for the duration. There would be no more liquor and no more women. The men began to discipline themselves. They made their beds in the unfinished car bodies on the assembly line, dubbing these makeshift homes "Hotel Astor" or "the Ritz." Each man showered once a day, did his share of cleaning and sweeping in the plant, and was careful to do no damage to General Motors' private property.

In January the men in Flint Fisher No. 1 heard rumors that General Motors was removing tools and dies for transportation to plants where union strength was negligible; 1,500 men at Fisher No. 1 sat down. They quickly organized a strike committee, which assigned specific duties to each striker. They set up a post office and a public-address system so that men could communicate with one another and with the picketers outside. To while away their time these strikers played cards or listened to the daily concert offered by the workmen's band.

The sitdown epidemic spread from the Detroit area to auto plants in Anderson, Indiana; Kansas City, Missouri; Norwood, Ohio; and Atlanta, Georgia. But it was in the Detroit constellation of plants that the fate of the union was to be decided.

On January 12 General Motors tried a pressure tactic. The heat was shut off in Fisher Body Plant No. 2. Management followed through by sending its own private police to surround the plant and to prevent food from reaching the men inside. News of the freeze-and-starve technique reached union leaders. Victor Reuther—one of three Reuther brothers all active in organizing the U.A.W. strikes—drove to the plant with a loudspeaker attached to his car. Reuther's voice boomed out a polite request to the General Motors guards—please let the food carriers pass. When there was no response, Reuther changed his request to a demand. Again there was no response. Reuther's third message was a threat: Violence would follow if the guards did not make way.

Within minutes pickets had rushed the police guards, had broken through their lines, and were hoisting coffee pails and buns to the hungry men inside. But the guards regrouped, charged the pickets, and drove them into the building. The strikers inside responded with a barrage of available objects. Coffee mugs, pop bottles, and two-pound auto hinges were thrown. From Reuther's sound truck a voice could be heard shouting: "We wanted peace. General Motors chose war. Give it to 'em!" [6]

The workers carried the day. They drove the police back with spray from a huge fire hose. As the guards retreated from the scene, the workers cheered their victory, dubbing the episode "the Battle of the Running Bulls."

Little time was lost in calling the National Guard to Flint, but General Motors was anxious to try persuasion once more before turning to force. Late in January the company reopened all unstruck plants. A back-to-work campaign was on. Labor leaders realized that they had to make a spectacular and crippling move soon.

The key Detroit area plant was Chevy No. 4, where engines were manufactured. If labor could take this plant, General Motors could be brought to heel. But the U.A.W. had no more than fifty loyal men in No. 4, discounting company spies and recent recruits. Then Roy Reuther came up with a plan. By diverting attention to a nearby plant, Chevy No. 9, union men could draw guards away from No. 4.

On January 29 Victor Reuther was again in his sound truck, this time circling Chevy No. 9. On signal Roy and a band of men began a noisy attempt to take this plant over. General Motors troops rushed to the rescue, pouring out of all nearby plants to check the attack. Only a skeleton crew remained at the real target, No. 4. While guards triumphed over Reuther's men at No. 9, the heavy machinery at No. 4 slowed to a halt. The engine plant was silent.

Barricades were put up; gondolas loaded with thousands of pounds of iron and steel blocked the doors. A union man climbed a fence around the plant to address the crowds below: "We want the whole world to know what we are fighting for. We are fighting for freedom and life and liberty. This is our great opportunity. What if we should be defeated? What if we should be killed? We have only one life. That is all we can lose and we might as well die like heroes as like slaves." [7]

General Motors capitulated. On February 11, 1937, the strikers marched out of the plants and down Chevy Avenue. The union had actually won very little for the men, but the successful act of defiance seemed sufficient for these workers to claim a great victory.

Detroit's troubles were not over, however. The sitdown had caught on. In March 192,000 men and women took part in sitdown strikes, and most of them were in the auto city.

The sitdown became a common means of protest. Everywhere strikers sang the praise of the union and its methods:

> When they tie a can to a union man,
>   Sit-down! Sit-down!
> When they give him the sack, they'll take him back,
>   Sit-down! Sit-down!

> When the speed-up comes, just twiddle your thumbs,
>   Sit-down! Sit-down!
> When the boss won't talk, don't take a walk,
>   Sit-down! Sit-down! [8]

Across the country, workers were sitting down. It became a national craze. Soda jerks in corner drugstores seized control and locked the bosses out. Five-and-dime employees sat down in Woolworths all over the country. And in Chicago Negro wet nurses sat down for higher pay per ounce of milk. The workers had found their form of protest.

While the workers in Detroit were winning their protest, the diamond-decked proletariat of Hollywood was mustering its forces for a grand display. During the "Red Decade," Beverly Hills stars identified closely with fellow wage slaves everywhere. On New Year's Eve, amid champagne and caviar canapés, the workers of Hollywood sang the "Internationale."

Communism and Marx had come to the West Coast, and the movie crowd, eager for leading roles in any great drama, turned left. To capture the stars' imagination and appeal to their love of intrigue, the Communist Party introduced its Hollywood supervisor as a "scarred veteran of the European underground." Actually the veteran was a Los Angeles taxi driver. He must have been successful, however, for the number of delighted converts increased. Hundreds of people in the movie industry signed up for formal study groups in Marxism, taking pseudonyms for their party careers. And they made proselytizing speeches between takes on the set.

Tirelessly the stars gave time and money for radical causes. Their fund-raising galas had the glamor of movie premieres. They were devoted egalitarians, but invitations to one fund-raising party for antifascism excluded anyone who earned less than $1,500. Protest followed the pecking order in Hollywood.

The screenwriters were the most intellectual and the most seriously committed of the Hollywood Communists. In the 1950s many of them were to pay for their connection with the party by being blacklisted, which ruined many careers. There was a sad irony to this fate, for, although they had given of their time and money to the party, their political protests had not shone through on celluloid. Hollywood was full of revolutionaries who wrote screenplays that members of the D.A.R. found delightful family fun, like *Radio City Revels* and *Sorority House*. The peak of protest came in a now-forgotten film, in which a devoted Communist filled in a blank moment by whistling the "Internationale." In the early 1940s two movies evincing admiration for Stalinism were made in Hollywood—*Mission to Moscow* and *Song of*

Russia. But by then the Soviet Union was an ally of the United States.

During the first half of the 1930s, liberals and socialists in Britain and the United States had watched the rise of Nazism and fascism with steadily growing anger and fear. The Spanish Civil War provided an outlet for their hatred of totalitarianism and militarism. Support of the Spanish Republic against Franco and the Falange became the most important way in which Anglo-American liberals protested the menace from the Right between 1936 and 1938. They did not inquire carefully into the labyrinthine complexities of Spanish politics and society that had brought on the Civil War. Nor did they reflect on the Soviet Union's motivation for its aid to the Republic and on Communist tactics during the war. They did not ponder the significance of Spanish leftist massacres of priests and nuns but only the atrocities perpetrated by the Falange. It was enough for these liberals to know that in Spain the forces of democracy were fighting for survival against fascism. Spain became the Holy Grail of men of good will, and the Civil War the Armageddon of democracy.

In 1936 the Hollywood revolutionaries raised money to send an ambulance to Spain to aid the Loyalist forces. Many of the big stars autographed the shiny new vehicle. Across the country in swank East River apartments wealthy New Yorkers in formal dress and jewels played roulette, blackjack, and craps to raise money for the Spanish Loyalists. In West Side apartments men and women of more moderate means danced to radio music and drank punch at twenty-five cents a glass. The punch money was donated to the Loyalists. And in England men and women collected funds for Spain with the plea "Give—give until it hurts. It will not hurt so much as a bullet in the belly. . . ." [9]

For many the Spanish Civil War was the most important and the most tragic event of the decade. It seemed to be the moment of truth for young men and women who had sworn support for Communist ideals and resistance to fascism. From England four thousand men went to fight in the International Brigades. Many were actually militant members of the working class, English and Scottish, often Jewish, many unemployed. They were not men of heroic appearance; they were ordinary men, "very much like the men you meet at any football match, and still more like the men who march in a May Day procession." [10] It was these ordinary men whom Auden had spent years championing but could not bear to be with.

Yet there were also English intellectuals, many of whom had sat at the feet of "Uncle Wiz," who chose to go to Spain precisely because it offered the opportunity to make real contact with the working classes. The chance to leave the ivoried towers of Eton and Oxford, to share a genuine experience with the proletariat, moved young poets and writers to cross the frontier into Spain.

Julian Bell was one such young man, and he became a heroic symbol for his generation. Born into the detached intellectual world of Bloomsbury, he was raised to be an artist and a pacifist. His father, Clive Bell, was a brilliant and influential art critic; his mother was the sister of Virginia Woolf. Yet when the Spanish war broke out, Julian's sense of commitment defeated his heritage of detachment: "It is impossible to let other people go and fight for what one believes in and refuse the risk oneself." [11] Julian Bell repudiated the *summum bonum* of Bloomsbury. He could not devote his life to art alone or to the perfecting of a private life of taste and culture. And he could no longer treat a vow of pacifism as a sacred pledge. Nonresistance to Franco and fascism meant certain death to all that he valued and to all that his pacifist family exemplified. In 1936 Bell went to Spain as an ambulance driver for Spanish Medical Aid. He had no desire to be a hero or a martyr; he intended eventually to return to England and to begin a career in British politics. But on July 18, 1937, the first anniversary of the outbreak of the war, he was killed in the bombing of Brunete.

A second young Briton, John Cornford, followed a similar path to Spain. Cornford was a poet, the son of an eminent authority on Greek philosophy, and was at Cambridge among his Elizabethan histories when the war broke out. He was a Communist and a leader of the left-wing political organizations at the university. When news of Spain reached him, he decided to make the journey south, not to fight but to observe. He merely wanted to see what was happening; he wanted to see in action that war against the Right and the concurrent revolution on the Left of which he had often dreamed.

Cornford went to Spain in 1936. On the third day of his visit in Barcelona he enlisted in a militia unit organized by the Trotskyite Partido Obrero de Unificación Marxista (Workers' Party of Marxist Unity), or the P.O.U.M. After several months in the army he fell ill and returned to England to recuperate. In England he organized a group of volunteers to return with him to Spain. Behind him he left a career and a fiancée. Sometime between December 26 and 28 John Cornford was killed in the battle for Lopera. He had just turned twenty-one.[12]

Before the 1930s had ended, Europe was at war with itself, and protest had been submerged in patriotism. Hollywood stars still went to gala fund-raising events, but they were for Liberty Bonds. Students enlisted to fight the Hitlerian hordes. Many radical intellectuals reconsidered and renounced their ideological commitments. In the 1950s ex-radical Daniel Bell declared an end to ideology and thus to the fierce commitments that had inspired picketing, marching, and calls for social revolution not so long before. In the confident and prosperous 1950s the only effective means of protest was to drop out of society.

CHAPTER

10

Anticolonialism: Gandhi and the Indian Experience

THE British Raj: imperialist aggressors, exploiters of the Indian subcontinent, repressive tyrants betraying the principles of their own civilization. Or the British Raj: benevolent despots, peacemakers in India, enlightened rulers bringing order and efficiency where chaos had reigned and training in the most precious element of the Western tradition, democracy. Two views: one couched in the rhetoric of Indian nationalism, the other in that of the British administrators of India.[1]

The theme of economic distress and oppression was a fundamental part of the rhetoric of Indian nationalism. Nationalists pointed to India's poverty and charged—but did not prove—that this poverty was the fault of the British Empire. The authors of this charge were themselves generally middle-class Indians enjoying at least fair economic security. Their argument was simple: India was poor; it was ruled by Britain; British interests took goods and money out of India to Britain; therefore India's poverty was caused by British rule.

To describe the source of the charge is not to prove it false, but the failings of British economic policy in India show evidence of negative rather than of positive harm. Nineteenth-century Indians spoke often of the "drain" on India caused by the British by which they meant that there was a steady flow of gold and goods out of the country which was not balanced by an equal influx of goods of any kind. This drain, they claimed, impoverished India and caused the rural poverty and periodic famines that plagued the country.

There had been an actual drain of goods from India during the latter part of the eighteenth century and probably extending into the nineteenth, but it resulted less from British actions than from failures to act. Tariffs are a good example. British economic policy, the famous laissez-faire, prevented the creation of protective tariffs on goods coming into India; emergent Indian industries were thus left to the mercies of general competition. Only once did the British government take positive action directly against Indian interests—and that was to establish a tariff on Indian cotton in order to protect the Lancashire wool industry. But this move was the exception. British economic failure in India was generally the result of the absence of any action at all.

Not that the British Empire in India did not operate in the long run against the interests of Indians. The destruction of village industries through European competition and the failure to establish modern industries are probable evidence of the destructive effects of British rule. It has been argued that the passion of the British governors for caution and economy kept them from undertaking programs that would have been beneficial to the country and policies that might have led to the eventual industrialization of India. But if India failed to progress, it seems fair to say that it was less because of the conscious policy of its rulers than because of the combination of current economic fashion and the unconscious, though consistent, British pursuit of imperial interests. British policy *may* have damaged the Indian economy, and India's poverty *may* have been a function of British rule. But twenty years after independence and partition, it is more difficult and less convincing to charge British imperialism alone with the responsibility.

If the theme of poverty and economic oppression was fundamental to the rhetoric of nationalism, that of "enlightenment" was at the heart of British imperial self-justification. The British viewed themselves as civilizers (later and more politely as modernizers), as the mentors of a country in political apprenticeship. They constantly stressed their role in bringing first peace and then democracy to the turbulent subcontinent. At times—after the catastrophic Mutiny of 1857 and in the twentieth century—this argument was put forth with less self-confidence and conviction than at other times during their two-hundred-year rule. But it was never abandoned as the statement of British purpose and the justification of British presence in India.

Most interestingly, it was adopted to some extent by Indians, as well as by English writers, both before and after Independence. The Indian obverse of this theme was that India sought, demanded, pressed for independence from a reluctant though benevolent Empire. Its demands were not made, however, with the violence and bloodshed of other (lesser) revolutions but with the force of reason, conviction, and moral purity; India employed those nonviolent methods fundamental to Indian nature and basic to Indian tradition to obtain the liberal and democratic processes that the West had taught India to value.

The emphasis on these themes, mutually flattering to both India and England, has given twentieth-century Indian politics a peculiarly friendly tone, at least in retrospect. It has certainly led to a de-emphasis, if not an ignoring, of the reality of psychological oppression carried out by the imperialist power in the country that it ruled, a form of oppression at which the British, with a sort of national genius for imperial arrogance, excelled.

British rule was only sporadically oppressive *politically*. The general political atmosphere in colonial India, which the British sought to encourage, was one in which free discussion and debate were tolerated if not enjoyed. This policy coincided both with the British self-image and with British political ideals. The political atmosphere was freer in the nineteenth century, however, when the threat of Indian opposition was smaller. In the twentieth century, when opposition was growing among the Indian communities, the British responded with increasingly repressive measures. They did so, however, at a cost to their own self-respect and to the image of themselves that they had built in Indian eyes.

Nevertheless, in psychological terms, British rule was always oppressive. (To do them justice, the British were only rarely aware of the traumatizing effect of their presence on the Indian population.) They assumed their own moral and political superiority and expected the Indians to do the same. The manner in which this attitude was expressed varied according to the subtlety of the personalities involved, but the basic attitude—unconscious racism—did not vary greatly. Nor did the British consider that this attitude might affect the way in which Indians behaved. Their definition of "Indian" was of an inferior; they did not consider that such a condition could be created.

Not even the passage of twenty years, which has softened many animosities into a more romantic benevolence, can mask the evidence that twentieth-century Indians were aware of the British opinion of them and that this awareness affected their behavior. Mohandas K. Gandhi talked and worried about the emasculation of his race. Jawaharlal Nehru spoke of the fear and inability to act that paralyzed Indians under the Raj. This psychological oppression extended beyond personal relationships. The British system of education in India provided instruction in Western subjects in the English language; its effect was to instill in native students a sense of intellectual tutelage and insecurity, the consequences of which were both complex and extensive.

British assertion of superiority in all areas and general acceptance of this assertion by the educated Indian elite created in the latter a need to win British approval and a corresponding need to escape from British domination and therefore rule. The legacy of disdain for things "Indian," for Indian traditions and beliefs, which is still found among English-educated Indians may well be the most durable feature of British imperial rule.

The British always maintained that the Indians, the "real" Indians, did not care who governed them as long as they were governed well. The corollary was that the Indian nationalists were representative not of the real Indians but only of themselves. The masses of Indians, if they were to speak, would not speak with the voice of the nationalist Congress Party. To that charge the party replied that it was indeed representative of the real India, that it spoke for the masses, who were not content with the British government.

Anticolonial protest in India usually took the form of nonviolent movements initiated and participated in by a relatively small group; there were also large-scale and chaotic mass riots, murders, and other violence, however.

The Sepoy Mutiny of 1857 was the single most violent episode in the long history of surface peace between the British rulers and their Indian subjects. Mass hysteria, mass murders, and mass revenge characterized the Mutiny. No historian has discovered significant evidence to substantiate the charge that an India-wide plot had precipitated the Mutiny. Rather, the violence seemed to occur spontaneously in different regions, set off by local incidents; it would then be fed by rumors about what was happening in other areas. The outbursts arose from anger and frustration against European authority, which had been growing in the period of British rule.

The Mutiny was not a planned revolution but a series of violent, chaotic outbursts. Indians turned on Europeans and attacked them in a racial struggle. Because of their own liberal and rational attitudes toward administration, the British officials had eliminated, or thought that they had eliminated, open conflict and violence in the society that they governed. But they had not fully appreciated the extent to which fear, frustration, hatred, and potential violence made up the dark side of such a paternalistic relationship. The English regarded the uprisings as a betrayal by the Indian population that they had taken under their protection and guidance and from whom they had expected gratitude and affection in return. Instead, they had suddenly experienced the full force of hatred and murder. One legacy of this struggle was increased bitterness and fundamental distrust among the English ruling group toward Indians in later years of the Raj.

After much debate the British government in India had established in 1833 a system of higher education in India: The language of instruction was English, the subjects to be studied Western humanities and science. The original intent of this system was partly practical—to bring into existence a group of Indians competent enough in the English language to work in the administration of the British Raj. But besides such practicalities there was also the romantic belief that, through this system of education, the Westernization of India could begin, that the knowledge and technology of the West imparted first to this small class would filter down through Indian society and would eventually penetrate to all levels.

In the end, the results were not that neat. The lessons of both Western propaganda and Western technology were isolated and separated from the mass of Indian society by the rapid and effective functioning of the caste system, which the British failed to anticipate. Over the next twenty to thirty years, however, English education did create a class with a common intellectual background and common aspirations. Known as the English-educated elite, it continued to exist throughout the British Raj and provided the core membership for later political movements against the government.

The first signs of the emergence of this class appeared in the 1840s and 1850s in Calcutta. Western-oriented Indian clubs and societies began to be formed, and there began to be reports that the older, more traditional generation was being scandalized by the pranks of the Western-educated students. The English-educated elite was romantically devoted to the British government, with whom its interests were strongly identified. During the Sepoy Mutiny the Calcutta elite's loyalty to the British Raj was total. Although perhaps the oft-quoted prophesy of Lord Macaulay that the education system would create a class of Indians "Indian in blood and color, but English in taste, in opinions, in morals and in intellect," had not been completely fulfilled, certainly the system had created a group with a particularly "British" point of view. This group soon began to develop also in Bombay and Madras and later throughout India.

In 1885, at the suggestion of A. O. Hume and with the encouragement of the Governor General, Lord Dufferin, the first all-India National Congress was held. Initially the Congress was to be composed of those Indians with an interest in politics; its purpose was not, at least in British eyes, to serve as an Indian Parliament but to provide an institutionalized forum for the expression of Indian opinions. ("Indian politicians should meet yearly and point out to the Government in what respects the administration was defective and how it could be improved," the Governor General said.[2]) In addition, it was hoped that if potential demagogues were given the outlet of such meetings, they would be prevented from seeking other, more dangerous forms of expression.

Clearly the Indians who attended in 1885 and those who came to later sessions perceived the Congress in another light. Saturated as the English-educated elite was with eighteenth- and nineteenth-century writings on the British system of government, they could not help but see in the Congress a "national" body and (according to one statesman, looking back from 1925) a group that could agitate for power and its own interests.

The first generation of Indian politicos arose at the end of the nineteenth century and were identified by their successors as the "moderates." Tied to British ideals and values that they had been educated to think were better than their own, they had faith and confidence in the rulers of their country. The tone and emotion of the moderates' writings bring the term "sycophant" to mind, but the label is somewhat unjust. British power over India and British education in the schools had created a relationship less self-serving than sycophancy. It was not simply self-interest that caused these men to speak to the British with praise and devotion, although certainly many must have found it both pleasant and prestigious to associate with the mighty. But behind their rhetoric was a devastating sincerity, the product of a generation of romantics and also, unfortunately, of a generation marked by insecurity and self-abasement, convinced of the inadequacy of its own tradition. Eager to re-create Britain in India, these men accepted their places in the Raj as tutelaries, fully believing that when on some distant day they had learned well and fully the lessons of self-government, they would be rewarded with the greatest gift that the British could give: self-government.

In 1905, for reasons of administrative efficiency, the Governor General of India, Lord Curzon, decreed the partition of Bengal into two provinces, one to be primarily Muslim, the other Hindu. It was in Bengal that "nationalism" had had its beginnings and that newly aroused loyalties and emotional ties to provincial culture were strongest. The belief that these new nationalist feelings were being attacked, as well as fury at the arbitrary manner in which the decision had been carried out, set off sharp local protest, which turned in some areas into communal riots. The Bengalis boycotted British goods in an attempt to force a reversal of the decision. In the ensuing debate among the educated elite over the degree and nature of support to be given to this movement, a marked difference in approach became increasingly apparent among the delegates to the Congress.

Since the last decade of the nineteenth century the rise of an "extremist" wing had been apparent. Leadership was growing, in both Bombay and Bengal, that did not accept the beliefs and practices of the moderates. In part, the differences between the two groups resulted from the maturing of a new generation more impatient and less trusting than its predecessor. Gopal Krishna Gokhale, one of the leading moderates, spoke of the disaffection from moderation and British aims among the young. In the late nineteenth and early twentieth centuries in both Bengal and Bombay a terrorist movement, composed largely of young students, developed. Its efforts were not unified but consisted mostly of random acts of violence directed primarily against the British Raj. The terrorists' object was to cause the disintegration of the governmental functions of the Empire through chaos and random destruction. The movement, particularly in Bengal, was an interesting amalgamation of Western revolutionary ethics and Indian religious traditions. Technically it was organized into loosely connected revolutionary cells. The cells, their structure, and the relations between the members and their leaders had deep roots in the religious tradition of Bengal. The cell leaders were semireligious figures with disciples in the tradition of Bengali mendicants; each disciple was bound to the leader—not to the others or to the group—by loyalty and devotion similar to those that bound religious disciples to their gurus. The cells, or *dals*, as they were called, were much involved with the worship of the Bengali goddess Kali and with sacrifices and initiation rites connected to this goddess.

These cells were successful in creating an atmosphere of terror, but because their ties to one another were so tenuous they frequently suffered from internal and intercell competitiveness. As the loyalty of the cell members was to the leaders, the cells easily disintegrated when leaders died or were arrested. Many cell members later in the 1920s joined the activities of the Congress Party itself.

There was a definite tendency in the younger generation not to follow the moderates' lead, but the difference between moderates and extremists was one of temperament as well. The moderates essentially believed in British liberalism, as they had been taught to do. The extremist leaders did not have the same romantic faith in British benevolence. Their appraisal of power relations was more realistic. The division between the two groups was exemplified by two leaders from the high-caste Chitpavan Brahmin community of Poona: Bal Gangadhar Tilak, until his death in 1920 the leader of the extremist faction, and Gokhale, leader of the moderates. Although members of the same generation, the two exhibited a marked difference in temperament. Gokhale was mild, sensitive, shy, and concerned with people's opinions of him; he was diffident on the subject of the British Raj and his position in it. "Perhaps in ten years time," he told one Englishman, "we may get provincial self-government, but for that we must educate ourselves and the educated class is very small." [3]

Tilak, on the other hand, was much more interested in power, specifically in political power. Foreshadowing the techniques of Gandhi, he turned Hindu festivals into political rallies and meetings and made conscious appeals to Hindu images in order to win wider support for his political goals. The moderates appealed to an idealized Western image that lived only in the imaginations of the English-educated elite, but the extremists reached into deeper levels of the Hindu mind and called on older loyalties and emotions identified with ancient Indian images. This technique, as well as that of the boycott and the ensuing Hindu-Muslim conflict, were foretastes of the Gandhian movement of the 1920s.

Congress met once a year after 1885. Its composition in the first twenty years was largely of high-caste Indians, predominantly professional men, that is, lawyers and teachers. During the last years of the nineteenth century, however, the difference in point of view between the moderates and extremists within this group became increasingly severe.

Debate in Congress over the Bengal boycott of goods brought this split even more into the open. In 1906 extremists demanded that the Congress support the Bengal boycott movement with the understanding that ultimately all things British, governmental as well as material, would be boycotted. The moderates, however, as Gokhale expressed it, felt that "our duty at this crisis [was] to put forth the whole of our strength and make it clear to the world that whatever a small knot of unthinking men may say, the Congress as such has no aspirations except such as may be realized within the British Empire." [4] The conflict was not resolved. The statement finally drafted was that Congress supported the "legitimacy" of the boycott movement. Each side interpreted this statement in its own way.

The final confrontation took place at the Congress session of 1907.

Originally it was to have been held at Nagpur, a stronghold of extremist activity. But the moderates, who held the majority of voting power in the Congress' central committee, refused to convene it there, for the structure of the Congress was such that members from the host city were given a heavier vote on the central organizing committee. The moderates were unwilling to lose control of the Congress and therefore used their voting strength to switch the meeting to Surat.

The final split occurred in the latter city. As the moderate president began to deliver his acceptance speech, Tilak, who had been refused the floor on a procedural point, mounted the platform to demand the right to speak. "Congress volunteers" threatened to force him to sit down. The house broke into rival chants of "Shame! We don't want you to speak!" and "He must speak! He must be allowed to speak!" An eyewitness describes the rest of the incident in incomparable style:

Suddenly something flew through the air—a shoe!—a Mahratta shoe!—reddish leather, pointed toe, sole studded with lead. It struck Surendra Nath Bannerjea on the cheek; it cannoned off upon Sir Pherozeshah Mehta. It flew, it fell, and as at a given signal, white waves of turbaned men surged up the escarpment of the platform. Leaping, climbing, hissing the breath of fury, brandishing tong sticks, they came, striking at any head that looked to them Moderate, and in another moment, between brown legs standing upon the green-baize table, I caught glimpses of the Indian National Congress dissolving in chaos.[5]

Although the moderates retained official control of the Congress, the split at Surat left both sides totally powerless. Without the moderates, the extremists (more closely connected with the terrorist movement than was wise) lost their protection from the repressive forces of the British Raj; without the extremists, the moderates became again an isolated, obsequious, and Anglicized clique. The split and thus the effective paralysis of the nationalist movement lasted until the advent of Gandhi.

On April 13, 1919, news circulated through the city of Amritsar in the Punjab that a big meeting was to be held. Between ten and twenty thousand people gathered in Jallianwalla Bagh, a small common meeting-place surrounded by a low wall with one small entrance. The crowd, unarmed except for sticks, had gathered in defiance of a British order prohibiting meetings and was being addressed by a speaker. Reports of the meeting had reached General R. E. A. Dyer, the British officer in command in the area and the author of the prohibition. Dyer, fifty soldiers, and two armored cars arrived at Jallianwalla Bagh; twenty-five soldiers were placed at either side of the single entrance (which was too narrow for the cars). No order was given to the crowd to disperse. The soldiers simply began to fire, letting off 1,650 rounds. According to official British estimates, 379 people were killed and 1,137 wounded.

General Dyer explained to the commission investigating the massacre that "it was no longer a question of merely dispersing the crowd, but one of producing a sufficient moral effect from a military point of view, not only on those who were present, but more especially throughout the Punjab. . . . I thought I would be doing a jolly lot of good." [6]

The Amritsar massacre occurred against a background of riots throughout the Punjab. The tension leading up to the tragedy can thus be partially understood. After World War I the British legislature in India had passed the Rowlatt Acts, extending wartime governmental powers of arrest and imprisonment. Gandhi had recently returned from South Africa and was rapidly becoming one of the leading forces in the Congress movement. He had called for a nationwide *hartal*, or strike, to protest the extension of these powers. Two strikes, held on March 30 and April 6, 1919, were peaceful. But in the Punjab on April 9 the coincidence of the deportation of two Congress leaders for political activities and the date of a Hindu festival sent mobs roaming through the streets. Three Europeans were killed, and a European woman, Miss Sherwood, was attacked. Attacks on European women always aroused tremendous anger and fear among the British in India —or perhaps only brought into the open fears that were always present. In reaction to the attack on Miss Sherwood, Dyer prohibited mass meetings, and at about the time of the Amritsar massacre several other proclamations expressing British fear and fury were issued. The "crawling order" declared that any Indian passing the street where the assault had taken place was to go down on all fours and applied even to those Indians who lived on neighboring streets. Indians on animals and vehicles were to dismount and, if carrying umbrellas, were to lower them and bow if they happened to pass a British officer. A whipping post was erected on the spot where Miss Sherwood had been attacked for the purpose of flogging violators of these orders.

The Amritsar massacre was not typical of the British Raj, but it did give expression to one aspect of that rule, the ever-present underlying combination of British hostility and fear toward the people they ruled. Perhaps these fears had not existed before the Mutiny. Perhaps they had always existed, the inescapable heritage of an imperialist ruling class. But the fears appeared most clearly when British rule was threatened, as during the Mutiny. At such times the British compelled symbolic demonstrations of Indian subservience to British power. By demonstrating the weaker position of the Indians, the British reassured themselves.

This element of fear was the reverse side of British paternalism in India, just as hatred and frustration were the reverse of Indian subservience. Another, more oblique, indication that the British were aware that they might not be altogether welcome in India was the frequent statements they made justifying their rule. In the last years of the nineteenth century and the first years of the twentieth these statements were often made in self-defense against Congress charges of misrule and demands for more power and government positions. These demands were made first for positions within the Indian Civil Service, later for power within the government itself. The British insisted that their rule was welcome in India and good for the people because it was efficient and just. But Lord Curzon, Governor General from 1898 to 1905—and the archetype of the imperialist Governor General—gave the classic justification of British rule: "When I am vituperated by those who claim to speak for the Indian people, I feel no resentment and no pain. For I search my conscience and I ask myself who and what are the real Indian people. . . ." [7] In Curzon's mind and in the minds of many British imperialists, the "real" Indian people were not those in the Congress. Congress represented only a small elite, whose demands were, furthermore, self-seeking and whose presence in government work was actually a burden to the British. The undercurrent of contempt for Western-educated Indians is one of the least pleasant features of imperialist writing. When asked why the government did not employ natives, Curzon replied: ". . . because they are not competent and because it is our constant experience that when placed in authority, if an emergency occurs, they lose their heads or abdicate altogether." [8] It is significant, in view of such alleged incompetence, that one of Curzon's defenses of the government's refusal to hold examinations for the civil service in which Indians would have an equal chance to compete was his fear of the "extreme danger" that posts would be "filched away by the superior wits of the Native. . . ." [9]

The importunate Congress members, then, were not regarded as representative Indians, and their protest was not considered to have any broad significance. To British imperialists both before and after the Mutiny, the "real" Indians—that is, the Indians who understood, appreciated, and desired British rule—were always the "simple" but honest and hardworking peasants. It was with the peasants that the British civil service had its paternalistic relationshp, and from them that it claimed gratitude and devotion. Whenever the romanticism of this view was shattered—by mass violence in the Mutiny or by more restricted rioting in the Punjab—the British community reacted by demanding physical proof of its power over India.

From the 1860s on, the British government in India periodically offered "reform" programs to those Indians interested in politics. In the late nineteenth century the general trend of such reforms was to include Indians in the Indian Legislative Council: First, they were allowed to listen to debates, later to participate in them, and only much later to vote (but always as a minority). The original purpose of the nineteenth-century legislative reforms was to enable the British to hear what the Indians had to say about government and hopefully to neutralize protests by bringing them within the structure of government. The Congress Party was founded by the British for much the same purpose.

In the twentieth century, as the number of Indians interested in politics grew and as the Congress developed more extensive organization, the demands and pressures on the British government for more significant reforms grew. In 1909 reforms increased the numbers of Indians on the Legislative Council and allowed more discussion of government business; as always, however, the government retained an official majority to ensure control. The moderates, who had had great expectations from these reforms, were disappointed. But as the British Secretary of State for India had rather unkindly prophesied before the reforms had even been passed, "if their political acumen had been greater, their enthusiasm might have been less." [10]

The 1919 reforms were simply a more complex extension of the same principles: increased participation and reserved power. The British had expressed in 1917 the imagined purpose of these reforms: gradually to train Indians in the mysteries of self-government through a series of increased responsibilities. This fantasy was repeated not only to Indians but among the British themselves with hypnotic frequency. One of the most complicated attempts to realize this goal was the structure set up in the 1919 Montagu-Chelmsford reforms. Dyarchy, the name given to the provincial system of government outlined in the reforms, was designed to give Indians practical experience in the art of self-government. On the provincial level Indians were to be elected indirectly through the legislatures to form provincial governments and to be given charge of certain provincial departments like health and education. Other departments like finance and police were reserved to the British. The significance of dyarchy, however, was that all real power—money and enforcement—was reserved by the government and that only the problem areas were allowed to the Indians. The Indian ministers, then, were to have the problems but not the means or resources to solve them. Pointing out that funds for the much-needed expansion of education were small, a government statement of 1919 went on to note ingenuously that "fortunately" education was a transferred subject and that the Indian administration might be able to discover new sources of income.

Congress well appreciated the significance of this division of labor. Originally the leaders had refused to participate in the reforms. Their refusal was a mystery to the British, who could explain it to themselves only in terms of extremist recalcitrance. When a visiting British nobleman made a "personal" appeal to the Indians in 1919 to "join hands and to work together to realize the hopes that rise from today" and his appeal went unheeded, British administrators professed not to understand why. The British failed to comprehend why the Indians lacked enthusiasm for dyarchy, as they consistently failed to understand why their words and pledges were not trusted by the Congress. When the repressive Rowlatt Acts were passed, a British administrator wrote of their reception, "It was in vain that member after member of the Government solemnly pledged his word that the provisions of the Bill would be used merely for the purpose of checking anarchical and revolutionary crime." [11] The British administrators of India, particularly those in high positions and therefore far from the actual application of power, failed, or perhaps refused, to recognize the real nature of the relations between themselves and the Indians. They regarded the Amritsar massacre as merely an unfortunate incident, not as an expression of the reality of British-Indian relations. The moderates had similarly refused to recognize existing power relations, and as a result they had been singularly ineffective in gaining more power within the government. What they had won in the nineteenth century with their methods had been the tenuous right to express their opinions on political matters to those in power. In addition they had garnered some British approval, but only on the most superficial level, judging by the condescending manner in which the British talked about the Indians among themselves.

The extremists were more realistic in their appraisal of the relative position of Indians and British. Tilak wrote, "No nation rules another for altruistic reasons; the British imperial government is not of whites and blacks, but only of white people and it is consequently for the benefit of the whites alone." [12] But the extremists had been too isolated; they were still primarily an educated elite without mass support and without means of paralyzing British government—and thus were relatively helpless before the government's power to imprison or deport them for sedition. It was Gandhi who found the solution: "We may attack measures and systems. We may not, we must not attack men." [13] It was part of his genius that he was able to unite in his own political efforts mass support, a realistic evaluation of power relations, and a subtle but powerful appeal to the British romantic vision of their own role in India.

"Our non-cooperation is with the system the English have established, with the material civilization and its attendant greed and exploitation of the weak. . . . Non-cooperation is not anti-English in spirit. It is a religious movement, it is a purifying movement. It is a movement intended to resist injustice, untruth, terrorism and to establish Swaraj [self-rule] in India." [14] Such were Gandhi's principles.

In 1915 Gandhi had come from South Africa, where he had led a successful campaign against the government for the purpose of bettering the lot of the Indian community there; his war service and self-sacrifice had won him prestige in the eyes of both Britons and Indians. The elements that combined to make up the power of Gandhi and his campaigns were his own personality, Hindu symbolism, and political acumen. The manner in which these complementary elements were used was neatly demonstrated in his first campaign.

It was at the 1919 Congress meeting in Delhi that Gandhi first suggested applying his method of noncooperation against the British government. After the Montagu-Chelmsford reforms had been passed and dyarchy proffered to India, he reversed his original opposition to the reforms. But after the Amritsar massacre, when it appeared that no punitive measures were to be taken against General Dyer—he was let off with censure—Gandhi reversed himself again. (At that time a small group of moderates broke with Congress and formed the Liberal Party; it consisted mostly of elder statesmen of the Indian nationalist movement and continued to hold conferences, cooperate in British reforms, and generally represent and speak only for its own members for the next twenty years.)

On August 1, 1920, the Congress session at Nagpur declared the beginning of noncooperation. Gandhi returned to the Indian government the medals that he had earned in South Africa. Several of the Congress high command, including Motilal, Jawaharlal Nehru, and Sardar Vallabhbhai Patel (later some of the most powerful leaders in the Congress Party) resigned from the British law courts. Gandhi began a seven-month tour of the country, with the purpose of converting people to support of the Congress movement. He also began to spin cloth; for a half-hour each day he worked on homespun cloth called khadi. Khadi—"the livery of our freedom," as Nehru called it—came to be commonly worn by nationalists; as an indigenous product it symbolized India's independence of the Western world. "I regard the spinning wheel," Gandhi said, "as the gateway to my spiritual salvation." [15] As it symbolized India's independence of the West, spinning also measured individual devotion and commitment to the Congress cause. It was an element of Gandhi's genius that he could invent a symbol that would permit mass action and visible mass support for his movement. "Any single district," he said, "that can be fully organized for khaddar [making homespun cloth] is, if it is also trained for suffering, ready for civil disobedience." [16]

At the villages where he spoke Gandhi told crowds that they must learn to spin and weave. He asked them to take off whatever foreign clothing they were wearing and to place it on a pile in front of the group. The pile was then set on fire, and while the clothes burned, Gandhi spoke of the nationalist movement. It was during this tour that Gandhi urged the formation of local Congress organizations. He designed a Congress flag with a spinning wheel in the center. He wrote for two weekly newsletters—*Young India* in English and *Navajivan* in Gujarati—that had been founded in 1919. In 1921 he adopted the traditional dress of an Indian mendicant, wearing a loincloth and carrying a bag made of khadi.

The first major noncooperation campaign was announced in October 1921, when the Congress Working Committee called upon all Indians to sever their ties with the government. Riots broke out in Bombay; Gandhi fasted for five days. The government began to arrest Congress leaders, and by December 1921 twenty thousand Indians had been jailed for civil disobedience and sedition. By January ten thousand more were in jail. "No matter what you do," Gandhi said, "no matter how you repress us, we shall one day wring reluctant repentance from you." [17]

Civil disobedience had not yet been tried, although the Congress leadership was eager to begin a campaign. But Gandhi was reluctant. He allowed Congress to pass a resolution that it would undertake mass civil disobedience, but he insisted on a promise not to do so without his consent. It was his idea that the method of civil disobedience should be tested on a small scale in one place, and for this purpose he chose Bardoli, a district of 87,000 people in Bombay Province. He informed Governor General Rufus Reading that the campaign would begin in that district. Gandhi feared that mass civil disobedience would trigger large-scale violence, for which he would feel responsible, as he had in 1919, when his call for a *hartal* had sparked riots in the Punjab.

The Bardoli campaign was to begin in February, but on February

5 in the village of Chauri Chaura in the United Provinces police began to attack several stragglers in a procession of nationalists. The crowd turned on them and chased them back to the police station, where they barricaded themselves inside. The mob then set fire to the building; when the police ran out, they were attacked and beaten, and their bodies were thrown back into the flames.

Shocked and revolted by this violence, Gandhi suspended the Bardoli campaign before it had begun. Congress leaders protested loudly, claiming that the suspension was politically suicidal; Gandhi, they believed, had betrayed the nationalist movement. In his defense Gandhi said only that "the drastic reversal of practically the whole of the aggressive program may be politically unsound and unwise, but there is no doubt that it is religiously sound." [18]

The British Governor General, Lord Reading, had been deterred from arresting Gandhi only by the fear of a mass uprising and had previously stated that there would be an arrest only if Gandhi took direct action. Once the Bardoli campaign had been canceled and his fears of mass riots somewhat assuaged, Reading consulted with the provincial governors. Gandhi was arrested March 10, 1922. There was no mass protest.

Gandhi was brought to trial and charged with seditious political writings. He pleaded guilty, and his statement at his trial was typical of his manner of dealing with the opposition, including a characteristically astute assessment of the British Raj:

I am here to invite and cheerfully submit to the highest penalty that can be inflicted upon me for what in law is a deliberate crime and what appears to me to be the highest duty of a citizen. . . . I am satisfied that many English men and Indian officials honestly believe that they are administering one of the best systems devised in the world and that India is making steady though slow progress. They do not know that a subtle but effective system of terrorism and an organized display of force on the one hand and the deprivation of all powers of retaliation and self-defense on the other have emasculated the people and induced in them the habit of simulation. . . .[19]

He was sentenced to six years in prison. The Congress movement slowed to an apparent halt. By 1926 the temporary alliance between the Hindu and Muslim communities (which had been initiated in 1916) had collapsed; Gandhi was still in jail, and Congress was torn by internal strife. British official opinion, shared by many Congress members, was that the time of noncooperation as a tactic and Gandhi's power as a political leader were over.

"In my opinion, non-cooperation with evil is as much a duty as is cooperation with good." [20] The degree to which Gandhi's political beliefs arose from intense religious conviction was the source of the tremendous power that he was personally able to wield in India. To a degree Gandhi himself became a symbol. His personality and his presence echoed forms and ideals from the far reaches of the Indian past. His way of life grew increasingly simpler as he grew older; he ate more and more sparely. At first he was simply a vegetarian (although in his youth he had eaten meat); later he would eat only nuts, some fruits, and juices. Although during his youth in England he had dressed as an English gentleman, he had now adopted the traditional garb of the mendicant, a simple loincloth. He had assimilated himself to the Indian idea of the hermit, the mendicant, who seeks after truth, who seeks union with the underlying principle of the universe rather than involvement in the passions and desires of the world, and who thus escapes the cycle of rebirth to which the rest of humanity is bound. It is the ideal of Hindu civilization to seek this course in the fourth and final stage of life. The man who does so is honored by his society and believed to have powers greater than those of other men.

"To find Truth completely is to realize oneself and one's destiny, that is, to become perfect." [21] Gandhi's search for truth (his autobiography is entitled *The Story of My Experiments with Truth* and describes his culinary and ascetic experiments) and the sincerity of his desire to "live truth" gave him a power over the Indian masses the depth of which is difficult to assess and the mechanics of which are even harder to describe. His use of this power—the degree to which he consciously exploited it and the degree to which he acted ingenuously—is one of the mysteries of the man. For instance, on numerous occasions, when violence erupted for which he felt responsible or when a policy failed, Gandhi would impose a fast upon himself. Those whose actions had brought on the fast were placed under tremendous pressure to yield, in order both to assuage their guilt and to avert the riots that would have attended his death. Understandably people so pressured were inclined to regard Gandhi's actions as consciously and deliberately coercive; the British called it moral blackmail.

Gandhi's technique was to use his moral power for political ends. He took concepts that in older Hindu tradition had applied to the individual's quest for salvation—concepts like *ahimsa* (nonviolence) and *satyagraha* (soul force—strength to pursue truth peacefully)—and reinterpreted them to have communal, political meaning. Asceticism and sacrifice had always characterized religious devotees who withdrew from social contacts in order to work out their personal spiritual destinies. These weapons—fasting in particular and the technique of civil disobedience—were now adapted to the social context to help attain social and political ends.

There were Indians who believed that their interests were threatened by Gandhi's views and actions. In 1932 the British offered the Untouchables special communal representation in any future electoral system that the government might offer. Gandhi's statements on the Untouchables and their lot shifted several times during his lifetime, but his personal response to them was always one of intense compassion. He lived in Untouchables' quarters on innumerable occasions, and he enjoined higher-caste Hindus not to exclude this community from their society but to treat them as *Harijans*, or children of God. But in 1932 he was convinced that separate elections for the Untouchables would wreck the entire structure of Hindu society: the very reason, in all likelihood, why Untouchable leaders favored such elections. Gandhi opposed special communal awards and began a fast to the death. The desperate negotiations that followed resulted in compromise, but such occurrences made more understandable the bitterness with which men like Dr. B. R. Ambedkar (leader of the Untouchable community) regarded Gandhi, who appeared to them a manipulator and a blackmailer.

Similarly the Muslim community felt threatened by the iron conviction concealed beneath Gandhi's tolerance and compassion. In the 1940s Gandhi took to reciting the Koran at his prayer meetings in the express belief that he was thus including Muslims in the meetings. He wanted to create greater political unity between the two religions. Hinduism had always recognized many paths to the truth, many valid ways of expressing the oneness of the universe. In reciting the Koran, Gandhi thus intended to bridge the gap between the two communities while acting in accordance with his own religious beliefs. Good Muslims, however, recognize the Koran as the expression of the *one* valid religion and could only be alienated by such an action. They were similarly alienated from Congress nationalism by Gandhi's consistent appeals to Hindu symbols and the Hindu past. *Swarajua* (self-rule), *satyagraha*, and *ahimsa* were all terms taken from old Sanskrit traditions with which the Muslims could not and did not wish to identify. Muslims believed that Congress nationalism was not secular but Hindu. Although the Congress and Gandhi denied this charge, the Muslims believed that they were deliberately lying.

How self-conscious Gandhi's protest techniques were is an almost unanswerable question. Some were more clearly deliberate than were others. For instance, he developed "silent days" during which he would talk to no one but would only pray and write messages. He admitted that he used these silent days to gain time alone for himself and occasionally to avoid speaking on matters about which he was undecided. But the motivations behind his fasting and his supposed basing of decisions on the promptings of an "inner voice" are more obscure. "They are a part of my being," he said. "I can as well do without my eyes, for instance, as I can without fasts. What the eyes are for the outer world, fasts are for the inner." [22] Gandhi's fasts thus seemed to be prompted not only by political expedience but also by his own inner needs.

There were certainly many aspects of Gandhi's psychology that appear decidedly peculiar to a Westerner. As with many famous men, his demands on both his wife and his two sons were extraordinary. He refused to allow his sons to attend college (although he had done so) on the grounds that such education was irrelevant to their personal development. His elder son became an alcoholic. His attitude toward his wife was decidedly ambivalent. In her final illness he refused to allow the doctors to give her the medicine that she needed because it had to be given by injection.

The whole atmosphere around Gandhi and his closest disciples exuded the faintly unpleasant air of constant manipulation through the twin controls of love and guilt. This manipulation extended beyond his immediate sphere. One anecdote, which Gandhi himself related, can illustrate the tone:

The army of my sweethearts is daily increasing. The latest recruit is Ranibala of Burdwan, a darling perhaps ten years old. I dare not ask her age. I was playing with her as usual and casting furtive glances at her six heavy gold bangles. I gently explained to her that they were too heavy a burden for her delicate little wrists and down went her hand on the bangles. . . . I must confess I was embarrassed. . . . I was merely joking as I always do when I see little girls and jokingly create in them a distaste for much ornamentation and a desire to part with their jewelry for the sake of the poor. [23]

Such anecdotes reveal Gandhi's brilliant use of others' guilt. But this trait can only appear unpleasant when abstracted from his genuine warmth, compassion, and courage. Furthermore, all his traits seem slightly distorted from a Western point of view. His real goal was an Indian ideal: *brahmacharya*, abandonment of the world and unity with Brahma, the underlying principle of the universe. Achievement of this goal demanded an extremism that appears fanatical to a Westerner. But to aim at such an ideal and to pursue it so intensely was a matter for praise and glory in Gandhi's own culture. What he sought was, in his own culture, a socially accepted and socially sanctioned goal.

However Gandhi's personality is finally assessed, his tremendous effectiveness, both in broadening the scope of Indian protest against British rule and in freeing those already committed to such protest from the fears that had formerly paralyzed them, can scarcely be overstressed. As Nehru wrote of the 1921 era:

Above all, we had a sense of freedom and pride in that freedom. There was no more whispering, no round about legal phraseology to avoid getting into trouble with the authorities. We said what we felt and shouted it from the housetops. What did we care for the consequences? Prison? We looked forward to it, that would help our cause still further. The innumerable spies and secret service men who used to surround us and follow us about became rather pitiable individuals as there was nothing secret for them to discover.[24]

Gandhi brought the nationalists out from under the pall of the moderates' desperate striving for British approval. He made protest against the British Raj respectable, a moral imperative. One way in which he accomplished this goal was by refusing to attack the British officials who ran the government; he attacked only the government itself. He thus maintained a stance of moral rectitude among the Indian educated elite. One of the strongest weapons that the British had been able to wield over that elite had been their claim to moral superiority. The British were supposedly by race, training, and nature better fitted to govern. Their sense of duty and honor had brought them to rule India as they did. To the elite, educated with British books and saturated with convictions of British greatness, it was painful to accuse the British of wrongs and frightening to act on those accusations. Gandhi obviated the need for the whole confrontation. By his willingness, even eagerness, to take suffering upon himself and upon the Indian people in order to make them free, through the method of civil disobedience and *satyagraha* (soul force), he shifted the burden of guilt firmly onto the shoulders of the British.

The intellectual essence of Gandhi's theory of *satyagraha* was that the means were as important as the ends and that no good could come from evil. In order to change the situation, he was willing to undergo any amount of personal suffering. "Strength," Gandhi said, "does not come from physical capacity. It comes from indomitable will. Nonviolence does not mean meek submission to the will of the evil-doer, but it means the putting of one's whole soul against the will of the tyrant." [25] Part of the devastating effectiveness of this technique, at least on a short-term basis, came from his total conviction of the correctness of his judgment; those pitted against him were usually both less convinced and less involved. They could hardly avoid being swayed or at least impressed by his conviction.

There were numerous instances in which Gandhi or his disciples successfully used *satyagraha*, for example with mill owners who underpaid their workers or in a protest led by Sardar Patel against a tax increase by the government of one district. The single most dramatic campaign, however, was against the British government in 1930: the Salt March to Dandi.

Political activities in the years preceding the Salt March had been uninspiring. The Congress in 1928 issued the Nehru Report, which had caused considerable intra-Congress feuding. The report demanded dominion status within one year or, failing that, complete independence. The British government had sent a parliamentary investigatory committee, the Simon Commission, to gather information on the situation in India. Congress had boycotted the commission, claiming that its methods were inquisitorial and that it contained no Indian member. In the ensuing stalemate Gandhi had finally emerged from self-imposed retirement. On March 2, 1930, Gandhi sent a letter to the Viceroy, Lord Irwin, informing him that in nine days a campaign of civil disobedience directed against the salt tax would begin. Many years before, the British government had instituted a tax on all salt. Gandhi's objection was that the tax represented a monopolistic manipulation of a commodity essential to life.

On March 12 he and seventy-eight members of his community began the two-hundred-mile walk from Sabarmati to Dandi, a village on the sea. It took them twenty-four days, walking along dirt roads through small villages, with frequent stops for Gandhi to speak to the crowds that gathered. By April 5, when they reached the sea, their numbers had swelled to several thousand. The next morning, after a night of prayer, Gandhi walked into the sea, then picked up some salt from the beach. He had broken the salt-tax law.

On this signal, protest and civil disobedience broke out all over India. Reports tell of five million Indians breaking the salt law in five thousand demonstrations along the coast. Salt was sold illegally at auctions. Mass arrests were begun by the government. One of the most dramatic scenes and terrifying examples of the strength of the *satyagrahis* was the confrontation between the police and protesters at the Dharasana Salt Works. Twenty-five hundred volunteers had marched to take salt from these works. They drew up in rows in front of the salt pans, which the police had enclosed with barbed wire and ditches. A United Press correspondent described the scene:

Suddenly at a word of command, scores of native policemen rushed upon the advancing marchers and rained blows on their heads with their steelshod lathis. Not one of the marchers even raised an arm to fend off the blows. They went down like ten-pins. From where I stood I heard the sickening whack of the clubs on unprotected skulls. The waiting crowd of marchers groaned and sucked in their breath in sympathetic pain at every blow. Those struck down fell sprawling, unconscious or writhing with fractured skulls or broken shoulders. . . . The survivors, without breaking ranks, silently and doggedly marched on until struck down. . . .[26]

Two men died that day, and over three hundred were injured; the protest continued for several days. By June 30 Gandhi and almost 100,000 other Indians, including all the major Congress leaders, were in jail.

"I think every European and Indian would tell you that he was surprised at the dimensions the movement had assumed," Lord Irwin said. "I certainly am myself—and we should delude ourselves if we sought to underrate it."[27]

The Dandi Salt March was a dramatic event, a great success in the application of Gandhi's techniques of protest, and an effective means of altering the moral climate of the country. Hindu poet Rabindranath Tagore wrote: "Europe has completely lost her former moral prestige in Asia. She is no longer regarded as the champion throughout the world of fair dealing and the exponent of high principle, but as the upholder of Western race supremacy and the exploiter of those outside her own borders."[28] In terms of purely political success, in gaining immediate political concessions, however, the march was almost a complete failure.

The British organized a round-table conference in 1930 to be held in London and to be attended by both Britons and Indians. The purpose of the conference was to discuss the Indian situation in an atmosphere of equality. Congress was unrepresented at this conference. Only Muslims and Indian Liberals were present, yet the conference was not wholly barren. "No fair minded Indian," one British observer wrote afterward, "who took part in the Conference could henceforward entertain any doubts as to the entire good faith and good will of the representatives of all English parties. . . ."[29] But comforting as this reassurance was, little of substance could be achieved without Congress representation. After a series of talks between Gandhi and Irwin, it was agreed that political prisoners would be released, confiscated property restored, and picketing allowed. In return, Gandhi would stop the civil-disobedience movement and attend a second round-table conference.

The immediate result of Gandhi's civil-disobedience campaign, in political rather than in moral terms, was stalemate; the same was true of the second round-table conference. The debates centered around what were to become the main themes of all British-Indian discussions: the communal (Hindu versus Muslim) question and the question of whom Congress represented. Said one British delegate to the conference, "When we abandon the governing of India, to whom are we going to hand it over, to the Brahmin or to the people?" [30]

Nehru had said: "There are only two forces in India today—British imperialism and Indian nationalism as represented by Congress." [31]

Gandhi's visit to England and his appearance in his usual attire at the conference prompted Winston Churchill to remark in dismay on the sight of a "half-naked fakir" seated in the councils of the great British Empire. One British writer thought it a great advance that the two groups were meeting on equal terms. But the terms were only symbolically equal. The fundamental power relationship had not changed. In Gandhi's absence a series of militant movements had started up in India: the Red Shirt movement in the north, a no-rent campaign in the United Provinces, and renewed terrorist activities in Bengal. On his return in 1932 Gandhi announced that he intended to begin a new civil-disobedience campaign. The government promptly jailed him.

In 1906 a deputation of Muslim leaders had sought and received an interview with the Governor General, Lord Minto. Having heard that discussions about approaching governmental reforms were in progress, they were anxious to protect themselves and their community. They presented Minto with a petition asking that Muslim representation on the enlarged Legislative Council be ensured and that it "should be commensurate not merely with their numerical strength, but also with their political importance and the value of the contribution which they make to the defence of the Empire. . . ." [32] The 1909 reforms contained a provision, reached after considerable discussion between British officials and the Muslim delegation, for a number of seats for Muslims on the Council. It was the first official legislative recognition of the Muslims as a community distinct from the rest of India. Did the British create this division by their legislative policy, or did they merely recognize a division that already existed? In one sense the Muslims were a separate community, and in another sense they were not. Their religion, the fierce self-consciousness and puritanism of Islam, and the isolating tendencies of the Hindu caste system, as well as their political supremacy before the British arrived, had maintained the Muslims' sense of communal identity in India. But centuries of living in close contact with Hindu culture had also changed them. When contrasted with non-Indian Muslims, they seemed more readily identifiable as Indians than as Muslims. Still, within their own community, they were conscious of the past glories of Islam, the Moghul Empire, and the hostility and threats to their position and prestige from the Hindu community. A sense both of danger and of pride prompted their appeal to Minto to ensure that "in any case the Muslim representatives should never be an ineffective minority." [33]

The British argument in favor of British rule had long been that only a "neutral" third party could govern equitably the many cultures of the Indian subcontinent. Muslim leaders of the nineteenth and twentieth centuries shared this belief. It was also shared by the British authors of the 1909 reforms; they never intended, and they made this point explicitly, their reforms as a prelude to the establishment of a parliamentary system in India. But such protestations were forgotten (or ignored) by later British statesmen, under pressure from Congress and enamored of their vision of leading the Indian savage into the world of modern liberal civilization.

Neither the establishment of the Muslim League in 1906 nor the reservation of seats for certain Muslim groups in the 1909 reforms received much attention from Hindu politicians at that time. Until a few short years before Independence, Congress leaders paid little attention to Muslim protests and claims; they grossly underrated both the intensity and the seriousness of these claims. They were also simply much more interested in the British. The Congress image of itself was that of an organization of "untainted nationalism and secularism." [34] Leaders like Nehru, a sincerely secular and highly Westernized man, refused to consider the claims of those who asserted that Congress was a Hindu-oriented and Hindu-dominated group. He recognized only Congress and the British as forces in India. To do otherwise would have disrupted his vision of the parliamentary state that he thought it possible to create in India. Other Congress leaders like Patel were less idealistic, more opportunistic, but equally unwilling to consider Muslim claims for a voice in negotiations separate from that of Congress; it served their own interests to refuse to do so.

For a long period before independence the main thrust of Congress's efforts was aimed at the British. This attitude was less than flattering to the Muslims, especially to their main twentieth-century leader, Mohammed Ali Jinnah, a man composed of equal measures of ambition and vanity. It is often suggested that it was when Jinnah discovered that the Muslims as a group and he as their leader could gain no significant power within the Congress that he withdrew from the

organization to reform and strengthen the Muslim League as a separate, extra-Congress force.

Some contemporaries and many later historians have claimed that
from 1909 on the British deliberately used Hindu-Muslim differences
to drive the communities apart and thus make their own rule in
India more secure. On one level the British did use the technique of
divide and conquer, less as a conscious policy than as the natural
reaction of a government besieged on all sides by demands and eager
to escape from some of the pressure. As one former British official said
to another, "You yourself must occasionally have heard British officers,
perhaps even me, say with mingled relief and amusement, 'Now
they've begun to fight among themselves.' " [35]

But on another level the British were quite innocent of the charge.
In the continual negotiations between the Congress and the British, the
latter repeatedly reminded the former that there were groups and interests in India that it did not represent. The British were not dividing.
They merely recognized existing divisions. Nor were they conquering
—at least they never persuaded the Congress to modify its claim to
represent a united India.

Behind those claims lay a belief often expressed by Congress leaders
and spokesmen: If India's internal divisions could be kept from articulation until after independence, they could then somehow be more
easily worked out. Independence was somehow miraculously to bring
with it instant modernity. India would become what Congress was
already claiming it was—a modern secular nation. This belief was an
analogue of the belief that Britain was the cause of all India's problems.
The minority communities, however, were less free to fantasize. Aware
of the realities of Hindu hostility and nepotism, aware too of the
power of the rich industrialists who provided the capital for Congress
efforts, the minorities had less faith that the millennium would come
with the British departure. Aware of Hindu numerical superiority,
they feared that, in an independent India ruled by Congress without
safeguards for minority communities, their claims would be ignored,
their rights denied, and their property destroyed.

Muslims found it more and more difficult to subscribe to Indian
nationalism as expressed in the rhetoric and personality of Gandhi.
Gandhi had initially done much to shape the united movement, but his
own strongly Hindu image and appeal left no room in his nationalist
philosophy for the Muslims' own identification with Islam and drove
them from him. The very quality that enabled Gandhi to capture the
Hindu masses made it next to impossible for the Muslims to follow him.

The Congress refusal to concede any power to the Muslim League was based not only on a secularist aversion to religiously based political parties (as in Nehru's case) but also and much more simply on the fact that the Congress Party was bigger than the Muslim League. It did not think that it had to accommodate the League, for the latter was too weak to insist. On the other side, the Muslims could see no hope for power or even for communal survival in an independent India. Only in their own state, in a Pakistan, did they believe that they could be secure.

The communal problem, the question of who would rule India and how, was posed repeatedly between 1936 and the end of World War II. The British governors of India had been promising eventual self-government since 1917. With the outbreak of World War II and the threat of a Japanese invasion of India, they again sought help or at least a promise of nonobstruction from Gandhi and the Congress. Sir Stafford Cripps headed a mission to India in 1942, offering new—and this time definite—promises of dominion status once the war was over. Gandhi and the nationalist leaders replied, "Quit India!"

The demand for immediate self-government and Gandhi's announcement that he would begin a new civil-disobedience campaign catapulted Congress leaders into jail. Violence erupted all around the country. It was largely spontaneous, for all the leaders were in jail. By the time that the worst of the "August rebellion" was over, 100,000 Indians were again in custody.

The Congress leaders remained in jail for the duration of the war, but by then the British were thoroughly tired. During the twenty years or so of the Indian struggle for independence, British administrators in India and British imperialists in England had been gradually losing self-confidence, losing faith both in their right and in their ability to govern India. Commenting on the government's censure of General Dyer's role in the Amritsar massacre, one former Indian civil-service man reflected the insecurity of a later age when he complained that it "had a disheartening effect upon the services engaged in the thankless task of maintaining law and order. It is difficult to get officials to act with promptitude and independence of judgment unless they are assured of support from the authorities." [36]

At the end of World War II, with a Labour government in power and the clear approach of Indian independence, the morale of the Indian civil service dropped even lower. The British wanted out. Since 1917 the question had been whether or not the British *would* leave India; the answer, reflected from the format and concessions of the various reforms, had been "yes but not yet." At the end of the war, the question was *how* the British would leave. The struggle in the years between World War II and actual independence was not between Indians and British but between Indians and Indians, a struggle among factions. The protest movement that Gandhi had led had become increasingly superfluous as the achievement of its goal, the end of British rule, had become inevitable. The political maneuverings and manipulations that preoccupied Nehru and other Congress leaders more and more and Gandhi less and less as the years passed were becoming more important. Protest was giving way to politics, or so it seemed.

The irrelevance of Gandhi and his movement in the postwar maneuvering increased as independence drew closer. In 1945 Sir Stafford Cripps again went to India, this time to offer one of the most complex alternatives ever presented to Congress and the Muslim League: the Cabinet Mission Plan. This plan called for a three-tiered government of provinces, "groups," and nation. It was designed to protect Muslim interests by guaranteeing them majorities at certain provincial and group levels and to appeal to Congress by providing for a united, independent India. The details of the plan are less important than the negotiations that resulted from it. After a long conference both the Congress representatives and Jinnah, speaking for the Muslim League, accepted the plan. Both sides had, however, chosen to interpret it in their own interests. An interim government was to be formed; elections were to be held; and a convention was to work out the details of government for independent India. But at that point Nehru, newly elected Congress president, publicly stated that the government of an independent India would in no way consider itself bound by previous agreements. The Congress Party, he said, would enter the Constituent Assembly "completely unfettered by agreements and free to meet all situations as they arise." [37]

The Muslims regarded this statement as further evidence of Congress treachery. In July Jinnah rescinded his agreement to the plan and called on Muslims to participate in Direct Action Day on August 16, 1946. The riots that broke out in Calcutta on that day were more serious than any that had preceded them. When the violence had spent itself, six thousand people were dead.

The Cabinet Mission Plan was dead too. Although various efforts were made to revive it, none succeeded. In the endless debate that has ensued over why Nehru made his speech when he did, several points have emerged. Agreement on the Cabinet Mission Plan had been tenuous at best; Nehru and Congress were committed to the idea of a strong central government in India, for the idea of a weak federation of states seemed to them unworkable. Furthermore, they gravely underestimated Muslim determination to have Pakistan and Muslim ability to make it work. They believed that the British and the Muslims would eventually accede to Congress insistence on a strong, united India.

Nehru's speech was not politic, but it was characteristic of the hostile, aggressive nature of the power struggle that the Congress and Muslim leaders had been waging. The Muslims were no less politically uncompromising than was Congress. They were only weaker. The suggestion of one writer that the commitment to democracy within the Congress and among the educated Indian community extended only to the point at which democracy would ensure their own continued rule has much to recommend it. Consensus government, the art of conceding power to weaker groups in order to ensure their support of central authority, does not seem to have been recognized or understood by Indian leaders. Occasionally the tactic was tried, but such instances were rare and not followed through.

The Western ideologies of nationalism and democracy were unquestioningly espoused by Congress leaders. Similarly they accepted the goal of an independent India to be the establishment of a modern, secular, and democratic state. But the process of establishing a national identity—in part, the point of Gandhi's whole movement—had anchored this identity so firmly in Hinduism that it effectively prevented the Muslim community from participating in the Congress movement. The deeply ingrained nepotism in Indian society also contributed to exclusion of Muslims.

During all these negotiations where was the founder of Indian nationalist ideology? Where was Gandhi? As independence drew closer and closer, he became less and less involved in the struggle. Whereas he had regarded the *satyagraha* movement as religious, Congress leaders, even Nehru, had regarded it only as political. Once the goal of independence had been gained, the political movement itself became less important. Not that Gandhi had lost his personal influence or the reverence that he had long commanded. In an internal Congress struggle in 1939 he succeeded in ousting a rival, S. K. Bose, from the party. In personal conflicts his power remained great, as did the respect of Congress members for him. But on the policy level his influence was declining.

His commitment had always been, paradoxically, to a form of government more democratic than that sought by the supposedly Westernized Congress members. He had sought the personal involvement of all Indians in their own politics. His economic program—calling for a return to basic village industries, with the village as the focus of life—

had been less utopian than expressive of his understanding that peasants could understand and learn to control the political spheres of their lives more easily at the village level than at remoter levels. His civil-disobedience campaigns had sought to arouse personal commitment to their means and goals among those who participated. The English-educated elite had supported Gandhi's civil-disobedience movement because it was an effective means of protesting against the British, of forcing them to turn over political power to Indians (primarily to the elite).

The Congress Party supported the civil-disobedience movement because it involved the masses in a protest against the British, and mass protest was not only a good thing in itself; it also provided a more convincing argument for independence than did the demands of a small elite. But once power was to be granted, the elite was satisfied to have it fall to them. The elite sincerely wanted, or believed that it wanted, democracy—but democracy in which the elite would wield power. Gandhi differed from other members of the elite on this point. He wanted power to be shared by all Indians. In a conversation with his American biographer, this exchange occurred: "There are four hundred million Indians," Gandhi said. "Subtract one hundred million children, waifs and others; if the remaining three hundred million would spin an hour each day we would have Swaraj."

"Because of the economic or spiritual effect?" his biographer asked.

"Both," Gandhi replied. "If three hundred million people did the same thing once a day, not because a Hitler ordered it but because they were inspired by the same ideal, we would have enough unity of purpose to achieve independence." [38]

When the Cabinet Mission Plan was offered, Gandhi played no active role; he did not like the plan, but he refused to attempt to force the other Congress leaders to accede to his wishes. His biographer regards it as evidence of his greatness that he did not try to force his views on Congress members when he saw that they opposed him. But he may simply have been astute enough to see that he would not succeed and unwilling to precipitate an open break with the Congress. Gandhi was unalterably opposed to partition. He always believed it the wrong course, and although he declined to speak against it at the end (from respect either for others' decisions or from lack of an alternative), he never spoke in favor of it. As the course of negotiations seemed to make partition more and more inevitable, Gandhi withdrew further from involvement in them.

With the final collapse of the Cabinet Mission Plan, Governor General Archibald Wavell was recalled, and British Prime Minister Clement

Attlee appointed Louis Mountbatten, a career naval officer with great personal charm and aristocratic family background, as the new Governor General of India. Accounts differ, but partly because of Mountbatten's reluctance to interrupt his naval career for a long period of time and partly because of Attlee's view that a time limit might shock the Indians into some resolution of their conflicts, the deadline for Indian independence was fixed for June 1948.

Mountbatten had not been in India a month when he decided, first, that partition was the only solution to the Indian dilemma and, second, that independence must come soon or the country, already racked by communal struggles, would fall into civil war, which the British administrators would be helpless to prevent or control. His task became that of convincing the Congress leaders of his view. Gandhi was excluded from the negotiations that followed, for he was deemed too idealistic to share in practical political decisions. He was also unalterably opposed to partition. He believed that the British should withdraw from India and leave the Indians to solve their own problems. The British believed that they could not simply withdraw, although it is at least questionable that the results would have been more calamitous than was the actual course of events. Although Gandhi did not lessen his opposition to partition, he did remove himself from the scene of negotiations in Delhi and devoted himself to touring riot-torn areas of India in an attempt to restore peace.

Mountbatten's efforts to convince Congress to accept partition were somewhat facilitated by the recent experiences of Congress leaders with the reality of sharing power with Muslims. Wavell had declared an interim government, and after some wrangling Congress had agreed to allow the Muslim League to appoint one minister. Finance was the portfolio that had been offered to the League, on the grounds, as Patel had argued, that the Muslims would have to reject it, for they had no one qualified to handle it. To their astonishment, the League accepted and appointed Liaquat Ali to the post. Far worse, the new Finance Minister proceeded to establish a heavy income tax—a development doubly embarrassing to Congress. Not only did the tax fall most heavily on the rich capitalists whose financial aid supported Congress, but in view of Congress claims to be a socialist organization, it was difficult to argue coherently against the tax. After such experiences, some writers have argued, Patel became convinced that it would be impossible, as well as undesirable, to attempt to share government with the Muslim League.

But there were other reasons too. After twenty years of fighting for independence, the men who had led the movement were tired; they dreaded the thought of jail again. If they waited for another solution, there was the possibility that it would be worse than the present one. "And so we accepted," wrote Nehru, "and said, let us build up a strong India. And if others do not want to be in it, well, how can we and why should we force them to be in it?" [39]

Congress, led by Nehru and Patel, agreed to partition. The Muslim League, somewhat shocked at actually having been conceded Pakistan, agreed to partition. This was in June 1947. The details remained to be worked out—in two months! Independence was set for August 15, 1947; the announcement of the specific borders of the country in the east and in the west was set for August 17, 1947.

"I shall give you complete assurance," Mountbatten said to Azad in a discussion of independence and partition; "I shall see to it that there is no bloodshed and riot." [40] The violence that erupted during partition left more than 600,000 dead and 14,000,000 homeless refugees. Whole villages were slaughtered by neighboring villages. There were stories of trains filled with refugees crossing the new borders with only corpses on them. On August 14 one British former civil servant commented, "This was no longer rioting; it was war, purposefully organized and fought by trained soldiers, many of them ex-members of the British Indian Army." [41] In the Punjab the Sikhs were responsible for much of the organization. They were a large, strongly organized community whose interests lay with India but who found most of their lands going to Pakistan; they retaliated with organized violence. But violence was not theirs alone: In every region the stronger communities attacked, murdered, and drove out the weaker, and violence was fed by desire for loot, hatred, and stories of atrocities in other areas. The army, which might have been used to preserve the peace, was wholly unreliable. Among Indians there were no nonpartisans.

Although the scope of the riots was beyond anything that could have been predicted, it seems likely that at least their occurrence could have been predicted. Although the secret service had broken down, officers in the border areas knew what was going to happen. Before August 17 there was already a sense of inevitable catastrophe approaching. "The communal feeling I found," one of Mountbatten's advisers said, "I just did not believe possible. It tore at you, all the time. There was slaughter everywhere. We British had all the responsibility and none of the power. The police force was already undermined and the civil service were frustrated and madly anxious." [42]

Precautions were lamentably inadequate. A proposal to reorganize the army was pigeonholed and not acted upon. A fifty-thousand-man Punjab Boundary Force was established to keep peace among a population of fourteen million. If those in command—Mountbatten, Nehru, Jinnah—did not know what was going to happen, it was at least partly because they chose not to know. One year earlier, on Jinnah's Direct Action Day, the riots in Bengal, and particularly in Calcutta, had left six thousand people dead. But in 1947 "no one foresaw the magnitude of the Punjab migrations," as one British officer said. "In part this was due to the belief that once Pakistan was conceded, the basic cause of communal violence would vanish." [43] Little thought had been given to those left on the wrong side of the border. The strongest support of the Muslim League had always been in the Muslim minority areas of India; when Jinnah flew to Pakistan, he left those areas heir to stronger, newly awakened feelings of communal hatred and violence. Congress, unable and unwilling to make concessions, left its adherents vulnerable in areas where they were in the minority. One writer speaks of the "surrealistic air" [44] surrounding preparations for Independence Day; those involved knew that general massacres and migrations would follow the formalization of partition and the announcement of the dividing lines, but they pretended that nothing untoward would happen. The announcement was delayed two days; the pageant of the passing of power from the British Empire to the Indian state was thus permitted to take place in peace before the holocaust. The myths of the nonviolent Indian revolution and of the rational surrender of British power were thus dominant at the festivities of August 15. They were not connected in the minds of the participants with the violence, chaos, and horror that began two days later.

The political process and the political participants were as distant from and as inaccessible to the Indian masses as they had always been under the British Raj. The Indian style of protest had combined total acquiescence with total violence: acquiescence because the forces of power were at once too strong and too unapproachable for any other posture, and violence because only in the safety of a mob could Indians express their frustration and their fear. The Indian style of protest— in the Mutiny, in the communal riots throughout the twentieth century, and in the final carnage of 1947—involved vicious, chaotic, unplanned mob attacks on the weakest representatives of those who held power over them. The mob turned in fury against the isolated British army officer; the lone European woman; the Muslim or Hindu cripple, woman, or child. The nineteenth-century British imperial government had had to deal with the mob; in 1947, in an overwhelming upheaval to which the riots throughout the century had been only the slightest prelude, mob fury, fear, and revenge were turned loose upon the new India, thanks to the remoteness and irresponsibility of its politicians.

Only Gandhi and his disciples had any success in calming the violence that raged throughout India. In Calcutta he and the Muslim mayor lived together in the Untouchables' section and managed to quell the riots that threatened to tear the city apart. Gandhi toured villages throughout Bengal, living with Muslim families and bringing at least temporary relief to the festering hatreds and resentments. In Delhi Gandhi fasted—and threatened to fast to the death—in order to force Hindu and Muslim leaders there to reach an accord and establish peace.

Gandhi employed a traditionally Indian kind of protest, usually applied only in personal matters. In Indian tradition, if a man behaved unjustly to another, the second man sat on the doorstep of the transgressor until he gave in—or the victim starved to death. It was this personal tactic of moral persuasion and guilt which Gandhi had turned into the political tool of protest—*satyagraha*, soul force, civil disobedience, noncooperation. His army of *satyagrahis* had consisted in theory, and sometimes in fact, of personally committed individuals protesting nonviolently against political injustice. In the whole of his method, Gandhi differed from the Indian tradition of violence. But the habit of violence reasserted itself again and again during the twenty years of the nationalist campaign against the British. Again and again Gandhi would abandon his civil-disobedience campaigns, telling politicians who complained that the movement had gone out of control and could not be continued because he would not be responsible for violence. There was a twenty-year struggle between Gandhi's nonviolence and the violent Indian tradition. In the end, after independence and partition, it was clear that nonviolence and individual commitment, the essence of Gandhi's protest movement, had conquered only for a moment, had held the field only briefly against the elitism and communal violence which were traditional in India.

On January 25, 1948, Gandhi was awaited at a prayer meeting in the garden of Birla House in Delhi. He was a few minutes late. As he moved through the crowd toward the platform, Nathuram Vinayak Godse stepped into his path. Godse was a Chitpavan Brahmin from Poona, thirty-five years old and a member of the Mahasabha, a conservative Hindu organization formed for the protection of traditional Hindu society. He was incensed at the recent fast that Gandhi had undergone to protest the treatment of the Muslims in and around Delhi and was convinced that Gandhi's "pro-Muslim" policies would bring the destruction of India and Hinduism. Godse made an obeisance to Gandhi. As the Mahatma raised his joined hands to his forehead to return the salutation and give a blessing, Godse fired a pistol, and Gandhi fell dead.

PART FOUR

THE ERA OF
PERMANENT PROTEST

INTRODUCTION

THE decade following World War II was characterized in Europe and the United States by conformity, political conservatism, and passivity; in the United States there was also a right-wing reaction against the left-wing movements of the 1930s. In Asia and Africa, however, liberation movements in the late 1940s and the 1950s accomplished the virtual extinction of the major European empires. At the end of the 1950s renewed dissent and protest emerged in the Western world, and by the late 1960s the rhythm of protest and rebellion equaled in intensity the radicalism of the 1930s.

We have entered an era of permanent protest, in which one group or another is always laying claim to liberation. Protest in contemporary society appears to go beyond assertions of the rights of particular groups toward demands for liberation of the individual from any kind of political order and social restraint. Communism has been attacked, along with capitalism and imperialism. Previous protests in the twentieth century were aimed at the authority of the established classes over other groups in society, often of the old over the young.

The black liberation movement in the United States, inspired by the emancipation of African and Asian peoples from imperial rule, inaugurated the contemporary era of protest. The emergence of new values among young intellectuals undermined, as in the 1920s, the values and self-confidence of the older generation. Protest again became a popular life-style, and the rhythm of dissent and rebellion produced the Communist protest against Stalinism, world-wide student upheavals in the universities, and the French crisis of 1968.

CHAPTER

11

Black Liberation in
the United States

BLACK protest against slavery began with enslavement itself. In many cases the only form that this protest could take was self-destruction: Many black men and women sailing on slave ships for America threw themselves into the Atlantic Ocean. Through suicide the slave freed himself from bondage and degradation, exercised choice, and effectively struck out against his oppressor by depriving the slave trader of his profits. On plantations throughout the South, the practice of self-mutilation among field hands was not uncommon, for damage to the slaveholder's "equipment" harmed the slaveholder.[1]

Black protest in early America was often openly aggressive, attempting to alleviate oppression by revolt. Insurrection and revolt run through the history of the American South from the earliest days of Spanish exploration. White historians long painted pictures of docile, even happy, field hands, houseboys, and mammies, but modern scholars are uncovering the extent of anger and rebellion. There were 250 known slave revolts—against insuperable odds—before the Civil War, as well as the persistent, though less dramatic, daily rebellion of broken tools, feigned illness, and false pregnancy.

The white man dealt with protest by increased repression. After the discovery of each insurrection plot, there was a tightening of regulations on black life. Throughout the South blacks were not permitted to leave plantations without passes. They were forbidden the right to congregate; often even their churches were shut down to prevent them from gathering. Very little effort was made to relieve the slave's condition, the cause of his protest.

The Southern slave's immediate and all-consuming desire was release from slavery. It was the free black man, however, who had to face the question of his relationship with white Americans. Many blacks had attained their freedom during the Revolution, by fleeing the South, by enlisting in the American or British army, or in the wake of land and property confiscation by the enemy. Some blacks managed to buy their freedom by renting themselves out after their chores were done. Before the Abolition movement, Southerners were not averse to these occasional grants of individual freedom. Many blacks were manumitted during the Revolutionary and Federalist periods, when the Southern statesmen who propounded the principles of freedom and equality with respect to their own treatment by the British extended the Declaration of Independence to black slaves as well. Ironically, the author of the American credo, Thomas Jefferson, continued to hold slaves; he was unable to accept blacks as human beings, rather than as the economic units the Colonists had made of them. Manumission societies were numerous in the Northern states, and as early as the 1790s statesmen like Alexander Hamilton and John Jay were urging individuals to free their slaves. In these various ways a free black population arose, scattered throughout the North and even in Southern cities like Charleston.

These blacks had to face the difficult problem of defining their rightful place in American society. After generations in this country they were less African than American. Unlike natives fighting for emancipation from colonial power, they were not seeking independence or the exile of old masters; American blacks were freed *into* the society of the old masters. Even that freedom was not complete. Whites were not willing to accept blacks as equal citizens. Instead a new class was created in America, neither slave nor citizen, with rights arbitrarily granted or denied. Blacks became, in the familiar phrase, "second-class citizens." The basis for this arrangement was racism, sometimes mild, sometimes vicious, ranging from a South Carolinian's belief that blacks were subhuman to a Bostonian's conviction that they were intellectually inferior.

Did black men want total acceptance in white society, or did they want to be separate from it? Black attempts to enter society always took the form of "cultural whiteness"—that is, complete emulation of white mores and manners and adoption of white standards. Such emulation was demanded by their white superiors, and blacks obliged, either willingly or grudgingly. The price of "cultural whiteness" was denial of their own identity.

The blacks' role and fate depended on white initiative, and almost all black gains resulted from white assistance. In the 1830s and 1840s this assistance took the form of a strong Abolition movement led primarily by churchmen and professional reformers. Abolitionists opposed slavery on moral grounds but were divided over the eventual fate of the emancipated blacks. Few whites could wholeheartedly support black leaders who sought first-class citizenship for former slaves. Instead white reformers proposed to rid the country of the black problem by ridding the country of the blacks. Organizations like the American Colonization Society proposed emigration to Haiti or to Africa. Abraham Lincoln believed that voluntary emigration of American blacks to Libya was the optimal solution. A tacit agreement that blacks would not—and could not—be absorbed into American society bound these reformers together. Many well-meaning crusaders for black freedom were not unwilling to endorse compulsory emigration. The freed black thus fought two battles: in cooperation with the Abolitionists against slavery but at the same time against the Abolitionists' emigration policy. In 1863 the leading blacks of Boston issued a manifesto that made clear their intention to remain in America. "If anybody else wants us to go, they must compel us." [2]

More militant blacks wanted less defensive maneuvering and less reliance on white humanitarianism. At the National Convention of Negroes in 1843, Henry Highland Garnet appealed to his people to rise up in resistance: "Brethren, arise, arise! Strike for your lives and liberties. . . . *Rather die* freemen than live to be slaves. . . . Let your motto be resistance! *resistance!* RESISTANCE!" [3]

It was, however, through the efforts of white men that black slaves eventually gained their freedom. The Civil War put an end to legal slavery. Yet white Americans were unwilling to initiate the full-scale programs of economic and educational assistance necessary to bring black men into "first-class" citizenship. Instead a haphazard program of humanitarian—and patronizing—assistance, usually coupled with political exploitation, typified Reconstruction.

In the late 1870s Reconstruction ended, and the status of the Southern black sank from an artificial peak entirely owing to the artificial props of the army and the Federal government into a condition of segregation only slightly better than slavery. Southern whites systematically disfranchised the blacks through out-and-out intimidation or such legal ruses as literacy tests and grandfather clauses (which disqualified blacks if their grandfathers had been slaves). By 1883 Alabama had only 3,742 registered black voters, out of 140,000 who had formerly been registered. By the end of the century the "separate but equal" doctrine had been developed through a series of Supreme Court decisions culminating in *Plessy v. Ferguson* in 1896. White lawmakers had passed the Fourteenth and Fifteenth Amendments, but political changes and the atrophy of the reform spirit had permitted black codes implementing legal segregation to replace effective application of the Amendments. A reign of terrorism and lynching settled over the South. Black protest existed in a vacuum, unheeded by white Americans, who were tired of the war and of unsolved postwar problems, insulated by a racist philosophy expressed in Darwinian terms, and busy with territorial and economic expansion. Once again blacks found struggle futile until a white humanitarian movement came to their support.

The turn of the century brought the Progressive Era and revived interest in egalitarianism. Again white men organized to aid blacks. The Springfield riots of 1908, a bloody pogrom against Illinois blacks, moved reformers like Jane Addams, Mary White Ovington, John Dewey, and William Dean Howells to issue a call to "all the believers in democracy to join in a National Conference for the Discussion of present evils, the voicing of protests, and the renewal of the struggle for civil and political liberty." [4] The interracial conference, held in 1909, produced the National Negro Committee. In May 1910, this committee was renamed the National Association for the Advancement of Colored People. Its goals were promotion of racial equality and acceptance of American blacks into American society. The N.A.A.C.P.'s orientation reflected the Progressive outlook; it was humanitarian yet patronizing, conservative in style and philosophy. The Progressives placed the highest premium on education and on legally oriented protest. The N.A.A.C.P.'s most intensive campaign throughout the early years was lobbying—unsuccessfully—for an antilynching law. Nevertheless, through such legal challenges it laid the foundations for the civil-rights movements of the 1950s.

Many black leaders refused to support the N.A.A.C.P. Southern black leaders like Booker T. Washington viewed it as radical and detrimental to black progress. These men preferred not to risk annoying white men by challenge and open protest. Instead they hoped to attain improved status in American society through hard work and humility. It was the dream of Booker T. Washington, the most influential black man of his day, that emulation of the white man, elimination of as many offensive differences as possible, and modest goals and requests would improve the blacks' position. When Washington accepted the presidency of Alabama's Tuskegee Institute, he conceived of the college as a training ground for "first-rate mechanical laborers and moral men and women." He believed that the creation of a skilled or semiskilled Negro labor supply would enable black men to bargain their way into society. His emphasis on black humility endeared him to white leaders, and he made no demands for social integration. He sought a subservient but improved economic life for black men. The races were to remain "separate as the fingers on my hand," but black men would at last be permitted to prosper. Washington gratefully acknowledged that black progress resulted from white largess; his own alma mater had been founded and funded by the American Missionary Society.

But most of the men and women educated at Tuskegee or at similar Southern institutions did not want places in a black labor force. Most preferred the most easily accessible profession: teaching. This growing cadre of educated blacks aspired much higher than careers in manual labor. From its ranks came men like W. E. B. DuBois, a distinguished historian with a Ph.D. degree from Harvard University, editor of the N.A.A.C.P. news organ, *The Crisis*, and a militant in comparison to the Washington group. DuBois' goal was fuller integration of blacks into society on all levels, and he urged that a vanguard of the "talented tenth" attempt to take their rightful places in that society. Through the achievements of the exceptional black—as doctor, lawyer, teacher, writer, artist, athlete, statesman—the entire race would thus be upgraded.

Neither Washington's dream nor DuBois' plan had much success. Labor-union discrimination effectively blocked black economic mobility, and no Southern-trained black labor army materialized. When blacks migrated to Northern urban areas immediately before and during World War I, they came as unskilled refugees from lynchings and poverty. The N.A.A.C.P. battle for better jobs and education for blacks was discouragingly slow, and the fight for equal treatment suffered setbacks under Southern-born President Woodrow Wilson.

The failure of both Washington's and DuBois' schemes, combined with disillusionment of blacks who had migrated north in search of greater opportunities, brought discontent and despair. At the same time the experience of World War I infused a new militance into black protest. Military service gave black men new assertiveness and a taste of independence. Furthermore, it produced bitterness and cynicism: The fight to make the world safe for democracy quite clearly did not apply to the United States itself.

Although many returning blacks were militant, it was the nervous white citizens who initiated racial violence after the war. A rash of lynchings broke out immediately after the Armistice in 1918; usually the victims were returning black soldiers. Racial tensions in the ghettos of urban areas also increased, with incidents of white attacks on blacks.

In 1919 black communities all over the country spontaneously began their least accommodating protest: Black Americans began to fight back. Echoing Garnet's 1840 call to resistance, a twentieth-century black poet, Claude McKay, urged his people to

> meet the common foe. . . .
> Like men we'll face the murderous, cowardly pack,
> Pressed to the wall, dying, but—fighting back! [5]

When white sailors from a naval training base near Charleston, South Carolina, began a fight with local blacks, the latter not only defended themselves but counterattacked as well. In Washington, D.C., tensions were aggravated by "opportunistic journalism." On July 19 two blacks jostled a secretary on her way home. After making a few insulting remarks to her, they fled. *The Washington Post*, however, headlined the incident: "Negroes Attack Girl . . . White Men Vainly Pursue." Angered and exctied by this affair as it was reported, the girl's husband, a sailor, and about two hundred other sailors and marines took to the streets to avenge her honor by lynching the culprits. They marched into the ghetto area of the ciy, beating all the blacks they encountered. But blacks organized counterattacks on the seamen, and for four days Washington struggled to contain a race riot.

Only a few days later violence exploded in Chicago. On July 27, 1919, a black swimmer accidentally crossed the invisible line separating the white and black swimming areas at a Chicago beach. White swimmers stoned the offending boy; he drowned. The white policeman patrolling the beach refused to make any arrests, despite charges lodged by black witnesses. Instead he arrested one of the blacks charged by a white with some minor offense. Angry blacks attacked the policeman, and soon black mobs were fighting white mobs throughout the city. Police and black men fired at each other. Only the arrival of the militia ended the battles, leaving fifteen whites and twenty-three blacks dead.

White reaction to the "new black" glimpsed in these riots was not sympathetic. Whites were frightened and disturbed by the violence, which they interpreted as aggressive, rather than defensive. They were only vaguely aware of the realities of ghetto life—and not particularly interested. Few were willing to consider racial equality as a solution to racial unrest. Nor did many propose even the most basic reforms in order to placate blacks. The most common response was a demand for "law and order," enforced if necessary by an enlarged police force. White supremacists capitalized on the riots, claiming that the violence proved the need for more effective subjugation of the blacks. Although many liberals shrank from blatant persecution and repression, they equally evaded any real confrontation with the economic and social problems of their biracial society. They sought outside scapegoats for racial unrest: Bolsheviks, it was claimed, had taken advantage of the postwar confusion to excite the blacks. Blacks, "naturally peaceful, kindly, good-natured, and loyal," were viewed as dupes of Communist agitators. The implication was clear that white men thought black men insufficiently intelligent or independent to evaluate their own situation and to act upon their own conclusions.

Ironically, in the 1920s whites took a faddish interest in black culture and black life. Black writers enjoyed a vogue, and Harlem provided favorite night spots for whites. Their interest and "understanding," however, were painfully superficial. The denizens of the Roaring Twenties found in Harlem a "gay," "happy," delightfully "primitive" subculture, whose poverty and despair seemed merely picturesque. But the blacks were still called "Negroes" and treated with condescension as primitives.

The "Harlem Renaissance" meant something far different to the blacks. The riots of 1919 gave impetus to a black nationalist movement that flowered in the 1920s. The blacks retreated from conflict with the whites; Marcus Garvey gave this withdrawal meaning and shaped it into a constructive exploration of black culture, black history, black identity. His organization, the Universal Negro Improvement Association, was founded on racial pride, on belief in the dignity and beauty of blackness. Millions of blacks, in the North and in the South, joined it.

Garvey was convinced that blacks must unite to help themselves. He was frankly mistrustful of white sympathizers. "It is strange that so many people are interested in the Negro now, willing to advise him how to act and what organizations he should join, yet nobody was interested in the Negro to the extent of not making him a slave for two hundred years. . . ." [6] Garvey espoused a black nationalism in which black men would control their own economy through cooperative ventures. The goal was black-run, -owned, and -patronized business. When whites and conservative blacks argued that this ideal was racism in reverse, Garvey replied, "We are organized not to hate other men, but to lift ourselves, and to demand respect of all humanity." [7] Yet the U.N.I.A. goals reflected the eternal black ambivalence toward the United States. On one hand, it encouraged colonization in Africa; on the other, it developed a plan for economic independence that would not only permit coexistence within American society but would also provide a bargaining wedge with which to enter its mainstream.

By 1925, however, Garvey's movement was dead. Its leader had been convicted of using the mails to defraud and had been deported. Its economic program had proved unfeasible, and it had failed to draw the attention of white Americans to black problems. The African nations, which were later to bring racial conflict to world attention, had not yet begun their revolutions. In the United States the white public was still able comfortably to ignore racial issues.

Black protest was once again left in the hands of the lawyers. Throughout the 1930s, 1940s, and early 1950s the N.A.A.C.P. continued its fight for legal equality. Progress was slow, yet the advantage of such legalistic protest was that its success or failure did not depend only on the mood of the masses or on the awakened interest and support of the white or black community as a whole. The groundwork was thus laid over some thirty years for the civil-rights movements of the 1950s and 1960s. The N.A.A.C.P. concentrated its efforts on education, a continuation of the old Progressive idea that education was the key to mobility and social acceptance.

The attack on the moral validity of the "separate but equal" doctrine began with a test of its practicability. In 1938 the Supreme Court ordered the State of Missouri either to admit blacks to the University of Missouri Law School or to provide them with equal law-school facilities. In 1948 the Court ordered Texas to admit a black man to the University of Texas on the grounds that black educational facilities in the state were not equal. And in 1952 the N.A.A.C.P. took up the cause of the Brown family, of Topeka, Kansas, in a legal battle to enroll their daughter in an all-white high school. For two years the case dragged through the courts. Finally, the Supreme Court handed down its decision in *Brown v. Board of Education*: The "separate but equal" doctrine was dead. The Court ordered school districts to begin—following one year of grace—to integrate education.

The *Brown v. Board of Education* decision was the beginning of the modern civil-rights movement. It set the style and direction of black protest for almost ten years. First, it concentrated protest almost exclusively in the South. Second, it reinforced black leaders' propensity to view progress in terms of legal protest. This Southern concentration and legal tone made it possible to attract the indispensable participation and support of Northern white liberals. The nature of Southern discrimination and intimidation made moral commitment a clear-cut issue for these liberals. Finally, the movement gained white respect by adopting from the start the Gandhian principle of nonviolence and Christian emphasis on love and patience, which allayed white fears of disruption.

American blacks felt that their moment had come. The 1954 decision seemed to be a great thaw after seventy years of legally sanctioned discrimination. A sizable number of blacks were ready in the 1950s to endure the inevitable discomforts and dangers of transforming law into practice. Although in 1919 they had been aware of no revolutionary traditions but those in the United States and Russia, by the late 1950s they could look to the independence movements of Africa for strength and hope. Furthermore, black Americans shared with other American reformers a naïve reverence for the magical powers of the law. They believed that law could change conditions—and that the law would automatically be carried out. Mississippi Senator James Eastland warned that "the people of the South will never accept this monstrous decision. I predict this decision will bring on a century of litigation." [8] Yet blacks relied on the average American to obey the law. Their faith in the larger white society was reflected in their willingness to move slowly and to prove themselves at every step. In short, black men, believing in their eventual success, were ready to face sacrifices along the way.

The battle of Little Rock best exemplified the protest movement of the 1950s. It was clear that in some states in the Deep South defiance, stalling, intimidation, and violence would be used to prevent "mongrelizing" of the white race, which Southern logic placed a hop, skip, and jump from integrated classes in algebra. In Arkansas, however, moves toward compliance with the law were being made. Five days after the Court decision, Fayetteville, Arkansas, announced that six black students who had been commuting to a high school sixty miles away would be admitted to the local school. Other small towns also announced fall integration plans. Arkansas colleges would accept black applicants in the fall. Governor Francis Cherry set the tone by declaring that "Arkansas would obey the law."

In Little Rock the school board proposed a three-phase integration plan. Step one was integration on the high-school level, step two on the junior high-school level, and step three on the elementary level. Not surprisingly, the board showed some reluctance actually to initiate the program. A vague promise of a beginning in 1957 was offered. A legal dance began; in 1955 the Arkansas N.A.A.C.P. filed suit on behalf of thirty-three black parents for immediate desegregation of grades one through twelve. A Federal judge ruled against these parents, arguing that the school board was acting in good faith in scheduling an integration program for fall 1957. The N.A.A.C.P. appealed, apparently less in the hope of winning a reversal than to ensure sufficient pressure on the Little Rock school board to meet the 1957 deadline.

Yet by then the tone of the state government had changed greatly. Cherry had been defeated in 1955 by Orval Faubus, who declared that "Arkansas is not ready for a complete and sudden mixing of the races." In the spring of 1957 four prosegregation bills were introduced into the state legislature, including a blanket grant of power to a State Sovereignty Committee to protect Arkansas's rights against encroachment by the Federal government, a bill making attendance at integrated schools noncompulsory, and a bill giving school boards permission to use school funds to hire lawyers in integration suits. Despite protests by religious leaders, politicians, and the N.A.A.C.P., these bills passed both houses of the legislature. It was clear that segregationist forces had consolidated and brought pressure to bear and that liberals and moderates, through indifference, fear, or unconscious racism, had relinquished their role in directing Arkansas's actions. The vacuum in leadership had been filled by Governor Faubus, the White Citizens' Councils, and the Ku Klux Klan.

The blacks were thus confronted with both "legal" opposition tacitly condoned and with intimidation. Yet the major moves were still played in the courtroom. In August 1957, a few days after a rock had sailed through the living-room window of Daisy Bates, state president of the N.A.A.C.P., a white mother filed suit for an injunction against integration. Mrs. Thomason alleged that she sought to protect innocent children from the terrorism that threatened if Little Rock's Central High School were opened to both races in September. Governor Faubus himself took the stand to testify that he personally knew that guns had been taken from black and white students alike. The injunction was granted. To celebrate, segregationists rode past Mrs. Bates's home, honking horns and shouting: "Daisy, Daisy, did you hear the news? The coons won't be going to Central." [9] The Federal District Court, however, overruled the injunction. Integration was to proceed immediately.

Nine black students—Carlotta Walls, Jefferson Thomas, Elizabeth Eckford, Thelma Mothershed, Melba Patillo, Ernest Green, Terrence Roberts, Gloria Ray, and Minnijean Brown—were to register at Central on the first day of school. Governor Faubus, however, moved to override the court decision in the interests of what he called safety. The day before school opened he ordered Central High surrounded by National Guardsmen. At first no one was certain whether this action had been taken to protect the nine black students or to prevent their enrollment. The Governor soon made his intentions clear. In a televised address to the citizens of Arkansas he declared Central off limits to blacks. In a cynical gesture of impartiality he declared Horace Mann, an all-black high school, off limits to whites. Faubus, with all the force of state law at his command, claimed that he could not control protesting white supremacists. "Blood will run in the streets," he said, if the nine black students insisted on entering the white school.

The nine did not try to register the next day, but the N.A.A.C.P. and Superintendent Virgil Blossom agreed on enrollment the following day. Blossom asked that the children arrive without their parents, which he felt would make their protection easier. Reluctantly the leaders agreed, but Daisy Bates arranged for local ministers, both black and white, to escort the children to Central's gate, arriving all together in a police car. By accident one of the new black students was not notified of the plan to enter Central in a group. Elizabeth Eckford, fifteen years old, arrived alone at Central, where she faced a mob of hundreds of screaming adults and teen-agers gathered in front of the National Guardsmen. She made her way through the crowd, but Guardsmen refused to let her enter the school. The crowd shouted obscenities and insults: "Go home, you bastard of a black bitch!" The women sent up a continuous chorus, urging their men to "lynch her, lynch her!" The Guardsmen made no effort to control the crowd as it pushed toward Elizabeth, blocking her way and shoving her. She was finally helped onto a bus and away from the crowd by *New York Times* reporter Bernard Fine and a local white woman. As the bus pulled away, a middle-aged white woman urged the mob to grab Fine and "kick him in the balls!" No one was arrested.

Meanwhile Elizabeth's eight friends had also been turned away by the National Guard, acting on Faubus' orders. Two school days had passed, and Central remained segregated.

Little Rock blacks sought legal redress. Thurgood Marshall and Wiley Branton went before a U.S. Federal District Court to ask for an injunction against interference with integration by Faubus. At the hearing Faubus' lawyers staged a walkout. Despite this display of Perry Mason dramatics, the injunction was granted. Faubus responded by dutifully withdrawing the National Guard. It was clear that he would use his powers to protect whites from nine black children but would make no effort to ensure black safety from the growing mobs.

On September 23 the black students were spirited into Central by a side entrance and registered. The mob "guarding" the school entrance was furious. Unable to get at the children, they attacked black reporters: Jimmy Hicks of New York City's *Amsterdam News*, Alex Wilson, and Earl Davy. Women in the mob screamed to their children: "Come out! Don't stay in there with those niggers!" Fifty students fled the classrooms, hysterically crying, "They're in, they're in!" The black children were removed before noon, for police chief Gene Smith realized that he could not hold back the mob with his men.

The white mob, thwarted at the school, roared through the city, beating up blacks at random. After this outburst the Little Rock Mayor requested help from President Dwight Eisenhower. The President immediately Federalized the entire ten-thousand-man Arkansas National Guard, and by 6:00 P.M. trucks, jeeps, and soldiers were arriving in Little Rock. The next day, escorted and protected by Federal troops, the nine children walked quietly through Central's main doors.

They continued to attend Central, at first escorted to classes and to and from school by the military. They were continually harassed by fellow students in a petty but vicious manner: kicked, tripped, pushed, threatened, insulted. When Minnijean Brown poured a bowl of chili on tormenters who had spilled soup on her, she was suspended. Black students were permitted to remain at Central only on the condition that they not "retaliate, verbally or physically, to any harassment." Minnijean left. The next day a group of students wore placards boasting, "One down, eight to go."

Yet on May 27, 1958, Central High School graduated its first black student, Ernest Green. This event was greeted by white liberals and many black leaders as a major step toward breaking down the barriers of Southern custom. It was an important symbolic victory. But symbolic victories educate few black children. In 1961, after years of perseverance in the face of danger, humiliation, and expense, fewer than 7 per cent of the South's black children were attending integrated schools.

The *Brown v. Board of Education* decision struck down the "separate but equal" doctrine only as it applied to education. Its immediate effect, however, was to unleash a battle against all forms of segregation, for in the minds of American blacks it legitimized their demands for racial equality. Even before the test of school integration at Little Rock, the blacks of Montgomery, Alabama, had begun hammering away at the segregation that burdened their everyday life. The civil-rights movement actually began on December 1, 1955, when Mrs. Rosa Parks, a seamstress for a downtown department store, boarded the Cleveland Avenue bus after a long day at work. She took a seat toward the back of the crowded rush-hour bus, for Southern custom decreed that whites seat themselves from the front and blacks from the back of the bus. When the white section of the bus was filled, the driver ordered Mrs. Parks to relinquish her borderline seat to a white passenger and to stand. Such an order was not unusual, but Mrs. Parks refused to comply. The driver had her taken off the bus and arrested.

Why had Rosa Parks refused to give up her seat? Whites in Montgomery speculated that the trouble-making N.A.A.C.P., in which Mrs.

Parks had once held office, had put her up to it. Others labeled her a "Communist agitator." In fact, Mrs. Parks was simply and quietly protesting her role as "nigger." It was a protest against a centuries-old kind of treatment that other Montgomery blacks easily understood. What surprised the country and the world was the spontaneous support these people gave to one individual gesture of protest.

An ad hoc committee was formed by local black women immediately after her arrest. They urged clergymen to call for a total boycott of public buses. A community meeting was called by the clergy, and it proved to be the largest gathering of Montgomery's black leaders in that city's history. The bus boycott was agreed upon. It was to begin on Monday, three days away.

The major problem was communication; word of the boycott plan must be spread to the seventeen thousand blacks who rode to work each day. The clergymen used their Sunday pulpits to publicize the boycott, but the committee took no chances, and in one weekend hurriedly mimeographed and distributed thousands of flyers to the city's fifty thousand blacks. The man who organized the leaflet campaign was Martin Luther King, a young minister, a graduate of the Boston University Divinity School, and new in town. On Monday morning the black boycott took the city by surprise. It was almost 100 percent effective. On Monday night the black community elected Martin Luther King president of a permanent boycott organization, the Montgomery Improvement Association.

The association formulated a set of demands that were surprisingly mild: courteous treatment of black bus riders; seating on a first-come, first-serve basis, with blacks taking seats from back to front, whites from front to back; and employment of black drivers on predominantly black bus routes. So moderate were these demands that the local N.A.A.C.P. refused to join the movement until more stringent demands were made.

White reaction to the successful boycott was bitter; violence and terrorism marked the following weeks. King was jailed. Yet the boycott continued, infuriating the whites; the only result of the terrorism was an increase in black demands. The M.I.A. now sought an end to segregated seating. When the protest took this new direction, the N.A.A.C.P. willingly stepped in to aid the movement. On May 11, 1956, N.A.A.C.P. legal counsel Robert Carter argued the case against segregation on public facilities before the Federal District Court. On June 4 the court ruled that segregation on municipal buses was illegal. Four months later the U. S. Supreme Court upheld the ruling. Montgomery's blacks had won.

The victory encouraged similar protests against segregated facilities all through the South. The lessons of community cooperation were not lost. Most important, this type of protest—against the petty, day-to-day discrimination endured by all blacks—directly involved more people than did N.A.A.C.P. court battles or N.A.A.C.P.-sponsored and -directed school integration struggles. A much larger segment of the black community now seemed willing, even eager, to participate in protest movements.

It was King who understood most clearly the lesson of Montgomery. He realized the potential of mobilizing Southern black masses in the cause of civil rights. His realization inspired the formation of a new organization, the Southern Christian Leadership Conference. The S.C.L.C. was a loose affiliation of local groups, led by community clergymen and organized around the most familiar and effective organizational unit in the Southern blacks' experience, the church. By making practical use of the existing social structure, King sought to reach the people. He was twenty-seven years old at the time, a well-educated theologian and minister of the Ebenezer Baptist Church of Atlanta. He was neither a great intellectual nor a great organizer, but, as Louis Lomax explained, he "was the foremost interpreter of the Negro's tiredness in terms which the mass Negro [could] understand and respond to." [10]

It was King who incorporated the Gandhian principle of nonviolence and the Christian doctrine of "love thine enemy" into the civil-rights movement. King believed that patient and dignified protest would awaken the conscience of the nation. His organization worked in counterpoint to the N.A.A.C.P. Like the older organization, the S.C.L.C.'s goal was total integration, but rather than drawing upon the black bourgeoisie and black professionals, King mobilized the masses on a regional basis. While the N.A.A.C.P. continued to concentrate on education, he sought concessions that would affect the average Southern black more directly. Despite the differences in constituency and leadership, the two organizations worked in concert, with the N.A.A.C.P. supplying the ever-necessary legal assistance.

On February 1, 1960, four freshmen from the all-black Agricultural and Technical College at Greensboro, North Carolina, initiated a new phase of the civil-rights revolution. They decided to carry protest against racism into the enemy camp; they quietly entered a Woolworth store and sat down at the all-white lunch counter. When they refused to leave, the manager closed the counter. The four opened their school books and began to read. Greensboro's radio stations broadcast the news immediately, to blacks as well as to whites. Within the hour other A. & T. students were pouring in to join the original four.

Later in the day black students called upon the head of the local N.A.A.C.P., Dr. George Simpkins, seeking help. Dr. Simpkins debated with himself and at last decided not to mobilize his own organization, which was unequal to the task in Greensboro. Instead he called the Congress of Racial Equality, a little-known but well-established organization founded by pacifists in 1942 and critical of the N.A.A.C.P. for being insufficiently aggressive in the case of black liberation. C.O.R.E. perfected the techniques of nonviolent direct action employed by Gandhi against British rule in India. It had already staged unpublicized sit-ins. If any group could ensure the students' success, it was C.O.R.E., which then sent Len Holt to Greensboro to train student volunteers in "passive resistance." Holt seated them at long tables resembling lunch counters; then he and his assistants played "whitey" to their "nigger." "Whitey" blew smoke in their faces, called them "coon" and "nigger," pushed them, hit them. Any student who responded angrily or fought back flunked the test.

News of the events in Greensboro spread quickly, and soon other organizations were offering help. King came to the small North Carolina town to encourage the sit-ins. His presence was a boost to the students' morale, for although C.O.R.E. had developed the techniques of nonviolence, it was King who had established it as a guiding principle. N.A.A.C.P. headquarters sent Herbert Wright, its youth secretary. Both organizations supplied needed money and advice. A pattern for protest activity was emerging: Local Southerners started demonstrations; then national organizations sent money and advisers.

The Greensboro sit-ins did not immediately succeed in integrating Woolworth's lunch counter, but eventual success seemed certain. Black pressure meant bad publicity, which a national company could ill afford. A thousand miles away, Northern liberals could sit-in, boycott, or picket local Woolworths in sympathetic protest. The sit-ins, illegal in the strictest sense, proved in fact much more effective than legal methods. The issue of segregated eating facilities reached the U.S. Supreme Court in October 1961. The Warren Court's decision favoring integration was handed down one month later. But in many areas of the country the issue had already been settled practically, by sit-ins.

Greensboro popularized C.O.R.E.'s nonviolent direct action technique and proved its effectiveness. Greensboro also initiated black youths into the civil-rights movement, and they promptly took the lead. Students formed their own organization, the Student Nonviolent Coordinating Committee (S.N.C.C., or "Snick"), to mobilize students on campuses across the South for sit-in demonstrations.

S.N.C.C. had a shoestring budget. Its first director, James Forman, took on his duties for sixty dollars a week. The money needed to get S.N.C.C. started came from S.C.L.C. and from the Northern Students' Movement. Although formed originally for campus-based action, S.N.C.C. quickly developed community projects and spun off summer projects throughout the South.

On March 13, 1961, C.O.R.E.'s new national director, James Farmer, announced plans for a "Freedom Ride," an integrated bus trip through the South to challenge racial discrimination in interstate terminals. Three years before, the Court has expanded a 1946 ruling against segregation on interstate carriers to include segregation in terminals. C.O.R.E. intended to test that ruling; it wanted to turn a paper victory into a practical one. The Rides were scheduled to begin on May 4 in Washington, D.C. The first Freedom Riders were a mixture of black and white, ranging in age from eighteen to sixty-one.

The Freedom Ride was not without precedent. In 1947 a "journey of reconciliation," cosponsored by C.O.R.E. and the Fellowship of Reconciliation, had carried blacks and whites on a two-week bus trip through the upper South. The journey had been undertaken to test the 1946 ruling against segregation in interstate travel. Bayard Rustin, a founder of C.O.R.E., had enlisted sixteen people to test Jim Crow seating and discourteous treatment of blacks by white drivers on Greyhound and Trailways lines. This early group was also trained in Gandhian nonviolent tactics. It met with some violence and achieved little success in the end. In 1947 the nation—white and black—had not yet been awakened to civil-rights issues. There were no reporters waiting to interview Rustin and his Freedom Riders at the end of that first journey. Few people—white or black—read about or saw pictures of the journey. Ironically, although the Freedom Riders found most drivers and passengers willing to accept integrated travel, the bus companies preferred to ignore the Court rulings. The 1947 group found few blacks ready to assert their rights to nondiscriminatory travel.

By 1961 the public attitude had changed radically; by then the world was watching the South. Television, radio, and press reporters followed the 1961 Riders. Black and white assistance came readily. The Federal government was prepared to put pressure on Southern state governments to protect the Freedom Riders. Blacks who took part needed no encouragement or cajoling to take seats in the front of the buses. And this time the Riders were headed into the Deep South.

The 1961 Rides were pilgrimages through petty harassment and nasty violence. The farther south the Riders went, the greater the resistance they met. At Danville, Virginia, restaurant facilities were integrated without incident, but in Charlotte, North Carolina, a Rider was arrested for trespassing when he demanded a shoeshine at the bus station. Some terminals simply closed their white waiting rooms or their restaurants. In Atlanta Riders found terminals complying with the *interstate* ruling by supplying one integrated waiting room but enforcing segregation for *intrastate* travelers, forcing blacks to wait in a separate room.

In Alabama the long-expected violence broke out. Southern whites were unwilling to end those segregation practices that assured them all, rich or poor, educated or illiterate, their comfortable, unearned sense of superiority. They were also infuriated by Northern "agitators," Northern busybodies, "uppity Northern niggers," television cameramen, and the Federal government's mounting attack on the bulwark of Southern racism, the doctrine of state sovereignty. Alabama complied with the demand of the Department of Justice for protective escort for the Freedom Buses en route, but it left the bus terminals themselves unguarded. At Anniston, Alabama, Greyhound Riders were met by a mob; no one was allowed off the bus. The Trailways bus carrying Riders was bombed and burned; the Riders escaped, but some were beaten.

On Sunday, May 14, the first Freedom Buses arrived in Birmingham. There was not a single policeman at the Trailways terminal. The reason given by Birmingham Police Chief Eugene ("Bull") Connor: It was Mothers' Day, and most of his men were off duty, visiting their mothers. Many of Birmingham's citizens, however, were less sentimentally inclined. A mob lined the sidewalk near the bus-loading platform. Most were young; some carried iron bars. Two Riders disembarked and entered the waiting room. Within seconds they were attacked by six men swinging fists and iron pipes. One of the victims, James Peck, had been on the 1947 journey. In May 1961, he had to lie on the operating table for four hours while fifty-three stitches were taken in his head.

The next lap of the journey was from Birmingham to Montgomery. The Riders regrouped in the Greyhound terminal on Monday, but the drivers refused to take them any farther. The mob, which had become a familiar part of the journey, had already gathered. After much delay these Riders boarded a plane to New Orleans, and the first of the 1961 Freedom Rides was over.

The C.O.R.E. Ride had ended, but other groups began to send Riders into Alabama. From May 17 until the end of the month, Freedom Rides continued, sponsored by C.O.R.E., the Nashville Student Movement, S.N.C.C., and S.C.L.C. They were joined by clergymen, white college professors, and Northern white students. Along the way Riders were jailed "for their own protection" or on charges of trespassing or interfering with arrests. In Montgomery on May 20 hundreds of segregationists attacked a group of Riders at an unguarded terminal. The mob beat blacks in the terminal indiscriminately. Newspaper photographers were kicked, beaten, and left unconscious. After ten minutes the police arrived, but they at first made no effort to disperse the mob; in the end they arrested eight of the "integrationists."

The Federal government sent U.S. marshals to Montgomery. The courts issued injunctions against the Ku Klux Klan, the National States' Rights Party, and all individuals interfering with "peaceful interstate travel by bus." But the violence continued. The arrests of Riders also continued.

In most cases the Freedom Riders in Alabama and Mississippi did not themselves succeed in integrating facilities. Often they never had the opportunity to try. But the Freedom Riders were ultimately victorious. A thousand Riders had brought the South to its knees: On November 1, an Interstate Commerce Commission ban on segregation in terminal facilities became effective.

The Rides catapulted C.O.R.E. and Farmer to national fame. By 1962 C.O.R.E.'s biracial membership exceeded forty thousand. For the next few years blacks and whites continued steadily to wear down local legal barriers to integration, despite Southern resistance. To that bastion of lily-white education, the University of Mississippi, came black student James Meredith in 1962. In 1957 the nine students at Little Rock had been greeted by mobs; in 1962 Meredith faced a mob willing to destroy its own school rather than to permit one black to enroll. Like Faubus, Governor Ross Barnett was cheered as a hero when he blocked Meredith's enrollment three times. When in October President John F. Kennedy finally called in troops to occupy the campus and to uphold Meredith's right to enroll at "Ole Miss," there was a night of rioting as enraged segregationists attacked guardsmen. At first the crowd had attacked only newsmen, but when one of Mississippi's own National Guard units—Federalized by the President—appeared on the campus to protect Meredith, the Mississipians attacked it in a frenzy. Eggs were thrown, then rocks. There were several acts of arson. Someone threw a metal pipe, which struck and stunned one Federal marshal. Jim McShane, of the Justice Department, saw the marshall fall and immediately declared war on the mob. All through Sunday night Federal marshals emptied canister after canister of tear gas into the mob, which kept up a barrage of stones, bricks, iron bars, Coke bottles, chunks of concrete, gas, and bombs. They fired pistols and rifles. A French newspaperman, Paul Gruhard, was fatally shot in the back. A bystander was killed by a shot through his forehead. Sixteen of the Mississippi national guardsmen were wounded. The racist mob smashed, burned, and shot up much of the campus before troop reinforcements quelled the rioting.

Again in Mississippi sit-ins, pray-ins, picketing, and organized boycotts were used to "crack the Deep South." The Deep South responded with the murder of black leader Medgar Evers in June 1963. A Birmingham church was bombed on September 15, 1963, and four young girls were killed. In its aftermath a maddening perversion of justice and laws was perpetrated: Byron de la Beckwith, Evers' confessed murderer, was not even indicted for the crime.

At that point groups like S.N.C.C. inaugurated a new attack, which proved more threatening to racists than had individual acts like that of James Meredith. The sit-ins and Freedom Rides had been protests against the superficial aspects of racism; segregated facilities were regarded as only symbols of a fundamental attitude. S.N.C.C. realized that the power structure in the South maintained and guaranteed this attitude and as early as 1961 began to lay the groundwork for a revolution in substance, rather than merely in form.

S.N.C.C. began a series of Mississippi summer projects aimed at meaningful political emancipation. Robert Moses, a young black civil-rights leader, organized the first Mississippi project. He began in McComb, a town of thirteen thousand people, where he found a small number of local students willing to help S.N.C.C.—despite their fear of white retaliation—by providing housing, transportation, and publicity. They canvassed in black neighborhoods, helping Moses to determine the potential voting population. This estimate was compared to the actual number of registered black voters: The result was a picture of almost total black disfranchisement.

Other S.N.C.C. field representatives arrived. By early August they had opened the first of their voter-registration schools, where classes on the Mississippi constitution, the mysteries and hidden pitfalls of registration applications, and the nature and habits of white registrars were held for potential voters. The first few attempts at registration were enough to arouse the whites to awareness of the significance of S.N.C.C.'s new project. Intimidation, arrests, and fines followed, yet the voter-registration schools continued to draw interested, though often frightened, blacks.

By 1962 C.O.R.E., S.C.L.C., and the Mississippi State Conference of the N.A.A.C.P. had joined S.N.C.C. in its voter-registration project. That summer white students poured into Mississippi from campuses in the West and North. Yet the legal gains remained small. In 1963 S.N.C.C. made a significant change in its tactics. It held a freedom registration, parallel to the official registration, operating on the principle of "one man, one vote" and ignoring such legal requirements as poll taxes and literacy tests. About 83,000 blacks participated. Later they cast their votes for the biracial "freedom candidates" for Mississippi Governor and Lieutenant Governor. This registration was the beginning of political action parallel to, but outside, that of the existing structures. It revealed the potential strength—and menace—of an organized black community. It succeeded in involving blacks on the local level, as Martin Luther King had always urged. It gave them political experience that they could not have gained in a lifetime of attempts to enter the white-dominated regular Democratic Party.

The link between the freedom voting and earlier forms of protest like sit-ins and Freedom Rides was in the goal of racial equality. The voting, like the riding, according to Arthur I. Waskow, "consists of doing outside the existing local law what could have been done legally if racial equality had already been achieved." [11] But unlike the sit-ins and Rides, the process of establishing a parallel political structure necessarily awakened and reinforced separatist leanings toward specifically black power, rather than toward the diffusion of blacks into a salt-and-pepper political stream.

In 1964 Mississippi blacks formed a counter–Democratic Party, the Mississippi Freedom Democratic Party, "open to all Democrats in Mississippi of voting age, regardless of race, creed, or color." Freedom schools were again set up. Despite vicious harassment—which included the cold-blooded murder of three S.N.C.C. workers, Michael Schwerner, James Chaney, and Andrew Goodman—party organization proceeded. By July precinct meetings had been held all over the state. Delegates were chosen for county conventions, which in turn sent representatives to a state-wide convention on August 6. There delegates to the National Democratic Convention in Atlantic City, New Jersey, were selected. They planned to seek recognition and seating as the rightful Mississippi delegation and thus as the legal Democratic Party of Mississippi.

President Lyndon B. Johnson and the National Democratic Convention leaders hoped for an orderly convention. To prevent any disruption they offered the M.F.D.P. seating as "honored observers" while the regular delegation took its seats as usual. The M.F.D.P. refused this token concession. Instead it brought its case before the Credentials Committee, on the grounds that the regular Democratic Party of Mississippi had often abandoned both the national platform and the national candidates and was thus no more entitled to seating at the 1964 Democratic convention than the Mississippi delegation to the Republican convention might be. Conversely, as the only political group in Mississippi loyal to the national party and its candidates was the M.F.D.P., that group claimed the right to a convention seating. The regular Democrats relied on their long-standing legal recognition and on their ability to deliver—if they chose—"real" votes. The niceties of the legal arguments seemed strangely irrelevant compared to the reality of that Mississippi summer of violence and murder.

White-liberal sympathy for the M.F.D.P. was strong. The testimony of civil-rights workers from Mississippi and the presence of Martin Luther King strengthened their inclination to support the challengers. A favorable compromise proposal was drawn up by Representative Edith Green, of Oregon: An oath of loyalty to the national nominees and national platform would be demanded from both Democratic delegations. Each delegate who swore it would be seated; delegates who refused would be denied recognition. The allotted Mississippi vote would then be divided among all accepted delegates. The compromise was presented to the liberal members of the Credentials Committee, who cautiously agreed to support it. The M.F.D.P. also reluctantly accepted the Green proposal, which did after all still sanction the established structure. The compromise, however, was never carried to the convention at large—where it might well have been passed—for the administration had become aware of the strength of the M.F.D.P. and moved quickly to block open debate. Pressure was brought to bear on liberal supporters. When many held firm, the Johnson administration decided to steal the liberals' thunder. It proposed that a loyalty oath be required of the regular delegation; those who refused to pledge party fidelity would not be seated. Two members of the M.F.D.P. would be selected by the Credentials Committee to take seats as "delegates at large" with voting rights—but not as representatives of Mississippi. For the future, the administration urged provisions to ensure that delegations be chosen without racial discrimination.

Liberals accepted the administration's proposal. The M.F.D.P. was urged by many civil-rights leaders to accept also. These leaders saw the administration's concession to the challengers as a great victory and urged realistic compromise as the basis of mature politics. Others, however, argued that their basic moral position should not be diluted. They insisted that the *raison d'être* of the Freedom Party should not be compromised; practical victories at the expense of principle would not satisfy the Mississippi blacks whom they represented. To sit "at large," rather than as representatives of their Mississippi constituency, would be a denial of their own legitimacy. It was not a question of sprinkling a few black faces among whites on the convention floor but of gaining recognition as a party unit.

The M.F.D.P. rejected the administration proposal; it was chastised for being naïve, but it stood firm. The lesson of the convention was clear for many black leaders: Any coalition with white liberals was built on sand; blacks would have to rely only on themselves and on their united power. Consequently, S.N.C.C.'s next Southern effort was to build an independent, all-black party in Lowndes County, Alabama. Members of this Black Panther Party assumed the existence of a struggle for power between the races. By uniting to elect black mayors, sheriffs, and school boards, they hoped to win that struggle.

The days of "black and white together" in the civil-rights movement were coming to an end. The high point of cooperation came with the March on Washington in 1963, but it was also the beginning of decline. The march was conceived by civil-rights leaders as a means of pressuring Congress into passing a strong and effective civil-rights bill. It was also a gesture to awaken the conscience of the nation. The Freedom Marchers would bring protest to the heart of the very capital of the United States and would confront Congress and the administration with the continued denial of black liberation.

The idea had considerable historical precedent. In 1894 Populist leader Jacob Coxey had led an "army" of unemployed on a march to the capital to demand the creation of much-needed jobs. In 1932—within the memory of many of the 1963 leaders—almost seventeen thousand veterans had formed the "Bonus Army," which had descended on Washington and had camped in shacks on the Anacostia Flats, waiting for Congress to grant it military bonuses. Not until President Hoover sent in Federal troops had the shanty towns been emptied. As early as 1949 civil-rights leaders had envisaged a march on Washington similar to the one that took place on August 28, 1963, one hundred years and twenty-four days after the signing of the Emancipation Proclamation.

The march probably had little effect on the fate of the Civil-Rights Bill. Senate Majority Leader Mike Mansfield was the first to admit this lack of influence. The 1964 civil-rights package that Congress finally produced was hammered out according to the orthodox rules of political compromise. But the march fulfilled its own goals: More than any previous effort, it created—for at least one day—the biracial humanitarian community that was the dream of the civil-rights movement. Two hundred thousand people gathered to show their support. Six busloads of Alabama blacks made the 753-mile trip to Washington. They carried picnic baskets, water jugs, Bibles. Many had never left their home towns before. For some the bus tickets represented one-tenth of their weekly salaries. From Jacksonville, Florida, came the "Freedom Special," thirteen railroad cars carrying more than 750 people to the capital. Cars, buses, and trains from New York, Michigan, Texas, New Jersey, and Arkansas brought blacks and whites to Washington. The atmosphere was that of a dignified carnival and Sunday prayer meeting. There was no violence, but there was a pervasive sense that August 28, 1963, was an important day in history. "I was there," read the marchers' buttons, and in fact the march seemed to be a kind of head count, a "testifying."

The leaders were both black and white: They included King; Floyd McKissick, of C.O.R.E.; Whitney Young, of the Urban League; Walter Reuther, president of the United Auto Workers; A. Philip Randolph, founder and president of the Brotherhood of Sleeping Car Porters; Roy Wilkins, executive secretary of the N.A.A.C.P.; Rabbi Joachim Prinz, president of the American Jewish Congress; Dr. Eugene Carson Blake, of the Presbyterian Church; and Matthew Ahmann, of the National Catholic Conference for Interracial Justice. These men coordinated the march, but the day really belonged to the marchers. The plan had been to assemble around the reflecting pool at the Lincoln Memorial. From there the demonstration was to march at noon to the Lincoln Memorial. But by 11:00 the crowd had begun its march spontaneously; without its leaders it moved slowly toward the statue of Lincoln. On the speakers' platform sat an incongruous collection of movie stars, black athletes, and civil-rights organizers. Peter, Paul, and Mary sang; the Freedom Singers from Mississippi sang; Bob Dylan sang. Joan Baez preceded Ralph Bunche; no one thought the juxtaposition odd. Finally King spoke. As always, he captured the essence of peoples' feelings: "I have a dream," he said. "I have a dream that one day this nation will rise up and live out the true meaning of its creed: "We hold these truths to be self-evident, that all men are created equal.' I have a dream," he said, and the crowd roared with him, "that one day even the State of Mississippi, a state sweltering with the heat of injustice, sweltering with the heat of oppression, will be transformed into an oasis of freedom and justice."

The marchers pledged themselves to continue the fight for freedom nonviolently, patiently, and with love. But already the time of love was drawing to an end. The call for freedom was becoming a call for "Freedom now!" The patient confidence of "We shall overcome—someday" seemed so much whistling in the wind to many young blacks. The Civil-Rights Bill was properly liberal; it prohibited segregation and outlawed racial discrimination in hiring, firing, and union membership wherever interstate commerce was involved. It forbade Federal grants to state programs that were discriminatory and granted the U.S. Attorney General greater powers to protect civil-rights workers and blacks from denials of their Constitutional rights. But the gap between law and reality seemed always to be growing. The more promised, the less gained. And the blacks who were most disappointed were *not* the Southern blacks who had been denied seats in the front of the bus; they were Northern ghetto blacks. The new militant voices came from New York, Chicago, and Los Angeles. The "Negro problem" turned out to be not a regional one after all. Demands for a civil-rights bill including Federal aid to train and place unemployed workers and a fair-employment law reflected new awareness of urban race problems. More than that, it represented an end to the naïve belief that granting *civil* rights would end poverty and unemployment or eliminate ghettos. There were those, of course, who had recognized this hard truth all along, but most Americans had long confused the surface trappings of discrimination with the real problem.

In the face of such discouragement the Northern ghettos experienced a sweeping revival of separatist ideology and a militant resurrection of Garvey's "black nationalism." A militant movement had begun in the 1950s, when Elijah Muhammad had declared himself the Black Prophet of Islam in America. He preached total rejection of European customs, culture, and religion; Black Muslims wanted to eradicate all traces of the "cultural whiteness" that had been painstakingly learned over the centuries. Initiates of the sect abandoned their "white" surnames. They donned African robes and stopped painful hair-straightening—called conking—in favor of natural styles. They developed a greater identity with Africa, which they considered a proud and independent society, and rejected any role in American society.

The eclectic Black Muslim theology was only vaguely related to genuine Islam. Its unique central doctrine was that the white man was the devil incarnate. An uncomfortably large number of blacks found this tenet easy to accept. The Black Muslims envisioned the ultimate destruction of this collective devil. Their eschatology included a sort of racial judgment day on which nonwhites would win a final victory over their oppressors and celebrate their glory. In preparation for that day, the Muslims demanded that an independent black nation be established, by violent means if necessary. By 1963 Martin Luther King's sermons of integration through love were already being drowned out by the fiery rhetoric of Muhammad's lieutenant, Malcolm X. Despair combined with this growing racial assertiveness of the 1960s to bring the nation full circle from 1919: Riots were the newest—and the oldest—form of black protest.

The years of rioting began in New York City on July 16, 1964, when a black teen-ager was shot to death by an off-duty white policeman. The killing intensified angry demands for a civilian review board, an issue that was being hotly debated in New York at that time. On Saturday, July 18, several C.O.R.E chapters called a rally to demand a civilian review board, and to pressure City Hall into replacing the New York Police Commissioner, an outspoken opponent of such a board. C.O.R.E. mustered about one hundred protesters, who marched to a Harlem police station to present their demands. In front of the station they staged a sit-in, insisting that they would remain until their demands were met. When the police tried to push the crowd back, fighting broke out. C.O.R.E. leaders were arrested and dragged into the station house, leaving the crowd leaderless and angry. Many outside claimed that they could hear the arrested men inside crying out as they were beaten by the police. Soon bricks and bottles were flying at the station house and the police. Policemen charged and scattered the crowd, but the struggle was not over. The angry blacks continued to mill about in the streets. At 10:30 P.M. a bottle of flaming gasoline was thrown at a squad car, and the police responded with shooting. It was the beginning of a race riot.

Throughout the night the exchange continued, and by Sunday morning twelve policemen and over a hundred blacks had been injured. One black man had been killed by the police. Looters ran rampant. For four more nights the violence continued; it finally died out in Harlem, only to flare up in Bedford-Stuyvesant, Brooklyn's ghetto area. By Thursday it was over, at least in New York. But race riots followed in nearby cities: in Rochester, New York; Jersey City and Paterson, New Jersey; and Philadelphia.

The authorities sought refuge in a conspiracy theory. New York's acting mayor blamed the violence on "fringe groups, including the Communist Party." [12] J. Edgar Hoover, chief of the Federal Bureau of Investigation, agreed that Communist influences were especially important. But the official F.B.I. reports conceded that not radical infiltration but living conditions in the ghettos had led to the outbreak of violence. The American public was shocked by the riots—and frightened. Ironically, whites were most aroused by the looting of stores—by disrespect for property—rather than by personal injuries.

In August 1965 a black neighborhood of Los Angeles, Watts,

erupted into violence. And in July 1967 another major riot broke out in Newark, New Jersey.

The Newark riot and the conditions that caused it were typical of such protests everywhere. Newark could be called America's model failure. In January 1967 the city's own business leaders admitted that Newark's problems were "more grave and pressing than those of perhaps any other American city." [13] Newark had the worst housing, highest crime rate, and highest incidence of venereal disease of any city of comparable size in the United States; its maternal mortality rate made childbirth seem a medieval gamble. In the ghettos unemployment was 15 percent.

Newark's middle-class leaders wanted to revive the city by making it attractive for business, commerce, and middle-class living. Urban renewal was sought in order to "overwhelm the creeps." Blacks had justifiable suspicions that the plan to save Newark was intended to save it *from* them, not *for* them.

As in almost all the other riots, violence was sparked by an incident of police brutality. On Wednesday, July 12, a black taxi-driver named John Smith was stopped and charged with "tailgating." Police charged that Smith began to use abusive language and to strike them, so that they were forced to "subdue" him. A total of seven policemen "subdued" John Smith on the street and in the precinct house; as a result he suffered caved-in ribs and a ruptured hernia. Civil-rights leaders rushed to the precinct and saw Smith within two hours after the arrest. They had him removed to Beth Israel Hospital. Then they began to organize a peaceful but angry protest demonstration. But the ghetto people, among whom word of the incident had quickly spread, had other ideas. The rally turned into a riot. By 11:00 that evening bottles had begun to fly at the windows of the precinct house; at midnight two Molotov cocktails exploded against the building's west wall. The classic battle between the blacks and what they considered the private army of their oppressors had begun in earnest.

The front line of the riot was always a youth brigade, people between fifteen and twenty-five years old who had been born in ghetto projects, unemployed "young people with nothing to do and nothing to lose." [14] But the older generation was there too, providing numbers, encouragement, and refuge for fleeing youths. This kind of generational participation conformed to the pattern of previous twentieth-century protest movements against imperial oppression, beginning with the Irish Rebellion in 1916.

By 1:00 A.M. the looting had begun. The shrill whining of hundreds of burglar alarms filled Seventeenth Avenue. Liquor, easily portable, went first, then furniture. Police were deployed in small teams but soon realized that they were outnumbered at any given point. They became jittery. Their own discipline collapsed, and police violence began. Police treatment of the blacks was roughly analogous to cowboys' treatment of a herd of cattle. "All you black niggers get upstairs," cops shouted to bystanders sitting outside a housing project. If a black appeared in their path he was beaten or arrested; because black people were rioting, all black people were treated as rioters. Nevertheless, the police lost control of the situation. That rioting did not spread rapidly to other areas was not to their credit but probably a result of the unorganized nature of the rioting itself. By 4:00 A.M. the streets were almost empty, except for the police, who stood on guard at the already-looted stores on Seventeenth Avenue.

On Thursday Mayor Hugh Addonizio assured the public that the riot had not really been a riot but only an "isolated incident." He then called for discussions with civil-rights leaders and a resolution of the issues. In the end some concessions were made: A black man was appointed a police captain, the first in Newark's history. A blue-ribbon commission modeled on the McCone Commission, which had investigated the Watts riot, was established. But Addonizio and other politicians were operating in a vacuum; they were out of touch with the mood of people on the streets. Some civil-rights leaders sensed that the protest was far from over and tried to channel it. A rally was called for 7:30 that night. The people who attended proved as uninterested in conventional protest as they were convinced that the politicians were uninterested in justice. A black detective tried to disperse the hostile demonstrators, shouting, "Why don't you people just go home?"; he was answered with a barrage of rocks and bottles. The police were more than eager to respond in kind. The door of the precinct house opened and white patrolmen poured out, yelling, "Let's go get these mother-fuckers!" Newsman David Crooms reported following policemen as they ran to the housing development called Hayes Homes. On the way they stopped to pull a black newsman aside and beat him. They chased a black into the project; it took twelve or fourteen of them to "subdue" him. Croom's account trails off here, for he is black and was their next target: "Get that black mother-fucker!" [15] The provocative language so offensive to Chicago's Mayor Richard Daley in 1968 seems to be as common a shortcoming among the men in blue as among protesters.

The looting spread to Springfield Avenue, the commercial main drag. The young led the way, breaking windows and chanting "Black Power!" Thousands followed. They entered stores a few at a time, took what they could carry, and fled. Those who disapproved did not interfere. The looters argued that the stolen goods rightfully belonged to them, that the liquor and furniture were their due—payment for years of outrageous markups, unfair credit terms, repossessions, trick contracts, inferior food, and price hikes on welfare-check days. The middle-class blacks joined with their "soul brothers" to loot and to superintend the looting. These blacks found racial ties stronger than class ties, but this reaction had been to a great degree forced upon them. White treatment of *all* blacks—rich or poor, educated or not— had forced these people to put class interests second to race interests.

There is in most group defiance of law or custom a delicious sense of community. During the Newark riots this sense was especially strong. For a few days the people owned the streets and everything on them. Economic injustice could be righted for the moment—not by government projects, church-sponsored help programs, or economic investment plans, but by robbing the merchants. Children who had never had two pairs of anything carried home armloads of dresses or jackets that had caught their eye; beds replaced cots or second-hand mattresses in many a home; new irons, televisions, dishes, and toys were selected, without easy-credit plans or carrying charges. The whites saw Armageddon, but the blacks were celebrating Judgment Day.

As in all ghetto riots, the attack on whitey centered in a black neighborhood. There was no organized invasion of white residential areas, no looting of white shopping centers. So strong were the ghetto boundaries, so strong was the young blacks' feeling that the "known" world was limited by these boundaries, that all activity took place within their own community. The attack was on the only white men with whom the blacks had daily contact: neighborhood businessmen and cops.

The hostility of the police equaled that of the blacks. By midnight on Thursday the police had received the desired carte blanche; "all necessary means—including firearms" could be used in self-defense. The first casualty occurred shortly afterward: a spectator who had gone to inspect the damage to the bar where he worked. By Friday morning more than 250 people had been treated in City Hospital. Over four hundred were in jail. At least two had been shot dead. Mayor Addonizio called on Governor Richard Hughes for help, and by dawn the black community was under military occupation.

Governor Hughes meant business. "The line between the jungle and the law might as well be drawn here as any place in America," [16] he said. Blacks had better choose the side of law and order, for it would prevail. By the following Monday it had. Twenty blacks had died in the name of law and order, most under police guns; a thousand more had been injured, and a thousand jailed. Police had destroyed black-owned businesses, which looters had left untouched.

The average outsider, hearing only official reports, might think that such measures, though tragic, were necessary. Left-wing observers like Tom Hayden, the leader of Students for a Democratic Society, disagreed. They believed that the police were more interested in retaliation than prevention. Most of the looting had ended by Friday morning; the ghetto business district had been picked bare. If national guardsmen and police were in Newark to protect property, they arrived on the scene too late. Nor were they stationed in downtown and white business areas. Sniper attacks were the most highly publicized danger cited to justify police firing. Yet there were only two white deaths from shooting after the troops came in, and they may well have been caused by stray shots of the police or military. Of the black dead, none was proved to have been a sniper, and no snipers were arrested. It is true that national guardsmen were tired, edgy, and confused over that long weekend. Many were therefore trigger-happy: At one point they fired at policemen, and another time Newark police and state police fired on each other. Yet much police and military violence was clearly the result of animosity toward blacks. "What do you want us to do," a guardsman asked a witness to the shooting of a teen-age looter, "kill all you Negroes?"

A policeman responded, "We are going to do it anyway, so we might as well take care of these three now." [17] The racial epithets flung at blacks—rioters or not—revealed distilled hatred. Among the dead were women and children; people were even killed in their homes.

Those arrested were not treated according to the best traditions of American law. When friends and relatives brought food to the jail, it was not permitted to reach the prisoners. Defense of law did not include defense of prisoners' rights under that same law; visitors were forbidden, as were telephone calls for legal aid. Relatives could not be notified. On Monday, April 17, Governor Hughes ended the occupation. The Newark riot was over.

There was more to black protest in the years after the March on Washington than spontaneous and unorganized rioting. Martin Luther King was killed. There was new leadership, and organizations like the N.A.A.C.P. and S.C.L.C. could no longer speak to or for many young blacks. A new black ideology was being developed by thinking black men like Stokely Carmichael, H. Rap Brown, Huey Newton, and Eldridge Cleaver. This new ideology was called Black Power, and it

—

was both romantic and grimly realistic. It was rooted in ideas as old as Garvey's black nationalism, as extreme and militant as Elijah Muhammad's Black Muslim movement, and as contemporary as African independence and theories of anticolonialism and anti-imperialism. Black Power was a call for separatism, based on what black leaders considered empirical proof that integration would mean at best assimilation, "painless genocide." They believed that racism was irrevocably built into the American political and social structure, an essentially colonial structure. Carmichael, like Malcolm X before him, was telling America that it was really two nations: a white mother country and a black colony. This country was like Africa in the 1940s and 1950s, with the overwhelming difference that both colony and mother country occupied the same space.

Black Power leaders were ready to fight for independence, yet they faced the dilemma of a revolution that would bring freedom *into* the conqueror's land and bring black men independence without a country of their own. The result was a serious appeal, officially voiced in 1967 at the Conference on Black Power in Newark, New Jersey, for a partitioning of the United States. These leaders called for a final, honest, and honorable separation between two nations—in physical reality, just as there had always been such a separation in social, economic, and political reality.

Until such time as partition could be accomplished, however, Black Power leaders would refuse to permit persecution of their people to continue. Blacks in the cities were organizing into mainly defensive, but at the same time quite aggressive, vigilante groups. In 1967 Huey Newton and Bobby Seale decided that Oakland, California, blacks should stop begging for an end to police brutality. Instead they should organize and give clear warning to white and generally Southern-born Oakland policemen that the blacks would defend and protect their own. The group took its name from the independent black political party first formed in Lowndes County, Alabama—the Black Panther Party. Newton's group, uniformed in berets and leather jackets and carrying guns, called itself the Black Panther Party for Self-Defense. According to Newton, the panther symbol was adopted for his group because that animal's nature was not to attack anyone unless cornered and then to respond viciously.

The Panthers began policing the police. Whenever white officers stopped a black man, a Panther patrol car would appear on the scene, and Panthers would get out to watch and to warn the black man of his rights. The police responded with persistent harassment of Panther members. Every time that a robbery or burglary report came in, Panthers were rounded up as suspects and held for the maximum time possible without preferring charges. Despite such harassment and the hostility of the larger white community to what it considered a new gang of hoodlums and racial agitators, police brutality did in fact decline in Oakland. The Panther technique of active self-defense worked. In a hostile world that black men considered unsafe, men like Seale simply urged that "every black brother put a shotgun in your home. It's necessary." [18]

But the Panthers, with about 250 members in June 1968, were more than a defensive organization. They were building a political party and had adopted a political platform. They sought freedom and the power for black communities to determine their own destinies. They demanded full employment, decent housing, and good, black-centered education. They demanded exemption from military service for every black man, not only because the country that he would have to fight for did not accept him as a full citizen, but also because as a nonwhite he ought not to assist in a white war against nonwhites. The Panthers wanted all blacks in jails across the country released because they had not been tried by juries of their peers. They denied the legitimacy of the law that governed their lives, a law that they had not helped to make and that operated to oppress them. They demanded an end to police brutality, a demand heard in ghetto riot after ghetto riot, even from blacks who denounced the Panthers. Huey Newton summed it up: "We want land, we want bread, we want housing, we want clothing, we want education, we want justice, and we want peace." [19]

The Panthers believed that for American black men the road to political freedom was best traveled with a gun handy. They were trying to build a revolutionary party. They considered themselves heirs to the Organization of Afro-American Unity, a group that Malcolm X had established after his break with Elijah Muhammad and that had died with him when he was assassinated in 1964. Malcolm, said Panther Minister of Information Eldridge Cleaver, had been trying to create a government in exile for people in exile. The Panthers asked for admission of Afro-Americans to the United Nations as a people in exile. Their eventual goal was national liberation. Not all radical blacks accepted Cleaver's analysis of American society or the goals of his party, but the concept of Black Power had penetrated into black organizations and ghettos everywhere. S.N.C.C., once a biracial organization in which white men like Mickey Schwerner and blacks like James Chaney had worked side by side, was methodically pressuring whites to leave. White staff members were no longer allowed to vote at staff meetings. And S.N.C.C. leader H. Rap Brown dismissed his organization's earlier efforts with the comment, "That whole non-violence thing was nothing but a preparation for genocide." [20] C.O.R.E., primarily a Northern white organization since its foundation in 1942, moved its headquarters to Harlem. Its 1967 convention voted to strike the word "multiracial" from its constitution. Only the N.A.A.C.P. and the Urban League repudiated the separatist philosophy of Black Power.

Martin Luther King's successor, Dr. Ralph Abernathy, carried on the old-style protests. But the Abernathy-directed Poor People's March on Washington in April 1968 and the organization of a massive sit-in in "Resurrection City" for several weeks were miserable failures that further discredited the nonviolent form of protest.

The Panthers' call for self-determination was picked up by community groups in urban ghettos. In New York City the Ocean Hill-Brownsville black and Puerto Rican community sought ultimate authority to hire and fire public-school teachers in its district and a strong voice in the academic curriculum. Aided by the Ford Foundation and Mayor John V. Lindsay, the community gained control of the neighborhood board of education. The board's dismissal of several white teachers, however, frightened the United Federation of Teachers and resulted in a city-wide strike. New York white families who relied on the public schools were enraged at the black community, the school board, and Lindsay. For the first time New York City Jews expressed strong overt hostility toward blacks.

The fight among black leaders over the issue of coalition politics was bitter in the late 1960s. Young radicals like Stokely Carmichael denied the possibility of coalition between whites and blacks. Let whites organize whites and blacks organize blacks, he argued. He even opposed Abernathy's attempt to weld a coalition of the white and black poor in the Poor People's March on Washington in April 1968. On the other hand, well-known civil-rights leaders like Bayard Rustin argued that Black Power as propounded by Carmichael offered no positive value and would in fact be harmful to the civil-rights movement. It would both isolate the black community and alienate whites. Realistically, Rustin argued, one-tenth of the total population could not hope to achieve its goals without the assistance of other groups within the larger society. Perhaps the Lowndes County party could elect an all-black slate some day. Perhaps blacks could legally seize political power in several Southern counties by working as united groups. But how many counties in the fifty states had black majorities? The majority voice of Lowndes was still the minority voice in the Alabama legislature. Jobs and economic aid could not be achieved by one or two black senators alone. Rustin believed that blacks should continue along the path of the Mississippi Freedom Democratic Party, working for a place and a voice within a larger group, in coalition with whites.

To Rustin the Black Power movement seemed the product of pessimism and loss of faith. It hurled a defiant "We want out!" at a society that seemed to reject blacks. Rustin believed that an integrated society was still possible and that most blacks still wanted to be in rather than out of American society. But the question of American whites' willingness to take up the challenge of black demands for first-class citizenship remained unanswered.

CHAPTER
12

From the Beats
to the New Left

A NEW Bohemian community was established during the 1950s in San Francisco's North Beach area. "The Beach" became a haven for a self-constituted minority group that was greeted with only lukewarm enthusiasm by the resident Italians and Chinese. To North Beach, as to all American Bohemias, came artists, writers, philosophers, and pseudophilosophers, men who chose to remain outside the pale of society and men who were seeking merely temporary respite. With them came the hangers-on—the peripheral (and frequently the most vocal) members of any such group. The new Bohemians, like many before them, gathered in coffee shops and cafés to play chess, to drink, to talk, to argue, and to think. In the Cellar or the Coffee Gallery they began to read their poetry aloud. Poets like Lawrence Ferlinghetti, Allen Ginsberg, and David Meltzer offered their works publicly for the first time. After the readings the patrons listened to a different kind of poetry—jazz.[1]

Whereas in 1910 Greenwich Village Bohemians had costumed themselves in Wild West outfits or colorful hats and shirts, the new, bearded Bohemians preferred the more relaxed garb of the American businessman's long-lost weekend: T-shirts, khaki pants, and sandals. And like their predecessors they lived in a world of ad hoc finances, never sure of rent money, feasting on Monday and bumming bagels at the Co-Existence Bagel Shop on Tuesday. Insecurity was the price they payed for independence and for art and poetry that had no market. Their rent for crowded and messy "pads" in dilapidated buildings was cheap. Fortunately, the Bohemian took a relaxed view of dirt, dust, and clutter. Interior decoration ran to Salvation Army rejects: mattresses on bare floors, crates and boxes for chairs and tables, and odd pieces of unserviceable furniture in corners. The walls were covered not with family photographs or Winslow Homer reproductions but with graffiti, philosophical or comic: "Mona Lisa is a Plain Clothes Queer"; "Minnie Mouse is a Mulatto." Both epigrams were wry comments on the daily life of the Bohemians. Their refusal to conform, in a decade that considered conformity more American than apple pie, brought harassment from society's watchdogs—the police.

Most of the Beach community consisted of serious, if not exceptionally talented, artists. They were nonconformists by choice and, they felt, by virtue of their chosen life's work. They wanted only to be left alone to live by many of the "don'ts" of the larger society. But a vocal few took seriously the need to establish and live by a new philosophy, not merely the negative of society's code but a positive value system of their own. It was this group that found in the Bohemian community a sanctuary from which to contemplate and evaluate life. They gave a new name to the Bohemians: the Beat Generation. It was "beat" because war, imminent death, and the collectivization of modern life were beating its members down; "beat" because their music was jazz, and its rhythmic beat their tempo, its improvisation their credo; and "beat," according to spokesman Jack Kerouac, because beatitude lay at the end of their spiritual quest for endless love.

The generation that came of age in the 1950s, like the Lost Generation of the 1920s, was trying to make sense of a postwar world. Its members faced a world that seemed to offer no respite but only an eternal state of war: World War II, the Korean War, the Cold War. Reality, as the Beats saw it, left no room for the worship of Reason. Evil could not be legislated out, although perhaps it could be legislated in. Nature, history, and humanity could not be controlled. Progress, the victim of every war, was an illusion, and death was the central reality. Because progress was a false concept, future and past meant little; the present was all. Imminent death made planning folly, but though life could not be planned or controlled, it *could* be sampled to the fullest.

Just as the war had atomized life for men like Ernest Hemingway and made all experience seem personal and discontinuous, so, according to the Beat philosopher, each man stood alone; his challenge was to live with that knowledge.

The generation of the 1920s had been angered and disillusioned by this revelation, but the Beats seemed to accept it without struggle. They embraced what they considered true and inevitable; they laid aside traditional consolations and set out to harmonize themselves with this new reality. The path to this harmony was to be through inner exploration, the tools were receptivity to experience of any kind, and the rewards were ever-heightened perceptions through sensation, through nerve endings rather than through logic and reason. The goal was to flow *with* life, rather than to impose false order upon it. For those who took "to the road," the only commandment was "thou shalt dig everything." Experiences were not to be differentiated, rated, evaluated, for to care for any one moment or thing more than for any other was to create an artificial hierarchy blocking out other experiences. Man was to be a receptacle for sensations, his body a collection of nerve receptors for shock, pleasure, pain, or orgasmic relief. The dictum was no longer "I think, therefore I am" but "I feel, therefore I am." The Beat regarded man's only obligation and responsibility as to keep himself always receptive, to concentrate on honing his own senses so that he could "continue to improve his dialogue with existence." [2]

The Beat schema inevitably rejected organized society and organized authority; both seemed against nature and thus oppressive. The "square," the modern man who stuck to his illusions, was the enemy. Yet the Beat felt a certain sympathy for the square, whom he regarded as a dupe, unliberated and burdened with the task of role-playing in a crazy world. The Beat held up to the world as heroes society's outcasts: the junkie, the hoodlum, the poet. Yet none of these outcasts had really succeeded in setting himself right with nature, for one escaped through drugs, another only defied society, and the third sought reality through an effort of mind rather than through genuine experience.

The Beats canonized men like movie actor James Dean—wistful, young, reticent—who accepted his isolation from the older generation, lived intensely, and died suddenly. Also in their pantheon were cool-jazz trumpeter Charlie ("Bird") Parker and Welsh poet Dylan Thomas, who had given in to and given themselves up to sensation.

The leading philosophers of the Beat Generation were Jack Kerouac and Allen Ginsberg, both ex-Columbia University students, one a novelist and the other a poet. It was Kerouac who gave the world the perfect portrait of the Beat; of course, the hero of *On the Road* was archetypal and had no counterpart in real life. But the stereotype held in the public's mind, even after Kerouac retired from the Beat world to live with his mother in Lowell, Massachusetts. The public, by the end of the 1950s, was paying closer attention to the Beats and their cult.

Although Kerouac saw his confreres as purposeful men, the outside world, alas, was less certain. To the average American the "Beatnik"—a term of dubious affection coined by San Francisco columnist Herb Caen—appeared to be a bum, a dropout not to a higher state of harmony with the world but to frivolous and nose-thumbing immorality. The Beatniks seemed to lead lives of wild partying, miscegenation, bad citizenship, free love, liquor before 5:00 P.M., and drugs.

To literary and artistic mandarins the Beatniks seemed sham artists and sham writers whose style was not innovative but only a "relaxation of form." Critics like Norman Podhoretz—a leader of the New York intellectual crowd—found them hard to understand, not because their thought was deep but because their powers of articulation were slight. To a world that valued order and coherence, the Beats' art seemed careless and confused and the artist himself incorrigible, rejecting coherence and precision as artistic virtues.

The Beats' withdrawal from the world particularly dismayed intellectuals. Rather than protest society's ills the Beats had simply withdrawn, a whole group of Thoreaus saying "No thank you" to membership in society. They had repudiated reason and intellect in favor of sensation. The Beatnik was, in short, *alienated* with a vengeance and organized in his alienation, with a set of rules, a style of dress, a posture, that resulted in conformity to nonconformity. Beatniks seemed "fixed forever in a gross and banal Romantic gesture of self-alienation, self-pity, self-confusion and wordy confession. The *movement* is destructive, not only of rational, moral, and spiritual values, but even of itself." [3]

The Beats did not protest the label of alienation, nor did Kerouac himself deny the escapist and destructive qualities of the quest for beatitude. Insanity was, the Beats believed, the ultimate state of harmony, the condition most in accord with a chaotic world, and madness was therefore the surest way—next to death—of "stopping time, and splintering life into a stream of acutely felt sensations that impose no demands and bring no consciousness of guilt." [4]

The Beatnik was not a crusader. He did not seek to convert mankind but only to be released from obligations to social forms and customs to explore his inner world. Unfortunately, society would not leave him in peace. The Beats fascinated and repelled, amused and threatened society out of all proportion to their number and influence. Mass media and the consuming public exhibited an almost morbid interest in the Beatnik—not in his philosophy or artistic quest but in his moral deviance and life style. Daring college students adopted beards and sandals; the general public borrowed Beat slang, and middle-aged lawyers "dug" their martinis and became "hip."

Ironically, it was the Bohemians who were not members of the Beat cult but were more orthodox Beach inhabitants who suffered most from this attention. Obscurity had been their shield. Curiosity and exposure interrupted their lives and brought harassment. By spring of 1957 trouble had begun for the eighty or so San Francisco Bohemians. The obscenity trial that followed publication of Allen Ginsberg's *Howl* in 1957 was greatly publicized, and suddenly landlords who had thought that they were renting merely to weirdos and bums realized that they were renting to immoral Beatniks. "No Beatniks Wanted" signs went up all over the Beach area. As Grant Avenue became a tourist spot, rents rose. Gray Line bus-tour guides pointed out bearded men; Bohemians responded by taking a Gray Line bus to downtown San Francisco, wandering in and out of fashionable hotels and shops, and staring at and annoying the customers, but their point was lost on the squares. By September 1958 the police had declared North Beach a "problem area," and no new liquor licenses were issued there. By 1959 the Bohemian community was dissolving. Beats like Kerouac had already deserted; he had "split the scene" in 1957 and was safely at home in his mother's house in the East.

The Beat Generation's neoromantic ideal appeared to have died in its infancy. Kerouac had had a vision, but he had deserted it. Yet Beats like Ginsberg, Gregory Corso, and Leonore Kandel lingered on and were rewarded for their fidelity in the mid 1960s, when the philosophy of beatitude was revived and came to flower.

The new subculture was christened the Love Generation, its members "flower children." Another San Francisco newspaper columnist had the honor to label the new Bohemians Hippies. The Hippies were indeed "hip" to what their older brothers of the 1950s had discovered. Society *was* mad; nuclear holocaust had blotted out all sense of the future, and the only journey worth making was inside one's own head. The mantle of alienation fell easily upon the shoulders of a generation raised in the era of assassinations and in the shadow of still another war. The murder of John F. Kennedy sparked this second great rejection. Resignations from society began to trickle, then to pour, in, and migration to a new Bohemia was on.

Bohemia had moved to the park-rimmed Haight-Ashbury district of San Francisco and to the seamier Lower East Side of New York City. The coffee shops had new names, and giant dance halls replaced smoke-filled jazz cellars, for the music was no longer cool jazz but electric rock. Most important, the leisurely pace of the journey to truth "on the road" had given way to the jet-propelled trip on LSD. The Beat's addiction to experience and sensation had led him to view the body as a sensory apparatus. The Hippie saw it instead as a complex chemical system, which could, like an electronic machine, be jolted, "turned on," its trigger mechanism "tripped" by the proper inputs.

LSD began respectably enough. It had, after all, gone to Harvard University, where Professor Timothy Leary first academically "dumped the lump," or swallowed the LSD-soaked sugar cube, in the quest for scientific knowledge. Leary's experiments finally brought his dismissal from Harvard's Department of Psychology, but the word was out on the psychedelia of the acid trip: feeling colors, flying, floating, hallucinations, soul-searching and satisfying self-revelation, cosmic harmony, visions of God and of man as he really is. Through the looking glass and on to the inner journey, LSD "deconditioned" the mind of all that society had filled it with and freed the spirit.

Leary stood by his miracle drug; Allen Ginsberg sampled it and saw that it was good. Out of Leary's experiments a new religion was born: the League for Spiritual Discovery. And in San Francisco, a good old-fashioned American capitalist apothecary rattled his laboratory test tubes and came up with commercial LSD. Augustus Owsley Stanley III, "Owsley" to his customers, promoted his product with free samples and turned on many new residents of the Haight. When California's legislature outlawed the drug in October 1966, it was too late. Owsley, a law-abiding citizen, could be stopped, but LSD could not.

The drug transformed the Beats' drab, sullen kind of protest into the colorful, flashy, fantasy-laden outburst of Hippiedom. The Beatnik had criticized the staid, conformist clothing of the square by dressing it down, but the Hippie overpowered the tweed suit and striped tie by changing everyday dress into a costume ball. For the Hippie dressing was an adventure in identity. He rejected "straight" society's role-playing, which demanded that the same part be acted out every day from nine to five, the same role performed 365 times a year. He offered whimsy instead, dressing as a pirate today, a bedouin tomorrow, a Victorian lady in rustling velvet skirts, an Indian, a *samurai*, an army general. He made fuller and more daring use of appearance to shock society and to protest its arbitrary rules. Where the Beatnik had offended his neighbors by aggressively advertising his masculinity with a beard, the Hippie challenged the hallowed definitions of masculinity by growing shoulder-length hair and wearing necklaces of beads, bells, or flowers.

Drugs also worked their magic on rock 'n' roll, and out of California came a new sound: electric rock. The music was part of the total environment that the Hippie hoped to create, a psychedelic environment that would give one a permanent high. The rock was loud, almost above the human auditory threshold; it throbbed, it whined, it pounded, it captured, it overwhelmed. The assault of noise overpowered all the senses, and one really could get high on music from the Grateful Dead, Jefferson Airplane, Steppenwolf, or Moby Grape. These and other rock groups, which came out of the Hippie culture with names like Big Brother and the Holding Company and The Gross National Product, were past masters of the put-on. Their lyrics attacked and satirized everything. The Beats had struck out at society with poem and novel; the Hippies sang their protest, and the songs were clever, often bitter. A New York Hippie group, the Fugs—whose members include one-time Beat Tuli Kupferberg—sang cheerfully about the war and patriotism, urging listeners to enlist and "Kill, kill, kill for peace, kill for your President." Country Joe and the Fish philosophized in their "I Feel Like I'm Fixin' to Die Rag":

> There ain't no time to wonder why
> Whoopie! We're all gonna die!

The rock groups also sang about love and sex. Their songs about sex were often satiric, as groups like the Fugs parodied American fantasies of epic potency and sexual abandon with "What Are You Doing after the Orgy?"

The Hippie is concerned about sexual freedom, for sexual repression is a barrier to self-expression and self-realization. His arguments for free love are not original, nor are they shocking to their generation of straight suburban friends. But suburbia's folly is still clandestine, and the Hippies' is not. In the East Village City Living Center, a small office-apartment–store front, the Kerista Society—"Love Conquers All"; "Balling Through Life Is the Kerista Way"—operates in the manner of a Christian Science Reading Room. There one can learn of Kerista's origins, of the life of businessman-turned-prophet John Presmont, to whom Kerista was revealed in a theophanic revelation in 1956. The society advertises a future mass exodus of the faithful to a still unchosen island, where Keristans will "create a green paradise for a special breed of people." [5]

The Hippie newspapers, beginning with the *San Francisco Oracle*, covered all the psychedelic news that *The New York Times* thought unfit to print. They editorialized on abolishing jails and legalizing pot, ran daily astrology columns, advised on macrobiotic diets, gave information on Eastern religions and meditation-study groups, accepted advertisements for sexual companions, and carried comic strips like *Captain High!* Their magazines, like their music, were agglomerations of protest and put-on. *Fuck You: A Magazine of the Arts* was dedicated to

. . . pacifism, national defense through non-violent resistance, dope-law defiance, freedom for hallucinogens, the Stroboscopic Mind Zap, street-fucking, the LSD Communarium . . . Acapulco Gold . . . the slithering psychopathic Lower East Side young lady pacifist snapping pussy, the Jergens Lotion Freak-bugger . . . Total Assault On the Culture, and to all those groped by J. Edgar Hoover in the silent halls of Congress.[6]

It was "Edited, Published, Zapped, Designed, Freaked, Groped, Stomped and Ejaculated by Ed Sanders [a Fug] at a Secret Location in the Lower East Side." The location was secret because New York City police confiscated Sanders' magazine whenever they could. Yet the "underground" Hippie press—largely staple-and-mimeo productions—was Rabelaisian rather than sadistic like its respectable counterparts sold above ground and by subscription.

It did not take long for the news media, the social analysts, and the general public to discover the Love Generation. For one thing the Hippie stood out in a crowd. He had a flair for the dramatic and a love of spectacle. In January 1967 the "Hashberry" community advertised the first human be-in, a gathering of the tribes in San Francisco's Golden Gate Park. The occasion was a celebration of the winter equinox. The most fully represented tribe turned out to be the Great Press-Card Confederation, and from January on Hippies were widely photographed, inspected, dissected, analyzed, berated, praised, and pondered. The interest was not simply a matter of idle curiosity about long hair and free-love orgies or even pot parties and LSD. Somehow Americans demanded that the Hippies be explained. It was disturbing that white middle-class sons and daughters were deliberately rejecting split-level houses for tenements and giving up their places in the great majority to run the risks of a minority group. The Hippie was a deserter; he should have been, after all, among those to whom the middle-class heritage was passed. But he rejected, and thus threatened, the very heart of American ethics, the Puritan ethos: hard work, responsible planning, respect for private property, and success and achievement through healthy competition. The Hippie was determined, above all else, to abolish competition. Burton Wolfe, who lived in San Francisco's Hippie community in 1967, describes a Hippie game of touch football:

It was touch football such as nobody had ever seen, not even at the Kennedys' house. Like many hippie young men, these fellows enjoyed tumbling and acrobatics. So, every once in a while, they would interrupt the plays with rolls, head stands, and back flips. Somebody on the line who was supposed to be rushing the passer would suddenly get the urge to somersault over the sand, and so, he would. If it enabled the other team to score a touchdown, that was groovy. As a matter of fact, the two sides frequently let each other score anyway, after the appropriate amount of pranking. . . . For actually there was no score. No score, no winners, no losers. Just a game, running, exercise, fun, sand, sunshine, and salt air.[7]

During the spring of 1967 the press began to carry awful warnings of a full-scale summer invasion in San Francisco. A veritable emptying of suburbia was predicted; 100,000 disenchanted—or enchanted—teenagers were said to be planning to flock to the City of St. Francis. All over suburbia teen-agers read about their proposed pilgrimage for the first time—and decided to make it. The migration fell some 98,000 short of the prediction, but that summer in San Francisco did prove to be the greatest of the Hippie spectacles.

The old-timers, or Elders of Hashberry, tried their best to provide for the arriving hordes. The Diggers, who took their name from a seventeenth-century utopian sect in England, made preparations to feed and clothe the newcomers. They had been organized the previous summer by twenty-three-year-old Emmett Grogan as the vanguard of the antiprofit movement. They stocked their stores with clothing and food that they begged from merchants and neighbors. Then they gave it all away. "It's Free," read the price tags, and if anyone insisted on paying for something, the Digger salesman promptly gave away the money. During the summer invasion Grogan's Diggers set up a soup kitchen on the Haight's Panhandle, a stretch of park connecting two other parks bordering the district. Every day at 4:00 P.M. they served a meal, and all the hungry Hippie or non-Hippie had to provide was his own plate, cup, and fork. Sometimes the Digger meal was good; sometimes it was garbage.

But the summer scene proved to be a bad scene, a bad trip, despite Digger efforts; despite the Hip Job Corps, which found long-haired boys and barefoot girls jobs in post-office mail rooms where the public could not see them; despite the Free Medical Clinic; and despite all the love and flowers. The summer Hippie had nowhere to live but the streets. And the "street people" had come with *Time* expectations and illusions and no real commitment beyond a summer vacation of "doing their thing." They slept in the streets and in doorways. They begged from tourists, took impure LSD, got hooked on methedrine ("speed"). If they were lucky, all they developed was bad teeth, bad digestion, and acne; if they were less lucky, they caught venereal disease and hepatitis.

The Elders could not cope. As October approached, the Diggers' Free Store was folding, the medical clinic had closed, and tourists with ready money were gone. Haight Street was filthy, littered with garbage and people. Pickpockets, alcoholics, sex maniacs, thieves, and addicts mingled with the Hippies. The Elders decided to end it all. In October an announcement went out: "Funeral Notice. Hippie. In the Haight-Ashbury District of this city, Hippie, devoted son of mass media. Friends are invited to attend services beginning at sunrise, Oct. 6, 1967, at Buena Vista Park." The Elders tried to explain their mercy killing to the street people:

. . . Media Created the Hippie with your Hungry Consent. Be Somebody. Careers are to be had for the Enterprising Hippie. Death of Hippie End. Finished Hiippyee Gone Goodbye Hehpphee Death Death Hippie. Exorcise Haight-Ashbury. Circle the Ashbury. Free the boundaries. Open Exorcise. You are free. We are free. Do not be recreated. Believe only in your own incarnate spirit. Birth of free man. Free San Francisco Independence. Free Americans. Birth. Do not be bought with a picture. A phrase. Do not be captured in words. The city is ours. You are are are. Take what is yours. The boundaries are down. San Francisco is free now—free the truth is out out out.[8]

The coffin, filled with Hippie artifacts, was carried in a circle around the Haight. Then it was burned, the demon exorcised, the "Brotherhood of Free Men" proclaimed. Many of the Elders left the city for communes in the California hills.

On New York's Lower East Side, the groovy idea of love, flowers, and brotherhood was also fading. In October 1967, a Hippie named "Groovy" and a speed freak named Linda Fitzpatrick (who also happened to be a wealthy college girl from Greenwich, Connecticut) were murdered in the basement of a tenement building. Suddenly the East Village Hippies realized that they were living in a ghetto slum. Slums were dirty, ugly, and dangerous: The Diggers in the Village began to carry guns. And drugs, drug addicts, and drug pushers were dirty, ugly, and dangerous. Taking LSD remained a sacrament to the Hippie, but he admitted that "speed kills." The Village Elders, Hippies with a genuine philosophical commitment, faced up to the consequences of the life that they had chosen and the poverty and danger it entailed. The plastic, or temporary, Hippies were leaving.

The Hippie protested the effects of society upon his own life, but there was another small group of young people concerned with society's effects upon others. This humanitarian impulse was directed into the arena of politics.

The political radical was the product of the middle-class environment, and like the Hippie he was not motivated by his parents' desire for status and wealth. These goals had already been realized. In fact both the political and the apolitical protesters were willing to give up material comforts in order to improve the quality of their lives.

The radical student was neither entirely an adolescent rebelling against his parents and society nor merely a second-generation activist following in his father's footsteps. He came from a home environment characterized by warmth, familial closeness, and idealism. He had weathered the adolescent storm long before he became committed to radical action. He was among the brightest and most able of the nation's young people, and through his academic achievements and the good fortune of birth successful careers were open to him. He was not a malcontent unable to succeed in society but a young man or woman who felt keenly his inability to satisfy his own needs or standards through success. His priorities included adherence to the dictates of a strong ethical and moral sense, and he felt personally responsible for correcting the injustices that he saw in his society.

Where had the radical acquired his principles, his ethical imperatives? From his parents. His radicalization process had not involved acquisition of new values but commitment to translating his parents' moral assumptions into political realities. These values were neither bizarre nor new to American society. What made the radical different from his parents and contemporaries was that he took these values seriously and proposed that his society live by them.

The radical had no counterpart in the early 1950s, a dark period for political radicalism. It was only at the end of the decade that English university leftists began to revive radicalism with the publication of two new journals and the founding of radical clubs among college students and working-class youths. In the United States the waning of McCarthyism and, more important, the rise of the civil-rights movement gave impetus to the new radicalism. By the turn of the decade radical organizations had been formed on campuses around the country, particularly at the universities of Wisconsin, California at Berkeley, Michigan, and Chicago. At Wisconsin, the most important of the new journals, *Studies on the Left*, was founded by radical historian William Appleton Williams.

The New Left of the 1960s bore little resemblance to the Old Left of the 1920s and 1930s. In fact, "new" meant more than "revived"; it was a purposeful distinction. The new radical's commitment was emotionally and morally, rather than intellectually, based. His movement was nonideological, for he was determined to avoid the handicap of rigid models and inflexible doctrines. The new radical, unlike the old, did not agonize over the dichotomies of Communist versus anti-Communist, Russia versus the United States, or Stalin versus anti-Stalin. He was concerned with American society and with the quality of American life. From this point of view, the New Left resembled pre-1917 progressivism.

It was the disturbing absence of quality, the emptiness of modern life and the fragmented urban environment devoid of a sense of community, the failure of American society to live up to its traditional values and ideals, its promises of equality and freedom, that the New Left protested. The young radical held the liberal "establishment" responsible for these failures, and it was this attitude that forever separated the New Left from the Old. For the former believed that yesterday's radicals had betrayed their ideals. They argued that the Old Left died not because of McCarthyism but because commitment to radical change and socialism had faded into the genteel meliorism of men who pursue power and prestige rather than ideals. By the 1950s the Old Left—speaking through one of its leaders, Columbia University sociologist Daniel Bell, a former editor of *Fortune*—had pronounced the "end of ideology" and thus the necessary and logical abandonment of commitments. But the New Left was unwilling to accept this analysis. C. Wright Mills, another Columbia sociologist and a prophet of the new radicalism, found Bell's pronouncement only "a weary know-it-all justification . . . a slogan of complacency, circulating among the prematurely middle-aged, centered in the present, and in the rich Western societies." [9]

The New Left accepted an end of traditional ideologies as an organizing principle, but it insisted that the moral *raison d'être* of a radical politics remained. The men who should have continued to fight for structural changes in society had let themselves be captured by it. These corrupted intellectuals joined a new American oligarchy; the coalition between the Old Left and its former enemies produced the liberal establishment of the 1960s.

Consequently liberalism was the radical's main enemy, for it had reduced ideals to platitudes; its members mouthed commitment to reform and equality yet had too much at stake in the status quo to function as anything but a conservative force.

The intellectual father of the New Left was Mills, who first focused the attack. He called to task an older generation of intellectuals for failing to remain honorably and proudly alienated from the mainstream, for failing to fulfill the intellectual's role as critic and moral exemplar of society.

Mills's analysis made sense to a new generation, which believed that technology and science had made possible the solution of society's problems and which was disturbed at the failure to undertake these solutions. The young radical could conclude only that these solutions had not been undertaken because the liberals in the power elite had chosen not to undertake them. The world was full of violence and injustice, in the radicals' view, less because evil men were blocking the efforts of good men than because liberals and their institutions had sacrificed justice, truth, and idealism on the altar of power and prestige. The Hippies called it "the fantastic ego trip."

In 1965 Carl Oglesby, a founder of Students for a Democratic Society, spoke at the SANE peace march on Washington:

> The original commitment in Vietnam was made by President Truman, a mainstream liberal. It was seconded by President Eisenhower, a moderate liberal. It was intensified by the late President Kennedy, a flaming liberal, Think of all the men who now engineer the war—those who study the maps, give the commands, and tally the dead: Bundy, McNamara, Rusk, Lodge, Goldberg, the President himself.
>   They are not moral monsters.
>   They are all honorable men.
>   They are all liberals.[10]

The radical's identification of the liberal establishment as his enemy leaves him without allies. It creates a dilemma that he is not able to resolve. If he believes with philosopher Herbert Marcuse that the liberal state is incapable of reform and capable of absorbing protest without noticeable damage to the status quo, then the only channel for change must be revolution. What cannot be transformed must be destroyed. Yet Marcuse and some of the radicals are realistic political and social analysts, recognizing that revolution cannot take root in a country that continually absorbs its dissidents and minorities into the mainstream. The absence of a radical American working class and the ultimately conservative goals of the average black may make a revolutionary situation in the American society permanently impossible.

Perhaps the radical's devotion to ad hoc projects with limited objectives can be better understood in the light of this dilemma. Such projects did not have to be integrated into a revolutionary scheme; they could stand alone. Yet even then the radical's work might be at odds with his own professed long-range goals. He participated in programs that were melioristic because they were humanitarian: The civil rights of the black man had to be won even if the black man would then willingly be absorbed into the liberal mainstream; the ghettos had to be dissolved even if the radical would then be without even his allies in poverty.

Few allies could be found among the American middle class. Its members were either satisfied or had been lulled into apathy by the very liberal institutions that they had created. Yet the radical continued his commitment. Perhaps the nonprogrammatic nature of the New Left—its emphasis on short-range effectiveness and limited goals— arose less from stubbornness or lack of organizational talent than from psychological necessity. To contemplate the distant future, to plan for it, to assess the actual possibility of the great change in modern life that the New Left desired, was to court paralyzing frustration and despair.

What remained for the New Left was the old Progressive idea of educating the people, of increasing their social and political consciousness through the articulation of dissent and moral example. The radical's tactic for educating the public was to force confrontations between himself and the institutions and power elite that he opposed. By honest confrontation and dialogue, he hoped to force his enemy to expose its true nature to the people.

To fulfill his role as moral exemplar, the radical became a constant watchdog of his own purity. From self-criticism he came to view the journey to the new world as a sort of Pilgrim's Progress. It became important in itself, and each step was a test of his commitment and his fortitude. This conception of the radical's role led Old Left spokesman Irving Howe to despair that "personal endurance thus becomes the substance of, and perhaps a replacement for, political ideas. . . . To create, by trials of courage, a tiny heroic group is in effect a strategy of exclusion. And it reduces differences of opinion to grades of moral rectitude." [11]

Yet the new radical believed politics to be only the means to realize ethical imperatives; to compromise standards could thus only ensure the creation of imperfect political institutions. The radical sought a new political and social structure in which individual uniqueness could be accommodated and mass collectivization avoided. He sought new political organizations whose institutional forms would *include*, rather than exclude, their citzens, and new political tactics demanding participation and honest confrontation rather than repression and artificiality. On none of these demands did he feel that he could compromise, for they represented his moral commitments acted out in politics.

The radical was naturally inclined to seek support from his fellow dissenters, the Hippies. He usually met with failure and frustration, for the Hippie exhibited an ostrich syndrome that denied the relevance of politics by ignoring it. In the fall of 1967, however, a new political activism seemed to be stirring in the East Village and Haight-Ashbury, which raised radical hopes. A politicized Hippie emerged, usually a member of an organizationless organization called Youth International Party: the Yippie. Yippie leaders seemed actually to be political activists gone underground or awakening from long slumber. Among them were Jerry Rubin, a former Berkeley activist, and Abbie Hoffman, a one-time civil-rights worker. Regardless of which came first, his radical or his Hippie experience, the Yippie proudly declared in himself the successful merger of New Left politics with the psychedelic life style.

The Yippie believed that the revolution had been realized in himself. "Our life style—acid, long hair, freaky clothes, pot, rock music, sex—is the Revolution." [12] A generation that had grown up with Marshall McLuhan was ready to declare that the medium was the message.

The Yippie was dedicated to mocking and shocking American society. He was confident that his very existence mocked the larger society, but to shock and arouse a public so satiated with vicarious violence and sex and absolutely thriving on protest was a more difficult task. He relied upon the construction of gigantic fantasies, sensational lies, and spectacular threats. In the fall of 1967 proto-Yippies marched with peace demonstrators on the Pentagon, but the Yippies did more than protest. They came up with a tactic to end the war. They solemnly measured the Pentagon, circled it, and exorcised its evil spirits.

> Ring around the Pentagon, a pocket full of pot
> Four and twenty generals all begin to rot.
> All the evil spirits start to tumble out
> Now the war is over, we all begin to shout.[13]

Just in case any evil spirits might still be lurking about, the Yippies were armed with their highly publicized wonder weapon, LACE.

LACE, not to be confused with MACE, was a purple spray composed of LSD plus a secret ingredient, DMSO, which when applied properly immediately impelled its victims to "make love, not war."

In August 1968 the Yippies joined political activists in their invasion of Chicago. Their united purpose was to protest proceedings at the Democratic national convention. The Yippies, of course, went further. They held a parallel convention at which they nominated a pig for President. To the ever-eager newsmen they leaked terrorist plans to burn Chicago to the ground and to turn on its entire population by adding "acid" (LSD) to the Chicago water supply. Worried city officials placed a guard around the entire reservoir system. Yippies had only to hint that their next Presidential candidate might be a lion for extra protection to be placed around the local zoo.

The Yippie was, of course, "putting on" his opponents. He had no intention of replacing fluoride with acid. He was trying, rather successfully for the moment, to arouse the public from its stupor, to scare it into thought and involvement, a task that he found all the more necessary because his more restrained colleagues could not persuade the public into dialogue.

The Yippie was above all else an actor. He sought through his own actions to dramatize the idiocy he found in the organized society around him. It was there that the true political radical and the politicized Hippie parted company. The Yippie was not centrally concerned with politics or political institutions. For him American politics was merely the most obvious example of the idiocy of any organized and structured social life. In the days of assassinations, television makeup for Presidential candidates, and senators who had sung and danced, what better opportunity for living theater than politics?

On one issue alone the Hippie, the radical, the liberal, and even the apolitical could agree: opposition to the Vietnam war. One might oppose the war because the draft was an infringement on personal freedoms, another because it seemed an imperialistic and exploitative venture, another on pacifistic grounds, yet a fourth because the draft interrupted his career. Yet all these paths eventually led to an antiwar position, and the possibility of an anti-Vietnam coalition had been present from the beginning.

Protest against the war and the draft grew steadily from 1965 on. And participants were an increasingly catholic mixture. Although SANE, a radical group, led the 1965 peace march on Washington, the ranks were swelled by mothers with baby carriages and college boys in three-piece suits. The Vietnam Summer Project in 1967 was organized by radicals, but they sought liberal support. Their goal was coalition rather than confrontation. They employed the usual protest techniques of marches, demonstrations, and teach-ins. But as early as 1965 a new tactic and new movement were developing; they aimed at redirecting energies from symbolic protest to actual attack on the military system.

The new tactic—resistance—was really old. Even in the United States there was precedent, for in 1863 Civil War recruitment had sparked bloody antidraft riots in New York City. Closer in history and in kind, French students had helped bring an end to the Algerian war by organizing resistance to induction in 1956. The theory was simple: A war machine cannot run without fuel to feed it; wars cannot be conducted without men who will fight.

The first acts of resistance were by small groups or single individuals. In 1965 a few religious pacifists publicly burned their draft cards in New York City's Union Square. In 1966 the president of the Stanford University student body, David Harris, left school to tour college campuses and to urge students to set aside their 2-S deferments and to turn in their draft cards. He met with little success then, yet by 1967 resistance was becoming a viable political alternative. Open support was growing among religious leaders and leftist intellectuals. In the early part of 1967 such spokesmen for the intellectual community as Noam Chomsky and Paul Goodman debated antiwar tactics in *The New York Review of Books*. Having reaffirmed their antiwar positions, they recognized that support of resistance was a logical, moral, and political imperative. In the course of their debate, they articulated a justification and an explanation for resistance, and their support brought able spokesmen and essential publicity to the movement. When a Cornell University group decided to stage the first mass draft-card burning at the April 15, 1967, peace march in New York, *The New York Review of Books* publicized the event and also encouraged young men to join in this action. Between 150 and 200 draft cards were burned on Central Park's Sheep Meadow that day. This event was the real beginning of The Resistance.

The men who organized The Resistance were both idealistic and practical. They combined the radical's moral sense and flexibility of tactics with insistence on realistic political analyses and the search for optimal political effectiveness. They organized not because they believed that a hundred thousand men would actually rise up against the system but to ensure that those who *did* would find allies and advisors and that those who were undecided would be persuaded by example. And they organized to force the mass of apathetic or inactive middle-class citizens to face the crisis of the war and take some action.

The Resistance was not a cure but a catalyst, an agent for public education. It was a coalition for political effectiveness.

The movement's basic appeal was originally—and remained—centered on the issue of personal freedom. Resistance literature conceded that the draft could be avoided by other means: A draft-age man could retain his 2-S classification, take a job with priority exemption, "go underground," or emigrate. But all these alternatives, supporters of The Resistance argued, were not only compromises with and even tacit approval of the Selective Service System and the larger system; they also represented surrender to a form of military control over individual life. This control was believed to be no accidental consequence of a preferential draft system; the government was said to have planned to use Selective Service to direct the lives of citizens, whether or not they serve in the armed forces. An official government pamphlet entitled *Channeling* had explained the virtues of the system:

Throughout his career as a student the pressure—the threat of loss of deferment—continues. It continues with equal intensity after graduation. . . . He is impelled to pursue his skill rather than embark upon some less important enterprise and is encouraged to apply his skill in an essential activity in the national interest. The loss of deferred status is the consequence for the individual who has acquired the skill and either does not use it or uses it in a non-essential activity. . . . The psychology of granting wide choice under pressure to take action is the American or indirect way of achieving what is done by direction in foreign countries where choice is not permitted.[14]

It was this control over the individual's life, subtle yet engulfing, that The Resistance urged men to be aware of and to reject. "Liberate yourself" was The Resistance appeal, echoing the Beat-Hippie credo and the radical's political imperative.

But the movement sought more than personal liberation; it had been formed not only to protest American policy but also to force change in it. Although it advised on emigration, for example, The Resistance did not endorse it. Emigration might cut into the military manpower pool, but resistance could disrupt the system itself.

On October 16, 1967, over one thousand draft-eligible men in almost thirty cities turned in their cards. On November 4 and December 6, almost six hundred young men followed suit, and on April 3, 1968, almost a thousand more cards were returned. Individual resistance grew daily, steadily if not spectacularly. In St. Louis two men a month refused induction, in New York City two a week, and in Boston three a week. Los Angeles averaged seven a week, and in San Francisco sometimes thirty men risked jail each week. The Resistance tried to have demonstrators at the induction center to support each resister and to distribute leaflets among the other inductees, disrupting the smooth processes of Selective Service and forcing the military establishment to go to court to clarify the provisions for military service.

The Resistance never glossed over the unpleasant consequences of defiance: The inevitable penalty facing each resister was imprisonment from three months to three years in accommodations from minimum-security prison farms to San Quentin cells. By fall 1968 at least a thousand men were serving such sentences. Yet each case offered an opportunity to take the military into court, to challenge conscription laws. In 1969 the Supreme Court was considering a challenge to the constitutionality of reclassification as punishment for participating in a political demonstration.

Technically The Resistance included only draft-eligible men who had refused to cooperate with Selective Service. But resistance to the military system and support for the movement came from others as well. Early in 1968 Dr. Benjamin Spock, William Sloane Coffin, Marcus Raskin, Michael Ferber, and Mitchell Goodman were indicted for conspiring to hinder the draft. Dr. Spock's arrest catapulted the movement to wide public attention. Middle-class citizens, already bewildered by defiance among clean-shaven young men, were amazed by the good doctor who had guided them through the care and feeding of their children. Perhaps more than the mass draft-card burnings, more than the trials of resisters, the approval and encouragement of such a man forced many people to examine the war and the draft issues—and to act. Appeals went out in newspapers and magazines for complicity statements: "Have you ever conspired with Dr. Spock? In word, thought or deed have you ever opposed the war?" At a rally following the indictment five hundred people walked to the stage at Town Hall in New York to sign such statements of complicity. Among those who spoke out for Spock and The Resistance was Martin Luther King. King put it simply: If Spock was found guilty, all who shared his views must be guilty.

After Spock's conviction The Resistance became more militant in its tactics. In May 1968 nine Roman Catholic pacifists took 378 files from the Catonsville, Maryland, draft-board office and burned them with homemade napalm. The "Catonsville Nine" were not young men, not Hippies or radicals; they included three former missionaries, a nurse, an artist, and two priests. The "Nine" argued that certain kinds of property had no right to exist and that the draft files, instruments of an illegal and immoral war, were such property. A Federal jury found them guilty of destroying government property and interfering with the administration of the Selective Service System. They faced up to eighteen years of prison and $22,000 in fines.

On September 24, 1968, fourteen draft resisters entered the Milwaukee Selective Service Headquarters and destroyed 25,000 records with homemade napalm. Six of the fourteen were clergymen. The charges against them under state law were burglary, arson, and theft (they took keys from a cleaning woman); under Federal law, they were charged with burning draft records. Why had they burned the files? "The service of life," said their spokesman, "no longer leaves any option other than positive action against what we can only call the American way of death."

Within the armed forces themselves "Liberate yourself" was becoming a popular motto. Soldiers deserted and took permanent sanctuary in Europe. The Resistance was there to give advice and aid. Sometimes deserters sought temporary sanctuary on college campuses, asking only time enough to hold press conferences to publicize their opposition to the military and to the war. The Resistance was there to arrange campus rallies and to notify the press. Even within the hallowed army barracks The Resistance was present, passing out leaflets to inductees while antiwar military men schemed to unionize enlisted men.

How did the dissenters of the late 1960s stand in relation to their society? The Hippie, like his predecessor, the Beat, was as the mercy of the larger society he had rejected. Ironically, only because that society had developed a high tolerance for dissent was he able to thrive. His life, theoretically so free and unfettered, was daily circumscribed by laws and regulations. Because he did not actively seek to change laws, he could only ignore or evade them. Drug laws made taking LSD risky. And although he rejected society, he was not necessarily free of obligations to it. Selective Service made the same demands on him as on his mainstream brothers. The Hippie's protest was passive, a life style in itself that was not easily translatable into institutional and organizational forms and programs. He could convert only by example. He could only play a waiting game, hoping that his way of life would prevail in the future.

The radical also belonged to a social minority subject to restrictions, bold or subtle, designed to blunt his attack or to force him to participate in precisely those institutional rituals that he wished to change. But the radical did not respond passively. His goal was to restructure institutions, and he was therefore less easily dealt with than was the Hippie. Institutions do not as easily absorb their antitheses; stockbrokers could adopt long hair styles and smoke pot without renouncing capitalism, but the stock market could not survive without capitalism.

Society could permit the Hippie to continue his marginal life, but the political radical had either to be cleverly wooed back into the mainstream or isolated, silenced, and possibly destroyed. The only alternative would be to undertake the vast restructuring that he demanded.

CHAPTER

13

Student Upheavals in American Universities

BY the mid-1960s a large number of young Americans were thoroughly dissatisfied with society and its institutions. Their alienation had many roots. The black liberation movement, first of all, had made activists of many sympathizers. Second, the Vietnam war symbolized all the ugliness and injustice of the contemporary United States. To young radicals, the bombing and burning of dark-skinned Asian peasants seemed a government-sanctioned expression of the same madness that had bombed children in a Southern Sunday school. Finally, as one and then another of the few heroes that the young had were shot down in acts of meaningless violence, "liberal" values as well as "liberal" institutions came under suspicion.[1]

Students, in particular, had grown increasingly hostile toward their own institutions: the universities. These universities had grown bigger every year, and many students felt themselves reduced to numbers on class cards, anonymous units in a mob. Like the workers in the early stages of the Industrial Revolution, who found the large factories forbidding and cruel, these students were angered by the vast size and impersonal demeanor of the large university.

The larger and more prestigious American universities, based on nineteenth-century German models, had been founded and administered to educate scientists and leaders to serve the community and to provide it with the knowledge and research of eminent scholars. Good undergraduate teaching had never been seriously rewarded in leading American universities; tenure and promotion always went to professors who published and to those who won recognition outside the school for scientific accomplishments or for service to government or to corporations.

Universities varied, of course, in size as in teaching practices, in social and political awareness as in faculty autonomy. The University of California at Berkeley was one of the biggest: With 27,500 students, it would be difficult under any circumstances to provide for effective outlets for individuality. Several Berkeley students had spent the "Freedom Summer" of 1964 with C.O.R.E. or S.N.C.C. in Mississippi, helping black voters to register. They returned to Berkeley dedicated to direct political action for social ends and led their fellow students in election work in California in the fall of 1964. They set up headquarters in a "free speech" area outside the Bancroft-Telegraph entrance to the campus, a traditional off-campus center for political activities. The university authorities suddenly discovered that the Bancroft-Telegraph area was actually part of the campus and therefore subject to the regents' ban on political activities.

The stage was thus set for the first of the big student-protest movements, a series of episodes more significant in their effects than in themselves. The Berkeley Free Speech movement not only won its goals; it also set a number of precedents: Students twice occupied an administration building and were forcibly removed by the police; the faculty pulled itself together and involved itself in university politics, generally on the side of the students; the leaders of the university administration proved their inability to handle protest and rebellion.

Mario Savio, the leader of the Berkeley radicals, became a national figure when he turned the Free Speech movement into a broadside attack on the whole concept of "multiversity." Clark Kerr, the president of the University of California, had introduced this image of the modern university as a huge, complex machine; Savio reacted with a violent attack on the machine. Kerr, once a labor arbitrator, had renounced arbitration in university management. He ran the seven campuses of the University of California as a centralized autocracy in which every decision and policy had to be approved by him. Although greatly admired in the educational world, Kerr turned out to be thoroughly incompetent to deal with student protest. His was one of the first careers to crash in the student-protest movement.

Berkeley provided a notable example of a condition common in most of the "great" American universities: The education of under-graduates was de-emphasized to the point of neglect. The brilliant or famous professors listed in the catalog saw few students. Some of them lectured to enormous classes, but few kept regular office hours or read students' papers. The graduate students ("T.A.'s," or teaching assistants) who did most of the work felt exploited by the professors and resented the entire system.

The argument over free speech at Berkeley implied the deeper question of the students' right to full citizenship and became an expression of widespread hostility toward "multiversity." When the demonstrators occupied Sproul Hall (the administration building) for the second time on December 2 and 3, 1964, the battle was escalated by the authorities into a genuine confrontation. The administration summoned city police to deal with a nonviolent sit-in, alienating faculty members, nonstriking students, and newspaper readers across the country. A few instances of brutality were reported, but by the standards of later events the police were fairly restrained. Nevertheless the teachers and students who watched the slow process of removal (it took twelve hours to clear the building) were appalled. The faculty passed resolutions demanding amnesty for the demonstrators and immediate implementation of liberalized free-speech rules. They also asked for a new chancellor.

Berkeley got a new acting chancellor—Martin Myerson—who announced settlement of the original free-speech issue in favor of the students. The students then splintered into many radical groups, including the short-lived Filthy Speech movement, which failed to attract enough support to become in itself an important issue. California legislators and the university regents, however, accorded it enough attention to bring about the temporary resignations of Kerr and Myerson, neither of whom supported filthy speech. They were both, however, concerned about outside meddling in university affairs—and with reason: State-wide reaction against the Berkeley radicals helped Ronald Reagan into the governor's mansion in 1968. Reagan cut the university budget, arranged for the dismissal of Kerr, and generally encouraged a marked increase in supervision of the Berkeley campus by state officials. Myerson resigned again, permanently, and was followed by several faculty members who were disgusted by the new atmosphere. The university had been, without question, profoundly damaged.

The effects of the Berkeley uprising were felt immediately. Between the winter of 1964 and the spring of 1968 student protests flared across the country. Between January and June 1968, 221 "major" demonstrations took place on 101 American campuses. Rebellion was in the air, and the events of the mid-1960s continued to provide cause for disgust and alienation. Berkeley had proved that young radicals could fight social and political battles on their own campuses and win. (They had to fight, however; in no instance were useful and meaningful reforms inaugurated by faculties or administrations in response to the events at Berkeley.)

Perhaps a large-scale confrontation was inevitable. The young people of the late 1960s seemed to represent a genuinely different kind of generation. Their drug-taking, long-haired life style, with its hostility toward traditional patriotism, was directly opposed to that of their parents and teachers, who had worn crew cuts and had marched willingly to war. The potential draftee of the 1960s was a very different young man, on his way to a very different war.

Columbia University was a logical site for a major confrontation. First of all, the university itself was in poor shape. Transformed by Nicholas Murray Butler in the early twentieth century from a gentleman's finishing school into an international center of learning, it had more recently fallen upon evil times. Butler had held all administrative power in his own hands. He had allowed the separate graduate schools autonomy under his supervision, and no university-wide faculty group existed to make policy or establish standards. After his death in 1945 weaker administrations (including that of Dwight Eisenhower from 1947 to 1952) lost control of the center, and Columbia became a collection of autonomous schools—some excellent, some very bad. Columbia College, the undergraduate division for men, was lost among the giants. The names of extremely distinguished scholars appeared in the college catalog, but many of them spent their time flying to Washington or around the world.

Furthermore, Columbia was located at 116th Street and Broadway, on the edge of one of the largest and poorest black urban communities in the Western world, Harlem. The university had an extremely bad reputation as a landlord and neighbor. Although it harbored some of the world's best-known and most-admired liberals, its administration evicted tenants from comfortable buildings to obtain offices and housing for its faculty and ignored the appalling needs of its Harlem neighbors across Morningside Park.

Grayson Kirk took over the presidency of Columbia from Eisenhower in 1952. He did little or nothing to limit the autonomy of the schools or to halt the decline of the institution as a whole. The faculty was regularly raided by more progressive colleges, and the students became increasingly alienated by the neglect of their teachers and the computer mentality of administration officials. The provost of the university, Jacques Barzun, demonstrated brilliance and style in his own writing and in picky points of administrative detail, but he did nothing to bring about massive reform.

In 1967 a new vice-president and provost appeared to offer hope for substantial change, however. David Truman, former dean of Columbia College, promised to rejuvenate undergraduate education and to reward fine teaching as well as scholarship. Truman's appointment was a hopeful sign, but he could not move fast enough to avert disaster.

The Columbia College 1968 yearbook was already at the printer when the upheaval began. No authority paid much attention at the time, but it was an extraordinary document. The yearbook—traditionally a testimonial to the fun of college life—was a violent expression of disillusion and alienation. Even the most popular teachers were held up to ridicule, and the university itself was pictured as a giant machine ready to distort and crush its students' individuality. A sense of betrayal and of the irrelevance of the liberal tradition stands out on every page. Presumably, liberal values had been handed on to the seniors in four years of classes, but their yearbook made it clear that they had learned to distrust those values along with the institutions that promoted them.

In early 1968 a revision of the draft law put an end to student deferment and inflamed existing hatred of the war and the authorities. Furthermore, the crusade and successes of Senator Eugene McCarthy, whose campaign had been manned by students, made protest and political action seem possible and desirable. The assassination of Martin Luther King in April deprived the young of another hero and once more illustrated the failure of the American dream. By the spring of 1968 a students' rebellion seemed almost inevitable; it occurred at Columbia because the university's location directly involved it in civil-rights issues, because its institutional weakness left it vulnerable to a major upheaval, and because it had unusually skillful and determined student radicals.

The organization most directly responsible for the channeling of student unrest into direct action was Students for a Democratic Society. S.D.S. had been founded in the early 1960s as an offshoot of the social democratic League for Industrial Democracy. It was a politically heterogeneous but profoundly radical organization based on rejection of American capitalist society, and its most effective work was on college campuses and in ghettos across the country. The Columbia branch of S.D.S. protested the university's "racist" approach to Harlem, its suppression of student political activity, and—

most vehemently—its connections with the military-industrial complex and the war in Vietnam.

Columbia belonged to the Institute for Defense Analysis, a group of universities organized to offer advice to the government in matters of defense, research on weapons and tactics, and riot control. Grayson Kirk's position on the board of I.D.A. offended radical students, and the entire relationship provoked valid questions about the propriety of an allegedly "free" university's accepting government projects of a quasi-political nature. Furthermore, the Columbia campus had been opened to Marine and Central Intelligence Agency recruitment, to the disgust of antiwar students.

The immediate impetus for the Columbia rebellion, however, came from resentment at the construction of a new gymnasium in neighboring Morningside Park. The trustees had raised five million dollars for a splendid new athletic facility to be built on leased public park land. There had been some opposition from the beginning, but Columbia—determined to enhance its Ivy League image by improving its athletic program—went right ahead with its plans. In deference to protests from the black community, however, arrangements were made to open some parts of the building to Harlem residents. But the location of the Harlem entrance—a back door—and the position of the gym as a sort of Berlin wall between Morningside Drive and Harlem infuriated black radicals. Columbia already had a very bad local reputation, and "Gym Crow" was suspected from the beginning; every stage in its planning and construction brought increased hostility.

Columbia had no official policy against student political protest, but in 1966, when such protest began to become effective—in the sense that it interfered with the educational process—confrontations between students and administration became frequent and noisy. In 1966–1967 there were demonstrations against C.I.A. recruiting and differences over subsequent disciplinary proceedings. In the fall of 1967 the university banned indoor demonstrations, but in March 1968 a demonstration against the university's affiliation with I.D.A. was held inside Low Library (the administration building) in defiance of the ban. Six out of a large crowd of demonstrators were suspended; all six were leaders of Columbia S.D.S. The organization now had an excellent reason to build furious and effective protest: It was fighting for its life as a viable organization at Columbia.

On Monday, April 22, S.D.S. announced that it would lead a march into Low Library on the following day. The S.D.S. leaders intended not only to advertise particular issues but also to seek a clash with the administration that would "radicalize" moderate students. The enemies of S.D.S., conservative fraternity men and athletes who believed that the radical minority was interfering with the peaceful education of the majority, declared that they would block any attempt to enter the administration building; on the appointed day they stood on its steps, waiting to meet the demonstrators.

The steps of Low Library rise from the central mall (College Walk) of the Columbia campus, which is laid out in stately geometric patterns entirely appropriate to revolution and melodrama. The radicals gathered around a natural soapbox on College Walk, a large, smooth sundial that makes an ideal speaker's platform. A crowd of about one thousand students, attracted by the prospect of a confrontation between the radicals and the "jocks," heard S.D.S. president Mark Rudd expostulate against the ban on indoor demonstrations. Leaders of the Students' Afro-American Society (S.A.S.) spoke against the gymnasium. Rejecting a late offer of a meeting with the administration, the students then marched on Low. But the building was locked, and the demonstrators—to avoid a major clash with the fraternity boys—marched to the gym site. There they tore down a section of the metal fence surrounding the excavation, thus attracting the attention of the police. There was a scuffle, or a series of scuffles, and some of the onlookers had their first glimpses of policemen's clubs in action.

There was little to be accomplished at the gym site, however, and Rudd soon directed the crowd back to the campus. At loose ends, the students wandered into Hamilton Hall (an undergraduate classroom building). There they hung around heckling one another until the acting dean of the college, the vice-dean, and the proctor entered the building and vanished into their offices, refusing to listen to any demands made under such circumstances. The demonstrators settled down, sent out for food and guitars, and passed the time eating, singing, and talking while their leaders drew up a program.

Six demands were proposed and adopted by the crowd: that work on the gymnasium be halted at once, that the university end its relationship with I.D.A., that indoor demonstrations be allowed, that a student-faculty judicial committee be appointed to make disciplinary decisions, that the university arrange to drop charges against those arrested at the gym site, and that everyone involved in the current demonstration be granted amnesty.

Dean Henry Coleman prudently remained in his office. It was not clear whether or not he was literally a hostage, but he and several members of his self-appointed (conservative) student bodyguard spent Tuesday night in Hamilton Hall. Many demonstrators spent the night there too, and by morning the nature of the occupation had been radically altered. White demonstrators were asked to leave, and S.A.S. took over the building; Hamilton Hall was rechristened Nat Turner Hall of Malcolm X University. Leaders of the adult black community had arrived during the night and had encouraged the black students to concentrate on their big issue, Gym Crow. The transfer of control in Hamilton Hall obviously affected the position of the Columbia authorities. They were very reluctant to risk a riot by calling in city police, and their reluctance was echoed by Mayor John V. Lindsay's administration, which was determined to avoid any large-scale racial confrontation.

After being dismissed from Hamilton Hall by the blacks, the white radicals had a choice of giving in (accepting suspension and probable termination of their academic careers) or of opening a second front. Mark Rudd chose the latter course, and in the early morning of April 24, S.D.S. members marched across campus to "liberate" Low Library. They broke into the building—an act not of demonstration but of revolution—and settled down in Kirk's own office. They used his office equipment, smoked his cigars, and congratulated themselves that their commitment rivaled that of their black colleagues, that they were in the vanguard of a war. Only a few leaders were hard-core radicals with fully developed social theories. Nearly all the student radicals came from middle-class homes in which "breaking and entering" was regarded as a sin as well as a crime.

The administration was stymied by the escalation of student protest into a demonstration of Black Power. The entire episode occurred in the full glare of publicity, and students and administrators across the country watched and waited to see what would happen. University officials tried at first to make a separate peace with the blacks, but S.A.S. stuck to the six demands of April 23.

Then the faculty stepped in. Lacking any university-wide organization, it set up ad hoc committees to discuss the crisis and make recommendations, envisioning its role as that of liberal mediator between radical students and reactionary administrators. Many faculty members sympathized with the students' grievances and some even with their radical philosophies, but most were horrified by the escalation of protest into revolt. They had no real power to negotiate a settlement, however, and they ran the risk of further alienating the students with meaningless promises. Most of the professors believed that work on the gymnasium should be stopped immediately, but they did not go along with the demand for total amnesty. They hoped to set up a tripartite board of students, faculty, and administration to make disciplinary policy, but they saw no reason why civil disobedience and disruption of the university should go unpunished. The faculty passed on its recommendations to Kirk, but he ignored them and took the problem to his trustees. These gentlemen, mostly leading members of the establishment, were asked to accept responsibility for the decisions facing the university.

The issue of amnesty was philosophically and practically bothersome to moderates and radicals alike. Civil-rights demonstrators in the South had accepted jail sentences as necessary sacrifices, but university law was after all much less well defined than civil law. The S.D.S. demonstrators regarded themselves as labor negotiators rather than as criminals. Amnesty was usually assumed in labor negotiations—unions were not held responsible for business losses during strikes—and they saw no reason why it should not be assumed in the negotiations of the student proletariat. They saw students as an exploited class, a new proletariat. Fundamentally, though, the radicals claimed that the university's authority was not legitimate because it was not based on representative democracy and that the authorities had to be forced to grant amnesty as a confession of illegitimacy.

Dean Coleman crossed the barricades at Hamilton Hall on Wednesday afternoon and reported that he had been treated very well. He was no longer a hostage—if he had ever been—but the pace of the rebellion did not slacken. Early Thursday morning another building was "liberated." Fayerweather Hall, the history and social-science building, was occupied by a group of students quite unlike the demonstrators in Low. These men and women, mostly graduate students, were far from radical; many were married, and most were well along in academic careers. Their occupation of Fayerweather was far more disturbing to conservative students than was the occupation of the administration building, for it signified that the rebels had effectively disrupted the educational process. Classes could not be held in Fayerweather, and those who disagreed with the radicals were thus deprived of their right to education.

The students inside Low Library spent Thursday keeping house and committing what might be described as student pranks, including mailing President Kirk's draft card to his local board. They also took letters out of his files and copied the ones pertaining to I.D.A. affiliation. Another building was "liberated" that evening; students in Avery Hall, the graduate architecture building, refused to leave when it was "cleared" by officials in the evening. Both architecture faculty and students had long been angry over the university's refusal to seek the opinion of the School of Architecture in university building and planning. In all the "liberated" buildings (eventually five) defense committees were formed to protect the inhabitants against invasion by police or conservative students.

A black community rally was held at Broadway and 116th Street on Thursday evening. The speakers denounced university racism, and the rally ended with a walk through the campus toward the gym site. A mass of antidemonstrators had collected inside the university gates, and when the police tried to clear a path for the marchers, the "jocks" fought back. They were finally persuaded to let the demonstrators pass, but the episode only increased their anger and frustration at the apparently successful takeover of the campus by radicals and blacks. Conservative students began to roam the campus, looking for suitable expression of their anger and disgust.

Mathematics Hall was taken at 3:00 A.M. Friday by a group of radicals, including Tom Hayden, a founding member of the national S.D.S. organization. Within minutes Vice-President Truman announced to a faculty meeting that the university authorities had summoned the police. The teachers, furious and worried, left the meeting to defend their students. After a brief and bloody confrontation in which professors were clubbed with nightsticks, the police entered Low Library. Not much else happened. A truce was called, the police left the campus, the students stayed in the buildings, and Rudd agreed to convey the administration position to the radicals. He did so on Friday morning; at that time compromise was still possible, and faculty members who had defended their students had more student confidence than they had had at any other time.

There were serious differences among the occupants of the liberated buildings, which were well aired during the truce period. Strike Central, an organization set up to coordinate separated groups, was dominated by the S.D.S. and its last-ditch philosophy of resistance. The radicals were not willing to moderate their demands in any way, they suppressed proposals put forth by the moderates in Fayerweather, and their high-handed approach irritated their allies. The fact is that S.D.S. preferred a "police bust" to negotiation. Its leaders sought "political clarity" and polarization, and they knew that a bust would win sympathy for themselves and their cause. The Columbia trustees played into their hands by making provocative statements denying any possibility of meaningful negotiation.

Meanwhile, the free-floating anger of conservative students had crystallized; a newly formed Majority Coalition led by fraternity boys and "jocks" was determined to force the faculty and administration to stop coddling the rebels. Eventually its pressure on moderate students resulted in further polarization; many students were pushed to the left in a forced choice between beards and crew cuts. Although on Friday morning compromise had been possible, by Friday night the campus had split into opposing teams, despite the efforts of faculty members to bridge the widening gulf. As individuals and groups, faculty members sent recommendations to the authorities and acted as emissaries to occupied buildings. They talked, argued, and debated, but they never persuaded officials or students to soften their stands. Professor Alan Westin, of the Department of Government, proposed a very reasonable compromise, but feelings had hardened to such an extent that it was accepted by neither side.

On Sunday, April 28, the Majority Coalition was out in force. It barricaded Low Library and refused to allow anyone or anything to enter except doctors and medical supplies. The conservatives were supported by a faculty cordon, which had become less a guard and more a police force. Food had to be thrown to the occupants over Coalition and faculty heads, and the scene took on a carnival aspect, as cans of tuna and jars of peanut butter flew in and out of windows.

The fun and games ended very abruptly in the early hours of Tuesday, when the police arrived in strength after having sent plainclothesmen ahead to infiltrate the buildings. Low Library was quickly and effectively cleared, with much punching of heads; then the police turned on heckling bystanders. At Hamilton Hall, however, there was no brutality or disorganization at all. The best men of the Tactical Police Force took the building with maximum respect for the black demonstrators' skulls and civil rights. The students were quietly marched onto waiting buses.

At Fayerweather Hall the bust took a nastier form. Faculty members who stood in front of their students were knocked to the ground and beaten with fists or rubber blackjacks. The building was emptied in an hour. At Avery, where the least radical group of students was in command, police brutality reached its peak. Clubs were used, and students were kicked downstairs. The brutality continued even after Avery and Mathematics had been cleared: The police turned against a crowd of spectators on College Walk, chasing fleeing students out onto Broadway or trapping and clubbing them against dormitory walls.

The bust was over at 5:00 A.M. More than seven hundred people had been arrested, five hundred of them members of the Columbia community. Eighty-four students and fourteen teachers ended up in the emergency room at St. Luke's Hospital, which looked like a field station in a combat zone.

The bust provoked violent rage among faculty and students alike.

Such a resort to force offended the deepest sensibilities of liberal professors, and even those who sympathized with the administration were horrified at the extent of police brutality. Some faculty members exasperated their colleagues by arguing that Kirk had had no choice but to call the police, but most set forth immediately to express formally their indignation and distress. As the day and its meetings wore on, however, the faculty position moved closer to the center. Early expressions of radical sympathies were moderated with time and reflection. The faculty did, however, announce cancellation of Wednesday classes. It also chose a group of representatives to meet directly with the trustees, an innovation in Columbia administration.

The students found a major outlet for their fury and frustration: They settled down under the leadership of S.D.S.—which claimed that police violence was inevitable in capitalist society—to a general strike. The call for such a strike had sounded even before the bust, and by Thursday it was a well-organized reality. The steering committee stated two prerequisites for further negotiation: legal and academic amnesty and explicit confirmation of the right of students to share in the restructuring of Columbia University. Granted these conditions, the strike committee would negotiate the six original demands of the first Hamilton Hall sit-in.

The next few days brought a remarkable burst of talk, music, "liberated" classes, and more talk. Sympathetic professors and ambitious students held classes outdoors, in apartments, or in the student union. Anyone could teach anything at the new Free University of Morningside Heights. Meanwhile, fearing a long strike, the college faculty made arrangements to extend the spring semester and to institute pass-fail grading. The strike *was* long. It worked much better than anyone had foreseen, and only the professional graduate schools returned to anything like normal operation before the end of the semester.

The strike also revealed differences within the faculty. Some members supported it wholeheartedly; others enjoyed the opportunity to stay home; still others defied it and continued to teach in regular classrooms. Even in "free" classes there were arguments over curriculum, since radical students reiterated their right to examine the "relevance" of subject matter to contemporary social problems. Graduate students in history and sociology especially made serious attempts to restructure their departments, in curriculum as well as in organization, to their own liking.

The faculty executive committee named a commission to study the causes of the crisis. Its chairman was Archibald Cox, a professor at the Harvard University Law School and former Solicitor General of the

United States. The students were not very enthusiastic about the commission; its members were mostly elderly men, and the radicals feared that they would simply whitewash the role of the university.

More significantly, members of various departments began to meet with students to discover and discuss their views on such matters as curriculum and degree requirements. This getting together was a slow business (too slow to satisfy many students), but it was a potentially useful and constructive approach to basic changes. It contributed to the difficulties of the strike committee, however. Moderate and liberal students—those who had been dissatisfied with the Columbia administration and horrified by the police bust—were ready to work for constructive change. Unlike the radicals, they did not despise the very institution of a university; they simply wanted to reform Columbia. Eventually the leaders of this moderate group left the strike committee. Although they continued to support the strike, they established their own organization (Students for a Reconstructed University, S.R.U.), which emphasized negotiation and reform.

S.D.S., deserted by the moderates, began to receive more and more criticism from the press and from the various commissions and committees at work on the Columbia problem. The radicals then turned their attention to what they viewed as their natural allies, the black community. They joined a group of black neighborhood organizations in "liberating" an apartment building owned by Columbia. S.D.S. and community members demonstrated in the building until the police arrived and took them downtown to be arraigned for trespassing. Mark Rudd was among them.

On May 19 the student-faculty committee on discipline made its first report to the university. The recommended disciplinary measures were extremely confusing at best, and bewildered students resented the committee's insistence on formal appearances before the dean. As part of the reaction, Hamilton Hall was "liberated" again on May 21, without the assistance of faculty buffers. When the Tactical Police Force arrived (under the personal supervision of Chief Inspector Sanford Garelick), the students were removed without brutality, and the episode was soon over. Sympathetic onlookers gathered around while students were removed from the building, however. Barricades were erected, and heckling turned to full-scale combat. Even Barnard girls from across Broadway joined in yelling obscenities at the police. The police returned to the campus at 4:20 A.M. They tore down the barricades, trapped students within the college walls, and even pursued them into dormitories. Injuries were numerous among policemen, as well as among students.

The second police bust won very little sympathy for the demonstrators except among those who were already committed to the radical cause. Fires had been set in faculty offices in Hamilton Hall by someone—S.D.S. members? police provocateurs? personal enemies?— and valuable research papers belonging to Professor Orest Ranum had been destroyed, which helped to harden faculty opinion against the vandals. Besides, it was nearly summer; the semester was over for practical purposes, and the Columbia community had begun to melt away.

Before the seniors and the faculty could leave, however, they had to undergo the ritual of graduation. In 1968 there were two such ceremonies. The official commencement (held indoors to discourage demonstrations) took place in the Cathedral of St. John the Divine; the S.R.U. organized a walkout from the cathedral to its own Free University graduation in front of Low Library. The radicals boycotted both ceremonies, but they managed to have included in the S.R.U. commencement—supposed to be a dignified affair—the burning-in-effigy of Grayson Kirk.

The official commencement address was delivered by a great historian, Richard Hofstadter, who spoke for the liberal intellectuals who had been shocked and horrified by the aims and tactics of the New Left. His own interpretation of American history as a history of continuation and modification of the liberal consensus had shaped the thought of a whole generation of historians. Without making any effort to interpret the causes of the Columbia uprising, Hofstadter denounced the iniquities of the S.D.S. He spoke for the traditionally nonpolitical university, above and beyond social problems, but he ignored its associations with the military-political establishment. Hofstadter's speech summed up and focused attention on the enormous gap between old liberals and new radicals.

The summer of 1968 was a period of reorganization on the Columbia campus. Seventy-three students were suspended, and a new dean was appointed. Carl Hovde was a popular choice among students and faculty alike; he was chosen for his apparent ability to work out a dignified compromise. Grayson Kirk resigned, and Andrew Cordier was appointed to the acting presidency of the university. No thoroughgoing solutions were offered or accepted, however, and the university community faced registration in September with forebodings of further trouble. Several faculty members accepted posts elsewhere.

The administration did formulate a plan to isolate the hard-core radicals from the rest of the students. By dropping criminal-trespass charges against most of the arrested students but refusing to drop more serious charges against 154 others (presumably extremists), it hoped to dispose of the hard core. At the same time, plans for extensive restructuring of the university were announced, including formation of a university senate to include faculty members, alumni, and students. The S.R.U. rejected this plan and announced that it would hold out for complete amnesty and for thorough study and reform of the university's relationship with society as a whole. The S.D.S. was, of course, violently opposed to Cordier's compromise. Fearing total exclusion from a moderately reformed Columbia, the radicals made several attempts to win over the student majority through another confrontation with authority. They had very little success. The Columbia rebellion was over, and the great majority of students and faculty were ready to return to normality. Mark Rudd went on a speaking tour of various universities, but he helped the S.D.S. cause little when he told a Boston audience that the issues in the Columbia crisis had been phony, concocted to guarantee a confrontation.

Let me tell you, we manufactured those issues. The Institute for Defense Analysis is nothing at Columbia. Just three professors. And the gym issue is bull. It doesn't mean anything to anybody. I had never been to the gym site before April 23. I didn't even know how to get there.

The Cox Commission published its report on October 6. It was extremely critical of the S.D.S., the faculty, the police, but most of all of the university administration and trustees. The report condemned the administration for authoritarianism that had demoralized the faculty and students. Most remarkable, however, was that the report had no practical effect at all. No resignations were demanded and none offered. The Cox report did not affect the university's facade of calm.

The uprising itself obviously, however, had significant consequences. The Columbia trustees and administration were forced to talk and act like liberals; high-handed pronouncements of their own authority would no longer be tolerated. Much more important, the restructuring of the university did begin. The faculty already had a larger part in administrative matters, as did the students. The Byzantine regime left by Nicholas Murray Butler was partially democratized, and an extensive reappraisal of the nature and function of a university was forced upon its leaders.

Old-fashioned liberals have stated that the S.D.S. would have failed without the cooperation of the black community, and there is truth in this assertion. It must be recognized, however, that the radical leaders were unusually courageous and unusually determined, that they knew exactly what they wanted while the administration ran around in circles. They were aided, of course, by the atmosphere at Columbia, where professors and students alike resented their dehumanization by the authorities.

The mass media, too, played a part in the Columbia story. Although the newspapers and television were slow to catch on to the significance of the rebellion, they took it up in a big way when they did grasp its importance. By September student radicalism had become a hot news item, and exhaustive coverage was being given to every "radical" manifestation. This extensive publicity made it possible for events at Columbia to exert all important effect elsewhere. University administrations all over the country (and in Europe) paid attention to student and faculty complaints. Even on distant campuses departmental rules were liberalized and joint faculty-student committees established. Presidents and deans became so wary of student unrest that they spent many hours drawing up battle plans in case students occupied a university building. The great issue facing university administrations and trustees now was whether and when the police should be summoned.

Liberal faculty members throughout the nation suffered through the crisis. The all-too-evident departure of the New Left from old-fashioned liberalism caused soul-searching on campuses everywhere. New Deal-oriented professors—including those who had stood up to Joseph McCarthy in the 1950s—believed leftist extremists to be as dangerous to academic freedom as rightists, and liberal Democrats were among the most violent critics of the S.D.S. The young radicals were equally violent in criticism of the liberals, whose "detachment" they viewed as abandonment of disadvantaged groups: black people, poor people, and students. It became increasingly clear to sensitive liberals that the ivory tower was crumbling, that a choice between defense of the traditional independence of the academic guild and active involvement with radicals and radical causes was being forced upon them.

One significant consequence of the student upheaval was the increasing polarization of the faculty between left and right wings. Professors who had great sympathy with the new student generation and at the same time regarded their own profession as sustaining the rights and privileges of an academic guild were caught in the middle. The student radicals had little or no respect for academic freedom: They sought to pressure the faculty into supporting their revolutionary political views, just as Joe McCarthy had tried to force academics to sustain his reactionary opinions. Student upheaval was causing the demoralization of the middle-of-the-road kind of academic, and as it continued, many moderates and liberals were taking conservative stands against the students. This process was also likely to drive many sensitive and brilliant men from academic life and to discourage younger scholars from entering the academic profession. American universities were following the miserable example of institutions of higher learning in totalitarian countries and becoming battlegrounds in which the passions and problems of society were daily visited upon the heads of the professors.

A more personal result of the Columbia uprising was the fall of David Truman, along with that of Kirk. Truman was just as judicious, charming, and intelligent as he had been before the crisis, but it was no longer possible for him to succeed Kirk to the presidency. Truman left Columbia abruptly in the spring of 1969 to become the president of Mount Holyoke College. He had failed to act effectively at the right time; he had stuck with compromise as a policy and a philosophy at a time when extremism was in control. With all his charm, Truman was not able to get through to the young radicals—nor they to him; his personal downfall, like that of Hubert Humphrey, was caused by the differences between the Old and New Left.

A new romanticism was sweeping the country in the 1960s, and whenever a new spirit is born the inevitable differences between generations are magnified. Students wanted to enshrine the individual and to tear down giant institutions, to return to humanism and to place emphasis on individual relationships—to make love, not war. Contemporary American thinkers (even those well over twenty-one like Norman Brown, Herbert Marcuse, and Marshall McLuhan) who expressed these students' inchoate feelings were denounced by the liberal establishment for romanticism and anarchism.

The very real generation gap of the 1960s was exacerbated by the apparent omnipotence of the elderly men in university administration. Inexcusably careless trustees and regents failed to appreciate the need to appoint to high office even moderately young men, men with some grasp of the new philosophy or at least an ability to accommodate its style. Typically, however, aging regimes fail to reform themselves until it is too late. Revolutions occur in badly run institutions that are neither strong enough to suppress insurrection nor sensible enough to institute reforms, and the revolt at Columbia followed the characteristic pattern.

If it did nothing else, the Columbia uprising served a useful purpose by triggering a continuing debate on the function of a university. Hofstadter expressed one point of view in his commencement address; student radicals expressed the opposite view in their claims that a university should work positively for the amelioration of social ills. According to the New Left, the American university had lost its political virginity long ago (as evident in its connections with the government); it could not therefore cop out of society on the false grounds of "academic freedom."

Student radicals were violent in language and action because they felt driven to call attention dramatically to their own needs and those of society. They felt isolated in what they felt were mechanistic institutions, and they were sufficiently articulate and well educated to express the rage of their black friends and neighbors. They were criticized for their apparent inability to offer constructive solutions for the problems they saw so clearly; it was asked whether or not the radicals could build as well as destroy, a valid question. The students at Columbia were too divided among themselves to agree on concrete proposals, and their very commitment to democratic procedures resulted in endless discussions and weak programs. Furthermore, many of them were deeply distrustful of anything resembling bureaucracy; ideals codified into formal plans often lose their attraction. The radicals knew that they were in a minority and saw their most important task as awakening others to the wrongs of American society. When more people were willing to defy institutions, the students argued, then they could turn their attention from destruction to rebuilding.

After all, the Columbia radicals were expressing a total rejection of society, not simply presenting a well-organized list of specific grievances like those of the liberals in the 1930s. American society, even that part of it that is enclosed by campus walls, was crowded and increasingly ugly. New Dealers genuinely believed that social ills could be cured by economic manipulation; contemporary radicals claimed that solutions had to be much more complex. Their alienation was not simplistic but represented an entirely new culture, a life style instead of merely a political platform. The Hippie movement expressed a part of the new total protest, but Hippies dropped out, whereas radicals acted.

The generation gap in the contemporary United States was not a phony creation of the mass media. Young people, whether pot-smoking flower children or austere followers of Che Guevara, did violently reject their environment. Their protest took a variety of forms, attaching itself to specific issues, whether genuinely felt or manufactured for the occasion. The protest was basically a moral one, however: The young were challenging the middle-aged on moral grounds. Their important and continuing quarrel with American life could burst out anywhere: on college campuses, in the ghettos, even in the squarest suburbs. The young simply refused to accept the values and institutions of their parents and teachers. Such a refusal was at the root of the

Columbia upheaval, and it is to be at the root of political, social, and aesthetic movements as yet unrecognized.

What was socially significant about the student radicals was the prominence in their ranks of a group that was relatively new on the American campus in large numbers. Before the late 1950s American students had either come from the established rich, for whom college was a finishing school, or from the upwardly mobile lower middle class, for whom the university degree opened the path to the learned professions and affluence. Many student radicals of the 1960s seemed to come from neither the very rich nor the ambitious lower middle class, but rather from the postwar suburban middle class. These students could neither look forward to heading big family businesses and naturally exercising leadership as a result of family position, nor did they have to worry greatly about economic security—one way or another, they had the connections to get a good job, if worse came to worse. If there was a class basis to the student revolt, it lay in the peculiar character of the suburban middle class, who could offer their children security without power. An impetus to student radicalism was a yearning for power by the comfortable postwar middle class of suburban America, which as yet had very little chance to exercise leadership in society. Perhaps this was why successful businessmen and matronly presidents of synagogue sisterhoods looked with such equanimity, even sympathy, upon the radical activities of their college-age children.

CHAPTER

14

Communist Protest
Against Stalinism

ALTHOUGH the magnitude and importance of the Russian Revolution of 1917 can scarcely be disputed, it should not be forgotten that Russia had had a long tradition of revolution from above, as well as from below. More often than not, radical change in Russian history had been the product of deliberate decision by the established authorities. In order to modernize Russia and to make it the equal of its Western neighbors and competitors, Peter the Great had, in the early eighteenth century, opened the floodgates to Western influence; the government of Alexander II emancipated the serfs in 1861 and set the stage for the remarkable industrial expansion of the last decades of the Russian Empire; and the government of Joseph Stalin manipulated and impelled the Soviet Union into the position of the world's second largest industrial power. Nikita Khrushchev's secret speech to the Twentieth Congress of the Soviet Communist Party in 1956, in which he exposed the barbarities of the Stalin era, can be regarded as the latest manifestation of this tradition, one that had far-reaching consequences for the Soviet Union, as well as its east European neighbors.

As in the past, Khrushchev's "revolution from above" evoked a swelling response from below, and his speech served as a signal for the loosing of long-repressed grievances. But this response in turn presented Khrushchev and his successors with the problem that had haunted many of their predecessors: how to control the pace and direction of change lest it undermine their own authority. Having unlocked Pandora's box with their criticism of the past, Soviet leaders found themselves beset by the plagues of dissent and even outright protest.

After the death of Stalin in 1953 a relaxation of fear and tension was inevitable, if only because there was no longer a firm hand to guide the apparatus of terror. Traditionally one of the most sensitive political barometers in Russia had been literature, and by 1954 it was signaling a "thaw"—as the title of a novel by the veteran writer Ilya Ehrenburg, published in that year, indicated. In a relatively bold manner *The Thaw* took up the theme of artistic freedom and integrity and touched upon subjects that could not even have been mentioned previously. The content of the novel, however, was of less lasting significance than the title. The image of the thaw, so appropriate in the Russian climate, perfectly expressed the widespread hope that the long political winter of Stalinism had at last come to an end.

Three years after Stalin's death that hope appeared to have reached fulfillment. On February 25, 1956, Khrushchev, in his capacity as First Secretary of the Communist Party, addressed the Twentieth Congress on the subject of the "cult of personality," the term that subsequently became the official euphemism for Stalin's despotic rule. Most of Khrushchev's revelations had long been known or strongly suspected in the West, but they had never before been admitted to a Soviet audience; his speech was not published in the Soviet Union, but its substance quickly became known and created an understandable sensation. Although he acknowledged Stalin's role in the development of the Soviet Union, Khrushchev catalogued in considerable detail the leader's many weaknesses: his arbitrariness and brutality, which had produced the mass terror of the purges; his refusal to accept warnings of the impending German invasion of 1941 and the "nervousness and hysteria" of his subsequent conduct of the war; his "mania for greatness." As Khrushchev described him, Stalin was "a very distrustful man, sickly suspicious," who saw spies and traitors everywhere. "Possessing unlimited power he indulged in great willfulness and choked a person morally and physically."[1]

Why did Khrushchev and his supporters take this fateful step? The precise motivations have remained a Kremlin secret, but they probably included several considerations in varying degrees. First, the denigration of Stalin undoubtedly was a tool in the jockeying for power then taking place within the Soviet leadership; if nothing else, it permitted Khrushchev to pose as a reformer and to tar his opponents with the brush of Stalinism. Second, without Stalin himself to control it, the machinery of terror that he had created might well have gotten out of hand; for leaders of lesser stature it was safer to dismantle it than to attempt to use it. Third, and most important, the Soviet system had to be relaxed and regularized less the tensions under which it had been operating explode and destroy it. According to Khrushchev's own testimony, officials faced with the perpetual threat of arrest "began to work uncertainly, showed overcautiousness, feared all which was new, feared their own shadow and began to show less initiative in their work." [2] Constant fear and repression were beginning to yield diminishing returns.

Khrushchev's speech marked the start of a campaign to efface not only the myth but also the very memory of Stalin. Stalin's name was expunged from history books, his image was removed from countless monuments, and his remains were transferred from the Lenin Mausoleum in Red Square to a modest site near the Kremlin Wall; like Trotsky before him, Stalin was on the way to becoming a "nonperson." Although there were intermittent attempts in Russia to achieve a more balanced appraisal of Stalin's rule after Khrushchev's fall from power in 1964, no concerted effort was made to restore the tarnished image of the dictator and his regime.

The impact of the "anti-Stalin campaign" on the people of the Soviet Union was truly shattering, for it amounted to nothing less than an indictment of the previous twenty-five years of their history. Although Khrushchev had taken care to praise past accomplishments and to promise justice thenceforth, the main effect of his revelations was to suggest to thoughtful Soviet citizens the magnitude of the lies and hypocrisy to which they had been subjected. Some of them set out to examine Soviet society and its processes in a searching effort to distinguish truth from falsehood, genuine achievement from sham, reality from appearance. This process of questioning and reappraisal was conducted most vigorously and vocally by Soviet writers and Soviet youth, and it was from those two groups that most expressions of dissent and protest emanated in the post-Stalin years.

Writers and young people tend to play greater roles in expressing dissent in the Soviet Union than in most Western societies because of the very nature of the Soviet system, in which virtually all formal channels of expression are under the control of the authorities and exclude unapproved or even merely unconventional views. Writers and youths, however, by their very nature retain a certain measure of independence from official points of view and are more likely to

articulate that independence. As Soviet writers themselves were asserting with increasing vehemence, art follows laws of its own, and the
creative artist has a duty to obey those laws rather than the dictates
of politics. Young people, particularly students still unburdened with
responsibilities and still working out their views of life, are socially and
psychologically freer than their elders to question the values of their
societies. In nineteenth-century Russia the autonomy of art and the
autonomy of youth posed persistent challenges to the traditional authoritarianism of the tsarist government. In the still repressive but no
longer terror-ridden atmosphere of post-Stalin Russia, they once again
posed such challenges.

The notion of the writer's high moral calling was deeply rooted in
Russian tradition. Although many Russian writers rebelled against a
conception of art that stressed social function as strongly as aesthetic
value, the conception had nonetheless proved a durable and important
element of Russian literature. The influential nineteenth-century critic
Vissarion Belinsky expressed it forcibly in 1847. The Russian public,
he wrote, "holds the Russian writers to be its only leaders . . . and
hence it is always ready to forgive a writer for a bad book but never
for a pernicious one." [3] More than a hundred years later the young
poet Yevgeny Yevtushenko, after Stalin's death, set himself the task of
emulating the civic spirit of Russia's great poets, who "were always
fighters for the future of their country and for justice," who had
"helped Russia to struggle against her tyrants." [4]

Imbued with this strong sense of responsibility, Soviet writers responded enthusiastically to Khrushchev's admission that errors of judgment and abuses of authority could occur in the Soviet Union. Instead
of painting Soviet life in uniformly rosy tones as thitherto prescribed,
poets, playwrights, and novelists felt free to add shades of gray to
their palettes. The dominant theme of the writing that appeared after
the Twentieth Congress was a plea for honesty and sincerity, in literature as in life, toward the present as toward the past. It was, in the
opinion of two well-informed observers, Hugh McLean and Walter N.
Vickery, "essentially a literature of protest—of moral protest, especially
against hypocrisy and falsehood." [5] This first wave of literary protest
culminated in the publication of Vladimir Dudintsev's novel *Not by
Bread Alone*. As in much of the new literature, the novel's moral integrity and the boldness of its subject matter were more impressive than
were its artistic merits. Its hero was the inventor of a new kind of pipe-
casting machine, and, as in the typical Soviet "production" novel of
the 1930s and 1940s, technical themes lay heavy on the story: The
average reader might well feel that he had been told more about casting

pipes than he wanted to know. But in its description of the obstacles that the young inventor had to face in trying to win acceptance of his design—misuse of authority, the stifling of individual creativity, the manipulation of Communist ideals by self-serving officials—the book exposed some of the fundamental ills of Soviet society. The ending in particular violated the usual norms of Soviet novels by presenting not the definitive triumph of good over evil but a more ambiguous image of perpetual struggle against dishonesty and careerism.

The appearance of Dudintsev's novel touched off a heated debate between liberals and conservatives. The sentiments of the former found expression in a speech delivered by Konstantin Paustovsky to a special meeting called by the Moscow Writers' Union to discuss the book. Until his recent death, Paustovsky was one of the most venerated figures in Soviet letters and an outspoken defender of liberal positions. Though he evidently had reservations about the literary quality of the novel, Paustovsky hailed its criticism of Russia's hidebound officialdom. In terms much stronger than Dudintsev himself had used, Paustovsky declared that the book had revealed the existence of a whole new social stratum of "profiteers and boot-lickers," of intriguers and traitors "who claim the right to speak in the name of the people. . . ." [6] They were the legacy of the "cult of personality," and, Paustovsky warned, they still survived. Such statements persuaded the authorities that the new wave of criticism was getting out of hand; it threatened to look beyond the "errors" of the past, which Khrushchev had attributed solely to Stalin's personality, and to raise more fundamental questions about the legal and political system that had permitted such abuses. In the summer of 1957 an article appeared in the Soviet press under Khrushchev's name, warning of "attempts to drag into our literature and art bourgeois views which are alien to the spirit of the Soviet people." [7] Such language served notice that official controls over literature, so recently relaxed, were being tightened once again. The first of the post-Stalin "thaws" was over.

After 1957 the history of literary censorship in the Soviet Union was an irregular series of chills, freezes, and new thaws. The publication in 1962—thanks to Khrushchev's personal intervention—of Alexander Solzhenitsyn's brilliant prison-camp novel, *One Day in the Life of Ivan Denisovich*, for instance, was followed in 1964 by the conviction of the highly gifted young Leningrad poet Iosif Brodsky on charges of "parasitism." (Brodsky was sentenced to five years' forced labor in Siberia but was released a year later.) Faced with the virtual impossibility of achieving authorized publication of unorthodox works —not only political but also purely artistic orthodoxy was generally demanded–younger writers in particular turned to illegal methods.

One of the more remarkable features of the Russian literary scene in the 1960s was the emergence of an "underground" literature, consisting of manuscript or typewritten materials reproduced and circulated clandestinely. Not only individual works but also whole journals, bearing such names as *Phoenix, Syntaxis,* and *The Russian Word,* were produced and circulated in this fashion.

An equally important development was the smuggling to the West—with or without the cooperation of the authors—of a considerable body of literature that was not publishable within the Soviet Union. Boris Pasternak's *Doctor Zhivago,* the writings of "Abram Tertz" and "Nikolai Arzhak," and most recently Solzhenitsyn's novels *The First Circle* and *Cancer Ward* were examples. Among the many ironies of Soviet cultural politics was the fact that some of the very best writing being produced in the Soviet Union received acclaim in the West but remained beyond the reach of its native audience. In 1966 the issue of unauthorized literary exports precipitated the most direct confrontation between the regime and the writers since the furor over *Doctor Zhivago.* In February of that year Andrei Siniavsky and Iuly Daniel were tried in Moscow. Their works had been appearing in the West for several years under the pseudonyms of Abram Tertz and Nikolai Arzhak respectively.

The charge against Siniavsky and Daniel was violation of Article 70 of the Russian criminal code, which placed a vague and elastic prohibition on anti-Soviet "agitation or propaganda." A transcript of parts of the trial was taken down by a sympathizer and spirited out to western Europe. It revealed the real issue of the trial: literary freedom. The prosecution insisted that the authors' works were subversive in content and that their publication in the West had lent aid and comfort to the enemy; the authors reiterated again and again that their writings were works of imagination and should be judged by aesthetic rather than political criteria. Whereas the defendants upheld the autonomy of literary expression, the state insisted on its right to interpret the political tendencies of literature and to reward or punish them accordingly. To quote Siniavsky himself, the prosecution held to the view that "literature is a form of propaganda, and that there are only two kinds of propaganda: pro-Soviet or anti-Soviet." [8]

Evidently as an object lesson to other literary dissidents, the two writers were convicted and given extremely harsh prison terms: Siniavsky was sentenced to seven years in a labor camp, and Daniel, possibly because he had expressed mild regrets over the illicit means he had employed to send his works to the West, was sentenced to five years.

To a Western observer, the dialogue and atmosphere of the Siniavsky-Daniel trial were reminiscent of a production of the theater of the absurd. In its effort to prove that works of fiction—some of them endowed with high degrees of literary complexity and sophistication —should be read as literal expressions of political points of view, the prosecution at times seemed to be trying the writings rather than the writers. Two considerations should be kept in mind in attempting to understand the meaning of the trial, however. First, in a system in which the state claimed the right and the duty to guide all forms of public expression, even nonconformist works could be construed as acts of political defiance. Second, as the Soviet government's constant preoccupation with literature indicated, the rulers of the Soviet state no less than the recalcitrant intellectuals were products of a tradition that attached immense moral and social significance to the written word. Ever since Stalin's famous dictum that writers should be "engineers of human souls," Soviet rulers had sought to turn that tradition to the purposes of the state, but they had not broken with it. Given its high respect for the authority of literature, it is not surprising that the Soviet government was peculiarly sensitive to the dissident voices with which writers sometimes spoke.

The banner of protest against literary censorship was finally taken up by Alexander Solzhenitsyn, whom many considered the most distinguished living Russian writer. Solzhenitsyn's finest works, like those of Siniavsky and Daniel, had been published only in the West, though in this instance against the author's stated wishes. In May 1967 Solzhenitsyn addressed an open letter to the Fourth Congress of the Union of Writers (to which he was not a delegate). Part of the letter was a bitter criticism of the Union itself for its consistent failure to protect its members and to represent their interests. Most remarkable, however, was his blanket condemnation of censorship: He called it a "survival of the Middle Ages" and demanded its outright and unqualified abolition in the Soviet Union. "Literature that is not the breath of contemporary society, that does not warn in time against threatening moral and social dangers—such literature does not deserve the name of literature; it is only a facade." [9] The only result of Solzhenitsyn's campaign, however, was the almost total withdrawal of his name from public discussion in the Soviet Union. Although no major sanctions seemed to have been taken against him, even his fiftieth birthday, an occasion when writers and other important public figures in the Soviet Union are normally honored, passed without mention in the press.

The persistent concern of Soviet writers with the issue of literary freedom should not be regarded as narrow or merely self-interested. Censorship not only cramps the writer's creativity but also humiliates him as a human being; a campaign against censorship therefore becomes inseparable from a more universal demand for individual rights and dignity. An example of this process was an unpublished letter to *Pravda* from the poet Andrei Voznesensky, complaining of the degrading manner in which he had been forced to cancel a scheduled trip to New York: "I am a Soviet writer, a human being made of flesh and blood, not a puppet to be pulled on a string. . . . Clearly the leadership of the [Writers'] Union does not regard writers as human beings." [10] The writer, more immediately and more painfully than most other members of society, comes into collision with a system that severely restricts the individual's right to express himself and fully manifest his personality; and the writer is obviously more capable than most of articulating his frustration and outrage. In fighting his own battle for freedom from literary controls, therefore, the writer necessarily fights the battle of all his fellow citizens for a greater measure of human dignity and respect.

Turning from literary circles to Soviet young people, one finds far fewer direct confrontations between them and the authorities than in the West. The risks of open challenge were great, and the channels were few. Nor were the majority of Soviet youths seriously dissatisfied with a system that had improved living standards and created opportunities for education and advancement that would not have been open to most of them otherwise. Nevertheless, since 1956 there had developed what can only be called a generation gap, less ideological than moral. The Soviet Union is one of the few modern states with an officially promulgated code of morality. In 1961 the Communist Party issued the "Moral Code of the Builder of Communism," a set of twelve principles supposed to govern both the personal and social conduct of every Soviet citizen. As an American observer, Richard T. De George, described it, "There is no room for the notion that man is a law unto himself in the sense that he must do what he thinks is right even if this goes against what he is taught or against his society. Such a concept and such an ideal are considered individualistic and contrary to collectivist, socialist morality." [11] The right to interpret socialist morality and to determine which actions conform to the goal of the building of communism is claimed exclusively by the Communist Party; in the light of revelations about the Stalinist era, however, that claim was inevitably called into question, particularly by the young. Without necessarily rejecting the foundations of the Soviet system or its ultimate aims, young people in the Soviet Union began to seek more satisfying rules of personal conduct and concepts of the "meaning of life" than those offered by official slogans now compromised by the exposure of past abuses. It was a vague and diffuse form of youthful rebellion, centered around a new emphasis on the values of individualism and skepticism.

Most of the external manifestations of this rebellion would be regarded as harmless in Western societies, as normal features of the painful process of growing up. In the Soviet Union, however, unconventional behavior is taken more seriously, for conventional behavior is not merely socially accepted but also officially sanctioned. The Soviet phenomenon most familiar in the West was the emergence of the *stiliagi* (the "style boys," what Americans in an earlier age would have called "zoot-suiters"), who adopted flamboyant styles of dress, often ineptly modeled on Western fashions. Though they were the objects of considerable abuse in the Soviet press, their motivation was primarily adolescent self-assertion. In addition, their efforts bespoke an intense longing among Soviet young people for some color and novelty in a society that seemed, from a Western point of view, unbearably drab and monotonous.

Another trend among young people in post-Stalin Russia was a growing interest in religion, an unusual form of youthful rebellion but understandable in an officially atheistic society. The extent of the religious revival in the Soviet Union was very difficult to measure, for it did not always manifest itself in confessional affiliation or church attendance. It was more spiritual than institutional, one form of the search for answers to larger questions of human existence that official ideology failed to provide. Once again the purely aesthetic element, in this case the appeal of church ceremonies, as in the growing popularity of church weddings among young people, should not be underestimated. Though its depth and breadth could not fully be ascertained, the persistence of religious feeling and its impact on Soviet youth could not be denied. It even affected Stalin's own daughter, Svetlana Alliluyeva, who accepted baptism in the Orthodox faith and for whom religion evidently filled a spiritual void.

The most pervasive form of youthful rebellion in the Soviet Union was the least visible, skepticism. Reappraisal of accepted values, insistence on the right to make personal judgments, questioning of established truths, were all viewed with alarm by a regime whose authority rested upon its purported monopoly of truth. The new tendency to ask questions rather than to accept ready-made answers was best reflected in Soviet literature, much of which had a tone of tentativeness and relativism in place of the absolutes of the past. Abram Tertz, for instance, in his essay "On Socialist Realism," argued for "a phantasmagoric art, with hypotheses instead of a Purpose" [12] as the form of literature most in accord with the contemporary mood. A century ago the young hero of Ivan Turgenev's *Fathers and Sons*, imbued with the spirit of scientism and positivism that distinguished the young intellectuals of the 1860s, delivered the opinion that "two times two are four, and all the rest is rubbish." Dostoevsky's "underground man" suggested that the formula "two times two are five" might also have its attractions. Given Soviet conditions, it was not without significance that one of the first literary responses to Khrushchev's revelations of 1956 was a poem by two young Soviet satirists entitled "$2 \times 2 = ?$"

As these examples show, literary dissent and youthful rebellion frequently overlapped in the Soviet Union. The writings even of older, more established authors reflected many of the sentiments prevailing among Soviet youth, and the rebelliousness of the latter often expressed itself in literary form. After the Siniavsky-Danial trial, however, the two appeared to draw much closer together and to join forces in a small but increasingly vocal movement of open protest.

The effect of the trial on Soviet society has been likened to the effect of the Dreyfus trial on French society at the turn of the century. Although the intention of the authorities was to cow the intellectuals, they succeeded instead in raising issues of fundamental concern and in polarizing Soviet public opinion on those issues. The response to the conviction of the two writers was a prolonged series of protest petitions to the authorities signed by some of the most prominent figures in the Soviet arts and professions. The petitions complained of glaring irregularities in the conduct of the trial and of the severity of the sentences; most important, they seconded the pleas of Siniavsky and Daniel for freedom of creative expression. One of the most eloquent of these statements was an open letter addressed by Lydia Chukovskaya, an author and literary critic, to Nobel laureate Mikhail Sholokhov. Alone among outstanding members of the Soviet literary community, Sholokhov had applauded the convictions and had even suggested that the sentences were too lenient. In her letter Chukovskaya charged him with violating the entire humanist tradition of Russian literature, as well as the laws of literary creation. Literature, she wrote, cannot be tried in any court but "the court of literature. . . . Literature does not come under the jurisdiction of the criminal court. Ideas should be fought with ideas, not with camps and prisons." [13] For the most part the petitions and complaints were respectful in tone and legalistic in their approach, but they were an unprecedented demonstration of unity and frankness among the Soviet intellectual elite.

The wave of protest generated by the Siniavsky-Daniel trial did not stop with the presentation of petitions but began to manifest itself in a series of public demonstrations. They were carried out primarily by people in their twenties or younger, but they received support from a growing number of older, more settled figures. Tiny as these gatherings were, they were the first truly spontaneous demonstrations of independent public opinion that the Soviet Union had seen since the 1920s.

Hardly to the surprise of the participants, such open displays of defiance led to a whole series of arrests and trials of nonconforming intellectuals. In January 1967 youthful demonstrators were arrested after meeting in Moscow's Pushkin Square to demand the repeal of Article 70 of the criminal code (the provision under which Siniavsky and Daniel had been sentenced) and the release of a group, headed by Alexander Ginzburg, that had been arrested for circulating underground literature. In late February or early March a large group of Leningrad intellectuals was arrested, including university professors, students, poets, literary critics, and editors; they were charged with participation in a terrorist network. In February and September 1967 participants in the January demonstration were brought to trial. And in January 1968 the Ginzburg group was finally brought to trial. Ginzburg himself was charged with circulating a "White Book" of materials on the Siniavsky-Daniel trial; a young man named Yury Galanskov was accused of editing the underground literary journal *Phoenix 1966;* and an even younger student, Vera Lashkova, was charged with typing clandestine manuscripts. (A fourth defendant turned state's evidence.) Ginzburg and Galanskov were also accused, on what appeared to be wholly trumped-up evidence, of collaborating with an anti-Soviet émigré organization based in Germany. Ginzburg, at thirty-one, was the oldest of the defendants. They were all convicted and sentenced to labor-camp terms ranging from one to seven years.

The Ginzburg trial generated a new round of protests and petitions, phrased in stronger and more indignant terms than those evoked by the Siniavsky-Daniel trial. The main themes were the violation of due process, distorted reporting of the trial in the Soviet press, and revival of Stalinist methods. Typical of the tone of moral outrage was an open letter signed by Pavel Litvinov, a physicist and grandson of the early Soviet Commissar of Foreign Affairs Maxim Litvinov, and by Larisa Bogoraz-Daniel, the wife of the imprisoned writer. "The judge and the prosecutor," they charged, "with the participation of a special kind of audience, have turned the trial into a wild mockery of three of the accused . . . and of the witnesses, an unthinkable happening in the 20th century." [14]

On August 25, 1968, Litvinov, Mrs. Daniel, and five others took part in a public demonstration. Armed with signs and placards, they stood in Red Square in the heart of Moscow to protest the invasion of Czechoslovakia by the Soviet Union and its allies. They were shortly set upon by plain-clothes police agents, several of them were severely beaten, and they were all hurried off to prison, though not before they had attracted a small crowd of onlookers. In October 1968, Litvinov was sentenced to five years of exile in a remote area of the country, Mrs. Daniel to four years, and several of the other participants to shorter terms of exile or confinement.

What were the aims of these bold protesters? They had no single specific objective. Their concerns ranged from such concrete issues as the demand for fair trials to a more general moral plea for the implementation of the "ideals of socialism." Basic to all their statements and actions, however, was the simple but fundamental quest for recognition of their right as Soviet citizens—and sensitive human beings—to speak out freely about those matters, both public and private, that affected their lives. Protest in the Soviet Union was still highly self-conscious, necessarily preoccupied with defending its very right to exist, and thus above all a campaign for basic civil liberties. Although the future of this protest movement is difficult to predict, the efforts of Khrushchev's successors to suppress it—their "policy of selective terrorism," [15] as Patricia Blake called it—do not appear to be succeeding. Unlike the victims of the purge trials of the 1930s, the defendants in the recent series of trials did not confess their guilt or recant. And one youthful protester not only refused to repent but also concluded his court statement with the defiant promise that "when I am free again, I shall again organize demonstrations—of course, in complete accordance with the laws as before." [16]

The loosening of controls and criticism of the past that began with Khrushchev's secret speech provoked a movement of dissent and protest not only in Russia but throughout eastern Europe, where the consequences were in many cases far more dramatic. In the twelve years between the Soviet invasion of Hungary and Soviet occupation of Czechoslovakia, a highly diverse and constantly shifting pattern developed in the nations of eastern Europe. Just as the tone and methods of east European communism varied widely from country to country, the dimensions and direction of dissent also differed according to individual circumstances; the events in Czechoslovakia brought a new element of unpredictability to an already fluid situation. We can do no more than sketch briefly the general framework within which dissent in eastern Europe proceeded and its indissoluble relationship with Soviet developments.

The impact of the "anti-Stalin campaign" in eastern Europe was considerably complicated by the issue of nationalism, an element that did not figure in the mainstream of dissent in Russia (although the ferment within the large Ukrainian minority was a significant adjunct to it). The period between the end of World War II and the death of Stalin brought various degrees of brutality and despotism, as well as Russian domination over an area where the struggle for national independence was a centuries-old preoccupation. The context within which dissent was generated and expressed was therefore more complex in eastern Europe than in the Soviet Union: determined not only by local governments and more vocal segments of the citizenry but by Soviet attitudes as well. The mixture proved unstable and occasionally explosive.

The strongest responses to the repudiation of Stalinism came in Poland and Hungary. There the intellectuals' hope that de-Stalinization would mean greater liberalization (including a return to traditional intercourse with the West) was paralleled by the hope of local Communist leaders for greater autonomy from Soviet control and greater freedom to map national development goals. The outcome in Hungary was the ill-starred revolution of 1956, which was followed by a vigorous restoration of authoritarian controls and Soviet hegemony. Gradually, however, a quiet process of relaxation and accommodation took place within Hungary and produced a measure of genuine popular support for leaders once regarded as mere creatures of Moscow.

The course of change in Poland was very nearly the reverse. Poland was spared the bloodbath visited on Hungary, and a number of liberal reforms were instituted under Wladyslaw Gomulka, who had previously been purged and imprisoned but was restored to power in October 1956. After 1956, however, the atmosphere of liberalization in Poland was gradually dissipated, and popular confidence in Gomulka—who walked a narrow path between the demands of his own people and those of the Soviet Union—waned. In 1968 open demonstrations, spearheaded by university students and supported by liberal intellectuals, erupted in Poland for the first time in more than a decade.

The confrontation began at the end of January, when the Warsaw authorities closed down a new production of *Forefathers*, a play by the nineteenth-century poet Adam Mickiewicz; they were evidently alarmed by the vigor with which the theater-goers were applauding the play's strong anti-Russian sentiments. This action stirred consider-

able public indignation. At the end of February an extraordinary meeting of the Warsaw branch of the Writers' Union condemned the closing of the play, as well as the general cultural policy of the regime.
Shortly thereafter a series of student outbursts began; they continued
for more than two weeks. On March 8 some four thousand chanting
students demonstrated at the University of Warsaw and clashed with
the police. The demonstrators, joined by sympathetic adults, quickly
moved beyond the specific issue that had sparked the protest and began
to present broader demands for cultural and personal freedom. Their
new complaints included censorship, press distortion of the student
movement, and police brutality; their war cries were "Democracy!"
"Constitution!" and "Gestapo!" The wave of student protest in Warsaw soon spilled over into other university towns: There were disturbances in Poznan (the scene of serious rioting in 1956), and on March
20 students organized a sit-in at Jagiellonian University in Cracow.
The following day some five thousand students at the Warsaw Poly-
technic School began a forty-eight-hour sit-in to demand that the government take up the students' grievances. Shortly before the scheduled
end of the sit-in, however, with the campus ringed by police, the Poly-
technic students left the buildings that they had occupied; as they did
so they distributed to passers-by copies of a resolution calling for
"freedom of expression, assembly, mass meeting and demonstration." [17]
Although some minor acts of defiance continued, this departure effectively brought to an end the succession of student demonstrations,
boycotts, and sit-ins.

The government's response to the student disturbances was repression rather than concession. In a speech on March 19, Gomulka dis-
closed that 1,208 people, 367 of them students, had been arrested in
connection with the protests; and 207 people, including 67 students,
had already been sentenced or fined. In addition, the demonstrations
had become a factor in the power struggle within the ruling Polish
United Workers' Party and served as the pretext for a vicious wave of
anti-intellectualism and anti-Semitism. The "Anti-Zionist" campaign
had begun at least as early as the Arab-Israeli war of June 1967, when
Gomulka, voicing his government's support of the Arab states, had
warned against Zionist "fifth columnists" in Poland. In the aftermath
of the demonstrations these charges were revived—apparently by
Gomulka's rivals—and intensified. The student movement was attributed to the instigation of Zionists, liberals, and discredited Stalinists
seeking to return to power. As the student protests petered out, the list
of officials purged from their posts grew; many of them were Jews,
including several tenured university professors.

While liberalization was regressing in Poland, actual democratization seemed to be approaching in neighboring Czechoslovakia. In January 1968 old-guard Stalinist Antonin Novotny was relieved of his duties as First Secretary of the Czechoslovak Communist Party (he was subsequently removed from the Presidency of the republic as well). He was replaced by Alexander Dubcek, who soon became a national hero, a status attained by no other Communist leader except Tito of Yugoslavia. It was in Czechoslovakia, which had the oldest and strongest democratic tradition in eastern Europe, that party and populace found themselves most solidly united on the need for reform. A revivified Communist party took the lead in voicing the fundamental aspirations of the people it governed. These aspirations were embodied in the party's "action program," which was adopted in April. Among its objectives were greater protection for the persons and property of citizens, greater freedom of information and expression, freedom to travel, greater independence for Czechoslovakia in the conduct of foreign affairs, economic modernization, and, perhaps most remarkable of all, curbs on the secret police on the grounds that the political convictions and personal beliefs of the citizenry were not the proper concern of such an agency.

Throughout the spring and summer of 1968 the whole of Czechoslovakia was engrossed in debate over national goals and priorities. Czechoslovak rejection of the brutality and hypocrisy of the past, which made itself felt at that time, was unique in eastern Europe, for it was truly nationwide. Both the people and their new leaders seemed inspired by the vision of a Communist government in communication with its citizens, responsive to their feelings and wishes, and even, perhaps, answerable to them for its actions. Whether the implications of the party position were fully realized or approved by its leaders remained unclear; what was clear was the strong fear among party leaders of other east European states that their own positions would be jeopardized by the implementation in Czechoslovakia of reforms that they had refused to grant in their own countries. The national unity forged in the Czech "spring" could not prevent the invasion of the country in August, but it did mitigate its effects and proved seriously embarrassing to its perpetrators.

The invasion of Czechoslovakia marked the most concerted effort since the suppression of the Hungarian revolt to slam shut the Pandora's box that Khrushchev had opened in 1956. The response of dissenters elsewhere in eastern Europe to the Czech "experiment" showed how closely the Czech criticism of their own repressive past and Czech hopes for a more liberal future reflected sentiments throughout the region. In Poland the student demonstrators of March demanded the introduction of Czech-style reforms and adopted the slogan "Long Live Czechoslovakia" as one of their rallying cries. In Russia, only a month before the invasion, a young man named Anatoly Marchenko addressed an open letter to several Czech and Western newspapers deploring Soviet efforts to hinder Czech reforms. The Soviet leaders feared the further progress of those reforms, he asserted, for "if Czechoslovakia should really succeed in organizing democratic socialism, then there would be no justification for the absence of democratic freedoms in our country, and then, for all we know, our workers, peasants and intelligentsia might demand freedom of speech in fact and not merely on paper." [18]

Contemporary protest in Russia and eastern Europe still seemed to wear nineteenth-century garb. The demands for freedom of political thought and expression, for cultural and intellectual liberty, for due process of law, and in the smaller countries for national independence were the fundamental demands of nineteenth-century protesters; they had long been voiced mainly by writers and students; and they were met by such nineteenth-century methods as commitment of recalcitrant writers to insane asylums and threats to induct student demonstrators into the army. Some aspects of contemporary protest in Russia and eastern Europe, to be sure, were similar to those of comparable movements in the West and arose from similar social, economic, and cultural forces: a tendency to question all established authority, a search for a postindustrial humanism and individualism, a simple desire to escape the boredom that seemed to be the price of increased leisure and prosperity in an unheroic era. Fundamentally, however, the dissidents and protesters of Russia and eastern Europe were demanding those basic personal and political rights that, whether used or abused, had long been taken for granted in the West. For this reason, the spirit and objectives of their protest bore a closer resemblance to those of their historical forebears than to those of their contemporaries in the West.

CHAPTER

15

The French Crisis

THE classic contemporary youthful rebellion—almost a case study in the escalation of student protest into violent insurrection—was acted out in Paris on May 3, 1968. About five hundred students, representing various shades of the political spectrum from communism to anarchism, gathered in the main courtyard of the Sorbonne to protest the closing of the University of Paris in suburban Nanterre (which had been closed by its dean in the face of demonstrations and rising unrest). The students were not a mob but an assembly of the leaders of hard-core French student radicalism. They made speeches to one another for the better part of an afternoon, attracting the attention of interested bystanders, uncommitted students, and right-wing student groups that had previously threatened the radicals with physical reprisals.[1]

The university authorities grew increasingly anxious, and with the consent or encouragement of the Ministry of Education they called in outside police. Quietly and efficiently the well-trained riot squad broke up the meeting and led students to waiting trucks. Onlookers reacted violently to the police action and gave vent to a ferocious outburst of hatred. Within minutes the academic courtyard became a bloody battlefield; within hours Paris was in a state of insurrection; within weeks all France was in chaos. The economy slowed to a crawl, political alliances formed and re-formed, and politicians rose and fell like marionettes. The apparently charmed life of the Gaullist regime came very close to a disastrous end.

The revolutionary spiral did not really originate at the Sorbonne, of course; it originated, as do all revolutions, in existing conditions. The whole French system of higher education contained plenty of combustible material, and the regime at Nanterre was particularly rigid. First, and perhaps foremost, the universities of France were critically overcrowded. Anyone who could pass the *baccalauréat* was eligible to attend a university (almost all universities were state-sponsored), and in a decade of rising affluence almost everyone did attend. Lecture halls and residences alike were jammed with bodies, and the supposed delights of French student life faded under the weight of numbers.

Nanterre was new, but it was overcrowded before it was finished, and it had never been popular among its students. Its huge, bleak buildings were set in a suburban desert, where it stood in ugly contrast to the ancient splendors of the Sorbonne and the metropolitan community and freedom of the Left Bank. The students, mostly self-confident children of the middle class, resented segregation from the lively world as much as the sexual segregation imposed by planners and administrators. The rigid system of parietal rules was one of the first issues between students and administration, and it symbolized student disaffection. Nanterre had its full share of the radical student groups that had proliferated in France during the previous decade. It may be that the revolution began where it did not because Nanterre was unusually bad but because some of its students were unusually skilled and dedicated to the radical cause. Certainly the student leaders at Nanterre were notably articulate and accomplished.

French left-wing student politics were almost incomprehensible to outsiders, but it is possible to characterize them briefly (at Nanterre as elsewhere) as well to the left of the French Communist Party. The radical student groups ranged from Maoist cells to social-democratic organizations; many of them, under the profound influence of resurgent Trotskyist philosophy, were strongly anti-Stalinist. These organizations were as torn by feuds and factions as were similar groups elsewhere, but they had been unified in recent years by overwhelming disgust at the Algerian and Vietnamese wars. These two manifestations of "capitalist imperialism" had brought left-wing students together as no domestic issue apparently could. The violence of student reaction to Algeria and Vietnam made plain their attraction to the concept of the "third world," their bitterness against what they regarded as racist aggression, and their yearning for peace.

In March 1968 a handful of student radicals was arrested for blowing in the windows of various American buildings in Paris to protest the war in Vietnam. On March 22 a group of students gathered at Nanterre to protest the arrests and support the insurgents, and the "Movement of 22 March" was born. The movement had a remarkable leader in Daniel Cohn-Bendit ("Danny the Red"), a German-born sociology student with the charisma that makes politics exciting and transforms protest into insurrection.

Cohn-Bendit was not firmly attached to any of the student groups, but his Movement of 22 March was supported, almost dominated, by the Jeunesse Communiste Révolutionnaire (J.C.R.), a powerful Trotskyist organization whose aim was the development of a revolutionary elite. The J.C.R. was university-oriented; it hoped to establish a trained cadre of professional revolutionaries, and its young leaders were highly skilled in the manipulation of crowds, although none claimed much control over the huge crowds that joined them in Paris. Another important group, the Maoist Union des Jeunesses Communistes Marxistes-Leninistes (U.J.C.M.L.), was oriented toward workers and factories, and it became important later in the revolution. The Comité Vietnam National (C.V.N.) mobilized antiwar feelings among various sections of the population, particularly in the *lycées* of France: The undergraduate revolutionaries were followed every step of the way by teen-age schoolboys. Other groups existed in confusing numbers, but these three were perhaps the most influential in the May revolution.

Outbursts of protest and violence disrupted the universities of France during March and April, and French administrators were not alone in their anxiety: Columbia University was working out its own problems when the dean of Nanterre shut down his faculty on May 2. On the same day the French Premier, Georges Pompidou, flew to Iran, leaving behind a President too proud to condescend to negotiations with students, and a government without real authority to act in a crisis.

The events of May 3 set off a revolution, partly because they produced revolutionaries. Uncommitted students and bystanders who attacked the police *became* revolutionaries as they fought. Violence tends to escalate in any conflict, and the excitement and solidarity of those first days in May revived the revolutionary heritage of Paris. The war never really stopped after May 3. Skillful leaders kept the fires glowing all over Paris, and provincial students fomented insurrections in their own cities. To those who watched policemen using gas grenades and pressure hoses on teen-agers, the representatives of authority looked like masked stormtroopers and their opponents like young heroes resisting brutality with only their bare hands and cobblestones. The wildest and most ferocious fighting took place on the night of May 10, which has passed into legend as the Night of the Barricades. The students built barricades out of heaped cobblestones or overturned cars. Red Cross workers had to fight through mobs and fires to reach the wounded; tear gas seeped through the windows of respectable homes; arrests and injuries mounted into the hundreds. There seemed to be no limit to the students' energy and determination.

On May 11 M. Pompidou returned to France. Adopting a reasonable and conciliatory posture, he reopened the Sorbonne and hinted at amnesty for the arrested demonstrators. But it was too late: The highest hopes of the revolutionaries seemed about to come true. Left-wing intellectuals universally desire meaningful alliance with the working class; after all, only the problems and aspirations of the proletariat give meaning to radical philosophy. Before the Premier's policy of conciliation could take effect, the most important French unions had joined the students; events then passed beyond the realm of academic demonstration and became something quite different.

The two largest labor unions called a strike for Monday, May 13, and on that day an impressive parade of 800,000 people marched through Paris. Exulting students led the way, while union bosses and left-wing politicians scurried along in the rear. It was abundantly clear that the youthful rank and file of the French unions—like their contemporaries in the universities—were going to try to drag their leaders into radical action for which the latter had little heart and less preparation.

The leaders of the political Left were even less well prepared than were the union leaders. Resigned to the regime of President Charles de Gaulle, they were waiting to take over when the General stepped down—and to take over within the democratic machinery, rather than outside it. The French Communist Party, which had spent the previous decade transforming its image from wild-eyed revolution to respectability, had come to seem in youthful eyes a bourgeois political machine. It no longer sought to subvert the capitalist economy of France but only to win a larger share for the workers. As industrialization and affluence spread in the 1960s, more and more French Communists looked forward to the possession of television sets and dishwashers rather than to the use of bombs and grenades. The French Socialists stood a better chance of taking over the revolution of the young, but they were too divided among themselves and from their potential allies among the Communists to exploit their opportunity.

There was an overwhelming response to the strike call on May 13. By May 22 nine million workers were out; many of them had occupied their factories and offices and had locked out the management.

In fact many strikers were joined by the lower ranks of the managerial class, who rejoiced in the opportunity to defy an outgrown system. French industry, like French schools, professions, and government, has remained strictly hierarchical, centralized, and bound in red tape. Respectable citizens of the middle class were all too glad to escape the prison of regulation and tradition. Orly Airport closed; mass transportation all over France was at a standstill; industry was almost completely shut down. Workers in aviation and auto factories turned off their machines and barred the doors against the owners.

While workers locked out their bosses, union leaders were equally careful to lock out student radicals. The union men, determined to continue to command the rank and file by means of economic gains, were terrified of the contamination of far-left ideas and of the repression that might follow continued insurrection. With the other old men of France, they were bent on preserving the framework that sustained their power.

The government responded to the strike by proposing large-scale reforms in wages and working conditions, to be negotiated immediately in emergency bargaining sessions. The talks began at Grenelle on May 25 in an atmosphere exacerbated by a useless and provocative speech by De Gaulle on May 24. He had called for a referendum to confirm his authority in the face of the insurrection; he was answered in the streets by a renewed outburst of desperate fighting by students, workers, and police. On May 27 Pompidou announced sweeping reforms: The minimum wage was increased by more than one-third, and fringe benefits of all kinds, from shorter hours to bargaining rights, were conceded by the government, which had previously been reluctant to establish national standards. It was a colossal victory for labor, and government and union leaders alike expected it to win the workers back from radicalism.

The triumphant labor leaders announced their enormous gains on May 27—the biggest package deal since Liberation. French industry traditionally had avoided big negotiations, preferring to work within small groups and factories. To the old bosses Grenelle seemed an unprecedented success. To the rank and file, however, it did not. Local leaders and petty bosses returned to their chiefs the unwelcome news that the workers had turned down the concessions, that they were not interested in negotiation and middle-class benefits. For a few days, then, at the end of May, it looked as if Nikolai Lenin's old dream had come true, as if the students had succeeded in igniting the workers to revolution. Democratic capitalism had always worked by drawing the top layer of workers into the middle class, where they would have a stake in the existing structure. Yet the Grenelle Agreements, designed on this principle, were rejected in favor of student-inspired revolt against the very structure of capitalist society.

All over France, meanwhile, students continued to march and fight and talk. At the Sorbonne, reopened by the Premier on May 11, they established an incredible atmosphere of noise, argument, laughter, and dirt. Students loved-in in the halls, played jazz in the courtyard, and argued radical philosophy in the lecture rooms. Bands of activists endangered their hold on public sympathy by bursting into surrounding streets to harass the police and upset the neighborhood. Eventually the Sorbonne became intolerable even to its own leaders, who moved out to plan the revolution in more peaceful quarters. Those who remained were divided—like the rest of young France—between reformers and revolutionaries. The former wanted to rebuild their institutions along more satisfactory lines, to negotiate with existing authorities for desired reforms. The revolutionaries, on the other hand, wanted to destroy the institutions as integral parts of a corrupt society. They rejected negotiation and piecemeal reforms as useless surrender to a wicked and discredited establishment.

The rejection of the Grenelle Agreements left the government, the union bosses, and the politicians of the Left in a dangerous and difficult position. The economy was in serious trouble, violent fighting still frightened citizens and tied up the streets, and events in the city of Nantes had provided the authorities with a dreadful example of what might happen all over the nation. There a Central Strike Committee had actually usurped municipal authority. The strikers had set up their own city government in defiance of Paris and had taken charge of food deliveries to the shops and of traffic in and out of the city. Peasants cooperated with workers, and together they eliminated the middleman and cut food prices. Students handed out leaflets, harvested crops, and provided encouragement and support to the strikers and their government. Nantes was a radical's dream of cooperation among worker, student, and peasant—a short-lived but memorable entry in the annals of revolution.

On May 27, the first day of the brief period during which France appeared to be in a state of genuine revolution (or anarchy, depending on the point of view of the observer), the student leaders organized a mass meeting at Charlety Stadium in Paris. They were delighted by the turnout of workers, which seemed to justify their belief in the revolutionary alliance. The meeting itself, however, exposed the real incapacity of the French Left. Many of the speakers expressed their scorn of the Communist Party, but none came up with a positive program for converting revolutionary momentum to real change. Pierre Mendès-France, who might have been able to exploit the movement, said nothing at all at Charléty; like other older leaders, he was not ready to commit himself to revolution. On May 28 Socialist leader François Mitterand announced that he would be a candidate for the Presidency after—as he confidently assumed—De Gaulle had been rejected by the national referendum in June. Mitterand did make a concrete bid for political power, but he was torn between the moderate Left of Mendès-France and the Communists, who were scorned by the radicals but had real power in the voting booth. Mitterand tried to propose a united front of the Left against the regime, but in reality the Left was far from united.

President de Gaulle, who had been ominously quiet since his disastrous speech of May 24, regained the initiative on May 29 and never faltered again. Announcing that he was leaving Paris for his country house, he flew secretly to the French military base at Baden-Baden for discussions with its commander. Nobody except the participants really knew what was said, but it was assumed that the President reassured himself of the loyalty of the army and the political support of its leaders. When he returned to France, he found that Mendès-France had announced his availability for public office; that is, a suitable leader for a popular front had declared himself. It is likely that this news only reinforced the President's determination to fight for his regime.

De Gaulle saw quite clearly that Communists would have a large share in any government that might replace his own. He fought his campaign on that basis, playing on the fear of Communism that exists in France as in any capitalist country in which large numbers of voters have a stake in the economy. De Gaulle made a short and impressive speech on May 29, announcing his implacable determination to resist "Communist takeover"; he offered no further concessions to the demands of workers or students, and he hinted that he would use force if necessary to bring an end to the Communist threat. Within minutes after the speech the streets of Paris were crowded with Gaullists of every description, waving the tricolor and shouting their loyalty to the regime. The mood of the streets told observers that the counterrevolution had begun.

Local authorities were given heart (and support) from Paris, strikers began to go back to work, and the police all over France began to win battles in the streets. The labor leaders, who had from the first been reluctant to depart from the safety of the economic realm, immediately erased political objectives and implications from their announced programs. The politicians of the Left, who had disappointed the radicals by their determination to remain within the democratic system, were accused by the government of having planned a *coup d'état*. As they had in fact withstood leftist demands to overthrow the system, this charge was highly unjust, but it worked.

Two sets of elections were held in France, on June 23 and June 30, and Charles de Gaulle returned to office with an unprecedented majority. He had more parliamentary support than he had ever had, more than any politician in a multiparty system could justifiably expect. The Gaullist victory was never really in doubt after the end of May, but in early June the revolution died in bursts of renewed and escalating violence. Its only fatalities occurred in June, one the death by drowning of a teen-ager who was running from the police. On the night of June 10 the violence in Paris reached a peak unmatched even on the Night of the Barricades.

The student leaders were expelled or driven underground, as were their organizations. Pompidou, the only really powerful political figure in France (besides the President), was fired in July and replaced by Maurice Couve de Murville. De Gaulle reigned alone, as he always had, and the strikers were back at work. Certainly the workers had gained what their leaders wanted for them—a larger slice of the economic pie—but the economy itself had been damaged: The franc was threatened, and the development of a nuclear force was delayed. The University of Paris at Nanterre was still overcrowded, but perhaps slow reforms within the democratic system would in time bring about a practical improvement in French higher education.

The radical students of France came very close to their goal of total revolution in politics, economy, and society, but the older Left failed to transform the energy of the young into concrete programs or political power. On the contrary, De Gaulle's grip on the nation was tighter than it had ever been. Whether the revolution had produced or would produce important and lasting changes in society or the economy remained a question; it was not yet certain whether or not brief freedom from traditional restraints had awakened lasting hopes of real reform. The only really certain outcome of the French revolution of 1968 was its reminder to the world that youthful protest can be effective, that it can shake the very foundations of modern society.

EPILOGUE:
THE NATURE OF PROTEST

Having examined major protest movements from the pre–World War I period through the spring and summer of 1968, what conclusions can we draw about the nature of protest in the twentieth century? What guidelines can be offered both to those who wish to foment successful protest movements and to those who wish to defeat and eliminate them? The lessons of the past are not inviolable. Changing social conditions and attitudes can alter the ingredients of protest, and the unpredictable personal abilities of protest leaders and of the prevailing establishments can never be discounted. Yet several generalizations can be attempted, and they are not only illuminating but also quite useful in current crises.

Characteristics of Protest

1. Protest per se is neither good nor bad; it is a common and generally effective means of achieving change in modern society. Most of the important political and social changes of the twentieth century have been accelerated, if not caused, by protest movements.

2. Protest is a vehicle of both the Left and the Right. Although in a community whose government is rigidly conservative, grossly incompetent and sluggish, or viciously authoritarian almost any kind of protest can have a therapeutic effect—in opening up the possibility of change—by and large the virtues of any particular protest movement should be judged according to who is doing the protesting and what their aims are.

3. Protest is a means by which unhappy, frustrated, and deracinated people can find at least momentary satisfaction. Protest movements offer release from the traditional and often tedious patterns of daily life in industrial society. For the participants in a protest movement (particularly an organized confrontation one) escape is provided from the routinized obligations of modern life. The movement also offers the joy that is gained from participation in a communal endeavor of idealistic cast. Even members of the government (state, city, university, and so on) opposed to the protest, though perhaps distressed and angered, can also experience release from routine and greater sense of community in the process of counteracting the radical movement.

4. At its most intense, protest becomes a way of life that absorbs all the energy, talent, and love of the participants and counterparticipants. It therefore provides the milieu for the romantic heroism that bureaucratized, rationalized, modern industrial society seems to have made obsolete.

5. There are two kinds of protest: generalized intellectual dissent and rebellion on the one hand, and organized confrontation on the other. The former is an invariable prerequisite for the latter: An ideology and a new cultural evaluation directly inspire the confrontation movement. More specifically, the confrontation movement takes advantage of the demoralization of the establishment effected by cultural upheaval and employs the new cultural rhetoric in its denunciation of the old regime.

6. Although most twentieth-century protest movements have professed, in one way or another, the liberation of the working class and the poor or at least amelioration of their conditions, in fact they have rarely been led by workers. Protest is a middle-class phenomenon. Not only the spokesmen of intellectual protest but also the leaders of confrontation protest have been almost without exception middle-class people, with good educations, professional opportunities if they cared to take advantage of them, and considerable leisure. Protest is thus a consequence of middle-class dissatisfaction and alienation from society and of ambition to take power away from the current establishment.

7. All protest movements center on moral issues, a consequence of the middle-class character of protest leadership; it is the bourgeoisie which par excellence concentrates on moral issues.

8. The middle-class character of protest leadership and the primary role of moral issues tend to stir a sense of guilt in the establishment. Without this paralyzing guilt experienced by those who hold power, protest movements could rarely succeed.

9. All major protest movements of the twentieth century have relied on force, whether mild or severe. But the force, even if it reaches the supreme violence of assassination and street fighting, is controllable by the leadership and is aimed at specific goals. When the violence is no longer controllable and ends no longer can be specified, a stage of revolution has been entered.

10. All protest movements are heralded in extreme language, which brands the opposition as monsters and certain institutions as thoroughly evil.

11. The rising effectiveness of protest movements runs parallel with the steady improvement in the means of mass communication. Television has been a big help, for protest feeds on publicity. That is why it is so difficult to deal repressively with protest movements in a democratic society with free press and broadcasting.

12. Protest requires enormous energy, as well as willingness to sacrifice careers and status. That is why most protesters are under thirty. Protest leaders are sometimes middle-aged men or women of great energy and determination. But protest is not for the old. As governments are usually led by at least middle-aged and frequently by old men, there is a pronounced generation gap between the protesters and any establishment, which not only impedes understanding and communication but also enhances the heroic image and egotism of the protesters. It is fashionable among conservative writers nowadays to attribute the protest movement on American campuses to the "permissive" unbringing of middle-class students by parents relying on the guidelines of Benjamin Spock. But current student protest follows the general pattern of protest movements in the twentieth century, and such movements have also developed in societies in which children have been treated in a rigid, authoritarian, and puritanical manner. Some commentators offer a Freudian interpretation of the sources of protest, claiming to find strong Oedipal attitudes among famous leaders of protest, particularly student leaders. But Oedipal conflicts, according to Freudian psychology, are generic in humans, and it is not easy to see why protest leaders should be more strongly conditioned by this psychological trait than anyone else. In any case, the biographical data seem at present too fragmentary to allow any firm psychological explanation of protest.

13. Protest begets protest. Successful confrontation by one group inevitably encourages other groups to "do their thing." As the world is now coming to be one community—and at least universal communication is instantaneous—the imitative phenomenon is now world-wide.

14. Twentieth-century protest movements belong to a larger cate-

gory of recurring phenomena in the history of Western civilization: the fragmentation of the elite. Dissent, rebellion, and revolution have not generally been, in the history of the West, the consequence of mass uprisings, whatever Marxist myth may postulate. The masses rarely rise—the workers and peasants are too depressed, disorganized, ignorant, and selfish—and whenever they have rebelled on their own, they have been crushed by the established order and those who hold power. Upheavals in government and society have usually come when a section of the elite—the comfortable educated classes—has become dissatisfied with the opportunities for power or personal happiness afforded by the prevailing system and has tried to force its way into the power system or to supplant the government entirely. In the long perspective of history, twentieth-century protest movements are revealed as the continuation of a pattern that began in the twelfth century and was given new impetus by the French Revolution in the late eighteenth century: the pattern of change by which newly prosperous and educated groups in society assert their right to political importance and power status consonant with their economic and intellectual capacities.

Guidelines for Successful Confrontation Protest

1. Organize carefully. Know the strengths and weaknesses of your personnel. Plan every step beforehand.

2. Choose the issue that has the widest and most ethical appeal—not necessarily the issue that you care most about.

3. Rely on simple rhetoric with vague meanings but highly emotional overtones: "Fascist!" "Racist!" "Liar!" "Traitor!" Constant reiteration will in time make these epithets part of daily language, and even the establishment will legitimatize them by use.

4. Publish incessant lists of demands, slowly increasing them.

5. Force is an inevitable technique. Choose your means—strikes, sit-ins, occupation of buildings, and so on—so as to achieve maximum publicity with minimum offense to middle-class shibboleths.

6. Seek by rudeness, violence, and escalating demands to force the establishment to respond with repression (preferably imprisonment or expulsion; a resort to the police is essential). Then claim that the authorities refused to negotiate or to listen to reason, that they misrepresented your position and resorted to police brutality. Denounce the establishment as fascists, pigs, and so on. At this point you are ready to use extreme violence (riot, assassination, and the like).

7. Demand amnesty (because you brought the great injustice in

question to society's attention), a new government with your participation, and complete surrender on original demands. Be ready to accept three-quarters of what you demanded plus public humiliation of leaders of the old regime.

8. Proclaim a new spirit of reform and community. Announce that you are ready to work for reform, pacification, and so on, but start planning the next confrontation, organized around an alleged breach of faith by the regime in keeping its promises. Cry "No compromise this time"; "Clean the rascals out"; and so on.

Guidelines for Establishments: How to Defeat Confrontation Protest

1. Keep abreast of social changes, intellectual fashions, styles. Be a swinger; use the new jargon and (moderately) the new modes of dress and hair style.

2. There are able moderates and conservatives among the rising generation and among restless and ambitious minorities. Seek them out and absorb them into the power elite.

3. Reply to initial extremist rhetoric and demands with sweetness and moderation. Then abruptly become extremist and use the same epithets as the protesters: "Fascist!" "Racist!" "Liar!" "Traitor!" (Note that "Communist" is no longer effective, though "Maoist!" is still useful, especially in the United States, and "Anarchist!" is always effective.)

4. Lay careful plans for the confrontation (riot, sit-in, and so on) that is sure to come. If police are to be called, it should be in the first hour after due warning has been given. Once crowds have gathered and reporters and television cameramen have arrived, it will be too late. Simultaneously deflate protest sails by announcing radical democratic restructuring of your institution. Play the charismatic ruler who is resolving the crisis by reforming the institutions of the community (state, church, university) from top to bottom. Stress the democratic process. Democracy means putting all changes to the vote of everyone in the community. The majority is always conservative and will give power to the prevailing elite. At the same time, much-needed reforms can be implemented, and incompetent fossils in the government can be removed. The most effective opposition to protest is to announce a more sweeping series of reforms than the protesters have asked for and to rely on the votes of the whole community, which will return you to power.

NOTES

CHAPTER 1

[1] This chapter has drawn heavily on the following works: George Dangerfield, *The Strange Death of Liberal England* (London: Constable & Co., Ltd., 1936); Roger Fulford, *Votes for Women* (London: Faber and Faber, Ltd., 1957); Christabel Pankhurst, *Unshackled* (London: Hutchinson & Co., 1959); Sylvia Pankhurst, *The Life of Emmeline Pankhurst* (New York: Houghton Mifflin Co., 1936); Sylvia Pankhurst, *The Suffrage Movement* (London: Longmans, 1931); Constance Rover, *Women's Suffrage and Party Politics in Britain 1866–1914* (London: Routledge & Keegan Paul; Toronto: University of Toronto Press, 1967).

[2] Emmeline Pankhurst, quoted in Sylvia Pankhurst, *The Life of Emmeline Pankhurst*, pp. 83, 116–117.

[3] Quoted in Dangerfield, *op. cit.*, p. 179.

[4] Christabel Pankhurst, *op. cit.*, p. 51.

[5] *Ibid.*, p. 76.

[6] Arthur Balfour, quoted *ibid.*, p. 58.

[7] Fulford, *op. cit.*, p. 285.

[8] Christabel Pankhurst, *op. cit.*, p. 254.

[9] Quoted in Fulford, *op. cit.*, p. 181.

CHAPTER 2

[1] This chapter has drawn heavily on the following works: Max Caulfield, *The Easter Rebellion* (New York: Holt, Rinehart and Winston, 1963); Redmond Fitzgerald, *Cry Blood, Cry Erin* (London: Barrie & Rockliff, 1966); Padraic Pearse, *Collected Works: Plays, Stories, and Poems* and *Collected Works: Political Writings and Speeches* (Dublin: Phoenix Publishing Co., Ltd., 1917); James Stephens, *The Insurrection in Dublin* (Dublin and London: Maunsell & Com-

pany, Ltd., 1916); William Irwin Thompson, *The Imagination of an Insurrection: Dublin, Easter 1916* (New York: Oxford University Press, 1967).

[2] Quoted in Caulfield, *op. cit.*, pp. 19–20.

[3] Quoted in Stephens, *op. cit.*, p. 38.

[4] Pearse, "The Fool," in *Collected Works: Plays, Stories, and Poems*, p. 334.

[5] W. B. Yeats, "September 1913," in *Selected Poems* (London: Macmillan and Co., Ltd., 1929), p. 115.

[6] Pearse, "Ghosts," in *Collected Works: Political Writings and Speeches*, p. 223.

[7] Sean O'Casey, *Inishfallen Fare Thee Well* (London: Macmillan and Co., Ltd., 1949), p. 165.

[8] "Eoin MacNeill on the 1916 Rising," *Irish Historical Studies*, XII (1960–1961), pp. 236, 239.

[9] Quoted in Caulfield, *op. cit.*, p. 90.

[10] Pearse, quoted *ibid.*, p. 352.

CHAPTER 3

[1] This chapter has drawn heavily on the following works: Henri Barbusse, *Under Fire (Le Feu)* (New York: E. P. Dutton & Co., 1917); Richard M. Watt, *Dare Call It Treason* (New York: Simon and Schuster, 1963).

[2] Barbusse, *op cit.*, p. 343.

CHAPTER 4

[1] This chapter has drawn heavily on the following works: Lionel Kochan, *Russia in Revolution 1890–1918* (London: Weidenfeld & Nicolson, 1966); John Reed, *Ten Days That Shook the World* (New York: Random House, 1960); Leon Trotsky, *The Russian Revolution*, ed. F. W. Dupee (Garden City, New York: Doubleday, 1959); Adam B. Ulam, *The Bolsheviks* (New York: Macmillan, 1965); Avrahm Yarmolinsky, *Road to Revolution* (New York: Macmillan, 1959).

[2] Ivan Turgenev, "The Threshold," quoted in Alan Moorehead, *The Russian Revolution* (New York: Harper & Row, 1958).

[3] Lenin, quoted in Maxim Gorky, *Days with Lenin* (New York: International Publishers Co., Inc., 1932), p. 52.

[4] Georgi Plekhanov, quoted in Yarmolinsky, *op. cit.*, p. 325.

[5] Lenin, *The Beginning of the Revolution in Russia* (Moscow: 1950), p. 6.

[6] Kochan, *op. cit.*, p. 76.

[7] Father George Gapon, quoted *ibid.*, p. 79.

[8] Quoted *ibid.*, p. 176.

[9] Trotsky, *op. cit.*, p. 49.

[10] Nicholas II, quoted in Kochan, *op. cit.*, p. 187.

[11] Reed, *op. cit.*, pp. 15–16.

[12] Trotsky, *op. cit.*, p. 336.

[13] *Ibid.*, p. 324.

[14] Quoted in Reed, *op. cit.*, p. 113.

[15] Trotsky, *op. cit.*, p. 366.

[16] *Ibid.*, p. 399.

CHAPTER 5

[1] This chapter has drawn heavily upon the following works: R. Page Arnot, *The General Strike, May 1926: Its Origin and History* (New York: Kelley, 1967); Wilfred Harris Crook, *The General Strike* (Chapel Hill, North Carolina: University of North Carolina Press, 1931); Charles Loch Mowat, *Britain between the Wars* (Chicago: Chicago University Press, 1955); Julian Symons, *The General Strike* (London: Cresset Press, 1957); A. J. P. Taylor, *English History 1914–1945* (New York: Oxford University Press, 1965).

[2] Crook, *op. cit.*, p. 11.

[3] Honoré de Mirabeau, quoted *ibid.*, p. 45.

[4] William Benbow, quoted *ibid.*, p. 8.

[5] Mowat, *op. cit.*, p. 33.

[6] *Ibid.*, p. 300.

[7] Quoted *ibid.*, p. 292.

[8] Arthur Cook, quoted *ibid.*, p. 296.

[9] Cook, quoted *ibid.*, p. 299.

[10] Jimmy Thomas, quoted *ibid.*, p. 319.

[11] Winston Churchill, quoted in Crook, *op. cit.*, p. 369.

[12] A striking sheet-metal worker, quoted *ibid.*, p. 412.

[13] George Orwell, *The Road to Wigan Pier* (New York: Berkeley, 1961), p. 135.

[14] Quoted in Mowat, *op. cit.*, p. 311.

[15] Crook, *op. cit.*, p. 448.

[16] Stanley Baldwin, quoted in Mowat, *op. cit.*, p. 334.

CHAPTER 6

[1] This chapter has drawn heavily upon the following works: F. L. Allen, *Only Yesterday* (New York: Harper & Brothers, 1931); Frederick J. Hoffman, *The Twenties* (New York: The Viking Press, 1955); Matthew Josephson, *Life among the Surrealists* (New York: Holt, Rinehart and Winston, 1962); G. Mowry, ed., *The Twenties: Fords, Flappers and Fanatics* (Englewood Cliffs, New Jersey: Prentice-Hall, 1963).

[2] Allen, *op. cit.*, p. 101.

[3] F. Scott Fitzgerald, quoted in Mowry, *op. cit.*, p. 174.

[4] Allen, *op. cit.*, p. 250.

[5] Ezra Pound, "L'Homme Moyen Sensuel," quoted in Hoffman, *op. cit.*, p. 10.

[6] Pound, quoted *ibid.*

[7] *Ibid.*, p. 308.

[8] H. L. Mencken, quoted in Allen, *op. cit.*, p. 232.

[9] Mencken, quoted in Hoffman, *op. cit.*, p. 310.

[10] Quoted in Allen, *op. cit.*, p. 238.

[11] Floyd Dell, quoted in Hoffman, *op. cit.*, p. 36.

[12] *Ibid.*, p. 33.

[13] Josephson, *op. cit.*, pp. 324–325.

[14] Hoffman, *op. cit.*, p. 49.

[15] Fitzgerald, "Babylon Revisited," in *Babylon Revisited and Other Stories* (New York: Charles Scribner's Sons, 1960), p. 229.

CHAPTER 7

[1] This chapter has drawn heavily upon the following works: Theodore Abel, *Why Hitler Came to Power* (New York: Prentice-Hall, 1938); Alan Bullock, *Hitler: A Study in Tyranny* (New York: Harper and Brothers, 1960); F. L. Carsten, *The Rise of Fascism* (Berkeley, California: University of California Press, 1967); S. William Halperin, *Germany Tried Democracy* (New York: Thomas Y. Crowell Company, 1946); George L. Mosse, ed., *Nazi Culture* (New York: Grosset and Dunlap, 1966); Robert Waite, *Vanguard of Nazism* (Cambridge, Massachusetts: Harvard University Press, 1952).

[2] Friedrich Ebert, quoted in Waite, *op. cit.*, p. 7.

[3] Quoted in Abel, *op. cit.*, p. 244.

[4] *Ibid.*, p. 123.

[5] Ebert, quoted in Waite, *op. cit.*, p. 2.

[6] *Ibid.*, p. 39.

[7] Quoted *ibid.*, p. 89.

[8] Quoted *ibid.*, p. 161.

[9] *Ibid.*, p. 221.

[10] Adolf Hitler, quoted in Bullock, *op. cit.* p. 88.

[11] Quoted in Waite, *op. cit.*, p. 209.

[12] Joseph Goebbels, *Michael*, quoted in Mosse, *op. cit.*, p. 104.

CHAPTER 8

[1] This chapter has drawn upon the following works: Daniel Bell, *Marxian Socialism in the United States* (Princeton: Princeton University Press, 1967); Irving Howe and Lewis Coser, *The American Communist Party: A Critical History (1919–1957)* (Boston: Beacon Press, 1957); Henry Pelling, *The British Communist Party, A Historical Profile* (London: Black, 1958).

[2] Howe and Coser, *op. cit.*, p. 6.

[3] *Ibid.*, p. 284.

[4] Granville Hicks, quoted in Bell, *op. cit.*, p. 138.

[5] Howe and Coser, *op. cit.*, p. 331.

[6] Quoted *ibid.*, p. 338.

[7] *Ibid.*, p. 359.

[8] Heywood Broun, quoted in Bell, *op. cit.*, p. 183.

[9] Howe and Coser, *op. cit.*, p. 392.

[10] Quoted *ibid.*, p. 434.

[11] *Ibid.*, p. 471.

[12] Quoted in Pelling, *op. cit.*, p. 10.

[13] *Ibid.*, p. 13.

CHAPTER 9

[1] This chapter has drawn upon the following works: Ronald Blythe, *The Age of Illusion* (London: Hamilton, 1963); Don Congdon, ed., *The Thirties, a Time to Remember* (New York: Simon and Schuster, 1962); Hal Draper, "The Student Movement of the Thirties: A Political History," in Rita J. Simon, ed., *As We Saw the Thirties* (Chicago: University of Illinois Press, 1967); Matthew Josephson, *Infidel in the Temple* (New York: Alfred A. Knopf, 1967); Murray Kempton, *Part of Our Time* (New York: Simon and Schuster, 1955); Peter Stansky and William Abrahams, *Journey to the Frontier* (Boston: Little, Brown and Company, 1966); Julian Symons, *The Thirties, a Dream Revolved* (London: Cresset Press, 1960).

[2] J. B. Matthews, quoted in Kempton, *op. cit.*, p. 160.

[3] Draper, in Simon, *op. cit.*, p. 156.

[4] Jack Conroy, quoted in Kempton, *op. cit.*, p. 135.

[5] Josephson, *op. cit.*, p. 356.

[6] Quoted in Herbert Harris, "Sit-Down at General Motors," in Congdon, *op. cit.*, p. 492.

[7] Quoted in Kempton, *op. cit.*, p. 287.

[8] Herbert Harris, "Working in the Detroit Auto Plants," in Congdon, *op. cit.*, p. 486.

[9] Symons, *op. cit.*, p. 119.

[10] *Ibid.*, p. 120.

[11] Julian Bell, quoted in Stansky and Abrahams, *op. cit.*, p. 300.

[12] For a full account of the lives of Julian Bell and John Cornford, see Stansky and Abrahams, *op. cit.*

CHAPTER 10

[1] This chapter has drawn extensively on the following works: Michael Brecher, *Nehru: A Political Biography*, abridged ed. (Boston: Beacon Press, 1962); Michael Edwardes, *The Last Years of British India* (London: Cassell, 1963); Louis Fischer, *The Life of Mahatma Gandhi* (New York: Harper & Brothers, 1950); Ram Gopal, *Indian Muslims: A Political History, 1858–1947* (New York: Asia Publishing House, 1959); Charles Heimsath, *Indian Nationalism and Hindu Social Reform* (Princeton: Princeton University Press, 1964); R. C. Majumdar, *An Advanced History of India*, 3rd ed. (London: Macmillan, 1967); Penderel Moon, *Divide and Quit* (Berkeley: University of California Press, 1962); Leonard Mosley, *The Last Days of the British Raj* (London: Weidenfeld and Nicolson, 1961); C. H. Philips, ed., *The Evolution of India and Pakistan, 1858 to 1947* (New York: Oxford University Press, 1962); H. G. Rawlinson, *The British Achievement in India* (London: W. Hodge & Co., 1948); Gorham D. Sanderson, *India and British Imperialism* (New York: Bookman Associates, 1951); Percival Spear, *India: A Modern History* (Ann Arbor: University of Michigan Press, 1961); Stanley Wolpert, *Tilak and Gokhale: Revolution and Reform in the Making of Modern India* (Berkeley: University of California Press, 1962).

342 NOTES

² Quoted in W. C. Bonnerjee, "The Establishment of the National Congress," in Philips, *op. cit.*, pp. 138–139.

³ Gopal Krishna Gokhale, quoted in Wilfred Blunt, "Estimate of Gokhale and Lajpat Rai, 1908," *ibid.*, pp. 167–168.

⁴ Gokhale, quoted in Wolpert, *op. cit.*, p. 106.

⁵ H. Nevinson, "The Surat Split in 1907," in Philips, *op. cit.*, pp. 166–167.

⁶ General R. E. A. Dyer, quoted in Fischer, *op. cit.*, pp. 182–183.

⁷ Lord Curzon, "Speech at Byculla Club, 1905," in Philips, *op. cit.*, p. 659.

⁸ Lord Curzon to Lord Hamilton, Secretary of State, 23 April 1900, *ibid.*, p. 564.

⁹ *Ibid.*

¹⁰ Quoted in Stephen Koss, "His Master's Voice: John Morley at the India Office" (unpublished dissertation, Columbia University, 1966), p. 275.

¹¹ "Statement Exhibiting the Moral and Material Progress and Condition of India during the Year 1919," *Accounts and Papers*, No. 8, *Parliamentary Papers* (London), XXXIV (1920), p. 28.

¹²Bal Gangadhar Tilak, quoted in Wolpert, *op. cit.*, p. 189.

¹³ Mohandas K. Gandhi, quoted in Fischer, *op. cit.*, p. 195.

¹⁴ Gandhi, quoted in Sanderson, *op. cit.*, p. 271.

¹⁵ Gandhi, quoted in Fischer, *op. cit.*, p. 231.

¹⁶ Gandhi, quoted *ibid.*

¹⁷ Gandhi, quoted *ibid.*, p. 197.

¹⁸ Gandhi, quoted *ibid.*, p. 198.

¹⁹ Gandhi, quoted *ibid.*, pp. 202–203.

²⁰ Gandhi, quoted *ibid.*, p. 203.

²¹ Joan Bondurant, *The Conquest of Violence* (Princeton: Princeton University Press, 1958), p. 17.

²² Gandhi, quoted in Fischer, *op. cit.*, p. 233.

²³ Gandhi, quoted *ibid.*, p. 228.

²⁴ Jawaharlal Nehru, quoted in Sanderson, *op. cit.*, p. 292.

²⁵ Gandhi, quoted *ibid.*, p. 290.

²⁶ Quoted in Fischer, *op. cit.*, pp. 273–274.

²⁷ Lord Irwin, quoted in Brecher, *op. cit.*, p. 68.

²⁸ Rabindranath Tagore, quoted in Fischer, *op. cit.*, p. 274.

²⁹ J. A. R. Marriot, *The English in India* (Oxford: The Clarendon Press, 1932), p. 296.

³⁰ *Ibid.*, p. 305.

³¹ Nehru, quoted in Brecher, *op. cit.*, p. 94.

³² "Muslim Address to Lord Minto," in Philips, *op. cit.*, p. 191.

³³ "Muslim Address . . .," *ibid.*, p. 193.

³⁴ Gopal, *op. cit.*, Preface.

³⁵ Penderel Moon, quoted in Sanderson, *op. cit.*, p. 295.

³⁶ Rawlinson, *op. cit.*, p. 203.

³⁷ Nehru, quoted in Maulana Abdul Kalam Azad, *India Wins Freedom* (New York: Longmans, Green, 1960), p. 181.

³⁸ Fischer, *op. cit.*, p. 430.

³⁹ Nehru, quoted in Brecher, *op. cit.*, p. 145.

⁴⁰ Louis Mountbatten, quoted in Azad, *op. cit.*, p. 222.

⁴¹ Edwardes, *op. cit.*, p. 215.

⁴² Mosley, *op. cit.*, pp. 109–110.

[43] Brecher, *op. cit.*, p. 140.
[44] Edwardes, *op. cit.*, p. 219.

CHAPTER 11

[1] This chapter has drawn upon the following works: Herbert Aptheker, ed., *A Documentary History of the Negro People in the United States* (New York: Citadel Press, 1951); Daisy Bates, *The Long Shadow of Little Rock* (New York: David McKay Co., 1962); Joanne Grant, ed., *Black Protest* (New York: Fawcett World Library, 1968); Tom Hayden, *Rebellion in Newark: Official Violence and Ghetto Response* (New York: Random House, 1967); Paul Lewinson, *Race, Class and Party* (New York: Oxford University Press, 1932); Louis Lomax, *The Negro Revolt* (New York: Harper, 1962); Arthur I. Waskow, *From Race Riot to Sit-in, 1919 and the 1960's* (Garden City, New York: Doubleday, 1966).
[2] Grant, *op. cit.*, p. 11.
[3] Henry Highland Garnet, quoted in Aptheker, *op. cit.*, p. 232.
[4] Grant, *op. cit.*, pp. 211–212.
[5] Claude McKay, quoted in Waskow, *op. cit.*, p. 176.
[6] Marcus Garvey, quoted in Grant, *op. cit.*, p. 201.
[7] Garvey, quoted *ibid.*, p. 200.
[8] Senator James Eastland, quoted in Lomax, *op. cit.*, p. 85.
[9] Quoted in Bates, *op. cit.*, p. 57.
[10] Lomax, *op. cit.*, p. 102.
[11] Waskow, *op. cit.*, p. 265.
[12] Quoted *ibid.*, p. 257.
[13] Hayden, *op. cit.*, p. 5.
[14] *Ibid.*, p. 17.
[15] Quoted *ibid.*, p. 28.
[16] Governor Richard Hughes, quoted *ibid.*, p. 38.
[17] Quoted *ibid.*, p. 46.
[18] Bobby Seale, quoted in *Ramparts*, June 28, 1968, p. 38.
[19] Huey Newton, quoted *ibid.*
[20] H. Rap Brown, quoted *ibid.*, September, 1967, p. 26.

CHAPTER 12

[1] This chapter has drawn upon the following works: Gene Feldman and Max Gartenberg, eds., *The Beat Generation and the Angry Young Men* (New York: Citadel Press, 1958); John Gruen, *The New Bohemia: The Combine Generation* (New York: Shorecrest, 1966); Paul Jacobs and Saul Landau, eds., *The New Radicals* (New York: Random House, 1966); F. J. Rigney and L. D. Smith, *The Real Bohemia* (New York: Basic Books, 1961); Burton H. Wolfe, *The Hippies* (New York: New American Library, 1968).
[2] Feldman and Gartenberg, *op. cit.*, p. 13.
[3] Rigney and Smith, *op. cit.*, p. 17.
[4] *Ibid.*, p. 153.
[5] Gruen, *op. cit.*, pp. 52–60.

[6] *Ibid.*, p. 65.

[7] Wolfe, *op. cit.*, p. 116.

[8] Quoted in "Autumn in the Haight: Where Love Has Gone," *The Village Voice*, November 30, 1967.

[9] C. Wright Mills, "Letter to the New Left," reprinted in Jacobs and Landau, *op. cit.*, p. 104.

[10] Carl Oglesby, "Liberalism and the Corporate State," reprinted *ibid.*, p. 258.

[11] Irving Howe, "New Styles in Leftism," reprinted *ibid.*, p. 292.

[12] *Ramparts*, September 28, 1968, p. 21.

[13] Abbie Hoffman, "How I Lost the War," *The Realist*, September, 1968, p. 22.

[14] Quoted in *Resistance* (a Resistance pamphlet), 1968.

CHAPTER 13

[1] For the Berkeley crisis this chapter has drawn upon Seymour Martin Lipset, *The Berkeley Student Revolt* (Garden City, New York: Doubleday, 1965). The discussion of the Columbia crisis is based upon information gained from interviews for a book I am preparing on the American university. Readers seeking a detailed account can consult the Cox Commission report, *Crisis at Columbia* (New York: Random House, 1968), and Jerry L. Avorn, *Up Against the Ivy Wall* (New York: Atheneum, 1969).

CHAPTER 14

[1] Nikita Khrushchev, quoted in *The Anti-Stalin Campaign and International Communism* (New York: Columbia University Press, 1956), p. 40.

[2] Khrushchev, quoted *ibid.*, p. 76.

[3] Vissarion Belinski, "Letter to N. V. Gogol," in Marc Raeff, ed., *Russian Intellectual History: An Anthology* (New York: Harcourt, Brace & World, 1966), p. 258.

[4] Yevgeny Yevtushenko, *A Precocious Autobiography* (New York: Dutton, 1963), p. 89.

[5] Hugh McLean and Walter N. Vickery, eds. and trans., *The Year of Protest, 1956* (New York: Vintage Books, 1961), p. 21.

[6] Konstantin Paustovsky, quoted *ibid.*, p. 157.

[7] Khrushchev, quoted *ibid.*, p. 6.

[8] Andrei Siniavsky, *On Trial*, trans. and ed., with an introduction, by Max Hayward (New York: Harper & Row, 1966), p. 146.

[9] Alexander Solghenitsyn, quoted in *Problems of Communism*, September–October, 1968, p. 38.

[10] Andrei Voznesensky, quoted *ibid.*, p. 55.

[11] Richard T. De George, *The New Marxism* (New York: Pegasus, 1968), p. 112. For the text of "The Moral Code of the Builder of Communism," see pp. 159–160.

[12] Abram Tertz, "On Socialist Realism," trans. by George Dennis, in *The Trial Begins and on Socialist Realism* (New York: Vintage Books, 1960), p. 218.

[13] *The New York Times*, November 19, 1966, p. 6.

[14] *Problems of Communism*, July–August, 1968, p. 43.

[15] Patricia Blake, "This Is the Winter of Moscow's Dissent," *The New York Times Magazine*, March 24, 1968, p. 122.

[16] Final trial statement of Vladimir Bukovsky, in *Problems of Communism*, July–August, 1968, p. 35.

[17] *The New York Times*, March 23, 1968, p. 1.

[18] Anatoly Marchenko, quoted in *Problems of Communism*, September–October, 1968, p. 60.

CHAPTER 15

[1] This chapter has drawn upon Patrick Seale and Maureen McConville, *French Revolution 1968* (London: Heinemann, 1968), and various news reports.

INDEX